FLICKIPEDIA

PERFECT FILMS FOR EVERY OCCASION,
HOLIDAY, MOOD, ORDEAL, AND WHIM

Michael Atkinson and Laurel Shifrin

CHICAGO
REVIEW
PRESS

An A Cappella Book

Library of Congress Cataloging-in-Publication Data

Atkinson, Michael, 1962–
  Flickipedia : perfect films for every occasion, holiday, mood, ordeal, and whim /
Michael Atkinson and Laurel Shifrin.
    p. cm.
  Includes index.
  ISBN-13: 978-1-55652-714-2
  ISBN-10: 1-55652-714-4
  1. Motion pictures—Catalogs. 2. Motion pictures—Plots, themes, etc. 3. DVD-Video
discs—Catalogs. I. Shifrin, Laurel. II. Title.

PN1998.A74 2008
016.79143'75—dc22

2007016467

Cover and interior design: Emily Brackett, Visible Logic
Cover image: Louie Psihoyos/Getty Images

First edition
Published by Chicago Review Press, Incorporated
814 North Franklin Street
Chicago, Illinois 60610
ISBN-13: 978-1-55652-714-2
ISBN-10: 1-55652-714-4
Printed in the United States of America
5 4 3 2 1

For our children, Molly, Riley, and Conor, and our parents,
with special gratitude to James Shifrin, who willingly sat through
Song of the South three times one summer afternoon in 1972.

CONTENTS

ACKNOWLEDGMENTS

This is a book that required a gargantuan amount of communal input—we never trusted ourselves as complete authorities on how and why other people might watch and love movies—and so, at the risk of overlooking someone who has contributed ideas, stories, whims, videos, or inspirations, we'd like to thank Frank and Susan Gallagher, Julie Liebow, Anuradha and Michael Magee, James Shifrin, Christopher Wales, Lisa and Tom Murray, Gae Miller, Yuval Taylor, Devon Freeny, Shari Crouch, Barbara Braun, Susan and John Leach, Laurie and Mark Wax, Robin Noble, Roberta Perry, and Nadine Kelly. And our children, who have acquainted us with our fair share of occasions, ordeals, and raptures.

INTRODUCTION

Now more than ever, movies are a way of life. Today it's difficult to remember that in previous eras, the cinema represented exclusively a destination—it was somewhere you went, a mini-vacation, a blind date with the sublime. Whatever movies were released to theaters on any given week dictated what you could see, simple as that. Come the late 1950s and beyond, you could catch old films on television, but which old films you could see and when they could be seen were variables the viewer couldn't control. If *Gunga Din* happened to be playing on one station while a new episode of *Gunsmoke* aired on another, somebody in the family had to lose the inevitable channel-knob knockdown. In any event, watching a movie via that old black-and-white cathode ray tube was a wretched experience, especially since the films were interrupted with commercials and often recklessly edited to fit into broadcast time slots.

In our pre-videocassette, pre–cable TV lives, movies were a stream we could only randomly raft, with no rudder, anchor, or map; we couldn't direct our viewing course. In this way, our experiences with cinema resembled those with theatrical performances or circuses—if the show came to town, we modified our schedules to catch it. ("*Lawrence of Arabia* is playing at the Rialto! And it's only playing at five and nine! Dinner's at four! *Go, go, go!*") It was the same with movies shown on television; they aired when they aired, and it was up to us to accommodate the schedule. Think about that: Then, as now, you could choose what food you'd like for dinner, and you could even revisit a restaurant and order a favorite dish over and over again. At bookstores and libraries, you could select any book to read, even if it had been written a century before you were born. You could buy a record of virtually any musical performance, bring it home, and play it any time you wished. But movies were neither easy nor cheap to catch, and they could not be "ordered up" so conveniently. Like the weather, they simply presented themselves on their own terms, heedless of how well or how poorly they meshed with the general substance of our lives. Movies were our masters, and we were merely the audience.

These days, it's a different game: we are in control. With megagoogooplexes showing popular new films on three or more screens every twenty minutes or so, the theatrical experience is now overtly impulsive—people go to the movies without even knowing beforehand which movie they're going to see or when it starts (as anyone who has witnessed the spectacle of patrons standing in line while indecisively scanning the ticket booth options knows). And the movie-as-outing dynamic constitutes only a sliver of the pie that is today's film-watching experience. A larger slice of that pie is served up in the form of DVDs, videos, cable and satellite television systems, and, increasingly, the Internet. Almost everyone has unlimited access to video rental stores, movies for sale on DVD, and subscription services that can whisk virtually any film on the market right to our mailbox the day after it's ordered. We have cable and satellite movie channels that run 24/7, nonstop pay-per-view services, and new technology that provides digitally piped access to a broadening selection of movies any time we want. These days it's possible (albeit usually illegal) to download, free of charge, many newly released films that have been uploaded to the Web and watch them on our laptops while we take the train to work, sit in stadium bleachers, wait in a Laundromat, or lounge in the park. Soon enough, we will be able to jack into a cinematic cyberstore and ask to see any movie, at any time, anywhere, on the insides of our eyelids. (By then, movies might not even be "movies" anymore.)

As it is today, you can, on a whim, rent a viewable copy of virtually any movie you can name for the price of a cheap sandwich; you can own any movie for the price of a restaurant meal—or less. Films are well on their way to becoming universally accessible, regardless of whether or not any given movie is a century, a decade, or a month old. For less than the price of a hardcover novel, you can go online and buy new and old movies, often in sterling digital editions, from Egypt, Brazil, Estonia, and the Philippines. DVD players that handle every international format can now be had for under a C-note.

Gone are the days of movies as fabulous occasions—events around which we must retrofit our busy routines. Today, they are as manageable and selectable to us as fashion, furniture, and food. As a cultural experience, movies now conform to *us*.

Which is another way of saying that today, movies are subject to the currents of our lives in ways they never have been before. Since the medium itself is at our fingertips, the very nature of film-watching is undergoing a sea change. We now often choose movies the same way we choose music: to accent, heighten, alleviate, expand, contrast, and enhance the flow, peaks, traumas, and doldrums of our daily existence. Certain films must be watched at Halloween, on the brink of baseball's Opening Day, before a wedding, and after a graduation. Times arise for each of us when we absolutely *need* to watch *Duck Soup* or *Casablanca* or *Hannah and Her Sisters*. Consider the contemporary Christmas use of *It's a Wonderful Life* and *Miracle on 34th Street*: these inexhaustible narrative cups of cocoa have become institutionalized rituals, replacing past eras' caroling sessions, passion-play pageants, and readings of Hoffmann's *Nutcracker*. They *mean* Christmastime to us now. Consider as well the irresistible kitsch tradition of watching *The Ten Commandments* on TV at Passover, the vivid evocation of summer electricity to be culled from *Jaws* (regardless of how many times you've seen it), the intense popularity of *National Lampoon's Animal House* among recreational drinkers, the becalming effect of costume dramas on women in labor (who know better than to watch anything more exciting *or* less distracting in their condition).

Family cine-traditions that are just forming will perhaps last generations. In our home, a summer cannot pass without revisiting *A Midsummer Night's Sex Comedy*, an anniversary means it's time to rewatch *My Man Godfrey* or nearly any other film starring Carole Lombard, and *A Room with a View* is trotted out on too many regular occasions to name. Whoever we are, wherever we are in life, there are movies to answer our needs, to remind us of time-honored truths, to submerge us in a season's atmospherics, to bring us to refreshing landscapes, and to temper our individual experiences with a multiplicity of vivid perspectives. Whether we need confirmation or schadenfreude, cathartic shock or assuagement, nostalgic rapture or immediate distraction, movies are at our beck and call. It's an idea whose time has come: movies are factors in the rhythm and course of our lives, and submerging into the right movie at the right moment can sustain us, amplify our daily blessings, and mark our memories like lightning marks the rings of a tree.

That's the theory, anyway. You probably don't fully exploit the potentialities of your own movie culture because, having a real life, you probably possess an ordinary civilian's small-scale grasp on the life-augmenting movie options available to you. Outside of calling upon memories of movies we've already seen or consulting an unhelpful A-to-Z video guide, we are purely at the mercy of the entertainment industry's publicity trumpets, which today are so loud they virtually obliterate all other forms of cultural discourse. What they happen to be hawking at any given moment is, to most of us, the beginning and end of our viewing choices. Movies that are not immediately and immensely profitable to somebody do not get hollered about from the media rooftops—precious few magazines, newspapers, and television programs bother themselves with yesterday's (or yesteryear's) movies. High-end publications like *The New Yorker* and *Harper's* routinely review the works and legacies of, say, Brahms, Zola, and Monet, but classic films and the artists who made them are simply not seen as being worth the ink—which means that movies that are, perhaps, a year or two (or seventy-five) years old will not reach our battered eyeballs unless we actively seek them out. But how do we do that? Movies have been opening a hypnotic window on human life for more than 110 years now, but where do we go to hunt down a movie we aren't already familiar with that may reliably answer the emotional reverb of a specific life moment?

Thus, the raison d'etre for the book in your hand. *Flickipedia* is structured by reality—by everyday stuff that occurs in our daily lives. We've endeavored to have every major landmark event, generalized social mood, and annual occurrence represented with recommendations herein. The book's broad categories cover holidays; seasonal passages (including the arrival and climactic rites of sports); life phases, from birthdays to marriage, childbirth, and retirement; common emotional trials and eruptions, including illness, heartbreak, depression, optimism, and party-heartiness; travel preparation; and reminiscences, whether of your own school days or of an entire bygone era.

How to use *Flickipedia* is simple: live first, and then pick a movie. We've striven to be entertaining as well as informative, and to include movies that readers may not be familiar with, while naturally acknowledging the tried-and-true standbys and popular classics. In addition, the films in a given section will differ in their approach to the subject at hand—just like people—and not every suggestion will fit every reader like a pair of old sneakers. Every life event, whether Thanksgiving, high school graduation, having a baby, or watching the Super Bowl, will provoke different emotions in one person than it does in another (think about the variables between men and women alone, just for openers), so we're there with movie-viewing suggestions to cover the waterfront.

This book has been written by a serious (sometimes too-serious) professional film reviewer and his opinionated, hard-to-impress wife, but the strategy we used to select the films discussed in this guide was not entirely critical—whether or not a movie is *good* was far from our only consideration. A film's application to life may count for more than its overall quality—indeed, there are movies included that we both think are dreadful, but we also think that they could be pertinent to your experience of Saint Patrick's Day or your divorce or your memories of the 1970s or what have you. Film may be a crucial art form *and* rampaging entertainment, but it's also living material, often factoring in our lives in ways that cannot be aesthetically assessed or appraised. By the same token, many perfectly terrific films have been left out because they don't readily rhyme with a life experience. We treasure Jean Renoir's *The Rules of the Game*, Jacques Rivette's *Celine and Julie Go Boating*, and David Lynch's *Blue Velvet*, but they just didn't fit in anywhere. Nothing personal.

Likewise, the categorizations don't represent our entire estimation of the movies—for instance, Bernardo Bertolucci's *The Conformist* is a much richer and more valuable piece of work than its inclusion in the "Doing Europe" section would indicate, but its electrifying evocation of a certain Mediterranean urban mood seemed to be its most powerful connection to a viewer's everyday life. Likewise, Orson Welles's *Touch of Evil* is a whole lot more than merely "Party Software," but that's the only category of this book in which that tortured beast seemed appropriate. This book aims to aid and abet cinephilia, not to define it for anyone (least of all us). We all watch cinema for all sorts of reasons, whimsical and otherwise, and often we meet the movie on its own plane, as a work of art that requires no context or justification beyond itself, our generalized preferences-of-the-moment notwithstanding. After all, wanting to see a "great film" is very different from wanting to see a movie that complements a real-life event, situation, or mood. Similarly, having a jones for a war movie isn't the same as choosing a viewing experience for Memorial Day.

With *Flickipedia*, we're trying to lend a hand for the latter moment; for the former, you're quite properly on your own.

We have also reserved the right to leave out films we could just never stomach. If you want to get primed for the Indy 500, say, you'll find the merely mediocre *Le Mans* suggested here, but not *Days of Thunder*, because that movie just stinks. Call the strategy selective subjectivity—or mediated objectivity. Part of our aim is to broaden the readers' range of movie options, but still: all of our lives are only so long, and we all have only so much time to waste on bad movies. Compulsive moviegoers both, the authors of this book have seen everything so you don't have to, and we will have to be forgiven for believing, in our film-drunk heart of hearts, that good movies should be given a place of preference over junk—that, for instance, everyone would be better off marking their Fourth of July by watching John Ford's *Drums Along the Mohawk*, not Roland Emmerich's *The Patriot*. If anything, we hope the book's scheme will induce readers to try little-seen, semiforgotten, or, more to the point, undercommercialized movies on for size—to, for instance, sit down to Luis Buñuel's *The Exterminating Angel* the next time they're rained in, or to Jean-Luc Godard's *A Woman Is a Woman* the next time they're in dire need of smile. We intend to serve not only the film viewer and the new mode of movie-watching, but also cinema itself, with all of its glories, warts, catapulting successes, and unfulfilled promise.

Just so you know, the vast majority of the movies described herein are currently available on domestic DVDs and videotapes, but a few aren't—which doesn't mean that you can't find older copies available for rental, that you can't tape these films when they play on one of many all-movie stations (a legally gray area, but no one's been busted yet in thirty years of home video), that you can't buy European or Asian DVDs online, that someone on eBay isn't willing to let you have an out-of-print copy for chump change, or that the films in question won't be released or rereleased someday soon. Be sure to consult the "Resources" section at the back of the book, particularly if you think Netflix can provide you with every movie you'd ever require (it can't), or if you've been wondering why you pay for five different versions of HBO and still never see anything worth watching.

It's a big, fat, new world of movie love and cinematic experience out there, waiting to intersect with our glories, our doldrums, our disappointments, and our joys. Godard famously said that movies are truth—twenty-four times per second. Brian De Palma and Errol Morris, for two, have maintained that movies are *lies* twenty-four times per second. You could debate it—but what's inarguable is that movies are, twenty-four times per second, *life*.

I II III IV V VI

HOME FOR THE HOLIDAYS

CHRISTMAS

"... isn't just a day; it's a frame of mind."
—Edmund Gwenn, *Miracle on 34th Street*

"The *mother* of all holidays" is how Jean Shepherd put it in his narration of *A Christmas Story*, and it's true enough—but Christmas is also the year's most demanding day (or fortnight, really) in terms of atmosphere, emotional temperature, and point of view. We don't feel a need to get all colonial or even terribly grateful on Thanksgiving; nobody talks about "getting into the spirit" of Mother's Day, Veterans Day, or even Independence Day. But for Christmas, there is a pervasive compulsion to summon reserves of tolerance, generosity, congeniality, and childlike optimism, and we go to extraordinary cultural lengths to make it happen. Hence, the phenomenon known as the Christmas movie. Films that fall into this category serve as narrative windows into that Edenic space in which cold hearts are warmed, charitable love dawns on the greedy, and, most of all, childhood memories and the purest notions of home become easier to grasp and hold. Old movies—those more closely linked to the idealized past from which all adult ardor for the holiday flows—are best; crassly commercial contemporary parables about crass commercialism (*Jingle All the Way, National Lampoon's Christmas Vacation, Christmas with the Kranks*, to name a few) are not, and we've largely left them behind. The season is short, after all.

***The Night Before Christmas* (1905)** This fabulously arthritic Edison production from the infancy of film history—directed by narrative pioneer Edwin S. Porter—is a dusty dream of Victorian faerieism, opening with Santa feeding a herd of real reindeer and teeming with antiquey landscape paintings and pretechnological toys. It's also the climactic short on Kino's DVD *A Christmas Past*, a collection of silent vintage holiday films that includes D. W. Griffith's fiercely moralistic *A Trap for Santa* (1909), the utterly lovely Edison film of realistic snowfall frolicking *A Winter Straw Ride* (1906), and *Santa Claus* (1925), an amateur film proudly shot on and around the Alaskan glaciers. A hypnotic time capsule and an effective premodern weapon in the war against shopping and accumulation for their own sakes.

***Scrooge* (1935)** It's a tiring parable, but Charles Dickens's chestnut *A Christmas Carol* is, in one form or another, all but unavoidable. Preachy, sure, but it's such an overused story that you can hardly watch an hour of November television without being pelted by a commercial's reference to it. Better to go to the source—the book!—or to this first sound version, British-made, starring stage vet Sir Seymour Hicks as Scrooge. A creaky, attic-webby beaut, choked with shadow and fog.

***Beyond Tomorrow* (1940)** A fiercely odd septuagenarian Christmas tale cowritten by Mildred Cram, the author of *Love Affair*, this forgotten dilly concerns three bachelor fogies (buoyant Charles Winninger, crusty yet affable C. Aubrey Smith, dyspeptic Harry Carey Sr.) who die and return as ghosts to facilitate the seemingly doomed romance of a pair of young 'uns. The star power of these three character actors alone makes it worth seeking out, but the story is also a fabulous lark. Sometimes retitled *Beyond Christmas*.

Remember the Night (1940) An overlooked screwball masterpiece from Hollywood's golden age, written by bad-boy satiric genius Preston Sturges and directed by beloved "woman's director" Mitchell Leisen, in which whimsical bachelor DA Fred MacMurray takes sexy shoplifting tramp Barbara Stanwyck with him to his homestead for Christmas. Sturges's dialogue, volleyed by these pros four years before *Double Indemnity*, is mint, but the idiosyncratic comedy slowly, organically seeps into melancholy. The film is as smart-mouthed as it is stunningly compassionate, and Sturges's fat heart comes through in ways that are unique in a Christmas film. The characters' feet are planted in the real world, and the season's triumph is rescue from the memory of a poisoned childhood.

Holiday Inn (1942) Possibly the best movie to watch while wrapping presents. Bing Crosby and Fred Astaire are a pair of showmen who decide to open a country inn that celebrates every holiday with song and dance. That's it for story. As you'd expect, most of the film is caught up with other seasonal occasions; Christmas is just one page on the calendar. It just so happens that the movie's endearingly canned studio "winter" and Irving Berlin's "White Christmas" are the most memorable things about the film. That's fine: you're busy looking for scissors and tape. Anyway, from today's perspective, there's something inherently Christmasy about the hat-wearing, crooner-loving, home-front 1940s, isn't there?

Meet Me in St. Louis (1944) As much as the saga of the bustling Smith family of 1903 St. Louis might seem, in many ways, to crest during the unforgettable Halloween sequence, the famous Sally Benson tale reaches its yesteryear climax with its Christmas scenes, and Judy Garland's inimitable warbling of "Have Yourself a Merry Little Christmas." That ultragingerbread Victorian house never seems as at home as it does in the snowy, gaslit evening.

It's a Wonderful Life (1946) Truly, no one who's owned a television set anytime in the last thirty years needs to be advised to see Frank Capra's tumultuous masterwork *It's a Wonderful Life* after Thanksgiving. To escape from the public-domain broadcast ubiquity it suffered from the mid-1970s to the early 1990s, you would've had to have been Bigfoot, living in the woods. So we won't linger—except to say, in case you've been oversaturated or distanced by televisual redundancy (far too many sympathetic viewers know this film in fragments, having happened upon signature scenes, on up to three stations at the same time, while channel-flipping), take a few years off (avert your eyes, as if from the sun), and then sit down and subject yourself to this movie's passionate vision once again. Much more than merely a Christmas film, Capra's magnum opus is an open exploration of midcentury American humanity, with all of its sacrifice, resilient humor, and dark self-pity, as it comes up against the inexorable hungers of postindustrial capitalism. But it's also, helplessly, a Christmas movie, the most heartfelt of all Christmas movies, free of cliches, shopping incitements, and the need to "believe" in anything but your neighbors. If you're not a kid—and you probably shouldn't be if you're going to watch this film, what with all its talk of bank runs and mortgage equity—Christmas is really about home, devotion, family, self-sacrifice, and the sometimes rueful passage of time, and this may be the only film ever made about the season that takes these simple realities as matters of fact. And it nails that snowy, small-town feeling *down*, despite having been shot in Encino.

Miracle on 34th Street (1947) Although not as badly wallpapered over December television as *It's a Wonderful Life*, nor anywhere as threatening, this is arguably the most beloved of all Christmas movies. Maureen O'Hara and eight-year-old Natalie Wood arch their eyebrows over a department store Santa's claim to being the real Kris Kringle, and a courtroom battle over his sanity makes believers out of us all. You'll get more than just a holiday heartwarming; this movie serves up a hearty dish of late-1940s New York City nostalgia, since the story centers around Macy's Department Store (which still takes up an entire city block after most of its competitors have vanished, and which still hosts a certain Thanksgiving Day parade) and stars the store's original owner as himself, waging the midtown-Manhattan battle of mass merchants against Mr. Gimbel (also played by himself) and declaring to all the world that he is one of the Santa faithful. Has any era in our lifetimes signaled a sense of holiday community as potently as the postwar years? (It's in those years that most classic Christmas songs were popularized.) The film is so powerfully familiar you probably can't believe Edmund Gwenn or John Payne in anything else, but try nevertheless to remain dry-eyed as Gwenn, at the head of a crowded "meet Santa" line of shoppers, sings a song in Dutch to a war orphan. Caution for family viewing: if your kids still set out milk and cookies on Christmas Eve, their world might be upended by the suggestion that believing in Santa Claus could land you in Bellevue.

Scrooge (1951) The most commonly revered version of the Dickens tale, the dreary sermonizing of which is thoroughly enlivened by the grumpy joie de vivre of Alastair Sim as Scrooge—Sim executes the supreme feat of perfectly judging Scrooge's inner misanthrope while at the same time giving us a grand, winking show of ham and cheese on wry. The titular creep never had it so good. This moody British adaptation—should there be any other sort?—has plenty of Victorian flavor, too.

The Holly and the Ivy (1952) A cozy, mature, and rarely-seen British heart-warmer in which an aging parson and widower (Ralph Richardson) convenes, with his three adult children and other relatives, on their village homestead for the holidays—to reminisce about the war, remember dead loved ones, and lay bare a few family secrets. Director George More O'Ferrall is no Frank Capra, but there's a lot of genuine warmth to go around.

***White Christmas* (1954)** In this semimodern quasi-sequel to *Holiday Inn*, the bounce is there, the Berlin songs are there, and Bing Crosby, Danny Kaye, Vera-Ellen, and Rosemary Clooney (aunt to George) are there, saving the old New England lodge from bankruptcy by hoofin' and croonin'. Relatively speaking, the film is light on old-fashioned seasonal vibe, but what it does have is an explicit paean to the American home front for the legions of vets exhausted from war.

***Rudolph the Red-Nosed Reindeer* (1964)** Baby boomers know this puppet-animated fable's scary oddities inside and out, from the Burl Ives snowman in a plaid vest and the icy toy mansion in the snow, to the feverish anxiety about reindeer employment, the Island of Misfit Toys' winged lion-king, and the too-chilling abominable snow monster Bumble, complete with giant shark teeth and autonomously mobile fur. Forgive us if we think this decades-old kid's fodder more than a little strange, from the song lyrics ("We all pretend the rainbow has an end," the key ballad says. "And you'll be there, my friend, someday . . .") to the ending credits, when a sleigh-riding elf, distributing umbrellas to the toys and then tossing them overboard, figures a toy bird can do without and drops him, not knowing it's a Misfit Toy alum and cannot fly. But that is all decidedly beside the point; for most intents and purposes, because we grew up watching it every year, it's now an annual must-see. Of course, the Rankin/Bass animation mill rapped out other seasonal staples, all of which are to some degree essential Christmastime viewing: ***The Little Drummer Boy* (1968)**, ***Frosty the Snowman* (1969)**, ***Santa Claus Is Comin' to Town* (1970)**, ***The Year Without a Santa Claus* (1974)**, and others far less memorable. But *Rudolph* is the genre's greatest head trip, a weird dream within which we all remain bewildered children.

***A Charlie Brown Christmas* (1965)** OK, but *this* is the most sublime holiday special ever mustered for TV. Just a few years after this modest, melancholy cartoon first aired on CBS-TV, it had acquired the status of a national carol, an anthemic cultural touchstone without which no home was truly seasonally attuned. By now, it's a landmark. No other twenty-five minutes of hand-drawn animation needs as little introduction; indeed, it's included here only for completion's sake. If you're holding this book, you already know this ditty by heart.

***A Christmas Story* (1983)** No one had use for this witty dose of ham-fisted yet clear-eyed nostalgia in 1983, but Bob Clark's realization of Jean Shepherd's immortal memoir *In God We Trust: All Others Pay Cash* has since acquired the patina of a godsend. Truly, Shepherd's fulminating narration and Clark's cartoony style take getting used to, but after you're acclimated, you'll appreciate that the saga of Shepherd's semifictionalized 1940s Indiana boyhood is blissfully funny, sharp, and sermon free. Christmas here isn't about charity or good cheer or "faith"—it's all about being a kid, getting presents, writing Santa letters, dealing with bullies, negotiating playground arguments, fearing the wrath of Dad, fantasizing comeuppances, suffering the ill-bought gifts of distant relatives, ad infinitum. It's the only film even to attempt to capture the cosmic allure that a particular toy—in this case, a very particular BB gun—can have on a lower-middle-class grade-schooler. The cast is uniformly excellent, but if Peter Billingsley is brilliantly eager as the hero, and Darren McGavin equally so as his irascible, distracted furnace fighter of a father, props must be offered as well to young Ian Petrella, as the younger brother with too many of the movie's most quotable moments. But it's Shepherd's enthusiastic asides, moist with amused memory and sardonic self-regard, that fuel the film. Without a crumb of sentimentality, he reminds us what Christmas is really about: our pasts, our childhood selves, our lost innocence.

Comfort and Joy (1984) Scottish director Bill Forsyth is—or perhaps was, since his only film since 1993 was never released in the United States—a master of gentle discombobulation, and his Christmas movie is appropriately wacky, but in a quiet, generous way. The holiday here is experienced by a middle-aged Glasgow radio personality (Bill Paterson), whose sexy kleptomaniac girlfriend walks out on a mysterious whim, and whose subsequent Christmastime loneliness is abated only by his involvement in a turf war fought between two rival ice cream vendors. With Forsyth, it's all in the details and rhythms, and the movie has a thoughtful, ruminative personality that could do wonders, as the title implies, for the sad-sacked and lonesome.

Falling in Love (1984) This is Christmas in New York City in the 1980s, where you can meet your soul mate in a shopping bag mix-up at Rizzoli, potentially the toniest of all the Manhattan bookstores, rich with wood trim, elaborate architecture, and holiday shoppers in designer businesswear. The lovers, a low-key Robert De Niro and Meryl Streep, find mutual attraction almost immediately, but they're each married to someone else. Within the year, they flirt with an affair, try, fail, surrender to the fact of it, hem and haw—nobody easily finishes a sentence in this movie—and another Christmas comes around. It's no *Brief Encounter*, for sure, but the actors are cooking on all burners, and the holidays-in-Manhattan feel is everywhere.

Gremlins (1984) A nasty, fantastically clever antidote of a film for those of us who think that Christmas commercialism has gotten completely out of hand. Here, seemingly innocent Christmas presents have a Hyde side, taking on carnivorous lives of their own and hunting down their recipients. The mayhem of Joe Dante's bad-time dream—in which adorable, Muppetish furball creatures are introduced into suburbia as gifted pets, then transform into raving homunculi—might be the most astute metaphor for holiday capitalism ever devised; what seems at first an ordinary act of giving becomes a bloodthirsty battle to the death. (Is there a more triumphant moment in all of 1980s Hollywood cinema than that when the hero's mom, faced with a kitchen full of malevolent harpies, gears into combat mode and dispatches the cackling creatures in the blender and the microwave?) Should we all have to fight our gifts? If we did, we'd certainly give the exchange, and the intent behind it, a lot more thought.

Nutcracker: The Motion Picture (1986) It may be one of America's best-kept secrets: we as a populace don't really love the *Nutcracker* ballet very much, and we resent having to ingest it every year as if it were a citizenship requirement. Most of us would be surprised to learn that the original E. T. A. Hoffmann tale has precious little to do with sugarplum fairies and all to do with a rather vicious war between toys and monster mice. Filming ballets has always been a bad move in any event, but this Carroll Ballard film version has a few saving graces beyond the score: it's designed by Maurice Sendak, and it has a bewitching opening act, shot in intricate close-up, in which Drosselmeier embarks on his epic toy-making venture. Then there's dancing.

The Dead (1987) Director John Huston may have been close to dying when he made this movie, but apparently no one else was going to film James Joyce's most famous short story and make it an indelibly mournful, old-world Christmas experience. Two spinster aunts host a Christmas dinner in turn-of-the-century Dublin, when ladies wore long skirts and high lace collars and guests entertained each other with stories, songs, and dances. Outside, horse-drawn carriages glide gently through the snow; inside, the holiday feast is an occasion to discuss scandals and politics before setting aflame the Christmas pudding. That is, before a plaintive singing of a sad Irish ballad, when suddenly the past returns, the present begins to decay, and the season's marking of time and age inspires a deep and universal melancholy. Something of a family affair (Huston's son Tony wrote the ingeniously expanded screenplay, and daughter Anjelica stars as the wife with a secret story), this dreamy adaptation refuses to be hurried, and Joyce's prose (narrated by Donal McCann, as the husband) is surpassingly eloquent. With logs for the fire and a toast in hand, it's a salve for those hungering for a more literate, and subtly powerful, holiday film.

Die Hard (1988) This prototypical kerblam–Rube Goldberg–esque action film—in which posturing New York cop Bruce Willis foils the elaborate heist of a high-tech L.A. office building—is silly and energetic enough for viewing under many circumstances, but it is set a) at Christmas time; b) during one of the most unsuccessful office parties in movie history; and c) in Los Angeles, where Christmas is something of a plasticized joke anyway. If your holiday stance is one of bitter irony, this is your baby.

Scrooged (1988) A contemporary, Reagan-era revamping of *A Christmas Carol* that feels less contemporary the farther away we get from big-hair 1988. The legendary cranky miser is now Frank Cross, a mercenary network executive producing soulless holiday specials (Michael O'Donoghue helped write the script), Bob Cratchit is his long-suffering, underpaid secretary, and Tiny Tim is her mute son. Bill Murray injects Cross's heartlessness with crispy, dry sarcasm, and he takes his lumps (literally) from visiting ghosts David Johansen and Carol Kane. There's plenty of tainted, dated, even somewhat soulless New Hollywood Christmas atmosphere, but Murray is, as always, a blessing, enduring Wile E. Coyote–like jeopardy as he learns to love Christmas and his fellow man.

The Ref **(1994)** Another great anti-Christmas Christmas comedy, wherein a burglar (Denis Leary) who busts into an upper-class, Noel-ed-up home and ties up its squabbling inhabitants (Kevin Spacey and Judy Davis) is the most sympathetic person in sight. He even gets to lay out the Man: "Great. I just beat up Santa Claus." Not a movie for kids, nor is it for kid-swaddled, holiday-impassioned parents, but the rest of you can have a ball.

Bad Santa **(2003)** Talk about anti. We live in hip, irony-saturated times, and Hollywood in general can no longer reliably warm the cockles of the December heart—so, instead, we get this, the most vile, relentlessly scatological, taboo-abusive Christmas film ever made, in which an incontinent souse (Billy Bob Thornton) works as a department store St. Nick (with his African American midget assistant, played with profane vitriol by Tony Cox) primarily for the purpose of robbery. Vomit, urine, and profanity flow like April rain. There's just no overestimating this film's dedication to bad-taste mayhem—when you think it'll soften its very bad manners and go for a mushy story twist, it takes the spew up a notch and pees on your shoes. Grab your barf bags: a longer director's cut—*Badder Santa*—is also available on DVD, extending virtually every major sex, robbery, and drunkenness set piece in this already densely offensive film.

Elf **(2003)** Christmas sappiness plus flat-out contemporary yucks, with Will Ferrell making himself a bankable star as a human raised as a North Pole elf who ends up, in *Miracle on 34th Street* and *Big* fashion, in contemporary New York City—which here isn't all that different from the old New York of our Christmas movie memories, down to Ferrell's employment at Gimbel's (the scenes were shot, it seems, in the survivor of the department store giants, Macy's). An unexpected surprise is Zooey Deschanel crooning "Baby, It's Cold Outside" in a voice rich enough to rival the original Esther Williams version.

THANKSGIVING DAY

"Let's eat dead bird."
—Robert Downey Jr., *Home for the Holidays*

Perhaps no national holiday is as well suited to theme-oriented movie viewing—no one's at school or work, but it's cold outside and the day itself has little to recommend it besides being a big buildup to a mountainous meal of poultry and vegetables. But there's a theme here, isn't there? Being thankful? Thanksgiving movies have largely overlooked this notion, so we've tried, while attending to the Hollywood treatment of the holiday's traditions, to suggest a few off-topic films. New family traditions might be born.

***King Kong* (1933)** Growing up a New Yorker in the TV never-never land of the 1960s and '70s, Thanksgiving meant one thing: giant apes. For some obscure reason, a local broadcast station (back when we *had* local broadcast stations) would always air, year after year, *King Kong*, *Son of Kong*, and *Mighty Joe Young* from noon to dinnertime. In some households it was the Dallas Cowboys; in others it was the Macy's parade. But in certain homes, the day was filled with images of black-and-white hand-animated gorillas rampaging through the respective jungles of Skull Island and midtown Manhattan. The Empire State Building instantly acquired a legendary aura for millions worldwide who had never been to New York, and we came to believe—in our movie culture's subconscious, at least—that the Third Avenue El disappeared because the famed subway actually was decimated by Kong. This counterprogramming against football and floats was so consistent that watching these flicks became an ersatz annual tradition for everyone we knew. Exactly why those anonymous, old-school TV programmers chose this very narrow subgenre of movies for this particular holiday is a mystery; *Plymouth Adventure* or *Drums Along the Mohawk* would've been more logical, if less captivating. But outsized, stop-motion simians? Whatever you say. Somehow today it makes sense, if for no other reason than because Thanksgiving, to kids, is often little more than a big meal. So, on a day that's dependably gray, cold, and somewhat dull, we were treated to grainy Depression-era urban camaraderie, holy-smokes wisecracker Robert Armstrong, foggy islandscapes, vertiginous cliffs (stalked by pterodactyls!), and horrific images of gargantuan chaos—escapism defined, and best seen on the living room rug with a good November rain rasping outside. Annual traditions certainly tend to be asinine and arbitrary in America, and there's no reason this one shouldn't catch on again. The loud, exhausting 2005 remake might suffice in some households, since it is nearly as long as all three films combined.

***Son of Kong* (1933)** See above. And try to not let that final image haunt your supper.

Heidi **(1937)** Another yearly tradition and TV-scheduling conundrum once upon a time, this Shirley Temple film has nothing to do with Thanksgiving. (Maybe the local networks of the day chose it because it heralded Christmas, with sleigh rides over the snow-covered Alps and *Weihnachten* in a wealthy Frankfurt home.) But the holiday spirit of appreciating one's fortune and tenacious family bonds is all over this children's standby; Temple, a little past her *Captain January*–cute days, was still a consummate actress and the reigning box office champ of the 1930s when this film was shot. The orphan-and-grandfather love story is a lock only if you can stand some more sweetness and warmth after the candied yams and pumpkin pie.

Mighty Joe Young **(1949)** This is, rather importantly, the happy coda to the giant-ape dynamic, which is otherwise freighted with doom. (See *King Kong*.)

Hans Christian Andersen **(1952)** For decades, this stiff-legged musical about the famed cobbler/fairy-tale spinner also served as local-station Thanksgiving counterprogramming in many states. If you know who Danny Kaye is, it might still fly.

Plymouth Adventure **(1952)** Hollywood's only feature-film shot at the Mayflower story, a pleasant mediocrity untempered by Spencer Tracy and Gene Tierney (here seen in their "rapidly aging" phases). It won an Oscar for its special effects—which are spectacular.

A Charlie Brown Thanksgiving **(1973)** The third of the Melendez-Mendelson *Peanuts* TV specials—and the first dud (too much Woodstock and Peppermint Patty, too charmless a script). Like the others, though, it may've been imprinted upon you as a child like a goose's southbound flight path, so you may not be able to resist it. All the same, is there a more eloquent portrayal anywhere of an American child's November afternoons?

Hannah and Her Sisters **(1986)** Woody Allen's great, sweeping, intimate, moving comedy-drama about a sprawling, neurotic New York showbiz family, their failures, cross purposes, heartbreaks, and hilarious obsessions, all of it spanning two Thanksgiving Day celebrations. And the festivities are not entirely unlike *your* Thanksgivings, either—witness the spite, drinking, betrayal, boredom, speeches, chitchat, and bustle, all wrapped in a family's unmistakable warmth. The film is segmented into brisk, poetically-titled chapters, scored with a mix of old show tunes and Puccini, and armed with brave performances (Oscar-winning and otherwise) from Allen, Mia Farrow, Barbara Hershey, Dianne Wiest, Michael Caine, Max Von Sydow, Maureen O'Sullivan, and a sadly semi-Alzheimer-ish Lloyd Nolan. It's one of those rare grown-up films—even from Allen—that summons a palpable sense of healing, joy, and resilience without for a moment pandering to the audience's sentimental wishes or surrendering to its sometimes harrowing relationship with the real world. You can tell the Woodman was happy in the 1980s—the movie glows with affirmative energy.

Avalon **(1990)** The third of Barry Levinson's Baltimore films is also the most ambitious, tracing the arc of a Russian immigrant family from 1914 into the 1960s. It's a tumultuous arc that's punctuated by Thanksgiving dinners—get-togethers that are fraught with generational hostility and growing pains. It's an ebullient film, but the course of the holiday celebrations allows Levinson to make a strong critical statement about modern life—as the years press on, the family dissipates and fragments, and the ever-present television slowly takes pride of place, edging out conversation and family intimacy. Armin Mueller-Stahl, Aidan Quinn, and Elijah Wood make up the three levels of fathers and sons.

Home for the Holidays **(1995)** Adapted from a bitter *New Yorker* story, this hostile, lower-middle-class dysfunctional-family comedy can't be anyone's idea of a yearly ritual, unless you're gay and your family isn't, and unless your folks still live in Baltimore. But give it a shot once, if you're priming for a trip to the tension-filled homestead—the tasteless wrangling eventually climaxes with a beautiful scene of quiet rue involving lost single mom Holly Hunter, her grumpy father Charles Durning, and a reel of old 8mm family home movies. If this movie seems to you less calibrated outrage and more docudrama, you have our sympathies.

CHANUKAH

"The special time of year between Christmas and Misgiving when all the bestest holiday shows are on TV."
—Cheryl Chase, *A Rugrats Chanukah*

It's hard to compete with Christmas, and for years Jewish people could only take bravado-tinged solace in the fact that their holiday was completely devoid of commercialism. Not anymore—now we have blue Chanukah lights adorning houses, public-square menorah lightings, and dreidel-shaped cookie cutters. There still isn't much in the way of films to fill us with the Chanukah spirit, but here are a few offerings to share over latkes and doughnuts.

The Golem **(1920)** The only German Expressionist staple—and the only horror-genre tale—of the Chanukah offerings, this Paul Wegener production (he's the director *and* monolithic star), which has its origins in ancient Judaic myth, details the magical creation, in sixteenth-century Prague, of a giant clay man to defend the Jews from persecution. Other versions, including a French *Le Golem* released in 1936 and a British thriller called *It!* (1966), aren't as memorable.

The Bible . . . In the Beginning (1966) John Huston got ambitious here, making a bombastic film out of Genesis—or, rather, a few chapters of it—that features a rather shy Adam and Eve, Richard Harris as an angsty Cain, a depressing and grungy version of Sodom and Gomorrah, Stephen Boyd gesticulating as Nimrod, Huston himself as Noah, and George C. Scott as a growling, titanic Abraham. Huston also plays the voice of God, which seems apt enough.

Hester Street (1975) Joan Micklin Silver's groundbreaking indie—a historical film about immigrant life in 1890s New York, made for next to nothing—re-creates the Russian-Jewish ghetto world with a savvy ear for dialect and distinctly unsilvery black-and-white cinematography. Other than the Yiddish films of Molly Picon, this may be the next best thing to being there.

A Rugrats Chanukah (1996) Arguably the best American TV series about small children, *Rugrats* was also one of the subtlest and wisest about Jewish family life in the United States. In this special, the toddlers imagine themselves into ancient Jerusalem. "A Maccababy's gotta do what a Maccababy's gotta do!" A richer meal, even, for parents than for tykes.

Eight Crazy Nights (2002) When Adam Sandler's "The Chanukah Song" hit the airwaves, it was original and funny enough to be instantly accepted as a seasonal favorite; if only one could say the same for the vile cartoon feature birthed from its success. There is unquestionably a dearth of Chanukah movies in the sea of Christmas cheer, but this may be asking too much. A movie fashioned from the song's actual sense of cultural spirit would be a relief for millions. If only.

NEW YEAR'S

"Only creeps and crazy people go out on New Year's Eve!"
—Julie Kavner, *Radio Days*

Here's another holiday wherein our usual rituals (parties, champagne, resolution making) outweigh the pragmatic significance of the day itself. Like New Year's celebrations, movies have their own ways of creating traditions, sharpening our awareness of our lives' annual landmarks, and backlighting the ruefulness of a year gone by. Anyway, not everyone has a party to go to, so a movie is good company on a cold December's eve.

Made for Each Other (1939) A vintage romantic comedy of the prewar years, this film is not distinguished by script or director, but it's hardy, funny, and sweet, and it's an energetic showcase for its vibrant stars, each of whom is at the peak of his and her charms and beauty: James Stewart and Carole Lombard, playing googly-eyed newly-weds whose life together is soon under siege by a vicious mother-in-law, problems at work, money shortages, and, most traumatizing, a sick baby. No matter; the turmoil culminates in a go-away-come-back New Year's Eve confrontation, in which "Auld Lang Syne" is used as the tear duct–inspiring brickbat it was written to be. Lombard's short-burning, twice-as-bright candle can thaw your soul.

Radio Days (1987) Woody Allen has seen career peaks and troughs like few other working filmmakers. His run of hits in the 1980s was remarkable, yet somehow this memoir-comedy—set in, around, and on top of radio culture as it was experienced by a nebbishy Coney Island kid (Seth Green), among others—was relatively unsung when it was released. Twenty years later, it's beginning to look like one of his masterpieces, and the enormous canvas of ethnic satire, all-American period flavor, eccentric char-acters, throwaway gags, high-octane nostalgia, and personal (for Woody) ardor makes for easy repeat viewing under a variety of circumstances. New Year's is one of those circumstances, as the film climaxes with a comic—and wistful—year-end celebration on a fabled snowy New York rooftop. Viewers may end up feeling that the film has encapsulated an entire crowded year of experience, memory, growth, and adventure.

When Harry Met Sally . . . (1989) Almost in a tribute to *Made for Each Other*—among a great many other movies that have wrapped up with scenes of revelers counting down to the new year—this popular Rob Reiner–directed romantic comedy ends its gender-disagreement tale of love, friendship, and fate amid midnight confetti and a proclamation of just-realized passion (everyguy Billy Crystal's, for longtime buddy Meg Ryan). It's a merciless sigh producer even for (or especially for) educated urbanites, and our advice is this: don't watch it, ever, if you're single and lonesome. If you're not, you've probably already seen it.

The Hudsucker Proxy (1994) The Coen brothers do midcentury New Yawk magical real-ism with this high-flying launch of poppycock, which revolves around a dolt with a dream (Tim Robbins), a huge corporation with management problems, and a clock-work cosmology that, in various ways, revolves rather wondrously around New Year's. Again, the holiday is at least half about what's bygone, so the evocation of a fantasti-cal, screwball Gotham, shrouded in late December snow, makes this film a seasonal shoo-in.

200 Cigarettes (1999) Downtown New York, late on New Year's Eve 1981—it's a neo–Brat Pack ensemble piece about know-nothing twentysomethings and their social plights. Mostly, though, it's a stomach-roiling reacquaintance with New Wave, mousse-and-"glittah" style, alien hair helmets, and post-punk accessories, worn by a huge cast of already-somebodies: Ben Affleck, Christina Ricci, Gaby Hoffman, Janeane Garofalo, Kate Hudson, Paul Rudd, Casey Affleck, Courtney Love, Jay Mohr, and more—*too* many likable stars, all doing little. But if this movie's about the old you, give it a shot.

HALLOWEEN

"Whatever walked there walked alone."
—Richard Johnson, *The Haunting*

Halloween rarely, if ever, lives up to its promise and reputation for those of us who are over age ten—except on film, where the world can still go irrationally, disturbingly mad. Appropriately, selecting the right horror film for the holiday has become a cultural ritual, and our list, though winnowed of chaff, is long.

Häxan: Witchcraft Through the Ages (1922) Benjamin Christensen's messy, crazy, thoroughly disreputable, frequently banned Danish silent has been resurrected as a creaky novelty at least three times since it was made—once, in 1968, with a narration read by William S. Burroughs. Hardly a serious work of art or even a visceral genre entry, the movie is nonetheless jam-packed with decaying Gothic imagery the likes of which you've never seen before, from black masses to possessed nuns to witch burnings to multiple Lucifers ruining the lives of innocents and sacrificing infants. You'll find no better ambient video for a serious Halloween party.

Nosferatu: A Symphony of Horror (1922) F. W. Murnau's classic silent version of Bram Stoker's *Dracula*—a German Expressionist milestone that is at the same time oddly realistic, shot not on shadowy sets but almost entirely at real, rotting medieval locations—may still be the creepiest. A large part of the reason is Murnau's way of making the genuine locales (northern Germany and Slovakia) seem otherworldly, but the lion's share of credit must go to Max Schreck, the skeletal, rodent-faced actor who plays the vampire. Freaky as he is, he doesn't seem to be wearing makeup, and for years rumors (abetted by his name, which translates as "max fright") swirled about who he really was, why he was never seen in anything else, and whether or not he was merely an . . . actor. (See 2000's *Shadow of the Vampire* for a satiric fictionalization of the myth.) The original Romanian definition of the film's title was "plague carrier," and no other movie has articulated that description as well as this one.

The Cat and the Canary (1927) The first true trapped-in-a-haunted-mansion-on-a-rainy-night-to-read-the-will movie, and hokey as all get-out, but marvelously musty, too, and pungently Expressionistic with a capital E. German master Paul Leni, transplanted

to Hollywood, served as director, and every inch of the movie is gloomily, ornately
trimmed out. It's a lovely, shadowy place to visit, and it's inoffensive for kids.

***Dracula* (1931)** So famous it's impossible to watch Tod Browning and Bela Lugosi's
pioneering version of the Bram Stoker novel (and the subsequent hit play that made
a star out of Lugosi) without confronting the more than seventy years of cheap jokes
piled up behind it—running from Lugosi's own late career to *Sesame Street*'s Count
von Count. The movie *is* a creaky early talkie, full of bad acting and canned sound. But
those factors also account for its allure: it's intended to be a rather tomblike experience, and the rough technology of the time and Lugosi's otherworldly melodramatics
only add to the creepy, claustrophobic atmosphere.

***Frankenstein* (1931)** Another pop-culture victim, but still a mysterious, moving old-world
nightmare, thanks to the patient direction of James Whale and Boris Karloff's seminal
performance as the Monster. Forget the decades of imitations if you can, and you'll
see that Karloff's patchwork nowhere man is one of cinema's most original and daring
creations. A walking metaphor for every existentialist predicament ever conceived,
the Monster is thoroughly modern, thrust without the benefit of childhood into a savage world he cannot fathom, resulting in an utterly convincing—and discomfitingly
realistic—portrait of feral, lost-child helplessness. Maybe it's not frightening today (it
was in the 1930s; our mothers remember being scared silly), but it still has resonance,
and the gray, set-bound vibe is unforgettable.

***Vampyr* (1932)** Austere cinema master Carl Theodor Dreyer—in his first sound film—
tried his hand at an outright horror film on assignment, but the end product cannot
be anything the dilettante producers anticipated. Gauzy, somnambulistic, and fog-
clogged to the point of dislocation, Dreyer's film is based on a Sheridan Le Fanu
story, but is less a tale told than a suffocating dream endured. But Dreyer produces
passages (such as a funeral march as seen from *inside* the coffin) that loiter in your
skull. Independently made and badly preserved, the sound is unreliable, and the multinational cast never seems comfortable with whatever language they're speaking,
which just amps up the disorientation.

***The Mascot* (1933)** Wladyslaw Starewicz was a Lithuanian puppet animator whose
sketchy career stretches from the pre-Revolutionary days to the Kruschev era; he is
roundly acknowledged as the grandfather of the stop-motion animation genre, which
has grown to encompass the works of Czech masters Jirí Trnka and Jan Švankmajer,
the brothers Quay, Tim Burton, and even the creators of Wallace and Gromit. This
inventive short—available on several video collections, including Milestone's VHS edition of ***The Cameraman's Revenge & Other Fantastic Tales***—presages the *Toy Story* films
as well; it follows the adventures of errant toys lost in a dark city, and climaxes with
a windblown, devil-haunted confrontation that is still chilling.

The Bride of Frankenstein (1935) If Halloween is more of a quasi-Gothic camp pageant to you—which is, more or less, how it has come to be thought of by most Americans—this may be the key film for your October. The mega-opus of the Universal horror sagas of the 1930s provides Boris Karloff's outcast creature a rudimentary vocabulary (and a desire for a handmade woman—"like me!"), and the viewer gets the double-trouble pleasure of Ernst Thesiger as a reedy, psychotic grande dame of a scientist and Elsa Lanchester as the Monster's mate, complete with electric-coil Afro. Viewers are also treated to the period's crowning achievement in smoke-machine atmospherics, medieval iconography, and creaky surrealism.

The Wolf Man (1941) In this, the first of several "Wolf Man" films, poor Larry Talbot (Lon Chaney Jr.) begins his despairing odyssey through the endless corridor of lycanthropy (which may be read to symbolize the body trauma or disease of your choice), only to have it end when he tumbles madly from a castle window in *Abbott and Costello Meet Frankenstein* seven years later. By this point in the 1930s–'40s horror-movie surge, period atmosphere had seriously begun to give way to contemporary details— modern clothes, cars, and lingo that infringed on the gypsy-caravan paganism—and the effect is that of a purely movie-movie universe, caught in the midst of history, pop culture, and fear. There's more dry-ice mist in these fake forests than there is fog in all of real Romania.

Arsenic and Old Lace (1944) Self-consciously campy about Halloween, this priceless farce continues to serve as a celluloid demonstration that being "stagy" is no handicap at all if the material crackles—and if you've got Cary Grant, Priscilla Lane, Raymond Massey, Peter Lorre, Jack Carson, and Edward Everett Horton to fill out the single set with their earnest energies. Crazy brownstone aunts who also happen to be serial murderers, Josephine Hull and Jean Adair are the straight men in this scenario, which director Frank Capra keeps whipping along like a relay race. A pungent evocation not only of the usual Hollywood backlot atmospherics, but also of the Brooklyn autumn of 1944, when this hilarious trifle was what the old neighborhood badly needed.

House on Haunted Hill (1958) William Castle's magnum opus involves Vincent Price, a cavernous house (actually miles of semianonymous poverty-row studio corridor, which is somehow just as creepy), a murder plot, and scads of "Boo!" effects. In 1958 Castle arranged for a prop skeleton to emerge above audiences' heads during a key scene, giving the postwar teenager's buck its biggest bang.

The Tingler (1959) Perhaps the most inventive of William Castle's cheapo postwar horror ditties, this barren, desolate fantasy posits a neurological bug that's attached to everyone's spine. Human fear incites the bug to grow to the size of a loaf of semolina bread (with rubbery caterpillar legs) and kill its prey (that would be you), and only an ear-piercing scream from the victim can disable it. Few things in matinee history compare to the look on Vincent Price's face as he finds the foot-and-a-half insectoid "tingler" in an autopsied cadaver, wraps his rubber-gloved hands around it, and pulls. Of course, the thing gets out—and then it attacks a cinema projectionist, breaks the film, and crawls across the white screen. In its initial release, as the creature "escaped" into the movie theater, Castle had certain seats in theaters wired to buzz and jolt their occupants. Those were the days.

***Horror Hotel* (1960)** A public-domain bad dream that surely lodged in the reptilian brain of every kid who ever saw it on local pre-cable TV, this otherwise forgotten British-made horror film was virtually remade as *Silent Hill* in 2006, but the original, however penny-ante and cheesy, still grips, with its shadow-and-cardboard New England setting, a palpable air of neglected-village dread, and a deftly written plot that begins with the Salem witch trials and proceeds to 1960s "present day." With Christopher Lee in a plummy walk-on, a king's ransom in dry-ice clouds, and a stirringly heroic denouement.

***The Innocents* (1961)** A fairly faithful version of Henry James's *The Turn of the Screw*, Jack Clayton's primally frightening film is a psychological nightmare masquerading as a classy, even typical literary adaptation—it lures you in, then sets the ghosts on you. It's a familiar story, yet one we had never truly seen before: Deborah Kerr plays a somewhat nervous governess who's appointed to care for two precocious children in a remote, empty country estate a year or so after the last governess killed herself in the nearby lake. Slowly the rather high-strung woman discovers that the crumbly manse is haunted by the ghosts of her predecessor and her sadistic lover—a brutish manservant—and that the children, who were infatuated with the two crazed lovers when they were alive, seem to carry on a secret relationship with them now that they are dead. Kerr's heroine is herself a wild card; no one seems to see the ghosts but her (are these strange kids lying, or are they truly "innocent"?), and her concern for the children's welfare quickly mutates into a mad obsession fueled by her implicit sexual yearnings. Are the ghosts real, or are they the governess's repressed libido in spectral form? Tasteful but goosebumpy.

***Burn, Witch, Burn!* (1962)** Another British genre toot, this Fritz Leiber Jr.–derived witchcraft opus is actually a sharp analysis of marital dysfunction, focusing on a churlish university prof (the rather windy Peter Wyngarde) who discovers that his wife of many years (Janet Blair) has long been a practicing sorceress. His first—and last—mistake is to pragmatically abolish the occult trappings from their life together: unbeknownst to him, the wife has been battling rivals and protecting her husband in a secret conjurors' war.

***Carnival of Souls* (1962)** Made for peanuts in Kansas (and at the Utah salt flats) by a company normally busy with industrial shorts, this ghostly orphan of the 1960s is one of those movies whose ill-exposed film, stiff acting, and general air of gray yesteryear poverty lend it a fantastic chill. A woman (an unforgettable Candace Hilligoss) gets run off a bridge in her car, but survives (*or does she?*) and accepts a job as the organist of a church—all the while being haunted by silent ghouls, and occasionally going unseen herself, like a phantom among the populace. Key plot points may have been cribbed from Ambrose Bierce's short story "An Occurrence at Owl Creek Bridge," but it's the dead-air sense of menace and dislocation that makes this film stick in your memory like a burr.

***The Haunting* (1963)** Of all the reflexive choices for Halloween self-programming found at your local chain video store, this Shirley Jackson–derived humdinger may come as the biggest surprise to genre fans born after 1970; this is a true horror film, dread-drenched and blood-chilling and old-dark-house atmospheric like none other. It is *not* a horror film as Hollywood has defined the genre over the last quarter century—that is, a decidedly unthreatening litany of F/X, gore, soundtracks bangs, and glib jokes. In terms of authentic Allhallows vibe, this movie is a treasure trove, full of chilly drafts, gray skies, dark hallways, rooms not to be entered, and sounds in the night. This haunted mansion is *not* cozy, the ghosts do *not* have problems the plot solves, and the heroine is *not* a plucky teenager. No one gets killed by flying objects; in fact, you don't *see* the phantoms at all. But the scenes of supernatural siege are nonetheless the most alarming and scarifying in cinema history. Try it on some "young adults" who think horror movies are just to be giggled at, and watch them get shaken at their roots. Not to be confused with the 1999 remake, which is less frightening than a car alarm.

***The Gorgon* (1964)** Perhaps the flat-out strangest of all of the Hammer Film Productions horror films of the 1960s, this film utilizes yet again the peerlessly cheesy old-village vibe, overlit histrionics, and garish monster melodrama so familiar from the British studio's Dracula and Frankenstein series. This time, however, the monster who's haunting a backward hamlet is . . . a figment from Greek mythology, literally: a snake-headed titan whose visage can, and does, turn men to stone. Peter Cushing and Christopher Lee stalk about contemplating the absurdities that abound here, and the old-world chilliness of the piece is fab.

***It's the Great Pumpkin, Charlie Brown* (1966)** A great, atmospheric childhood dirge about nonconformity amid the mild anarchy of "tricks or treats," this holiday special holds a place in many generations' hearts, not only for Charlie Brown's lament he "got a rock" instead of candy—Charles Schulz's unseen adults hit a new low in their affliction of the young—and Linus's dogged belief in a pagan pumpkin god and the "sincerity" of his neighborhood pumpkin patch, but for Snoopy's extended detour through a stormy, battle-pocked French countryside dressed as a World War I flying ace.

***Night of the Living Dead* (1968)** A silly movie made for beans in the outlands of Pittsburgh, yet even today it remains one of the most scalding experiences in American independent film history. The fact that it was the first film to feature flesh-eating zombies should not be held against it; the movie remains crashingly effective, an ordeal by documentary-style realism, *because* it was so cheap, shot so simply, acted so amateurishly, subjected to the grayest autumn skies North America has to offer, and, most importantly, conceived so savagely that no sacred tenet of social life is left unattacked. Just consider how contemporary horror films could never stomach the zombie child's matricide-in-the-cellar scene. It's been called the best film about the Vietnam War that was produced during the conflict, but it's the unrivaled claustrophobic menace that makes for great Halloween viewing.

The Exorcist **(1973)** What can you say? It's a decidedly modern, un-Gothic attack of a film—in which only a young girl, not even a whole house, is possessed by a demon—but one with so much meticulously crafted atmosphere and apocalyptic frostiness that it'd be virtually impossible to watch during any other time of year. The gritty realism and focused acting of the 1970s definitely gives this film's grim medieval scenario its extra bite. But who would've thought that the D.C. suburbs could've ever seemed so *haunted*? From its early domestic portents (the party urination scene is a grim experience, hinting at so much of the dysfunction *and* supernatural tumult to come) to its full-on confrontation between hellfire and mortal piety (in a refrigerated bedroom set), this movie moves like a shiver machine, and the ways in which it makes us uncomfortable about basic daily things—household spaces, children, furniture, and the like—are profound and daunting.

The Legend of Hell House **(1973)** Contrary to what you'd think, well-tuned haunted house movies are rare, and this might be the best of the subgenre in the decade that followed 1963's *The Haunting*, the template of which—research team finds itself amid ghosts—it updates (though not as extremely as Richard Matheson's source novel, *Hell House*). The film features a large and gruesomely ornate mansion, poltergeist craziness, British diffidence (especially in the form of trauma victim/telepath Roddy McDowall), the doomed attempts to rationally control the chaos of the netherworld— you name it.

An American Werewolf in London **(1981)** The preeminent Halloween party film, a delicious fusion of several key elements: sophomoric irreverence (personified by Griffin Dunne's masterful turn as a decomposing dead slacker), monster-movie shocks (being predigital, all of the transformation scenes are done with makeup, robotics, and sweaty actors), and superstitious mood—the misty moors, the cramped inn with secretive locals, the stranger-in-a-strange-land vision of London (and of English hospitals). Complete with a soundtrack made up of nothing but songs with "moon" in their titles, John Landis's movie is enough of a cultural reference point to have invaded real life—there has been for years a very real pub in Manhattan's West Village called the Slaughtered Lamb; it boasts the film's very same wolf sign hanging outside and a dusty cellar in which the owners have been known to show the film all day on October 31.

The Company of Wolves **(1984)** Another kind of werewolf film altogether—directed by Neil Jordan from the neo-folktale by Angela Carter, this dreamlike, story-within-a-story fairy tale uses the lycanthrope legend to take on, in all seriousness, the story of Little Red Riding Hood and its overbearing Freudian subtexts. The makeup technology isn't up to that of Landis's movie (or to that of its contemporary, Joe Dante's Californicated *The Howling*), but the trippy Grimm-ness and overt sexual imagery make for a much stranger movie experience.

A Nightmare on Elm Street **(1984)** At the time, it was an entirely new kind of horror film, and it was deserving of its small-budget success—if not deserving of the string of sequels that relied more on wacky effects, shock sounds, and bad puns than invention, and that made Freddy Krueger a harmless costume-shop monster. He's anything but that here, haunting teenagers' dreams in a surreal rip through that old canard that says if you dream of your own death, you die in real life, too. Scarily unpredictable and full of deranging images, Wes Craven's movie is hammy but off-kilter enough, in fact, to steal your sleep.

Jacob's Ladder **(1990)** Another gloss—spoiler!—on Ambrose Bierce's "An Occurrence at Owl Creek Bridge," this Adrian Lyne film may be an overlit phobiafest, but it nevertheless imbues its protagonists' New York postal worker milieu with a heart-stopping variety of the creeps (courtesy of uncredited artist-photographer Joel-Peter Witkin, among others) that brand themselves on your eyeballs, thanks largely to the film's commitment to in-camera effects (no postproduction digitizing here). The incursion of the tangible, serpentine demonic into everyday urban life is jolting and ferocious, and it makes a stroll through downtown a goosey experience.

The Halloween Tree **(1993)** Nobody ever sang the song of Halloween as passionately or as lyrically as Ray Bradbury. (A faithful remake of his novel *Something Wicked This Way Comes*, filmed dreadfully in 1983, is waiting to be made.) This Hanna-Barbera–produced cartoon version of Bradbury's young-reader novel is torn between a brooding plot (four children chase after the soul of a dying friend) and a rather trite and episodic tour of the holiday's traditions through the ages, but the man's rhapsodic sense of the season is unmistakable.

Tim Burton's The Nightmare Before Christmas **(1993)** Tim Burton becomes a trademark with this stopmotion holiday hybrid, in which the preeminent creature of Halloweentown, Jack the Pumpkin King, out of a kind of existential longing, crosses into the realm of Christmas and makes a royal mess of it. Few Allhallows cliches are left out, but pivoting the plot on the amoral behavior of trick-or-treaters Lock, Shock, and Barrel is inspired. The humor is all playground nihilism, where everything bad is good and vice versa, and the distinctive design is entirely of a piece, derived from Burton's unique sketch style. Unfortunately, the forgettable but grating Danny Elfman songs curdle the action.

The Blair Witch Project (1999) The real deal, a radical realigning of genre prerogatives, and a lean, mean, pants-soiling machine set in the very real American scrub forest of your forgotten preadolescent nightmares. Forget the astonishing hype, spin-offs, and spoofs this movie generated when it was released—this is the first movie that genuinely understands fear. It is, without a doubt, the all-time ideal Halloween renter—it's the audiovisual equivalent of every sleepover ghost story you ever heard, and *it really happened!* No, it didn't, but think about the 1999 Sundance Film Festival and that lucky, traumatized first audience who saw the movie *at midnight, in the mountains of Utah,* without being told it wasn't a documentary. Daringly, Daniel Myrick and Eduardo Sanchez's film is nothing more than the rough footage shot by a three-student documentary team who have decided to make a cheesy film about a chunk of Maryland woods and its accompanying witch legend. What happens is simple: they can't get out of the woods, the overnight hike turns into days of hysteria in the wilderness, and something—*something*—begins to reveal itself to them in ominous nighttime sounds, pagan signs, and worse. Throughout, the fact that we see only what the beleaguered trio manage to film, and often not even that, thanks to the limitations of light and focus in handheld moments of primordial terror, makes this more than just a horror movie—it's a return to your childhood's starkest memories of abandonment and dread. Saying *The Blair Witch Project* is a convincing experience is only scratching the surface. Because you believe it, because your vision is limited, because the actors are, in reality, alone in the dark—because it doesn't even seem to be a film, but rather somebody's home-movie footage gone terribly, sickeningly berserk—it might be the scariest film ever made.

Sleepy Hollow (1999) With this high-octane Gothic comic book, Tim Burton continues his unique, idiosyncratic, and very personal career project: to reexperience and revivify the toy chest of pop-culture effluvia that sustained him—and many of us—through our 'Nam-era childhoods. Burton has said he'd wanted to pay homage to the old British horror movies made by Hammer Film Productions; in typical Burton style, he beat them at their own game. No Hammer film ever looked this crepuscular, this grandly, rottenly ghoulish. Extrapolating from Washington Irving's nervous little ghost story "The Legend of Sleepy Hollow" (which was adapted, in animated form, not at all ineffectively by Disney in 1949), the movie dazzles us with one Halloweeny motif after another, from scarecrows with candlelit jack-o'-lantern heads to enough fog to choke L.A. However thin in the story department (like all of Burton's films), it's a fabulous hoot, and you feel the filmmaker's macabre delight in every frame.

Donnie Darko (2001) First timer Richard Kelly's film defies description—it's a wild, unpredictable beast that refuses to be caged by genre or expectations. Enveloped in a mood of cultural doom and psychological unease that is persistently haunting, this saga of teenage alienation is in a more or less constant state of cataclysm—internal or external; you decide. Donnie (the naturally affecting but abstruse Jake Gyllenhaal) is a high schooler in 1988, on the cusp of the Bush/Dukakis elections, attempting to navigate his terrain despite the fact that he sleepwalks, hallucinates, is becoming convinced that the world will end in twenty-eight days, and has decided to stop taking his medication. He's partnered by a skull-faced rabbit figure inciting him to destruction, and his suburban school is in the grip of a messianic self-help guru (Patrick Swayze), but Donnie's primary problem is his own flexible reality; he doesn't know, exactly (any more than we do), how much his mental disturbance reflects or *causes* the cosmic countdown to Halloween. A feverish fan cult has sprouted around this movie, and with its sense of ominous portent and middle-class-kid holiday ritual, it may be the best Halloween film ever made (even if it's not frightening, but is instead heartbreaking and mysterious). While the film seems clearly a free-fall study in psychological meltdown, by the end you're not so sure if it isn't revisiting "An Occurrence at Owl Creek Bridge" (again!) or, more aptly, simply culminating in a stunning, purely cinematic act of salvation.

Satan's Little Helper (2003) Forgotten genre freak Jeff Lieberman—his erratic career began in 1976 with the giant worm saga *Squirm*—manufactured this 1980s-style gore farce out of crummy horror-flick spare parts, but the result is conceptually maniacal and witty. A semidelusional kid, obsessed with a Satanic video game, meets and obliviously assists a psycho wearing a grinning-demon mask as the madman litters bodies through a prototypical suburb on Halloween—a setup that, at least, allows Lieberman to fill front-lawn graveyard displays with real corpses and bloodied knives. Never released to theaters.

Tim Burton's Corpse Bride (2005) A formal repeat performance of *Tim Burton's The Nightmare Before Christmas*, complete with identical character designs and Danny Elfman songs, this sumptuous Black Foresty animation virtually oozes with gray, toy-shop atmosphere. Of course, it's strictly for the irreverent Halloween renter, although this endearingly modest movie has some real poetry in it, as well as a concrete relationship with centuries of *Mitteleuropan* legend and Ukrainian peasant myth.

Monster House (2006) High-concept digital animation brought down, definitively, to a trick-or-treater's level. The myth of everyone's childhood neighborhood—of the darkened, unkempt house on the block that no one knows much about, and that may well be the site of unspeakable creepiness, or worse—is exploded into a carnivorous piece of rotting architecture, swallowing hapless children (or at least their toys) and inspiring endless prepubescent schemes and surveillances. In keeping with the Steven Spielberg model (he and Robert Zemeckis served as producers), the climactic battle is too long and too loud, but the draftsmanship is imaginative, the voices (especially those of Jason Lee and Steve Buscemi) are sharp, and the tunnel vision of kids on a self-scaring tear is splendidly evoked.

INDEPENDENCE DAY

"This is a revolution, dammit! We're going to have to offend *somebody*!"
—William Daniels, *1776*

It *is* July, a great time to be outdoors, and sure, you have your parades and fireworks and barbecues lined up to celebrate the holiday—but what if it rains? And what about the evening of July 3? You can't count on the movies to provide accurate history, but they can contextualize the Fourth of July celebrations.

Janice Meredith (1924) A pulpy silent romance in the D. W. Griffith tradition that positions its heroine, played by William Randolph Hearst protégé Marion Davies, as helping out with both Paul Revere's ride and Washington's crossing of the Delaware. Rarely seen or broadcast, with a sensational cast that also included W. C. Fields (as a drunken Brit officer), Tyrone Power Sr. (as Lord Cornwallis), Fatty's cousin Macklyn Arbuckle (as Davies's father), and, as Marie Antoinette, in one of only two known film appearances, one Princess Marie de Bourbon, a popular model and reputed relative of Italy's King Vittorio Emanuele III.

Ah, Wilderness! (1935) Small-town, turn-of-the-century life by way of Eugene O'Neill, so depression, alcoholism, and prejudice cut the sun-dappled optimism to some degree. But it's set at and near a nineteenth-century-style, midwestern Fourth of July celebration, and the exuberant, creaky, cracker-barrel priorities are in line, with Mickey Rooney and his little-rascal buddies setting off firecrackers underneath the grown-ups' various melodramas.

Drums Along the Mohawk (1939) Director John Ford, with his customary visual beauty and antiquated notions of women, manhood, Native Americans, and war, does up the Revolutionary frontier milieu, with New York farming couple Henry Fonda and Claudette Colbert meeting with range crustiness, savage injuns, and, eventually, the British infantry. Simpleminded but fun, in lovely three-strip Technicolor.

Lafayette (1962) A little-seen French historical pageant about the revolutionary hero, good for old-fashioned European attention to period sumptuousness, as well as a spot-the-star cast of internationals, including Orson Welles as Benjamin Franklin, Jack Hawkins as General Cornwallis, vet character star Howard St. John as George Washington, and Vittorio De Sica as Edward Bancroft, Franklin's double agent.

1776 (1972) Easily the most thoroughgoing War of Independence film ever made in Hollywood—there aren't many competitors, which says something about how interested Americans truly have been about their own history—this silly anachronism is also an eager-to-please Broadway musical put on film. Still, it has its devotees, and besides, the facts are there, a good deal of the dialogue consists of historically accurate attributed quotes, the cast is game, and the anticonservative number "Cool, Cool, Considerate Men" is included on video versions of the film, after having been initially cut by studio chief Jack Warner at the behest of President Richard Nixon.

Tom Sawyer (1973) Mark Twain's familiar touchstone gets a brash treatment as a musical, produced by Reader's Digest and written by Disney song vets Robert and Richard Sherman. Thankfully, the songs play over the action, so the plot keeps hustling despite them. Best of all, the film was shot in rural Missouri, and it basks in the early American glow of the childhood few of us really experienced but wish we had: running barefoot, rafting down a slow river, fishing with a stick and a string. And the Fourth of July is the perfect day to watch this film—and vicariously enjoy a town picnic, friendly tugs-of-war, and fireworks.

Blow Out (1981) Brian De Palma's tribute to Michelangelo Antonioni's *Blow Up*, Chappaquiddick, Watergate, JFK, sound engineering, and Philadelphia, all rolled into a crazy plot involving a political assassination that the hero (John Travolta, engagingly relaxed) may have accidentally recorded on audiotape. The background of a berserk City of Brotherly Love during the July Fourth fete is as central to the film, visually and ironically, as the national monuments used by Hitchcock in his works. All in all, a smashing, thoughtful, stirring piece of pulp, and probably the best movie for the holiday.

Revolution (1985) A rare attempt by the Hollywood studios to make a serious film about the Revolution, but boy, the engine dropped out of this lemon straight from the factory. Which makes it something like a comedy now, what with Al Pacino's meant-to-be-historical Brooklyn accent, Annie Lennox stalking around as "Liberty Woman," a sound mix that literally loses 50 percent of the mumbling dialogue, a stupefying lack of both history and action, and an impressive visual palette that runs from umber to sienna.

The Last of the Mohicans (1992) Though Michael Mann's buckskin-sex, tomahawk-to-the-head take on James Fenimore Cooper isn't about the Revolutionary War or national independence, it evokes, as few films do, the real wilderness of the time, a place at once homestead, battlefield, and frontier. Log cabins, cannon-stocked forts, gun smoke and mud, eating venison by candlelight—this may be the closest an American film will ever come to capturing the period. Plus it has Daniel Day-Lewis and Madeleine Stowe; as star-crossed lovers amid the warfare, they're the most convincingly hot movie pair of the 1990s.

VALENTINE'S DAY

"Kiss me. Kiss me as if it were the last time."
—Ingrid Bergman, *Casablanca*

Valentine's Day is a prime video rental day—once a relationship is past those first few rookie years, romantic movies are called upon across the land to warm this February evening. Roughly speaking, anniversaries can have more gravitas and natural sentimentality to attend to, but St. V's Day is time for pure movie-movie larkiness. Nevertheless, most of the entries in the "Anniversary" section—as well as those in "Dating," "Newlyweds," and "First Love"—are appropriate to the holiday as well.

***Peter Ibbetson* (1935)** Semiobscure and precious as a pearl, this woozy mid–Depression Era projectile is filmed like an old maid's opium daydream, but the story is what makes your head spin: after being separated as children, Gary Cooper and Ann Harding meet again with a husband between them, and after he's accidentally killed, Cooper's unpretentious architect goes to prison *for life*—but as the couple ages, they literally meet, forever young, in their dreams. For *decades*. French critic Georges Sadoul wrote, in his famous 1965 reference volume, *Dictionnaire des Films*, "It is difficult to discuss this film without tending to invent certain details more than 25 years after being burnt by its flame." He didn't invent much in his synopsis, but the movie's flame is very real.

***Ninotchka* (1939)** This Ernst Lubitsch comedy is pure bliss, and a paean to Parisian mad love and fun, which hedonistic American expat Melvyn Douglas pitches to steely, humorless Soviet comrade Greta Garbo, who's in town to reel in a few goofy Soviet agents who have become distracted by the Gallic pleasure principle. Of course, Garbo is masterful as the comically grim maiden in a gray suit, barely disguising a warm heart yearning for love that we can always see beating beneath the Marxist-Leninist ideology. A little champagne, a little Paris skyline, a little woo from the rather satyric Douglas, and she opens like a lily (figuratively speaking, at least; this is 1939). It doesn't hurt that Lubitsch had the subtlety and timing of a Hollywood Mozart, or that *Ninotchka*'s screenplay, penned mostly by Billy Wilder and Charles Brackett, is one of the wittiest and gentlest of Hollywood's entire golden age.

***Wuthering Heights* (1939)** Whatever can be said about *Wuthering Heights* as a romantic experience fit to kindle powerful emotions on Valentine's Day (or any other day), it can't possibly be enough. This is it, the seminally cosmic love story of all time. Cathy and Heathcliff experience a yen so powerful it can transcend jealousy, fate—even the grave. Samuel Goldwyn, director William Wyler, and screenwriters Ben Hecht and Charles MacArthur worked up an Emily Brontë reduction sauce, story-wise (the movie stops at the book's chapter 16, which is fine, because the rest of the story, about the next generation, never mattered anyway). But the combined natural forces of Merle Oberon (not a skilled actress, but a galvanic movie star), a young Laurence Olivier, the moors (actually Los Angeles County), and Brontë's fierce storytelling make this a larger-than-life experience. Ignore the few stodgy details, and submerge into its self-destructive passions.

Casablanca **(1942)** Novelist and semiotician Umberto Eco called it not "a movie," but "the Movies," and yet that still doesn't explain the deathless allure and hypnotic dramatic slam of this greatest Hollywood concoction, as much a still-vibrant myth system as a super-romantic wartime soap. Persistently popular for decades after its premiere, *Casablanca* ran the natural risk of becoming overly familiar. Although it has generated a storehouse of cliches and fabulous dialogue snippets that have found their way into everyday language without very many of us knowing where they came from ("I'm shocked—*shocked*"), the film rarely has occasion to show up on TV anymore, and teens no longer consider Humphrey Bogart a hip counterculture icon. Never mind; *Casablanca* is still the quintessential mating dance of tough-guy cynicism and heart-tugging yearning—of self-satisfaction and self-sacrifice, be they in the context of savoring a love affair or saving the world from Nazis (or, as is the case with this film, both). Which means that, unlike so many of today's romances, this is not strictly a "chick flick"—the sensibility at work here (primarily due to a remarkable screenplay that was written and rewritten a day at a time as the movie was being shot) acknowledges, caters to, and converses with both genders. Bogart has become virtually synonymous with the twentieth century's first definition of a man's man: ugly and short, but indescribably charismatic, and so cool he can run into his lost love (a daydream-inducing Ingrid Bergman), spar with Nazi officers, crack jokes, *and* subtly reveal a lifetime of bitterness and desire, all at exactly the same time. And Bergman, for her part, is intelligent, gentle, and fantastically desirable as the despairing hub around which the battle for the free world revolves. That's what makes this movie ideal for Valentine's Day viewing—neither partner is simply indulging the other, and both will easily be drawn into the tragic intercourse of love and history.

Lola **(1960)** New Wave romantic Jacques Demy takes to the streets of Nantes in his first café love tangle, in which Anouk Aimee is a luscious cabaret singer flitting above a messy but congenial web of lust and love, waiting for her true, idealized love to return to her.

Heaven Can Wait **(1978)** Warren Beatty's remake of 1941's pretty swell *Here Comes Mr. Jordan* is a wonderfully lighthearted love story of an aging quarterback who is plucked up to Heaven's way station before his time—and before his final Super Bowl. Too late to go back among the living as his old self, he gets temporary custody of a millionaire's body, becoming smitten with an Englishwoman (Julie Christie) in the bargain. Beatty and codirector Buck Henry cut the sweetness with plenty of satire, and Charles Grodin all but steals the show with his special brand of duplicitous diffidence. Hardly a moment in the movie isn't a pleasure.

Like Water for Chocolate (**1992**) Mexican culinary magical realism—this is a world in which salt for cooking comes from dried tears, where desire and lust can cause you to steam or burst into flames, where a single bite of quail in rose petal sauce can make you run naked out of the house in time to be fetched by a revolutionary on horseback. It's a seductive approach to a film, and this international hit—in which the daughter of a traditional family conjures metaphysical explosions in the kitchen when she is forbidden to wed her heart's desire—knows that, for women, food has magical qualities that are just as sensual as they are sensuous. If you know what you're doing, you'll cater your evening up grandly, without skimping on the caviar.

Sleepless in Seattle (**1993**) There's Romance with a capital R in so many aspects of this movie that you can overlook some of the more toxic Nora Ephron–esque things about it, including insufferably precocious children and scenes that seem to be built entirely of one-liners. Sam (Tom Hanks) and Annie (Meg Ryan) are both adorable and lovable: he, a grieving widower raising his son alone, bravely, on the watery banks of Seattle; she, beautiful, smart, and not quite willing to give up every woman's fantasy that "there's one guy out there for me, and he isn't a man who wears a bow tie." The homage to 1957's ***An Affair to Remember*** can only mean we're bound to see the Empire State Building sooner or later, but, arguably, the most memorable scene (stolen by Rita Wilson, the real-life love of Hanks's life) is a bright exchange about our attachments to certain movies and the way we love to shamelessly weep over them.

Shakespeare in Love (**1998**) A lighthearted and lovely tale of Shakespeare's own unrequited love story, which proved the inspiration for both *Romeo and Juliet* and *Twelfth Night*, as light on its feet as *Romeo and Juliet* is weighty with tragedy. The comic timing from a large and buoyant cast is impeccable, and the lovable energy of the movie is embodied in Shakespeare himself (Joseph Fiennes), who never seems to sleep and is in constant athletic motion. The players, sometimes in disguise, deliver masses of Shakespearean dialogue with complete conviction, wit, and speed, and there's enough heat between Fiennes and Oscar winner Gwyneth Paltrow to warm the home fires.

Serendipity (**2001**) John Cusack and Kate Beckinsale meet during a holiday shopping tug-of-war for a pair of cashmere gloves at Bloomingdale's and continue their flirting over the famous frozen hot chocolate at nearby Serendipity 3, following up with skating in the snow at Wollman Rink. Is it fate? She thinks so, to an almost psychotic degree, and so decides to test it, and thus the movie carries on through several years and many monstrous dalliances with destiny before the inevitable hookup.

Before Sunset (2004) The setting is Paris, the archetypal hub of romance, and we rejoin Celine and Jesse nine years after they left each other at the train station, swearing to meet in Vienna six months later, in Richard Linklater's *Before Sunrise*. With that movie, we were clearly supposed to wonder if they'd actually meet up—and, just as clearly, we weren't supposed to know for sure either way. But this sequel, coming a decade later, with a decade's wear and tear having accumulated on the actors *and* the characters, gives us a Valentine's Day–style answer we had no right to expect. *Before Sunset* is both intelligent and sexy, and whether you sigh dreamily over the notion of love at first sight or scorn it, the screenplay approaches the concept in such an original way that you won't have the heart to scoff: Celine and Jesse share humorous, offbeat musings on life while they meander around Paris in the late-afternoon sun, just as they did when they wandered Vienna, but now they avoid—until they're no longer able to avoid—the paths their lives have taken, because no, they never reunited as they'd promised. Ethan Hawke and Julie Delpy have invested so much in these characters that they share screenplay credit with director Richard Linklater; hard-bitten realists, the three of them are dogged about not letting anyone off the hook, romantically speaking, yet the movie comes booby-trapped with the sneakiest happy ending ever, a slow dawning as Delpy sashays around her apartment, impersonating Nina Simone. Irresistible.

SAINT PATRICK'S DAY

"When I drink whiskey, I drink whiskey; and when I drink water, I drink water."
—Barry Fitzgerald, *The Quiet Man*

In the United States, Saint Patrick's Day is the most widely celebrated ethnic holiday, and it's generally utilized as a cause for red-cheeked heritage pride, if you're Irish; as a reason to quaff robust amounts of stout, ale, whiskey, and cider, whether or not you are in fact Irish; or as a calendar-scheduled time for both. So, movies about the Irish and Irish Americans tend toward one of these options as well. Pick your poison.

Man of Aran (1934) Famed documentarian Robert Flaherty went to the rocky western Aran Islands of Ireland to shoot the preindustrialized, treacherous life of the region's fisherfolk. Unfortunately, he couldn't find any that lived and worked as they had in the past—in long, nonmotorized boats on the stormy seas. So Flaherty, as was his custom, made the locals act out the abandoned traditional way of life for his camera. The film is a magnificently shot and fabulously authentic portrait of a bygone culture that was probably intimately familiar to many an American family's long-passed immigrant patriarchs and matriarchs. Just don't mistake it for a documentary.

Kathleen Mavourneen **(1937)** A hard-to-find English ditty, based on the oft-filmed nineteenth-century poem by Thomas Moore and shot in Ireland, it involves a peasant love triangle. Worth locating, if only for the on-location imagery.

Odd Man Out **(1947)** Director Carol Reed and the Abbey Theatre players fill out a shadowy studio that doubles for war-torn Belfast, through which crawls James Mason as an IRA hold-up man with a bullet hole in his gut. More a portrait of a community coming apart under political pressure than a thriller, the film is rich with character bits, impassioned acting, and noirish anxiety.

The Luck of the Irish **(1948)** New York newspaperman Tyrone Power goes to Ireland and meets a leprechaun (Cecil Kellaway), who follows him back to the United States. The film is cute as a button, with Anne Baxter shining up the rear as an Irish lassie who just won't let the handsome American sell out, but squeezing Kellaway's rotund, 55-year-old form into our general idea of what a leprechaun is supposed to be gives the movie a cognitive dissonance. You can't buy it any more than you buy Lucky Charms commercials, but the cast and filmmakers act as if you do, so it works. What were the other options, superimposition or a midget?

The Quiet Man **(1952)** The king rooster of Irish American movies, this film employed virtually every Irish actor in Los Angeles and was directed by the erstwhile Sean Feeney (John Ford), making a mighty thick and affecting pudding out of the American idealization of the old country, complete with thatched cottages, rolling green hills, rascally old Oirish men in tweed, rebel songs, tempestuous redheaded women (Maureen O'Hara, carving out immortality for herself), and even the occasion to have a rousing, good-natured donnybrook. Once beloved, this boisterous comedy-drama can be a hard swallow now, what with its Stone Age treatment of women and the boozy silliness that runs through it (as is the case with so many of Ford's films). But John Wayne gives a terrifically modest performance, Victor McLaglen is a blubbering riot, and the twinkly-eyed atmospherics are spot-on. If you are in fact Irish, you can't resist this movie, but even if you're not, you'll still find it bullishly entertaining in an old-school way, and, naturally, even more so with a bumper or eight under your belt.

Darby O'Gill and the Little People **(1959)** The *other* leprechaun movie, this time with dated Disneyfied special effects that fill the screen with miniaturized actors scampering, dancing, and overacting like crazy. The Scottish Sean Connery shows up as a normal human, but otherwise, this may appeal only to very small and very undiscriminating children (who perhaps should not, in any event, be exposed to Irish folklore in just this way). Can't resist quoting the telltale poster tagline: "A touch O'Blarney . . . a heap O'Magic . . . and A LOAD O'LAUGHTER!"

A Terrible Beauty (1960) This forgotten oddity, a British film coproduced by star Robert Mitchum's independent company (and titled, of course, with a line from Yeats), looks at actions within the IRA during World War II in 1941—when the nationalist group's fight against the Brits coincided uncomfortably with the Nazis' assault. Mitchum plays a new inductee who eventually falls in love, and informs on his fellow soldiers after getting a taste of their mercenary brutality. Cyril Cusack, Richard Harris, Niall MacGinnis, and Dan O'Herlihy fill out the rather aimless story. Nationalists might balk, but no other movie touches on that period and those issues.

Ryan's Daughter (1970) Ireland has had the misfortune of being fantasized about too much by outsiders, and this World War I–set David Lean epic was and still is roundly considered to be the most Hollywood-bloated example. But however wobbly it is dramatically, the movie photographs the west coast of Ireland more spectacularly than any film ever has, and the acting—by Robert Mitchum, Leo McKern, John Mills, Trevor Howard, Arthur O'Sullivan, and Sarah Miles (as the fickle lass that breaks everyone's heart)—is fine. Still, Lean's monumental style, which is so adept at evoking southeast Asia, Russia, and Arabia, may be a misshapen fit for Irish landscapes—County Kerry feels a bit like Middle-earth.

The Field (1990) An Irish widow puts her farm on the auction block, and the old bloke whose family has been farming it for years dukes it out with the Ugly American who naturally shows up to buy it. An old sock packed with blarney, this hammy Jim Sheridan–directed yowler is enjoyable if, and perhaps only if, you toss back a pint of Guinness and picture here, in place of the actual cast, the Monty Python crew—all spouting outrageous brogues. Instead of Richard Harris as the blustery patriarch, picture a pipe-clenching Graham Chapman with eyes agog; John Cleese could replace Sean Bean as the long-legged son given to fits of rage. The thin-nosed priest would have to be a bright-eyed Eric Idle, and Michael Palin would be a vast improvement over John Hurt, who seemingly plays an illiterate leprechaun. And the perfect frumpy housewife isn't Brenda Fricker—it's Terry Jones.

The Commitments (1991) Roddy Doyle's novel comes by way of director Alan Parker, and it's merely the charming tale of a many-membered, soul-standards band's rise and fall in Dublin. But it's got great local pub flavor, Parker's smoky imagery, and an ensemble cast whose characters are uniformly allergic to pat dramatics. The music ain't Irish, but it's splendid.

Into the West (1992) A gritty but mannered Irish fairy tale, intensely appreciated by some, in which two contemporary boys from the itinerant Traveller minority, who live in the Dublin slums, are suddenly gifted with a large white horse. When goldbrickers steal the animal, they steal it back, and the three light out for the west coast. Faithful to the Traveller culture in which the boys live, and pleasantly stirring.

The Secret of Roan Inish **(1994)** Who saw this coming from John Sayles—a movie that deals seriously, and magically, with Irish fairy lore? Based on a 1957 novella by Rosalie K. Fry, the tale is beautifully conceived: after her mother's death, a ten-year-old lass returns to live with her grandparents on the western Irish shores, near the place where, a few years earlier, the girl's infant brother was lost at sea in a hand-carved cradle. Longing to reunite her family and return them to the island of Roan Inish, where they lived for generations, she seeks out the truth about her family and the whereabouts of her brother, whom she spots as a little boy sailing the rocky inlets in his ship-shaped cradle. The saga involves the authentic Irish legend of the selkie, a beautiful half-seal, half-human water fairy that can only be married if you steal its shed skin. Run through with mythic images and briny mood, it's a lovely experience, even if Sayles's visual choices are pedestrian. That the story and imagery are still moving is testament to how badly we need more movies that are seriously saturated in myth. Whatever this one's shortcomings, after watching it you walk away refreshed.

Michael Collins **(1996)** A lead-booted, sentimentalized view of Irish history, Neil Jordan's biopic is still the only film you'll find that's factually involved with the Easter 1916 uprising and its political aftershocks, which included the titular hero's (Liam Neeson) efforts to establish an independent republic despite the wishes of the British and the IRA.

Bloody Sunday **(2002)** No party movie, but if you're having an angsty, progressive, Bono-style Saint Pat's, you can hardly beat Paul Greengrass's meticulous, minute-by-minute reenactment of the famous slaughter in Derry, by British soldiers, of unarmed civilians during a peace march on January 30, 1972. This is as neorealistic a view of Ireland and Irish history as movies have yet given us; the period details are perfect, and the sense of outrage is blistering.

EASTER

"The other day you said, if a man hit you, you'd turn the other cheek. I didn't like that."
—Harvey Keitel, *The Last Temptation of Christ*

Another holiday with a modern deficit of things to celebrate—unless you take your Christianity, and your resurrections, very seriously, or unless you still live a preindustrial, agrarian lifestyle, when the arrival of spring was a matter of life triumphing over death. The ritual Easter egg hunts will only occupy the minions for a short while, though, so stock up on movies.

Ben-Hur: A Tale of the Christ **(1925)** The big-budget Hollywood silent version of the old-time Lew Wallace novel, in which the titular Jewish aristocrat (Ramon Novarro) suffers travails at the hands of a Roman friend, wins a bloody chariot race, and sees the Crucifixion. Until it was remade, this busy epic was the film that out-DeMilled DeMille. The race is still a thrill, and the story is less plodding than in the Oscar-heavy 1959 remake.

Easter Parade **(1948)** A secular, bunny-free musical with elegant fashions, flowers, and Fred. Pulling a Pygmalion, the story begins with the famed Fifth Avenue parade, and throughout the film, Astaire and Judy Garland manage to complement each other wonderfully—he floats on air while toodling weak, innocuous tones; she labors over every step while belting with that honeyed voice. Easter doesn't have much to do with the story, but it's a nice way to pass the evening with a belly heavy with ham.

Ben-Hur **(1959)** Big, big, big all around: this (lazily) William Wyler–directed mastodon is what your holiday ordered if in fact size matters above all things. And it can: there's no denying the pleasures to be had, even on video, from the huge, earnest Biblical melodramas Hollywood made in the 1950s—a time when movies were family events around which middle-class Americans of all ages could commune by the millions. And this film is long; no need for a Easter Sunday double bill. Charlton Heston won an Oscar for his performance in the lead role, and the chariot race, twice the size of the 1925 version's, is amazing and special-effects-free.

King of Kings **(1961)** There are many flat-out New Testament movies, and most of them are awful—besides, it's a pretty timeworn tale for many of us, isn't it? Here is Nicholas Ray's version, referred to by many upon its release as *I Was a Teenage Jesus* (Jeffrey Hunter made for a rather heart-throbby, rock 'n' roll Christ), and composed of complex wide-screen shots that have a hard time finding a home on most TVs. As usual with the Christ story, the actor playing Pontius Pilate has the most fun—here, the drippy Hurd Hatfield camps it up.

The Gospel According to Saint Matthew **(1964)** Director Pier Paolo Pasolini was a Marxist, a homosexual, and a Catholic—and he made arguably the greatest Christ movie of all time, using the eponymous gospel verbatim as his screenplay (which got him permission to make the film from the fiery Italian censors) and at the same time crystallizing the character as a people's revolutionary and the story as a political parable. Using the very real poverty of southern Italy to stand in for ancient Judea, Pasolini made the most believable film about Jesus, and the most incendiary. Brilliant, but not necessarily a comforting watch on Easter.

The Greatest Story Ever Told **(1965)** Filmmaker George Stevens, hitting his self-important bloat stage, manufactured what might be the most grandiose Christ film, but get past the looming sanctimony and the film is little more than an orgy of bizarre stunt casting, including the world's only Swedish-accented Jesus (Max Von Sydow), an outrageously brawny John the Baptist (Charlton Heston), Barabbas as a hard-bitten noir figure (Richard Conte), an honest-to-God Nubian (Sidney Poitier), John Wayne as a centurion on Golgotha (not kidding), and much more. Telly Savalas rebels against the fey Pilate stereotype, painting him as a bullet-headed militarist.

It's the Easter Beagle, Charlie Brown **(1974)** As the great works of Charles M. Schulz go, this perennial offers nothing close to the sublimities of *A Charlie Brown Christmas* and *It's the Great Pumpkin, Charlie Brown*. Linus dreams up another absurd holiday deity (a wish that Snoopy eventually fulfills), the kids color Easter eggs, Snoopy tries to find a new home for Woodstock, and—as is the case with *A Charlie Brown Thanksgiving*—there's just too much focus on Peppermint Patty). Negligible, unless you or your kids need an innocence fix.

The Last Temptation of Christ **(1988)** Martin Scorsese, America's premier conflicted-Catholic moviemaker, tackles Nikos Kazantzakis's masterful novel exploring the Jesus character through the lens of genuine human suffering, sin, psychology, and, sure, temptation. The whole paradigm gets a thoughtful rewrite: Judas (Harvey Keitel) is no longer merely a greedy betrayer, but a seditionist using Jesus (Willem Dafoe) as a weapon against the Romans; John the Baptist (Andre Gregory) is a raving evangelist. Mary Magdalene (Barbara Hershey) is a whore bitter over her lost love for Jesus, who for his part is never sure he's not simply going crazy. (Pilate, played by David Bowie, remains a swishy bureaucrat, as per cliche.) Most who protested this gravely redemptive film were knee-jerk reactionaries who hadn't seen it—*of course* Christ has to yearn for love, sex, and earthly satisfaction. Otherwise, what was he sacrificing? *The Da Vinci Code* has made an industry of this kind of interrogation today; unlike that commercial steamroller, however, Scorsese's film is purely emotional—and potentially conversional.

Bringing Out the Dead **(1999)** Just as, for perverse cinephiles, the alcoholic melodrama *The Lost Weekend* (1945) might be interesting to watch on Yom Kippur (Ray Milland's lush can't sell his typewriter because all of the Jewish-owned pawnshops are closed!), this Martin Scorsese semicomedy—about a burned-out New York EMT working the ambulance graveyard shift over Easter weekend—might be perfect anti-Easter programming. Features plenty of mordant humor, gore, Scorsese camera work, and Nicolas Cage.

PASSOVER

"Are her lips chafed and dry as the desert sand, or are they moist and red like a pomegranate?"
—Anne Baxter, *The Ten Commandments* (1956)

A belly full of matzo and brisket, recitations of the flight from Egypt, no cute dreidel games or presents to while away the time—sounds like a recipe for a family movie. Nothing too serious or hard to have fun with—enough suffering, already!

The Ten Commandments (1923) Cecil B. DeMille's career-making silent epic seems quite stodgy and unimpressive today, but it's worth watching if you're sick of the colorful, bombastic 1956 version.

The Ten Commandments (1956) Over-the-top Bible epics used to be so much campy fun before Mel Gibson came along and got all preachy; I'll bet Easter dinner at the DeMille household was a lot more enjoyable than it is at the Gibson ranch. Would Passover have been so entertaining over the years without televised visions of Charlton Heston's chin, John Derek's pecs, Anne Baxter's pouty kitten lips, or Yvonne De Carlo's heaving cleavage? Even if you haven't always made it to shul, you know the deal with this movie—Moses, Pharaoh, Red Sea, Edward G. Robinson growling, "Where's your messiah *now*?"—and you also know that it's a long enough movie to stretch over at least a few of Passover's nights, if not all eight. "So it shall be written, so it shall be done."

Exodus (1960) Leon Uris's bestselling novel covers much more history than simply the struggle in the late 1940s to establish a Jewish state, but you gotta give director Otto Preminger and long-blacklisted screenwriter Dalton Trumbo a hand for trying to winnow Uris's magnum opus down to a unifying dramatic thread. As Passover viewing, this long (more than three and a half hours), rhapsodic, muddling tapestry is sure to strike an emotional chord, even if you remain troubled by the way the Middle East has turned out since. Filmed on location in Cyprus and Israel, and starring Paul Newman as the perpetually pissed-off hero, Ari Ben Canaan.

Wholly Moses! (1980) Like Monty Python's *Life of Brian*, this Mel Brooks–ish Old Testament parody trails after a schmuck (Dudley Moore) who was *almost* Moses. Low shtick, with Madeline Kahn, Jack Gilford, James Coco, and Richard Pryor as the Pharaoh. Director Gary Weis began his Hollywood career doing hilarious shorts for *Saturday Night Live* in that show's infancy.

A Rugrats Passover (1994) As with *A Rugrats Chanukah*, this special episode celebrates American secular Jewishness in the wisest and most entertaining fashion; this time, Grandpa Boris regales the kids with an epic, albeit abridged, Exodus story.

The Prince of Egypt **(1998)** The *kinderlach*, their knowledge of Passover limited to macaroons and matzo balls, are falling asleep waiting for Grandpa to get on with the plagues, already—it was probably just such a dilemma at the Spielberg, Geffen, and Katzenberg seders that led to the creation of this cartoon Haggadah from DreamWorks. It's quite dramatic and stirring, and it's certainly a cut above many of the animated features that wind up being merchandised into our consciousness. Our kids were completely engrossed and acted as if they'd never heard the story before. The five-year-old said it best during the parting of the Red Sea: "Oh yeah! I want to be on Moses's team!"

Into the Arms of Strangers: Stories of the Kindertransport **(2000)** A conventional but heart-wrenching documentary about the shipment, in the year prior to the invasion of Poland, of some ten thousand European Jewish children from their families to the United Kingdom, where they waited out the war with foster families and then, afterward, tried to return home. Other chest-swelling nonfiction portraits of life and survival in the Holocaust era—a fairly recent breed of documentary—include *Fighter* **(2000)**, *Shanghai Ghetto* **(2002)**, and *The Danish Solution: The Rescue of the Jews in Denmark* **(2003)**.

When Do We Eat? **(2005)** Finally, a seder comedy, and, aptly, one likely to ignite heartburn. The father (Michael Lerner) accidentally consumes ecstasy, the Holocaust-surviving granddad (Jack Klugman) exhibits paranoia, kids are stoned, old wounds are reopened, and so on. Your family is probably funnier and a lot less obnoxious. But maybe not.

MOTHER'S DAY

"A boy's best friend is his mother."
—Anthony Perkins, *Psycho*

There are many movies about evil mothers, possessive mothers, conniving mothers, pesky mothers, unreformed old-world mothers at odds with modernity, yada yada yada, but why would you want to watch those? Instead, we tried to appeal to the purpose of the holiday—without being too naive about real mother-child relationships, which are seldom easy or simple.

Mother **(1926)** Master Soviet silent-montage propagandist Vsevolod Pudovkin adapts Maxim Gorky's patriotic novel, in which a grown son and his beleaguered mother battle the czar's police during the pre-Revolutionary days. If your mother is an unre-formed Party member, go for it.

Mrs. Miniver **(1942)** The peerlessly lovely Greer Garson is unjustly notorious as merely the prototype of genteel, stiff-upper-lip British resolve in wartime. That may be why she won an Oscar for this home-front melodrama, but today her character is a revelation—a wife and mother of three who radiates lusty playfulness, real-woman warmth, and prefeminist strength. Luminous, almond-eyed, and honey-voiced, Garson never sounded the acting trumpets like Katharine Hepburn or Bette Davis did; she just *was*, and here she's the ultimate mom, confident and unruffled by chaos, yet still stirringly sexy and sweet. William Wyler's movie is laced with propaganda and hokum, but between Garson's maternal light and Teresa Wright's performance (another Oscar winner) as her daughter-in-law, the movie veritably glows.

I Remember Mama **(1948)** The story of a dead-poor Norwegian immigrant clan living in San Francisco circa 1910, whose matriarch is wise, firm, funny, loving, and, of course, self-sacrificing. The family could just as well have been Scottish or Asian or shtetl-Jewish—mothers the world over want more for their children, and why should they have a new coat when the little ones need books? Irene Dunne, in her last significant role, flashes that ironic smile as she bustles about with her brood, but she's fully committed to her character's limitations and the feeling of family intimacy. There's no defense from tearjerking once she sneaks into a hospital children's ward pretending to be a nurse, just so she can croon to her sick daughter and, as it turns out, the ward's other young patients as well.

The Effect of Gamma Rays on Man-in-the-Moon Marigolds **(1972)** Joanne Woodward won Best Actress at the Cannes Film Festival for playing the batty, maddening, slightly crazy mother of two neglected teens (one of whom—Matilda—is played by Nell Potts, daughter of Woodward and director Paul Newman). From a play by Paul Zindel.

Italianamerican **(1974)** Early in his career as New York's signature movie voice, Little Italy–bred Martin Scorsese shot this lovely featurette composed of little more than a plastic-wrapped-couch interview with his aging parents in their apartment on Elizabeth Street, in which they detail their lives as second-gen Sicilian Americans and life in the lower Manhattan neighborhoods during the first decades of the century. The movie, like the Scorsese family itself, defers to gregarious, no-nonsense Mama Catherine on most counts, and that includes the credits, which feature her recipe for spaghetti sauce. Mrs. Scorsese appeared in several of her son's films, but this document is as thorough and priceless as portrait of mother-son love as any ever made.

Freaky Friday **(1976)** This Disney cheap-concept hit, which would be remade twenty-seven years later, explores the commonly felt certainty that if she could just be you for *one day*, your mother (if you're a teenage girl) or daughter (if you're the mother of a teenage girl) would finally understand you and what you're going through. So that's what happens: kid Jodie Foster and mom Barbara Harris swap bodies, endure varying comeuppances, and so forth. Watching this flick may give you a deeper appreciation for your mother or daughter, but mostly it'll just give you the gleeful opportunity to watch the other half suffer for a change.

The Joy Luck Club **(1993)** Amy Tan's multigenerational saga about Chinese mothers, Chinese daughters, and Chinese American daughters gets a shorthand Hollywood treatment, but the actresses are all dynamite, and the dramatic circumstances of their travails—feudal-era oppression, betrayal, infanticide, abuse, you name it—is a tell-your-mom-you-love-her emotional bludgeon.

Rugrats: **"Mother's Day" (1997)** Chuckie, you will recall if you were lucky enough to have children when this brilliantly inventive and eloquent cartoon series first ran, is the lisping, bespectacled scaredy-cat whose absent mother is eventually revealed to have died—and in this episode, which can hit you like a truck if you let it, the toddlers try to find, amid the Mother's Day gift giving, a mom for Chuckie, until it is realized that she is all around them already, in the garden she planted before she got sick. Whew. Featured on the ***Rugrats: Mommy Mania*** video release.

Lovely and Amazing **(2002)** A caustic film about a family of insecure women plagued by the same flaws and body image hang-ups nearly every woman has. The mother (Brenda Blethyn) subjects herself to liposuction while fantasizing about the dishy doctor, and each of the daughters flounders in her own life: the eldest (Catherine Keener) has a disastrous affair with a teenager; the middle child (Emily Mortimer) is helplessly vulnerable to anorexia and male criticism; and the youngest daughter, an adopted African American (the painfully genuine Raven Goodwin), overeats to assuage her confusion about life.

Rabbit-Proof Fence **(2002)** As European settlers took to slowly decimating Aboriginal society in Australia, what began as just one manner of oppression—kidnapping Aboriginal children from their families "for their own good" and training them as servants—became, in the case of "half-caste" children, official state policy. This program persisted, astonishingly, into the 1970s, but Phillip Noyce's film, based on a true story, is set in 1931, when three girls, aged fourteen, ten, and eight, were snatched from their family and sent to a slave camp hundreds of miles away. Indignant, they escaped; hell-bent on returning to their mothers, they walked for months back north along the continent-dividing fence that provides the film's title, always just one step ahead of the law. Based on a memoir by a grown daughter of the eldest girl and rarely digressing from the journey itself, the movie is a primal trial, visually arresting and sociopolitically devastating.

***Since Otar Left...* (2003)** A Georgian film shot in Tbilisi (apparently, the Frenchest city in the ex-Soviet regions), it paints a vivid portrait of a cultured, all-female family (cranky, reactionary grandmother; bitter, pragmatic mother; rebellious teen daughter) struggling to survive in the new nation after the clan's son/brother/uncle hightailed it to Paris. Among the three women (in masterful performances across the board), every love-hate tangle we've ever had with our own mothers is hashed out and healed.

***Volver* (2006)** Pedro Almodóvar's very campy, very gender-flexible, very female-friendly universe gets another workout, with Penélope Cruz as a single mom with mother problems, daughter problems, aunt and sister problems, and a masculine corpse to hide. Not only is the film essentially a love letter to feminine-family bonding and mother-daughter pathos, but its quasi-Hitchcockian plot is also unraveled almost entirely by way of womanly banter, chitchat, and heart-to-hearts.

▐

FATHER'S DAY

"Hey . . . Dad? You wanna have a catch?"
—Kevin Costner, *Field of Dreams*

Dad's Day movie choices are a little easier than those for Mother's Day: though it hasn't been clinically proven as far as we know, it seems that father-kid kinship is generally a less fraught affair—often more distant, perhaps, but also less haunted by expectations, old intimacies, and stuff like that. Generally. Anyway, movies can often serve as channelers for hard-to-express feelings, and they can offer context for relationships that have been, shall we say, sobered by masculinity.

***Life with Father* (1947)** Hard to believe that the memoirs of one Victorian-era Wall Street dad could be so fascinating and funny that they could fill a bestselling book, become the longest-running nonmusical Broadway play ever, and find their way onto the silver screen and into a television series besides. The bombastic Clarence Day (William Powell) thinks he rules the roost but harrumphs around the house wondering why no one heeds his orders. Irene Dunne is the unflappable airhead wife who believes the entire world revolves around her husband but still manages to make him do whatever she wants.

***East of Eden* (1955)** Elia Kazan's lopsided but passionately acted version of the John Steinbeck epic, about a dynastical meltdown in the Salinas valley during World War I, in which motherless, rebellious son James Dean and hard-line single father Raymond

Massey clash like titans. The relationship is more complex than you'd expect, given Steinbeck's Biblical code, and just as tragic.

***The In-Laws* (1979)** The ultimate daddy comedy, and an unsurpassed confluence of post-Catskills humor, post-Method acting, and flat-out farce. Alan Arkin, in his prime as possibly America's best-ever comic straight man, is a wealthy Manhattan dentist whose daughter is marrying the son of Peter Falk, an apparently delusional (or at least chronically mendacious) rogue CIA agent. A domino tumble of highly questionable circumstances sucks Arkin's safety-obsessed nebbish into his future in-law's cockamamy plots, betrayals, and screwups, all of it endured, in the end, for the sake of the kids. The absurd shenanigans are in well-trained hands (including those of screenwriter Andrew Bergman, and costar Richard Libertini as a daffy South American despot). Do not confuse this, the original, with the 2003 remake, which, by comparison, has the flavor of rising stomach acid.

***Kramer vs. Kramer* (1979)** This Oscar-weighted fave may feel a little dated; Dustin Hoffman's ineptness as a workaholic single father is more sitcom than domestic reality. (Even in the 1970s, men knew how to pour milk on cereal.) So Robert Benton's film is playing with a marked deck, but the rhythms of father-son bonding are performed with care and a sharp ear. It might be best as a Father's Day choice for men who are in Dutch with their wives; Meryl Streep's deadbeat mom is not just unhappy—she's a self-obsessed, mercurial bitch who walks out on her own son and then has the gall to try to win custody of him. No one would take her side, even on Mother's Day.

***Field of Dreams* (1989)** Father-son relationships can be stymied by emotional distance, and often enough games with balls serve as intermediaries. Because it is so unabashed about baseball's capacity to make wistful wimps out of manly men, this mush-minded sigh of a movie might seem to be a hard sell to your work-hardened, aging dad, but chances are, it'll win him over and make him drop a grudging tear. The tall tale's from W. P. Kinsella's novel *Shoeless Joe*: Kevin Costner is the Iowa farmer who hears voices telling him to carve a baseball diamond in the middle of his cornfield, seemingly so that Chicago Black Sox legend Shoeless Joe Jackson can return from the Big Bench in the Sky to play once more. How, why, what? It all leads up to a second chance at redemption, not only for Shoeless Joe and other unfulfilled ballplayers, but also for the delighted farmer's squandered relationship with his long-dead father. Even the toughest old coot will sniffle at the climactic line.

***Mr. & Mrs. Bridge* (1990)** An updating, in a sense, of *Life with Father*, but relatively humorless, this careful Merchant-Ivory adaptation of Evan S. Connell's novels about an emotionally repressed midwestern patriarch (Paul Newman), his servile wife (Joanne Woodward), and his three grown, rebellious kids (including fiery Kyra Sedgwick and lisping zero Robert Sean Leonard) isn't a dramatic powerhouse, but it's got meaty family-conflict material running through it like marrow. It works best, in fact, as a study of defensive, unshakable father domination—an old-school social mandate that, in the modern age, breeds only unhappiness and discord. A sensitively judged film that could justify for you the decision not to call your father on Father's Day.

Eat Drink Man Woman (1994) Ang Lee conjures a heartfelt generational saga about a traditional dad (is there any other kind?), his three grown daughters, and how, amid a battery of high cuisine (the father's a chef), their life together in Taiwan becomes discombobulated by modern contingencies and disagreements. Sensitive and insightful, but far from mushy.

Frequency (2000) The mushiness factor shoots off the gauge in this *Twilight Zone*–ish fantasy, in which modern-day lonely boy Jim Caviezel manages to have, via a cosmic screwup in the sky that magically bridges thirty years of intervening time, a ham-radio conversation with dead fireman dad Dennis Quaid. The time-travel plot twists like an old-fashioned phone cord, but the father-and-son heart-to-hearts are mercilessly effective in the hands of actors this good. Watching this, even the crustiest man's man will fold like a wet newspaper.

Riding Alone for Thousands of Miles (2005) Zhang Yimou's neglected heart-tugger, in which the estranged, unemotional father (Ken Takakura) of a dying Japanese filmmaker decides to go to China and finish his son's documentary about a celebrated folksinger. The journey takes on resonance of its own, of course, but the generational pathos is powerful.

NATIONAL GRANDPARENTS DAY

"Grandpa, if you had a chance to go back and do it all differently, what would you have changed?"
—Kathleen Turner, *Peggy Sue Got Married*

In 1978 President Jimmy Carter decreed that National Grandparents Day be celebrated in the United States every first Sunday after Labor Day. Now you know. Traditions are waiting to be minted—don't put it off.

Willy Wonka and the Chocolate Factory (1971) The first, and still the best loved, version of the Roald Dahl kid's novel clings to your memory for many reasons—the pastel-hued, cardboard set design, the bewigged-midget Oompa-Loompas, the fierce overacting by a raft of British character players, the quietly disorienting mania of Gene Wilder's

Wonka. But it's also a potent portrait of love between a sweet but beleaguered semi-adolescent (the earnest Peter Ostrum) and his dreamy, devoted grandfather, warmly portrayed by Jack Albertson.

***A Summer at Grandpa's* (1984)** An early and rare film from Taiwanese artist Hou Hsiao-Hsien, in which the two children of a terminally ill mother are shipped off to spend the summer at the country home of their grandparents. Stereotypes are dumped wholesale in exchange for emotional ambiguity: wonder and joy are undercut with anxiety and insecurity, love with grief.

***Cocoon* (1985)** This Ron Howard–directed, Spielbergian-blue-light-saturated smash, in which alien pods revive weary septuagenarians, does not hold up well today—it barely did in 1985. But the sci-fi scenario can have regenerative effects, and the film salutes its elderly cast (including Wilford Brimley, Jessica Tandy, and Don Ameche, who won his only Oscar for his performance) in a way that too few movies do.

***Peggy Sue Got Married* (1986)** Kathleen Turner is a disenchanted wife and mother who, during her twenty-fifth high school reunion, is mysteriously transported into her own past as a teenager in 1960, where she hokily reevaluates her life from an if-I-knew-then perspective. Nicolas Cage's courageously absurd portrait of a nasal-voiced eighteen-year-old is a bright spot, but the movie's central conceit only hits the gut when Peggy Sue meets up again with her long-dead grandparents. In just a few scenes, *Peggy Sue* captures, from a kid's perspective, the stinging reality of the generational bond.

***Hope and Glory* (1987)** John Boorman's award-winning semiautobiographical ode to his childhood experiences during World War II and the Blitzkrieg is a rangy, busy film (Boorman even packed in an Arthurian parable), but at its core is the joie de vivre shared by the nine-year-old Bill (Sebastian Rice Edwards), who is having a fascinating and surprisingly ecstatic time amid the chaos, and his vivacious grandfather (Ian Bannen's zesty performance netted him a British Academy Award nomination).

***The Way Home* (2002)** A shameless Korean tear-wringer, in which a spoiled urban brat is left with his rural grandmother while his mom looks for work. Naturally, the boy's destructive and bratty ways are no match for his grandmother's patience and love.

PRESIDENTS' DAY

"The president can bomb anybody he likes."
—Anthony Hopkins, *Nixon*

Though legally still called Washington's Birthday in the federal code book, this day has come to honor Lincoln (who also had a February birthday), and since the 1980s, unofficially, all presidents. That certainly expands your options for celebrating your day off from work; you could hail the presidential giants (if you are so inclined), decry the criminals (how *do* you fete the legacy of Richard Nixon or George W. Bush?), or recall the boondogglers (Warren G. Harding, *go*). Movies tend toward hagiography, but there are a few films in which we're treated to less-than-rosy pictures of our former chiefs.

Young Mr. Lincoln **(1939)** The easiest of U.S. presidents to idolize, Lincoln gets the John Ford treatment here. In keeping with the more simplistic grade-school-history texts, Lincoln's young, crafty-but-idealistic, self-made lawyer days (during which he argues a fictional case against lynch law) provide a moral template for his presidency. Henry Fonda does a fine, wary job, and the filmmaking is lovely. The editors of the renowned French film magazine *Cahiers du Cinéma* thought the film was significant—to the extent that their theory-choked, deconstructive 1970 "collective text" about it is now more famous than the movie itself.

Abe Lincoln in Illinois **(1940)** Raymond Massey, potentially the most underrated actor in 1940s Hollywood, does an enthralling Lincoln—perhaps the best in movies—in this version of the Robert Sherwood play, which travels from the president's woodsman days to his first election. Stirring and noble stuff (although it avoids the many difficult details involved in fighting the Civil War—a biopic on that subject is just waiting to be made), with Ruth Gordon stealing her scenes as Mary Todd Lincoln, a tradition for those who play First Ladies that carries all the way to *Nixon*.

Wilson **(1944)** There may be a limit to the extent that a movie should lionize a historically destructive president. This unwieldy biopic of Woodrow Wilson, a pet project for producer Darryl F. Zanuck, is more interested in the twenty-eighth president's personal struggles, widowhood, and disappointment over the failure of the League of Nations than it is in the disaster Wilson single-handedly contrived by persuading Congress and the populace (thanks to his newly formed propaganda office, the Committee of Public Information) into entering the European war and sending more than a hundred thousand American draftees to their deaths. He was a dedicated public segregationist, too. But, hey, the flick lavishly evokes the period, and Alexander Knox (as Wilson) isn't dull in every scene.

Bedtime for Bonzo (1951) For citizens who haven't forgotten the Reagan era's impact on the economy, Central America, the environment, and federal regulations, and who may still be dazzled by the reverence blithely directed at our first truly clueless president, what better way to spend Presidents' Day than with this idiotic comedy, starring a future world leader and a chimpanzee? (This is whom we willingly elect to run our country?) Reagan plays a dim prof who decides to teach a baby chimp the difference between right and wrong. And fails. You don't need to know more.

Sunrise at Campobello (1960) The obligatory lovefest biopic of FDR—who knows why it wasn't made earlier. Ralph Bellamy plays our only thrice-elected chief official in the 1920s, during his first polio battles and his rise to political fortune. The still-lovely Greer Garson plays Eleanor—a hilariously inappropriate casting coup that must've made the still-alive, ugliest-of-all-First-Ladies tipsy. A starry-eyed film that seems more like a play, but it's fun for old New Dealers.

PT 109 (1963) A wholesale dose of Kennedy-Camelot whitewash, in which JFK (Cliff Robertson) is lionized for his wartime heroics. The film was released five months *before* the November assassination, and therefore might be the most shameless gift Hollywood ever gave to a standing prez. But it's hard to begrudge the gesture now, and the movie is sure to have aging Democrats reaching for a tissue.

Millhouse: A White Comedy (1971) Nonfiction muckraker Emile de Antonio cobbled together this devastating portrait of America's craziest president out of Nixon press conferences and news footage, illustrating to all eyes how amoral, foolish, and pandering a man can be and still become the world's most powerful leader.

Give 'Em Hell, Harry! (1975) James Whitmore was, oddly, Oscar nominated for this filmed record of his Broadway one-man hit, in which he plays Harry S Truman as a lovable, quip-tossing, middle-American arch-uncle.

The Wind and the Lion (1975) A bit dated and politically silly, this broadly fictionalized historical epic traces the kidnapping in Morocco, around the turn of the century, of an American (Candice Bergen) by a Berber chieftain (Sean Connery). An international skirmish resulted that was ultimately managed, after a fashion, by President Theodore Roosevelt (Brian Keith). Writer-director John Milius is a self-professed hawk, so it's no surprise the portrait of Roosevelt is something of a saber-rattling whitewash, but Keith is convincing and great fun.

Nixon (1995) Oliver Stone applies his particular hammer-to-the-head style of filmmaking to the life of one Richard Milhous Nixon, with emphasis on the late, great psycho prez's rabid bigotry and manic paranoia. No insights to speak of, and the absurdly miscast Anthony Hopkins is never convincing as Tricky Dick (Dan Hedaya was born for the role, but, we assume, he didn't have enough star power to suit Stone's bankrollers, so instead he got stuck playing a fictionalized version of Bebe Rebozo, the Florida magnate and Nixon buddy). Still, Joan Allen reigns as a fracturing Pat Nixon, and the rest of the cast eats the story alive.

Thirteen Days **(2000)** Assiduous, temperate, and a lot more honest about government and politicians than any other Hollywood film of the last few decades, this docudrama about the Cuban Missile Crisis at least does the justice of dressing down the overly sanctified Camelot legend, even as it skips over vital history (like the small, precipitative matter of Operation Mongoose, the Kennedy administration's prolonged covert attack on Cuba before and after the crisis, without which we would've had no troubles there at all). Without actually beating him up, this film shows the most seemingly innocent twentieth-century president as a living, breathing, deeply flawed politician, susceptible to backroom dealing and virtually free of high principles. This is, however, about as political as director Roger Donaldson's movie gets—otherwise, it is a chronicle of the American system at work during one of the few international moments in which politicians and bureaucrats, from JFK (Bruce Greenwood) and RFK (Steven Culp) to advisor Kenny O'Donnell (Kevin Costner), came off looking like champions. Still, despite its professionalism and mature perspective, it elides whole truths. What rankles most, perhaps, is how the film makes heroes out of people like Robert McNamara (Dylan Baker), McGeorge Bundy (Frank Wood), and Dean Rusk (Henry Strozier), who may have acted heroically for that brief moment in time, but who made careers for themselves greasing the money chutes of the corporate elite, producing illegal triumphs for moneyed politicians, and working covertly (and sometimes not so covertly) to forcefully keep Central America, Africa, and the Middle East under the U.S. boot. But this *is* Hollywood.

VETERANS DAY

"Did you ever think life would turn out like this?"
—Meryl Streep, *The Deer Hunter*

In crafting this section we had to walk a fine line, choosing films that celebrate the men and women who have gone to war while avoiding movies that celebrate the wars themselves. In the end, we would argue, it is the antiwar film that realistically depicts combat experience and emotionally ties us to the people caught up in it. Thoughtless flag-wavers like 1949's *Sands of Iwo Jima*, therefore, can find their champions elsewhere.

***Grand Illusion* (1937)** Jean Renoir's classic, seminal antiwar film makes its position crystal clear without a single battle scene. Instead, Renoir's customary humane generosity extends here even to World War I prisoners of war, whose ethics and camaraderie in the face of incarceration backlights the essential evil of war the way a saint's beatific behavior implicitly interrogates our own petty meanness. Jean Gabin, Pierre Fresnay, and Marcel Dalio lead the French soldiers in stir; Erich von Stroheim, Teutonic as always, but old-world civilized and sympathetic, is the German commander. On this fringe of the global conflict, all exhausted souls wish one another well.

***J'Accuse* (1937)** Abel Gance's howling morality play follows a traumatized World War I vet (Victor Francen) who seeks to stop war for all time; as World War II approaches, his efforts are thwarted by the government, which incites him to summon the war dead in protest. Gance used hundreds of very real maimed and scarred veterans for the chilling climax, and as pacifist statements go, it's hard to forget.

***Hail the Conquering Hero* (1944)** Screwball king writer-director Preston Sturges even had it in him to lampoon World War II home-front fervor *during* the war, in this comedy about a nerd (Eddie Bracken) who gets discharged for hay fever but spontaneously encourages his crazy town to believe he's a wounded hero.

***The Story of G.I. Joe* (1945)** William Wellman's film dramatizes the famed warfront news dispatches of journalist Ernie Pyle (Burgess Meredith) during World War II's North African campaign. With Robert Mitchum in a star-making role as the coolest Army officer ever. This is how America saw itself during the war: not as flag-waving goons nor as bloodthirsty killers, but as men at hard work.

***The Best Years of Our Lives* (1946)** Probably the best film ever made about returning vets, William Wyler's small-town ode takes its time, cares for details, and attends to emotional ambivalences. Heroic and lovely. (See "Reliving the 1940s," p. 288.)

***The Steel Helmet* (1951)** Several Classic Hollywood directors went to war in the 1940s (if only to shoot propaganda films), but only Samuel Fuller, a hard-boiled tabloid reporter at the time, saw war for what it really was: "limbs everywhere," an irrational state of fear, and brutish chaos. Fuller's war films, of which the purest and nastiest is this noirish rat-pit drama, were distinctively unpatriotic and undiluted by idealism. In this, only his third film, Fuller grunts along with a few ragtag soldiers, and a little Korean boy, at the onset of the Korean War (the movie was filmed only months after U.S. forces began engagement). Among cineasts and a certain breed of vet, this is the greatest American war film ever made. Fuller's other war films all burn with vulgar conviction; check out ***Fixed Bayonets* (1951)**, the recently restored, semiautobiographical ***The Big Red One* (1980)**, and, if you can find it, ***Falkenau, the Impossible* (1988)**, a French documentary, narrated by Fuller in all of his glory, that centers around the footage Fuller shot as an infantryman of the liberation of the Falkenau concentration camp.

Men in War (1957) Anthony Mann's meticulous Korean war saga is all "boots on the ground," and is so awake to physical reality that, as critic David Thomson put it, "one could draw a contour map of the terrain." The enemy is never seen; Robert Ryan, Aldo Ray, and Vic Morrow hold the foreground.

Red Angel (1966) Obsessive Japanese auteur Yasuzo Masumura takes on the 1930s Japanese siege of China—a cataclysmic eight-year massacre mission in which at least twenty-three million Chinese died and which Japan, to this day, struggles to rationalize. The film follows the dire path of a young nurse (Ayako Wakao) who, in the first five minutes, is raped in a ward of recovering soldiers. The bodies of dead and wounded arrive in truckloads, and the medical choices are reduced to amputating various body parts or letting the bastards die; Masumura is not above cutting to a barrel stuffed with hacked hands and feet, or glancing at mass cremations for a transition shot. Too overwhelmed by carnage to align her emotions, the heroine instinctively trades sex for a pint of blood to help her rapist when he returns, near death, from the front, and half-willingly becomes horndog prey to virtually every man she meets, including a double amputee begging for a handjob, a platoon of death-facing soldiers who maintain their right to just screw anything, and a morphine-junkie surgeon who considers himself little better than a mass murderer. It's difficult to recall any American war film as horrified and cynical about the ripple effects of imperial war, or one as nearly suicidal with cultural guilt.

Winter Soldier (1972) If reality, not fond memories or propaganda, is on the agenda, you can hardly do better than this searing, radical documentary, which is really nothing more than the filmed record of a days-long press conference held by vets returned from Vietnam, in which they talk about the routine atrocities they'd committed and witnessed. This film, shot and edited by an anonymous collective, was essentially blacklisted for decades; only in 2005 did it finally get a video release. Other essential, and upsetting, documentaries of 'Nam vets include ***No Vietnamese Ever Called Me Nigger*** (1968), ***Interviews with My Lai Veterans*** (1971), and ***Hearts and Minds*** (1974).

Coming Home (1978) It had to be done eventually—a Hollywood love story between a cool paraplegic 'Nam vet and the innocent wife of a hawkish officer—but the filmmakers deserve praise for how beautifully it turned out—acted like crazy by Jon Voight and Jane Fonda, filmed with tons of grainy respect by Hal Ashby, and scored with scores of period tunes.

The Deer Hunter (1978) Politically, this is at best an ambiguous hot potato—an emotionally crushing portrait of how the Vietnam engagement devastates a small, working-class town (which is captured superbly in every detail). But the Vietnamese themselves are depicted as virtually an alien species, remarkable only in their rabid cruelty. In other words, some might consider it the perfect Veterans Day film, if also the one most likely to reduce you to sobbing convulsions.

Born on the Fourth of July (1989) Oliver Stone does his unsubtle dance on Ron Kovic's own story, in which the flag-waving kid from Long Island (played by Tom Cruise, working hard) went to Vietnam and returned, paralyzed, to translate his anger, bitterness, and shame into antiwar, pro-veteran's-rights activism. A brutally realistic portrayal of the devastation of Vietnam and of the shameful treatment of the soldiers who fought there and returned, broken in body, spirit, or both, to find the country ambivalent about what they'd done.

Capitaine Conan (1996) Based on a 1934 semiautobiographical novel by Roger Vercel, Bertrand Tavernier's electrifying antiwar epic bulldozes down a familiar path: it's a war-is-hell World War I message movie, a la Stanley Kubrick's *Paths of Glory*. But Tavernier never moralizes; although his movie is clear about the costs of war, the question of whether the titular hero (Philippe Torreton), the fiercely independent leader of a brutal guerilla platoon of Frenchmen fighting at the tail end of World War I, is a hero, a bullheaded rogue, or a dangerous psycho is a question the film never answers for us. The movie might also be the only film that deals with a rarely acknowledged aspect of the Great War's eastern front: the undeclared war in the Balkans—against the Turks, Bulgars, Serbs, and Greeks—that was fought by some hundred thousand Frenchmen for a full year after the armistice was signed. The politics of this "theater of external operations" aren't made any clearer to us than they seem to be to the soldiers; the story's crucial thread is the effect of guerrilla warfare on Conan and his men. Tavernier shot *Capitaine Conan* like no other war film—the action, whether it's a torrential battle or a stockade argument, often comes at you from a place you least expect it, deep in the frame, then disappears again.

Three Kings (1999) Four American soldiers embark on a hunt for Kuwaiti gold during the first Gulf War—it's symptomatic of this movie's dark humor that they find their treasure map sticking out of the ass of an Iraqi prisoner. George Clooney leads the band of thieves that includes rappers Mark Wahlberg and Ice Cube, and Spike Jonze (director of *Adaptation*). Along the way to finding the gold, they stumble across Iraqi civilians in danger from Saddam Hussein's army, and struggle with their own consciences as well. A strong antiwar statement tucked into a raucous comedy-adventure, director David O. Russell's film forces us to see the situation from the Iraqi point of view; depending on their politics upon returning, vets of either the previous or the current Iraqi war may either love or loathe this movie.

Flags of Our Fathers and Letters from Iwo Jima (2006) It's as if Clint Eastwood set out to piss off "the greatest generation" even as he gave it a back massage with this dead-serious diptych, which looks at World War II's Iwo Jima experience from the American side (*Flags of Our Fathers*: war horror, then hypocritical propagandizing), and the Japanese side (*Letters from Iwo Jima*: just war horror). The latter film—in which Americans are the menacing hordes killing good-hearted Japanese—is the tougher test for vets. Of course, Eastwood's point is that we all think of ourselves as righteous, even as we lay siege to thousands. But did it, and does it, play in Peoria?

MEMORIAL DAY

"Who lit this flame in us? No war can put it out, conquer it."
—Ben Chaplin, *The Thin Red Line*

Like Veterans Day, this emotionally charged commemoration of the American war dead can spark contention along political lines. Again, honor the difficulty and suffering of war; honor the martyr to it.

All Quiet on the Western Front (1930) Erich Maria Remarque's ubiquitous World War I novel gets an Oscar-winning, early-talkie treatment from director Lewis Milestone. The drama is clumsy, but the trench-warfare battle scenes are horrifying and traumatic.

The Fighting Sullivans (1944) One of World War II's saddest true stories, dramatized in this low-budget propaganda piece: five stick-together Iowa brothers enlist in the Navy after Pearl Harbor, and all five go down in the Pacific together. The film is, naturally, a real tearjerker; fifty years later, the tale of the brothers would inspire the core story of the fictional *Saving Private Ryan* (see below).

A Walk in the Sun (1945) Lewis Milestone returns to the battlefield, but unlike his *All Quiet on the Western Front*, this stylized, grunt's-eye-view follows a standard motley assortment of soldiers through Italy from their landing to their arrival at their destination, a nondescript farmhouse; the dialogue (and many of the monologues) take on the form of repetitious, singsong battle poetry. The enemy is never seen.

The Burmese Harp (1956) A haymaker of an antiwar film from Japanese moviemaker Kon Ichikawa, in which a soldier escapes death in Burma by masquerading as a Buddhist priest, then finds himself transformed by the horrors of war into a holy man dedicated to burying the countless dead.

Paths of Glory (1957) Stanley Kubrick's bare-knuckle screed about war and military injustice, set during World War I and amid the French. Kirk Douglas plays a colonel ordered to shove his men into a hopeless slaughter; when they eventually refuse, he's compelled to court-martial a handful of random infantrymen for cowardice. Muscular storytelling and unremitting moral outrage.

The Dawns Here Are Quiet (1972) This patient Soviet propaganda movie was nominated for an Oscar for best foreign film, then was summarily forgotten. It might just be the only war film in which the beleaguered infantry is made up entirely of women: it's World War II, and the horny male soldiers at a lonely outpost are replaced by ably trained female volunteers—all of them eager, fresh-faced comrades, each with her own fragile hopes for the future. Soon, a Nazi party presses them into armed conflict, with their avuncular C.O. torn between duty and guardian guilt. For the Soviets, an inspiring ending meant martyrdom, not salvation.

Overlord (1975) A low-budget British film that's half archival World War II footage and half low-budget, low-key dramatics, Stuart Cooper's all-but-forgotten film (a winner, nonetheless, at the Berlin International Film Festival) echoes *All Quiet on the Western Front* in structure and tone, but the very real sequences of bombing raids and smoldering urban craters leave their own welts.

Das Boot (1981) The greatest submarine film of all time, hands down. Exploiting claustrophobia and water pressure like no one ever has, Wolfgang Petersen (who's been stuck doing seafaring movies ever since) follows the experience of a German U-boat through battle. See the three-and-a-half-hour, undubbed "director's cut" if you can.

A Midnight Clear (1992) It's Christmas, 1944; the Germans have nearly lost, and everyone knows it. Six mostly inexperienced soldiers (including Ethan Hawke, Frank Whaley, and Gary Sinise) are selected for special assignment because of their high IQs, so we know we're in for a thoughtful movie—no "kill the Kraut" heroism here. After stumbling through the darkened, snowy forest they hole up in an abandoned mansion, wondering what to do; the Germans they meet feel likewise, and for a while—but not forever—it seems they won't exchange fire more dangerous than snowballs. This unjustly overlooked film is based on a William Wharton novel.

Saving Private Ryan (1998) The first and more orthodox World War II war film of 1998, Steven Spielberg's heroic yarn follows a troop of assorted all-American types through the European theater on what seems to them to be a fool's mission: retrieving a soldier (Matt Damon) from battle after his brothers are killed elsewhere. Tom Hanks rings true as an unlikely macho commander, and the opening D-Day sequence is justly famous for being gut-twisting.

The Thin Red Line (1998) The year's true World War II masterpiece, Terrence Malick's comeback film (after a twenty-year hiatus from filmmaking) takes place during and around the battle of Guadalcanal, but is in reality far more concentrated on the emotional experience of battle and the impact, poetically invoked here, of human warfare upon individuals and upon nature. Essentially a three-hour, nonnarrative experiment, there are no main characters—just an ensemble of thirty or more figures—and there's no story—just impressions, experiences, feelings (the complex weft of narrational voices often do not synch up with on-screen personas), and astonishing images. Oh, yeah—it's based on James Jones's 1962 novel, though you'd never know it.

9/11

> "Hi, Mom, it's me . . . this really kind woman handed me the phone and told me to call you."
> —Chloe Sirene, *United 93*

A few years ago, the idea of commemorating this anniversary with a movie would've seemed appalling, but the feeling toward addressing the tragedy in cultural terms has come around. Unfortunately, there's only one film that merits a recommendation.

United 93 **(2006)** Treat the toxic, disrespectful likes of Oliver Stone's *World Trade Center* (2006) and the French portmanteau mess *11'09"01: September 11* (2002) with lead tongs. This award-winning and perfectly judged Paul Greengrass film, depicting in meticulous detail the journey of the day for those aboard the plane that crashed down near Shanksville, Pennsylvania, and for the air-traffic controllers at work, stands alone. Don't expect to sit back and nosh.

LABOR DAY

> "They got you fightin' white against colored, native against foreign, hollow against hollow, when you know there ain't but two sides in this world—them that work and them that don't."
> —Chris Cooper, *Matewan*

Most of us are unaware of it, but Labor Day is in fact a day designated to celebrate the unionized working class—it's a socialist holiday from the ground up. President Grover Cleveland declared it a federal holiday in 1894 in an effort to appease the zeitgeist, concerned as he was that discontented labor groups—in the days in which such groups possessed real social power—would institute annual protests against the ownership class. Today, Labor Day is merely seen as a salute to the very work that the holiday allows everyone to skip, but even now the day has real significance.

Strike **(1925)** Soviet propaganda wizard Sergei Eisenstein's first film, a reckless montage frenzy revolving around a chaotic, pre-Revolutionary workers' strike.

Hindle Wakes **(1927)** A forgotten, but DVDed, British silent melodrama about factory girls, their lives of drudgery, and their romantic woes when, on holiday, they try to seduce their way out of the lower classes. For its time, a shockingly frank depiction of industrial labor.

Earth **(1930)** Early Soviet film poet Alexander Dovzhenko wasn't the politburo's favorite filmmaker; this lyrical homage to the Ukrainian peasantry, and the hopefulness of collective farming before Stalinism lowered the boom, attended more to the cycles of farm life and the rough natural beauty of the country than to propaganda.

Black Fury **(1935)** Warner Brothers, in its Depression-gangster heyday, does a crude job of this union drama, which has Paul Muni (as an immigrant with an accent as thick as a railroad tie) trying to talk reason to rebelling coal miners and management.

The Grapes of Wrath **(1940)** John Ford does John Steinbeck's dust bowl epic, and does it with little condescension and no romanticism to speak of. Did Hollywood ever before make poor people look this real? The film was stark and truthful enough to warrant a boycott call from banks and farming corporations, and its unionizing stance was forceful enough to get Ford, of all people, investigated by the House Un-American Activities Committee years later.

Bicycle Thieves **(1949)** A worker's horror story: a postwar Rome father obtains a rare job that's contingent on having a bicycle; soon enough, his vehicle is stolen, and he and his son go searching for it—in a devastated city filled with bicycles. The great Italian neorealist classic (often mistitled as *The Bicycle Thief*), and an unsentimental heartbreaker.

Salt of the Earth **(1954)** Independently made by real union miners and McCarthy blacklistees—at a time when the only "indie" movies were exploitation flicks—this clumsy but gutsy movie about Mexican miners organizing resistance against their white company bosses remains the premier American union film. The production met with federal interference at every juncture, and Mexican star Rosaura Revueltas was imprisoned and deported as a Communist. Stirring not just as a movie, but also as evidence itself of corporate injustice (this theme would be echoed in 1976's *Harlan County USA* [see below]), it's a movie that Noam Chomsky likes to note, saying that it's hardly a coincidence that *Salt of the Earth* is a little-known cultural pariah—while the antiunion *On the Waterfront* is an Oscar-awarded, AFI-approved landmark.

The Molly Maguires (1970) A ham-fisted depiction of a slice of labor history that has been, like so many others, largely excised from schoolbooks: Irish immigrant coal miners in 1870s Pennsylvania battle the injustice and oppression of the mining company with what amounts to terrorism—and their leader is Sean Connery.

Edvard Munch (1974) Radical genius Peter Watkins has made a great many revolutionary movies, most of which are distinguished by the small numbers of filmgoers who've actually been able to see them. This masterwork isn't one of them—its high-art hook got the movie on the TV, and on videotape, years before his other films. A nearly three-hour biopic of the angst-plagued Norwegian painter, the movie not only plumbs Munch's history and social situation, but also utilizes Watkins's frequently ripped off, but never bettered, signature method of framing the film as a fake documentary. The film depicts the vast spread of Scandinavian culture during the Industrial Age—its abuse of workers, wretched living conditions, and institutional injustice. The larger point of the film, of course, is that little has changed.

Harlan County USA (1976) An Oscar-winning socialist-cinema signature film, this shocking Barbara Kopple documentary follows a 1973 Kentucky coal miners' strike, in what amounts to a nerve-racking present tense of summary murder, gun threats, crowd madness, abject poverty, corporate greed, and astonishing communal solidarity. Kopple also looks back upon a century-long history of union battles and violence, a vast national story that still goes missing from most public-school history texts. The local communist ballads, Industrial Workers of the World sloganeering, and memories of robust early-twentieth-century worker networks makes the integrated state of today's unions seem pathetic.

Norma Rae (1979) Don't be fooled by the ad art, which features Sally Field leaping and beaming like a cheerleader. Her character, Norma Rae, is a poor, uneducated factory worker who's had children with men she barely knew; Field looks justifiably wan and sweaty through most of the film. Salvation comes in the form of a Jewish Brooklyn union organizer (Ron Leibman). Forget romance; this is all about workers' politics. Field won her first Oscar for her performance.

The Wobblies (1979) In the first decades of the 1900s, the Industrial Workers of the World (IWW) was condemned, brutalized, legislated against, campaigned against, and demonized; by 1979, American culture had been made to forget that the labor union existed at all. Deborah Shaffer and Stewart Bird's film stands, alongside a scant handful of books, as a testimony to the IWW's astonishing power and growth, with its newspapers and songs and sheer membership, as well as to the sickening history of suppression, murder, and criminal injustice that was brought to bear upon it.

Matewan (1987) John Sayles's earnest, moody, patient dramatization of a true 1920s incident—a coal company's brutal oppression of West Virginia miners and the efforts of a union organizer (Chris Cooper) to unite the disparate racial groups among the workers. It's merely another scary chapter in the story of American labor struggle, resembling many others, but here it's acted up nicely (David Strathairn is unforgettable as a local sheriff who boldly steps into the fight) and photographed with solemn honesty.

Roger & Me **(1989)** Michael Moore's much-celebrated debut film, which set him on an invaluable career course as the fearless, ever-cynical, derisive antidote to corporate-owned media monopolies. Each of his films is a truthful speaking to power (however he might've juggled facts to make them funnier), and here he analyzes the impoverishment of his hometown of Flint, Michigan, in the profit-earning wake of layoffs and factory shutdowns. Riotous and unsettling.

American Dream **(1990)** Barbara Kopple, with a team of fellow documentarians, returns to the striking life in this Oscar winner about the union workers of a Hormel meatpacking plant in Minnesota who buck up against the corporate headquarters' desire to cut their wages and benefits despite escalating profits. This is the reality of workers in the post-Reagan era, and it isn't pretty.

Riff-Raff **(1991)** The great British lefty Ken Loach had his first stateside hit, of sorts, with this film, his first comedy, about low-rung construction workers. His trademarked documentarian's POV, which elsewhere suggests squalor and hopelessness, is perfectly suited for the vinegary backbeats of construction site camaraderie; we witness the battery of roughneck Iron Johns working, lazing, joking, arguing, and frequently falling prey to their employer's insufficient safeguards and general disregard for the working stiff. A somewhat marginalized figure, Loach has been making politically committed films since the 1960s, and he continues to do so today.

Land and Freedom **(1995)** Both a Marxist rant and a cold squint at the consequences of political idealism, Ken Loach's film vividly surveys the psychic wreckage of one of the century's greatest and least remembered political shitstorms: the Spanish Civil War. A young Liverpudlian bloke (Ian Hart) goes to Spain to fight with the Loyalists on the dusty Aragon front, where the weight of righteous ideology is just as tangible and riveting as the battlefield grit.

The Awful Truth **(1999–2000)** Michael Moore's short-lived cable TV show had some lazy fat on it, and Moore's not to everyone's tastes, but nowhere else in American mainstream media are you likely to see active and fearless concern for real workers and real union solidarity. Besides that, it's wrenchingly, savagely funny. A key example: Moore's portrayal of a group of Mexican Holiday Inn maids who tried to unionize and got deported for their troubles. Moore throws them a farewell party (complete with INS-agent pinata!), then proceeds to document, on tape, the hotel's many health and fire violations.

La Commune (Paris, 1871) **(2000)** The latest film from sidelined progressive empiricist Peter Watkins, and a tribulation of righteous anger. Nearly six hours long, the film is a "faux" news telecast reporting on the Paris Commune's 1871 peasant rebellion, during which working citizens essentially took over huge chunks of Paris and set up their own, fastidiously democratic communal government. A long, unrelenting flame-thrower of humane rhetoric, with an all-amateur cast who occasionally step out of character to share political epiphanies with Watkins's restless camera.

GROUNDHOG DAY

"This is one time where television really fails to capture the true excitement of a large squirrel predicting the weather."
—Bill Murray, *Groundhog Day*

It was a minor, foolish, forgotten annual all-American semi-event, until *that* movie came to town.

Groundhog Day **(1993)** So there's only one viable movie choice for this peculiar American holiday; good thing it's an enduring beaut. This film has become a part of our cultural DNA, and it's gone a long way toward redefining the meaning of Groundhog Day in the vernacular. The day is still an odd showbiz ritual that centers on a rodent, a small town in Pennsylvania, and the presence or absence of cloud cover, but now, thanks to writer-director Harold Ramis and star Bill Murray, it also represents the opportunity to repeat something until you get it right. Murray plays an ultracynical weatherman plagued by his assignment to travel to Punxsutawney, Pennsylvania, and pay broadcast homage to the country's most famous groundhog. His comeuppance for being a selfish, coldhearted jerk arrives when he wakes up to find himself living that same day over and over again. Along the way, he discovers his own humanity and perky producer Andie MacDowell's irresistibly crooked smile; the nice thing is that Murray's too deadpan silly to get sentimental, so the movie never loses its edge.

EARTH DAY

"Where there is no intelligence, there is also no stupidity."
—Lawrence Pressman, *The Hellstrom Chronicle*

Another recently branded American holiday, Earth Day was federally declared for the March equinox by President Gerald Ford in 1975, in answer to the "ecology" movement. Few films made before the 1970s regarded nature with much reverence, which may well have been part of the holiday's broader cultural point.

The Hellstrom Chronicle (1971) Will insects inherit the Earth? Of course they will, eventually, but this feverish quasidocumentary, narrated by a fictional scientist played by Lawrence Pressman, makes the case that it'll happen sooner rather than much later, since bugs are shown to be many times tougher and more adaptable than any other life on the planet. The facts are disquieting by themselves, but the film whips up a frenzy of entophobia with galling sequences of insect warfare and predation. Yuk.

Frogs (1972) A cheesy ecological horror film in which swamp creatures of all varieties protest pollution by descending upon grumpy pesticide-hound Ray Milland, confined to a wheelchair and in deep amphibian trouble. The memorable poster image—a human hand hanging out of a giant frog's mouth—has nothing to do with the movie.

Day of the Animals (1977) Not many reasons to recommend this post-*Jaws* dime-store thriller, in which the wildlife of an ozone-depleted, irradiated North American woodland attack hikers, other than the simple fact that the animals—hawks, wolves, snakes, bears, cougars—are surprisingly expressive actors.

Koyaanisqatsi (1983) What used to be called a "head movie," this vast montage about technological progress and its impact on the planet (the title, pronounced to rhyme with "coy honest Nazi," is a Hopi word for "life out of balance") is little more than a frantic jumble of images of nature and human devastation, set to a rhythmic Philip Glass score. But its point is salient and hard to ignore.

The Bear (1988) A French film made with minimal dialogue and dubbed into scores of languages, this zoological odyssey follows a real orphan Kodiak cub who latches onto a full-grown male and attempts to steer clear of hunters. Tremendous unspoiled locales (Canada, the Italian Alps), cute animals, and at least one dramatic confrontation between man and animal that'll make your eyes bulge.

Gorillas in the Mist (1988) The biopic of naturalist and activist Dian Fossey, who spent the later years of her career observing and fighting for the African highland gorilla, which were and still are endangered by poachers (for, among other reasons, the ghastly international market in gorilla-paw ashtrays). Sigourney Weaver plays her with a rather simian fierceness, and the sequences shot with actual wild apes are mesmerizing. A woman with many enemies in Africa, Fossey was murdered in 1985; it's believed she was killed either by poachers or by other parties with economic interests in the gorillas' exploitation.

Lessons of Darkness **(1992)** Whether he's making a fiction film or a documentary, German director Werner Herzog always seeks out earthly landscapes that seem to be ready-made metaphors for man's folly and its disastrous collision with natural forces. For this film, Herzog went to Kuwait after the Gulf War and simply shot the burning oil fields—but the result is gut-wrenching, infernal, and howlingly eloquent about ecological ruin.

MicroCosmos **(1996)** A goggle-eyed French documentary about French insects, Claude Nuridsany and Marie Pérennou's captivating film is like an immersion in an alien world (even for Americans who know their local garden arthropods), including a breed of follow-the-leader caterpillar that gets confused and becomes trapped in a circular flow, and a pair of amorous snails, whose lovemaking is ridiculously squishy.

Princess Mononoke **(1997)** Among the hypnotic, wondrous animated films of global auteur-star Hayao Miyazaki, this burly pagan epic stands out for its ambition and uncharacteristically conflicted plotting. That it was released in the United States with an atrocious redubbing job featuring Billy Crudup, Claire Danes, Billy Bob Thornton, and Jada Pinkett Smith didn't help. Loosely based on an interesting hunk of Japanese folklore and blazing occasionally with bizarre, mythic imagery that can make your hair stand on end, the story concerns a young warrior, a rampaging demonic plague, a human war between a self-interested fort town and an army of freebooters, the forest maiden of the title, and an array of angry animal gods, who are wholly concerned with how the various modes of destruction are harming the wilderness. To keep all of this straight, enormous mountains of exposition are required—some it even delivered by enormous Boar Gods on the way to battle. The paramount conservationist message is expressed in truly grandiose terms, but *Mononoke* died at the U.S. box office. (For a time after its initial release in Japan, it was that country's second-highest-grossing film ever, after *Titanic*.) If you can find it in its subtitled (not dubbed) format, jump on it.

Kestrel's Eye **(1999)** A wordless, meditative wildlife documentary about a family of birds, Mikael Kristersson's offering is such a small, unassuming film that it's hard to believe anyone noticed it. The method was simplicity itself: using remote-control cameras and microphones, the filmmaker captured a full year's cycle in the lives of a family of kestrels (a common European falcon) as they nested in the steeple of a thirteenth-century Swedish church. That's it, and of course Kristersson's point is that that should be more than enough. We see the birds hunt, eat, and care for their young, and eventually we see the young bust their way out of the alcove and meet the world. It might be the quietest film ever made—seeing it in a theater meant getting enveloped in the timeless patience of wildlife on their own turf. (It wouldn't surprise us to discover the film lowers blood pressure.) Anyone feeling bludgeoned by contemporary movies might very well experience an epiphany watching this film.

Winged Migration (2001) A French documentary about birds, but one that, dazzlingly, flies with the creatures practically wherever they go. Great video wallpaper.

The Wild Thornberrys Movie (2002) Easily the most globally integrated entry in the post-mod New Cartoon Wave, this film, about a globetrotting, dysfunctional family of wild-life documentarians, made for a fairly rote feature, in which poachers are battled and defeated. Still, there's no denying the charm of bespectacled, braces-ridden, homely wild child Eliza (Lacey Chabert), who can speak to animals—and who emerges as one of the most stirring heroines in contemporary media.

Save the Green Planet! (2003) A South Korean whatzit that begins as a kidnapping psycho-comedy and evolves into something else altogether, then into something beyond that—to say more would douse its fire. Suffice it to say that the title's implicit concern for planetary health is earned with wild imaginative energy, not just glibly asserted.

The Wild Parrots of Telegraph Hill (2003) A touching documentary about a flock of par-rots that have made San Francisco their home and the near-homeless man that cares for them. Adorable, but be forewarned: tragedy strikes; our eight-year-old was inconsolable.

Mountain Patrol: Kekexili (2004) Panoramic and visually daunting, this Chinese film chronicles a very real band of paramilitary volunteers who, in the mid-1990s, patrolled the Kekexili highlands, prowling after poachers of Tibetan antelope.

Grizzly Man (2005) In this award winner, director Werner Herzog considers the case of one Timothy Treadwell, an egomaniacal, self-styled naturalist-slash-wildlife expert who spent scores of summers living in the Alaskan wilderness with only his camera and an array of wild, potentially deadly grizzly bears. Treadwell, along with a girlfriend, was finally torn to pieces in 2003; Herzog appropriates the man's own remarkable and often narcissistic film footage to ask: Did he do right by the bears, or did he endanger them? Was he a fool or a crusader? Did he get what he deserved?

March of the Penguins (2005) To date the second-largest-grossing documentary ever made (after *Fahrenheit 9/11*), this French-made, Morgan Freeman–narrated tribulation observes the Antarctic emperor penguins as they traverse miles of open ice to mate, lay eggs, and hatch chicks. Fascinating for at least a while, it also indulges in cutesy music cues, anthropomorphic stereotypes, and hilarious assumptions about the feel-ings of inexpressive marine wildlife.

An Inconvenient Truth (2006) Moon about penguins and parrots all you like, but Davis Guggenheim and Al Gore's dissertation on global warming sets up the big environmental picture, and gets the sirens going. The burden of unassailable evidence says the wheels have already been set in motion for making our planet essentially uninhabitable and no amount of corporate or political prevarication will make that fact go away.

MARTIN LUTHER KING DAY

"That's the double truth, Ruth!"
—Samuel L. Jackson, *Do the Right Thing*

This holiday (signed into holiday law by a reluctant, King-bashing President Ronald Reagan in 1983) is designated to officially honor the civil rights struggle of the postwar years. In terms of movies, it's also the day to choose whether to watch a recently released, righteously enlightened film on American race relations or an older, illuminatingly bigoted one—either choice may, in fact, impart the same lesson. Consider the following to honor Black History Month as well.

The Birth of a Nation **(1915)** Any concern about the history of civil rights in America ought to include a close study of this long-praised silent epic, the first full-length feature in Hollywood history and, by some estimations, the most-seen film of all time. It's grand filmmaking for its day, and director D. W. Griffith innovated all over the place, but there's no escaping this Civil War melodrama's massive racist assault and blistering bigoted caricatures. The climax, which features a rescue by the Ku Klux Klan, is just the cherry on a very large, very exhausting insult. Hardly a "classic," it stands as a shocking expression of institutionalized bigotry.

The Defiant Ones **(1958)** Director Stanley Kramer was known for years as a heavy-handed, social-issues ideologue, but in retrospect—and considering today's "serious" films about racism, genocide, environmentalism, and so on—much of Kramer's oeuvre now seems eloquent, passionate, and affecting. This film is a prime example: escaped convicts Sidney Poitier and Tony Curtis, chained together, are forced to bond as men despite their individual races as they scramble across the countryside. Hot under the collar and acted at a fever pitch, this movie makes even some Spike Lee films look cheesy and softhearted by comparison.

Shadows **(1959)** Indie great John Cassavetes's first film was made for peanuts on the streets of New York, and it displays a truth-seeking, improvisational style that would soon revolutionize American filmmaking. The story concerns an ill-advised interracial romance, but in fact deals with the psychosocial conditions of an entire black community in a subtle variety of ways. An epochal film event, however jazzily dated and technically crude, that realistically portrays the city's social landscape and the unspoken prejudices that lurk under even the hippest social intercourse.

Nothing but a Man (1964) Michael Roemer's modest, eloquent low-budget film, released just months before Martin Luther King Jr.'s March on Washington, involves a nomadic, pensive railroad worker (Ivan Dixon) born of a prototypically hellish place and time, who's determined not to be sucked into a racist society's traps. Once he meets a preacher's daughter (played with a wry smile and dazzling gentleness by jazz diva Abbey Lincoln), he decides to break the mold of his wretched circumstances, marry, and begin a family in the Deep South; steadily, his quiet resistance to the pervasive bigotry around him sends him on a downward spiral, causing him to resemble his own wife-beating, hateful, family-abandoning father. Like Dixon, the movie rarely raises its voice, and everything it says is therefore clearly heard—in contrast to Hollywood's idea of race relations, *Lilies of the Field*, released the previous year.

King: A Filmed Record . . . Montgomery to Memphis (1970) Essential viewing, this documentary portrait of Martin Luther King Jr. features virtually all of the memorable news footage of the leader's speeches. Narrated by a platoon of Hollywood stars and assembled by Sidney Lumet and Joseph L. Mankiewicz. Similarly, Arnold Perl's *Malcolm X* (1972) serves history by simply presenting the visual record of that civil rights leader in chronological order.

Do the Right Thing (1989) Spike Lee's breakout movie, the film depicts a vivid, no-holds-barred social engagement surrounding the troubled Brooklyn 'hood of Bedford-Stuyvesant, here pressure-cooked by summer swelter, poisoned by commingled racial spite, and made raw by the brutal white-on-black memories of Eleanor Bumpurs and Howard Beach. Shot right in Brooklyn—in hot primary colors, as if the sun had moved several hundred miles closer—Lee's movie is funny and bright and irresistible, even as it commits to a fearless dialogue between races that no American film had ever before attempted.

Daughters of the Dust (1991) Julie Dash's highly respected, but often dreamily aimless, period film preserves the Gullah culture of South Carolina's islands, a haven of African folkways that lingered deep into the last century.

Malcolm X (1992) Spike Lee's epic biopic on the radical civil rights leader is light on convincing characterizations and, strangely, on dramatic demonstrations of midcentury racism and strife between black and white. But it was not conceived as instructional entertainment so much as a monument to Malcolm's political recalcitrance, the unrelenting call for pride and defiance that he embodied, and the decades' worth of hard-won progress that enabled, among an infinite number of things, someone like Lee to go to NYU and make internationally acclaimed films. Denzel Washington doesn't even seem to be acting, but instead seems filled with the spirit.

ELECTION DAY

"Here was a man that not only had a brilliant mind and a wonderful wit, but could also sing!"
—Alan Rickman, *Bob Roberts*

Election Day isn't a holiday, of course, but it's certainly a day of reflection upon our nation's politicians and the myriad ways in which they have screwed, blued, and tattooed the citizens that vote for them. For this one day, at least, cynicism has no proper limit, and getting a handle on the inequities and critiques of the past can only be a good thing.

The Great McGinty **(1940)** Preston Sturges, already a revered scriptsmith in Hollywood by 1939, connived to direct this film, his first, by selling the screenplay to Paramount for ten bucks on the condition that he be made its director. Brian Donlevy plays a goldbricker who's hired by an urban political machine to abet election-box fraud and who is eventually elevated to a corrupt mayorship. When his wife—whom he married strictly for appearances' sake—convinces him to enact real reform, the machine beneath him begins to bite back. Sturges saw the American political system for what it was and still is: a for-profit corporation from which the odd honest and moral individual is systematically expunged.

All the King's Men **(1949)** Robert Penn Warren's Pulitzer-winning novel birthed an Oscar-winning film that's all but forgotten today—and not quite undeservedly so. Robert Rossen's movie has a thunderous postwar realism to it, and Broderick Crawford and Mercedes McCambridge are terrific, but the Huey Long–derived scenario—Louisiana hick reformer skates to the governorship on evangelical rhetoric and bullying, only to prove himself corrupt once he's in office—seems a little naive. If ignorant loudmouths were the primary threat to the integrity of the American system, the institution would be as clean, smooth-running, and honest as the day is long.

Advise and Consent **(1962)** This adaptation of novelist Allen Drury's big bestseller paints a refreshing portrait of federal politics in America: a rat pit full of egomaniacs, grandstanders, strategists, and pocket liners. Henry Fonda is the new Secretary of

State nominee under inquiry, Franchot Tone is the president under fire, and Walter Pidgeon, Charles Laughton, Don Murray, and Peter Lawford are among the jockeying senators.

The Manchurian Candidate **(1962)** John Frankenheimer grabbed author Richard Condon's berserk Cold War paranoid fantasy—of Korean War brainwashing, Sino-Soviet conspiracy, sleeper assassins, McCarthy-like demagoguery, election-year skullduggery—and went for broke. The film still thrills, still musters a creepy Oedipal jolt, and still seems shockingly prophetic, in light of the Kennedy assassination thirteen months after the film's release.

The Best Man **(1964)** Gore Vidal, no foreigner to D.C. or political families, takes a rougher tack in this perennially revived dose of poison, in which Henry Fonda and Cliff Robertson unleash a Pandora's box of underhand slimeball tricks on each other to insure their party's nomination for president. This might still be the bitterest, and most realistic, fiction film made in the United States about election politics.

Point of Order **(1964)** Documentarian Emile de Antonio didn't need to work hard fashioning this famous film, which is comprised entirely of the televised footage of the 1954 McCarthy–U.S. Army hearings, in which McCarthy was eventually censured for "conduct unbecoming" a senator because of under-the-table dealings that had little to do with his House Un-American Activities Committee witch-hunting, but everything to do with his demagogic public behavior. An invaluable window on political abuse, and a fascinating sequel-before-the-fact to George Clooney's ***Good Night, and Good Luck*** **(2005)**.

Medium Cool **(1969)** When Mayor Richard J. Daley and the Chicago police brought out the billy clubs on protestors and Democrats at the 1968 Democratic Convention, radical cinematographer Haskell Wexler was there with the cast and crew of this uneasy metafilm, about a comatose TV news cameraman (Robert Forster) who films the chaos instead of getting involved in it. The irony is, of course, that Wexler got more chaos than he'd bargained for.

Punishment Park **(1971)** Exiled film master Peter Watkins's most lacerating act of political cinema, this 'Nam-era dystopia—presented as a mock documentary—imagines the Nixon government actually acting on the very real McCarran Internal Security Act of 1950 (granting summary-judgment powers to the president in times of potential "insurrection") and shipping arrested war protesters out to the California desert, where they're tried, hunted, and shot like game. Stunningly convincing, and as applicable to the Bush era as it is to the civil rights protest years.

The Candidate **(1972)** On a gentler note, the early 1970s gave us this subtle and reflective satire from director Michael Ritchie, in which Robert Redford plays a young, idealistic lawyer enlisted to run for the Senate as a Democrat—not understanding that he's been chosen specifically because he doesn't stand a chance. The film is properly disillusioning, and so gritty-real it hardly allows you to laugh.

All the President's Men **(1976)** Alan J. Pakula, master of Nixon-era paranoia, was the right man to adapt the Carl Bernstein–Bob Woodward bestseller into an investigative procedural, in which the glamorized reporters (Robert Redford and Dustin Hoffman) keep digging at the Watergate burglary, even though everyone, including their editor (Jason Robards), thinks they're chasing rainbows. What's best about the film is its overall sense of creeping dread—as the Nixon administration's crime become clearer, it also seems that law and order and rightful ideas of democratic authority begin to decompose.

Bob Roberts **(1992)** Tim Robbins's first film as writer-director is an often sophomoric, but more often savagely funny, satire on neoconservative politics. Robbins plays a dimple-faced, folk-singing reactionary on his way up the ladder; around him, seen and interviewed in mock-doc format, are fawning handlers, pundits, and fans.

Feed **(1992)** A "found footage" film with a program: all of the images are culled from the televisual material surrounding the 1992 New Hampshire primary; as each of the various candidates from both parties appeared before the camera and waited for their cue to speak, vast stretches of broadcast "feed" were sent out into the atmosphere, in which the waiting candidates—including Bill Clinton, George Bush, Pat Buchanan, Paul Tsongas, Jerry Brown, and Ross Perot—would pick their noses, comb their hair, sigh, look bored, and so on. A bracing vision of politicians.

Manufacturing Consent: Noam Chomsky and the Media **(1992)** A lengthy, self-involved documentary profile of the world's most rigorous and morally incorruptible political activist, who firmly believes that ethical stature—both high and low—is earned by action, not rhetoric. Chomsky has devoted his public life to burning through the many layers of carefully engineered propaganda about corporate behavior and governmental action, using recent history, not theory, as his broadsword—so, naturally, he has been systematically sidelined and repressed in this country. Made in Canada because, as Chomsky himself would attest, no one in the United States would have had the nerve to back such a film.

The War Room **(1993)** From Chris Hegedus and emeritus documentary-maker D. A. Pennebaker comes this popular film portrait of the 1992 Bill Clinton for President campaign, from which came the temporary celebrities of George Stephanopoulos and James Carville. The backroom engineering will come as no surprise, especially to viewers who endured the subsequent presidential elections.

Bulworth **(1998)** Warren Beatty did the impossible: he got the word "socialism" into a Hollywood film—*two times* (here and in *Reds*). While this absurd farce may not count as a serious statement on race and poverty, it counts as a shoot-the-wounded satiric roast of political machinery, campaign bullshit, and even hip-hop culture. Beatty, who also directed, plays a broken-down senator who hires an assassin to kill him, then tries to cancel the deal, then becomes completely unglued and transforms into an aging white rapper. Beatty may seem to have been slightly unglued himself in some sequences, but the nerve on display is admirable.

Primary Colors (1998) Undeniably witty and well executed, this Mike Nichols version of the bestseller by "Anonymous" attempts to be cold-eyed about the political game by baldly offsetting the Clintonian "we'll make history" buffoonery with sex scandals, abject amorality, merciless ambition, and illegal maneuvering. Well, this is the reality of American politics, but if you look closely, the film seems terrified of commitment—pretending to be morally above the fray, it enjoys the scandal and gamesmanship for their own sake and never acknowledges, as most media are loath to do, that politics is not in fact a horse race, but is actually about the correct and ostensibly honest governing of the populace, with real misery, prosperity, justice, safety, jeopardy, rights, life, and death at stake. Ethically flip? A comment *on* the media's point of view? You decide. But, after September 11 and years of the Bush administration's scorched-earth policies, this film may have you fondly remembering the days when the country had only the infidelity of somebody else's husband to worry about.

The Trials of Henry Kissinger (2002) Based on the Christopher Hitchens book, itself a devastating accumulation of facts, this earnest centrist documentary details the role Kissinger has played in a harrowing array of global holocausts: Vietnam, Cambodia, Chile, and East Timor. Hitchens's book makes a thorough case for Kissinger being arrested and tried at the Hague, but Eugene Jarecki's film falls several steps short of that, preferring instead to pose the ethical question of how much a statesman can be held culpable for the war crimes he helps instigate. The moral leap required to answer that doozy is exactly where most American media fear to tread.

Fahrenheit 9/11 (2004) The most successful and widely seen nonfiction film of all time, Michael Moore's act of open defiance of the Bush administration and the Iraq invasion may seem like old news years after the fact, but at the time of its release it was news, no doubt about it—and the film remains a pungent, sardonic piece of discourse. Charges by right-wingers that it wasn't "objective" were risible, of course—what film is objective?—and they couldn't overshadow the fact that Moore showed things we should've seen on TV but didn't: the president's limo getting mass-egged in 2000, the extent of the Bush family's financial relationship with the Saudis, and dead Iraqis—lots of them. What Moore did in this one film is what the news media should be doing 24/7—keeping a watchful eye on the powerful and demanding accountability.

The Manchurian Candidate (2004) Jonathan Demme revamps, retools, updates, and Democratizes the Richard Condon potboiler for the Bush II era, with Denzel Washington as the Gulf War vet sniffing out a conspiracy surrounding a vaguely neoconservative political campaign and his former platoon mate (Liev Schreiber), a man everyone loathes but also, strangely, cannot help but adore. Slick and fun except for the central conceits, which have Schreiber's puppet-automaton as the candidate rather than the assassin, and surgical implants, not Cold War brainwashing, as the culprit. Since when has there been a shortage of willing bottom-feeders happy to take power in the name of profit?

One Bright Shining Moment **(2004)** Stephen Vittoria's portrait of George McGovern and his career leading up to his derailed 1972 presidential campaign is useful as history, but it's hyperbolic and hysterical, and far too worshipful. Still, if you were there, you may share a sniffle.

Giuliani Time **(2005)** In the works since Rudolph Giuliani was still mayor of the Big Apple—and still policing the city with totalitarian quality-of-life tactics, Kevin Keating's doc was released just in time to deflect the ex-mayor's 2008 presidential bid. Here's the reminder everyone needs about his public tenure, from boat-people corpses on Florida beaches (when Rudy was assistant U.S. attorney) to the incendiary experiences of Abner Louima and Amadou Diallo, all of which transpired amid a hailstorm of power-mad baloney. Faithful Republican thug, Giuliani may be our destiny in national politics—a man who's capable of boasting to a crowd that, upon seeing a body falling from the Twin Towers, he turned to Bernard Kerik and said, "Thank God George Bush is our president."

Masters of Horror: **"Homecoming" (2005)** This lacerating cable-TV featurette by Joe Dante has the recent war dead, fresh from Iraq, rise from their graves and flag-draped coffins with one purpose in mind: to register and vote in a presidential election. Not to be missed.

Bobby **(2006)** Emilio Estevez wrote and directed this hammy, erratic *Grand Hotel* riff, set in L.A.'s Ambassador Hotel the day Robert F. Kennedy was shot there in 1968, after winning the California primary. Plenty of inspired acting shores up the multitude of irrelevant stories (none of which involve Kennedy or Sirhan Sirhan), but the hopeful liberalism of the time is powerfully invoked with news footage—of an America bursting with rage and change, when citywide riots broke out almost every week.

INTERNATIONAL WOMEN'S DAY

"My problem is that, given complete freedom of choice, I don't *want* to squeeze the goddamn Charmin!"
—Paula Prentiss, *The Stepford Wives* (1975)

First observed in 1909 (initiated, like so many honorary days, by the early Socialist labor movement, and celebrated in years hence in particular response to the infamous Triangle Shirtwaist Factory fire in which so many ill-treated women workers lost their lives), the IWD was an official, day-off holiday only in the Soviet Bloc countries in the 1970s and '80s. But shouldn't there be one day, at least, that's devoted to the viewing of flat-out feminist cinema? Unsurprisingly, most of the qualifiers are European-made films.

***Bed and Sofa* (1927)** A famously radical act of filmmaking amid the ideology-fueled Soviet heyday of socialist cinema, Abram Room's lovely melodrama paints a lively symphony-of-the-city portrait of 1920s Moscow, then focuses on a sheltered, oppressed wife and her apish husband. When a friend moves onto the couple's couch and becomes as demanding as a second husband, the poor woman begins to look for a way out. The setup might sound screwball, but the film sensitively attends to the limited social opportunities of women in modern society, and it is something of a feminist landmark.

***Christopher Strong* (1933)** A romantic 1930s melodrama, but one directed by a woman, Dorothy Arzner, and one in which Katharine Hepburn plays an independent, single, self-possessed aviatrix caught, sympathetically, as the third wheel between mewling husband Colin Clive and suffering wife Billie Burke.

***Cleo from 5 to 7* (1961)** Agnes Varda's French New Wave breakthrough, this entrancing Gallic daydream centers on Corinne Marchand's pampered celebrity girl toy on the day she awaits the results of cancer tests.

***My Life to Live* (1962)** Significantly less optimistic, Jean-Luc Godard's analytical film chops up the life of an opaque young woman (Anna Karina) who leaves her husband and child and, for lack of funds, becomes a call girl. It's a tragic tale, but Godard and Karina never look for pathos or make us empathize with the character—they're more interested in the social dynamic and how it's created by exactly the sort of distance the film itself maintains. A masterful film that, because it does not manipulate the viewer's experience, raises many varied and even conflicting reactions.

***Diary of a Chambermaid* (1964)** Surrealist Luis Buñuel routinely treated humankind as if it were a comical species of foolhardy jungle fauna, and frequently the observer-protagonist of his films is a cool, amused woman, aware of her sexual influence but in control of her gifts and immune to the nonsense around her. This adaptation of

Octave Mirbeau's novel has Jeanne Moreau as a self-immolating aristocratic family's imperious maid, surrounded by cretinous men and loving it.

***Persona* (1966)** Two women in a beach house—or is it? Art film giant Ingmar Bergman takes on, in a strictly poetic and often ambiguously self-reflective fashion, the restless landscape of the female psyche in this masterwork, one of the enduring works of the form. Liv Ullmann and Bibi Andersson star.

***Riddance* (1973)** Hungarian-born Marta Meszaros has been the only uncompromised feminist voice emanating out of Eastern Europe for more than three decades. Her films, best taken one at a time, are lonely afternoons, dry-eyed visits to a bilious Europe of epic industrial mundanity, inhabited largely by inadequate men and inadequately loved women. Made of moments not privileged so much as exquisitely ordinary, her hard-bitten realism seems caught in the flow of the nearby Czech New Wave, but Meszaros has fought her own good fight, making films that bite back at the Communist state for the ruin it made of love lives, career ambitions, and female adolescence. This film deals with everyday young love; her others, including ***Adoption* (1975)**, ***Nine Months* (1976)**, and ***The Two of Them* (1977)**, deal with various social struggles, all of them feminist.

***The Stepford Wives* (1975)** Paternalist culture takes it in the kidneys with this high-concept pulp, in which independent women are swapped out by their husbands for subservient robots. See also "Ms. Lonelyhearts" (p. 195), for whom the plot could be a metaphor for marriage in general.

***My Brilliant Career* (1979)** From the 1901 novel by early feminist Miles Franklin, this Australian film details the social trials of a tempestuous girl (Judy Davis) who gives up the confines of a loving marriage for the sake of personal freedom. Bubbly and endearing, and the film that established Davis, costar Sam Neill, and director Gillian Armstrong.

***Entre Nous* (1983)** Reminiscent of Marta Meszaros's *The Two of Them*, this Diane Kurys film details a 1950s friendship between two wives and mothers (Isabelle Huppert and Miou-Miou) who are stuck with husbands they hadn't wanted, thanks to World War II; their spiritual kinship with each other outshines their otherwise disappointing lives.

***Vagabond* (1985)** Agnes Varda's most acerbic film, in which Sandrine Bonnaire plays a young homeless woman who, at the outset, is frozen dead in a winter ditch. From there, we tread backward to her last weeks as she loiters on the fringes of the rural community, endures the projected prejudices and desires of others, and, all the while, absolutely resists living by even the most fundamental rules. Because it's stripped down to the bone, it's a viscerally loaded statement of gender politics.

***Peking Opera Blues* (1986)** In the 1980s, Hong Kong movies were the wildest, fastest, least controlled, most absurd films on the globe, and this protofeminist spectacular, made by whirlwind Tsui Hark, is typically sky-high on pure moviemaking bliss. It might be the greatest of all peak-era Hong Kong movie-movies, which doesn't mean that you can't see the strings—you can—or that the movie undulates from pathos to violence to slapstick with anything resembling a measured pace. Set in the 1920s, amid the postimperial storm as Sun Yat-sen's underground movement gained steam, the film chases after three women (Brigitte Lin, Cherie Chung, and Sally Yeh) who crisscross each other's paths over a cache of errant jewels. The film's bug-eyed international premiere at the Cannes Film Festival is famously remembered as the moment the world understood what was glorious about Hong Kong movies.

***Story of Women* (1988)** Claude Chabrol's best film? Certainly his most socially charged. This film tells the tale of the last woman to be guillotined in France—for performing abortions during the Nazi occupation. The economic verities and wartime horrors are indelibly etched, and Isabelle Huppert again epitomizes an embattled womanhood under fantastic pressure.

***Female Perversions* (1996)** The first film of its kind, as far as we know—and, one hopes, the last: a feature fiction film based on a published volume of psychosocial lit crit. Here, Louise J. Kaplan's *Female Perversions: The Temptations of Emma Bovary*, is fictionalized into a horny bisexual odyssey filled with feminist theory and the cavorting sauciness of Tilda Swinton, as an attorney who vamps more than she litigates.

***Aimée & Jaguar* (1999)** A raunchy, fiery, and passionate *Masterpiece Theatre*–ish period tragedy, this World War II lesbian romance has the added allure of being based on an extraordinary true story: in 1943 Berlin, as the Allies are bombing the city and the last German Jews are being rooted out, Jewish gay underground spy Felice Schragenheim (Maria Schrader) begins a love affair with a promiscuous mother of four, Lilly Wust (Juliane Köhler), whose husband is on the front lines. The tale (based on Wust's oral history) is dizzying in its promise—what wouldn't the late New German Cinema juggernaut Rainer Werner Fassbinder have done to make this movie?—and director Max Färberböck makes crystal clear the costs of the women's love: family, community, and, ultimately, mortality. It's an actor's movie, and the two leads are terrific (they shared the Best Actress award at the 1999 Berlin International Film Festival). In particular, Schrader's predatory, vampy spy Jaguar is an unforgettable piece of work, alternately ravishing and horrific, but always dazzlingly larger than life.

***The Circle* (2000)** Jafar Panahi's lacerating work of interwoven narrative is a blackjack of thematic directness, a restless, wide-eyed *la ronde* bouncing, without warning, from one female character to another as the women find themselves trapped in an Islamic fundamentalist society that regards them as little better than criminals or slaves. It's a movie of labyrinthine alleys, obscure portals, and cages—the first thing we see is a window in a hospital delivery room door, through which a woman discovers that her new grandchild isn't the boy the ultrasound promised and the father's family expects, sending her into a mortal panic. We never see where her story goes; Panahi instead begins following two furtive women who are attempting to elude the police—on a temporary leave from prison, they have no intentions of returning. (Their crimes are unknown; in Iran a woman can be imprisoned for being suspected of having sex, for disobeying her family, or simply for appearing in public without a chador.) The spiral continues.

The Day I Became a Woman (2000) Iranian cinema—the world's premier art-film factory of the last two decades—is art born under pressure of Sharia law, and the only way Marziyeh Meshkini (the wife of Iranian powerhouse Mohsen Makhmalbaf, who produced this film) could make her debut feature was to film three shorts—only feature-length films need prior permission from Iran's censors to be made—and then conjoin them into one devastatingly feminist film. The three tales focus on womanhood in crisis: first a child emerging into the strictures of adult life, second a grown woman struggling for freedom, and third an elderly woman facing death.

I

COLUMBUS DAY

"The earth I walk upon sees me and quakes. But whoever follows me and the river will win untold riches."
—Klaus Kinski, *Aguirre, the Wrath of God*

The Age of Exploration! What would we know or care about such ancient history if it weren't always ripe fodder for movies? Whether they involve grand endeavors, imperialist injustice, or both, movies might be the only way to salute this oddest, and most historically oblivious, of official celebrations.

The Adventures of Marco Polo (1938) A risible, not-too-serious serving of Hollywood un-history, which has the Italian explorer (Gary Cooper—who could be more Italian?) travel to Peking, "discover" spaghetti, and fall for the Emperor's daughter (Sigrid Gurie—who could be more Chinese?). Cooper, though, was in his prime and arguably the handsomest man on the continent.

Stanley and Livingstone (1939) Twentieth Century Fox spared little expense to make this whitewashing saga about the New York reporter (Spencer Tracy) who plunges into Darkest Africa to find the lost British missionary (Cedric Hardwicke), and does. Not such a fabulous story, as it turns out, and reality is, in any event, told to hit the bricks.

Christopher Columbus (1949) The first straight biopic of the explorer, and a slow, drab English film at that, with only Fredric March in the lead to recommend it.

Hare We Go **(1951)** This is more like it—Bugs Bunny rides along on the *Santa Maria* and drives a diminutive Columbus batty. Robert McKimson directed.

The Far Horizons **(1955)** Donna Reed doesn't look much like the Sacajawea we have on our dollar coin nowadays, but this isn't history; it's Hollywood doing Lewis and Clark (Fred MacMurray and Charlton Heston), whose actual trip would've made an eventless movie in the traditional sense, and so dramas are invented involving tribal war, a scurvy French trader (Alan Reed—that's right, Fred Flintstone), and the love dance between Clark and Reed's dewy Indian maiden. Shot in Grand Teton National Park.

Aguirre, the Wrath of God **(1972)** German New Wave adventurer Werner Herzog stranded his crew, his cast, and himself in the Andes to film this magnificent parable on fascism, which looks as if it were shot in the sixteenth century. The tale of a mutinied contingent of Spanish conquistadors, lost on a Peruvian river and led by megalomaniac knight Klaus Kinski, it's a muscular, incredibly realistic experience (no safely dismissed special effects here)—a masterpiece.

Mountains of the Moon **(1990)** A terrific, overlooked revisionist epic of the Age of Exploration's last days, as the impossibly cool Sir Richard Burton (Patrick Bergin) and the not-so-impressive John Hanning Speke (Iain Glen) search Africa for the source of the Nile. If you're of an anticolonialist mind-set, you'll be happy to see that they get theirs; in addition, the spirit of Victorian clubs, British savoir faire, and National Geographic adventurism is intoxicating.

1492: Conquest of Paradise **(1992)** This Ridley Scott behemoth virtually drowns in its own grandiloquent beauty—it's glutted with compressed visions of unearthly sunsets, color-drenched landscapes, strutting stallions, and fluttering banners, all of it lumbering along like a monstrous Thanksgiving Day (or, we suppose, Columbus Day) parade, with Gérard Depardieu hovering over the pageantry like the Underdog balloon over Broadway. The chief conceit at work in this campy yet enjoyable mess is that of Columbus as frontier-intoxicated *übermensch* who pursues the New World for the greater glory of, well, glory; here it is evil, racist royalists and rampaging cannibals who spoil the Eden of Hispaniola. Scott glorifies Depardieu's massive, shaggy bulk in such a rapturous storm of golden heroic tableaux that Columbus comes off like a titan, a larger-than-life warrior-saint, without whom the world would still be flat. (When Depardieu falls to his knees on the beach, it sounds like a herd of elephants go down with him.) Though an improvement over the truly heinous *Christopher Columbus: The Discovery*, also released in 1992 to celebrate the five-hundredth anniversary of the famous Italian's landfall, *1492* is, on a trashy matinee level, actually less engaging—at least the other movie has naked native women running around, driving the sailors nuts, and there's some skid row buckle-swashing.

¡O No Coronado! **(1992)** The ultimate anticolonialist adventure epic is a featurette, made largely out of found footage by satiric avant-gardist Craig Baldwin, that scrupulously recounts the doomed and fruitless Southwest odyssey of the eponymous conquistador who slaughtered Indians, conquered villages, and returned in ignominy to government in Mexico.

The New World **(2005)** Terrence Malick's bleeding-heart romantic vision of the Pocahontas–John Smith saga is less interested in historical revisionism per se (it does Disney a step better, though) than it is in projecting a rhapsodic feeling for the unspoiled wilderness, frontier intoxication (Colin Farrell, as Smith, is as joyful and quivering as a child at Christmas) and the sun-burnished, beauteous glow of costar Q'Orianka Kilcher, whose Pocahontas should define the character in the popular culture for eons to come. (We'll forget, as everyone has, that the real Pocahontas was about eleven years old and naked, clothes being permitted among the Powhatan only after puberty.)

CHINESE NEW YEAR

"She has the face of Buddha and the heart of a scorpion."
—He Caifei, *Raise the Red Lantern*

Falling on a day in early to mid-February (it differs with the year), this truly international holiday is ripe for an annual, culture-evocative, movie-rental tradition, even if you don't happen to be Chinese. *Gung hei fat choi!*

Zu: Warriors of the Magic Mountain **(1983)** Ancient Chinese ur-myths, seen through the psychotic lens of the 1980s Hong Kong film machine and director Tsui Hark, don't get any crazier. (See "Party Software," p. 253.)

Yellow Earth **(1984)** The film that effectively launched the famous Chinese Fifth Generation filmmaking wave, Chen Kaige's sensitive epic examines the 1939 tribulations of a rural girl who looks to a visiting, folk-song-collecting Communist soldier to save her from an arranged marriage and a servile life. Propaganda is thwarted, finally, by real life and soured hopes. Shot by Zhang Yimou, who would go on to be the movement's global-circuit powerhouse director.

Dim Sum: A Little Bit of Heart **(1985)** Wayne Wang's film, about a San Francisco Chinatown family and its classic conflicts between tradition and modernity, is an exquisite, observant domestic miniature—a little bit of heart all by itself. Millions of first-generation Americans can find their family's cultural drama right here, expressed with sympathy and wisdom.

Peking Opera Blues **(1986)** Spirited, outrageous, historical-intrigue hijinks. (See "International Women's Day," p. 66.)

A Chinese Ghost Story **(1987)** Made by director Ching Siu-Tung and producer/genre-movie maniac Tsui Hark, this hyperactive, cardboard-and-chintz Hong Kong fantasy has more childish energy per minute of footage than any film made west of Nanning. The sequels (the first was released in 1990; the second in 1991) are just as explosively silly.

The Last Emperor **(1987)** Bernardo Bertolucci's lumbering, gorgeous Oscar winner is exactly the kind of expensive epic that nobody wants to see again after its award hoopla has died down, but it's the most lavish and visually splendid portrait of traditional Chinese pomp available. If you are of Chinese descent, you know to seek cultural veracity elsewhere.

Red Sorghum **(1987)** The Fifth Generation reached its international apex with a run of sumptuous, feminist films directed by Zhang Yimou and starring the impossibly lovely Gong Li—they were the first films made on the Chinese mainland to be widely circulated outside of the world's various Chinatowns. This peasant epic of arranged marriages, forbidden alliances, and clan revenge is the best of them, but ***Ju Dou*** **(1990)**, ***Raise the Red Lantern*** **(1991)**, and ***To Live*** **(1994)** are magnificent as well.

Once Upon a Time in China **(1991)** Tsui Hark, at it again—this time taking a run at the classic nineteenth-century martial arts legend of Wong Fei-hung like a house on fire. No ten American movies could keep up with it, or with its levitating first two sequels (the first was made in 1992; the second, in 1993), in a footrace; if Tsui made a movie out of our phone bills, we'd pay them twice.

Actress **(1992)** Hong Kong romantic Stanley Kwan made this neglected movie (sometimes titled *Center Stage*) about Chinese silent screen star Ruan Ling-yu, "the Chinese Garbo," starring porcelain beauty Maggie Cheung (whose performance won her a Best Actress award at the Berlin International Film Festival). The Hong Kong film industry's most impassioned love song, both to itself and to its own legacy (which dates back to the second decade of the twentieth century), this film creates a kind of Chinese box out of Ruan's archival footage, documentary-style glimpses of Cheung as the film is being made, lushly realized romantic fiction about Ruan's life, and recreations of cinematic history. Ruan herself died at age twenty-five in a mysteriously motivated suicide, so the long-lost time and radiance represented by her films and by Kwan's movie have a tragic and poignantly archetypal glow.

Farewell My Concubine **(1993)** Chen Kaige's peaking achievement, an epic tangle of romance—straight, gay, platonic, and/or suppressed—that centers on two Peking

Opera performers (Leslie Cheung and Zhang Fengyi) and the woman (the inevitable Gong Li) who comes between them. The story spans most of the first half of the twentieth century. Sweeping and seductive.

***The Gate of Heavenly Peace* (1995)** The Chinese New Year movie for you if you're a hard-core historical junkie: ethnographic filmmakers Carma Hinton and Richard Gordon take stock, in three hours, of the events of 1989 that resulted in the student protest and occupation of Tiananmen Square, using piles of incredible original footage. Heart-breaking—especially considering that after having seen it, you will know far more about those events than most Chinese.

***Comrades, Almost a Love Story* (1997)** Peter Chan's rueful, absurd romantic fable features Maggie Cheung and Leon Lai as two mainlanders making their way through the profiteering chaos that is 1986 Hong Kong. He is a starry-eyed innocent intent on earning enough to import his childhood sweetheart; she is a fervent capitalist with her fingers in a dozen small-time pots. They partner up, then go their separate ways; as the years roll on, they glance romantically off each other like moths, their paths eventually crossing again in New York. Dreadfully underrated and underseen.

***Crouching Tiger, Hidden Dragon* (2000)** Ang Lee's blockbuster gloss-up of the Hong Kong wuxia pian saga, complemented with digital touch-ups, might not have pleased genre purists, but it was *the* trippy martial arts movie for a middle-class world population that otherwise hadn't much cottoned to trippy martial arts movies. The combat that takes place high in the bamboo grove is entrancing, and Michelle Yeoh is fab. The film's success spurned Zhang Yimou, in a career funk since the mid-1990s, to make imitative, Crayola-colored epics like ***Hero* (2002)**, ***House of Flying Daggers* (2004)** and ***Curse of the Golden Flower* (2006)**.

***2046* (2004)** Swoon along with director Wong Kar-Wai to a vision of a lost postwar Asian urbanity that may never have existed. (See "Heartbreak," p. 193.)

THE GREAT AMERICAN SMOKEOUT

"A delivery device for nicotine. Put it in your mouth, light it up . . . and you're going to get your fix?"
—Christopher Plummer, *The Insider*

This health-minded occasion has persisted since 1977, thanks to the American Cancer Society. It comes down to this: if you want to quit, for the day or forever, maybe an antismoking movie will help get you through. It certainly can't hurt.

Cold Turkey (1971) Amid the postwar decades in which everybody, seemingly, smoked, and just one year after the Surgeon General's warning was put on cigarette packets, TV producer Norman Lear veered into movies with this satire about a town that's offered twenty-five million dollars if *everyone* in it quits smoking for thirty days. The results are slapstick—and surprisingly nasty, even with Dick Van Dyke starring as a priest.

The Insider (1999) Meaty, passionate, and executed with feverish commitment, this Michael Mann whistle-blower thriller is based on the true story of Dr. Jeffrey Wigand (Russell Crowe), a tobacco-industry turncoat who told *60 Minutes* that the companies had always known that cigarettes were medically destructive, and who saw his life collapse as a result. Mann takes on every aspect of the scenario, from the public compromises of Mike Wallace (Christopher Plummer) to the legal infighting and Wigand's own marital dissolution. Crowe may have won Oscars in 2000 and 2001, but he really deserved one for his performance here.

Bright Leaves (2003) Southerner Ross McElwee is a chronic self-chronicler, and his life project—which stretches over twenty-five years and twelve nonfiction films—is close to being Proustian in scope. A truer, funnier, and vaster portrait of an American life may not exist. In the life chapter that is this film, now-middle-aged McElwee (always behind the camera, never at center stage) explores his family legacy of tobacco farming, the ways in which that legacy intersects with the 1950 Hollywood film *Bright Leaf*, and the methods by which the tobacco industry itself has wreaked havoc on everyday America.

Thank You for Smoking (2005) A biting black comedy whose protagonist (Aaron Eckhart, with a newscaster's mug and an ex-quarterback's stature) is loathsome by any standards: he's a tobacco lobbyist rationalizing his work to Congress, the country, his adolescent son, and himself. Tobacco-related deaths are notches on his bedpost to be compared with those of the buddies who lobby for similarly fatality-prone pastimes (alcohol, guns)—the tougher the job, the more hardcore the salesman. Ironically enough, there isn't a single lit cigarette in the entire movie. It's a questionable strategy—did a lobbyist get to the filmmakers?—but if you're trying to quit, it may be the perfect film. There're certainly enough sobering facts lurking beneath the satire to make your breathing labored without help from Marlboro.

I II III IV V VI

MY FAVORITE SEASON

SUMMER

"Those beaches *will* be open."
—Murray Hamilton, *Jaws*

Hazy, lazy, crazy—our choices here, from a million possibilities, recall beach-bound days, hot nights, childhood matinees, sweaty exotica, and, notably, the sun-scorched way in which American movies captured summer heat in the 1970s.

Morocco **(1930)** A legionnaire (Gary Cooper) dallies with a world-weary desert-oasis diva (Marlene Dietrich), who isn't exactly as cynical and experience-toughened as she thought. The first, epochal American Marlene Dietrich–Josef von Sternberg film is the muggiest, woozy with hot, moonlit Saharan nighttime. Of course, it was all shot on the Paramount lot, with shadows. According to von Sternberg's uproariously self-aggrandizing memoir, the Pasha of Marrakech asked him, years later, why the film-maker had not visited him when making the film in Morocco, which he'd recognized firsthand; von Sternberg maintained he'd never been to the country, and Cooper, in his foreword to the book, expressed doubts that the windy director could've found the nation on a map.

Duck Soup **(1933)** Less a matter of weather than of unbridled élan, this preeminent Marx Brothers comedy—their most concentrated, fluent, and beautifully timed, which might just make it the greatest comedy of all time—is too much carefree fun for one 68-minute movie, and could stand to represent everything summery, young, impudent, crazy, and joyful in your life, if you watch it at the right time. Famously, the film savagely satirizes world politics, war, ruling-class pomposity, and ritual, but there are other things at work with the Marxes at the peak of their form—an essential hedonism and a life-loving respect for impulse, whim, mockery, and anarchy.

Beauty and the Beast **(1946)** Jean Cocteau's definitive incarnation of the fairy tale, and a supremely dreamy July daydream, shot with silvery shimmering by Henry Alékan and infused with nursery wonder. Jean Marais's leonine Beast is fab, but Josette Day's serene maiden is close to an ideal.

Smiles of a Summer Night **(1955)** Ingmar Bergman, summery? This famous art-house favorite isn't the Swedish moper's only comedy, but it is his funniest, largely restricted to intertwining boudoir farce reminiscent of *A Midsummer Night's Dream* (and rein-vented decades later as Stephen Sondheim's *A Little Night Music*), but occasionally embracing love in a haystack at dusk.

The Blob **(1958)** An alien jelly mold has invaded Eisenhower-era, drive-in-crazy Middle America, and only honest teen Steve McQueen (who was actually in his late twen-ties when the film was made) can save us. There's something quintessential here:

a potent feel for small towns at night, when everyone's home and looking toward bed—everyone, of course, except the pesky teenagers (those kids!) and the amused, lazy cops manning the local station.

Black Orpheus (1959) The most evocative tropical film ever made, this peacock of a movie transposes the Orpheus-Eurydice myth to Rio amid Carnivale, and the heavy dose of South American colors, nonstop samba music, sweat, dancing, copulation, and Brazilian zest can make you dizzy. The tale is tragic, of course, but one-hit-wonder director Marcel Camus determinedly turns on the juice, and in the end the story is spectacularly life-affirming.

La Collectionneuse (1967) The first feature-length entry in French New Waver Eric Rohmer's Six Moral Tales, this sun-drenched dalliance chronicles a typical Rohmerian triangle—two vacationing aesthetes, slumming in an absent friend's Saint Tropez chateau, philosophize self-destructively about potential sexual-romantic involvement with a young, bikini-clad mademoiselle. The action is acidic, but, ironically, the honeyed ambience is hazy and lazy; even if you've been there, you haven't seen the Côte d'Azur in summer until you've seen cinematographer Néstor Almendros's celluloid portrait. Also summery as a ripe peach: Rohmer's *Claire's Knee* (1970).

Once Upon a Time in the West (1968) Director Sergio Leone virtually invented the Italian-made "spaghetti western," and this hot, sweaty mastodon of a movie may be its crowning exemplar: it's the most overwrought, supercool, breathtakingly lavish, preposterously lyrical western ever made. The sets are huge (farmhouses appear to have twelve or more rooms), the story is absurd, the music is rapturous, and the faux desert sun is hot. Every aspect of this film swoons with a love of Movies, and every scene is a western standard jacked up into a feverish fit. The incredible opening credits sequence alone (Jack Elam, Woody Strode, a fly, a deserted train station . . .) is worth the rental fee—and, like the rest of this super-wide-screen mock opera, must have given the video transfer guys serious headaches. The story involves the westward push of the railroad, a mail-order bride (Claudia Cardinale), a rogue outlaw (Jason Robards), a mysterious man with no name (Charles Bronson) who's bent on avenging his father's murder, and the vilest western villain of all time (Henry Fonda, in a marvelous bit of countercasting). As exaggerated and berserk and self-conscious as it is, it's also profoundly sad—Ennio Morricone's crescendoing music makes the loss of the Old West seem a heartrending reality.

Planet of the Apes (1968) Before there was "the summer blockbuster" (a label that now describes a studio's box-office hopes rather than a film's actual success), there was the matinee movie, meant as a respite from summer heat for kids with nothing to watch at home (in the days before videos, DVDs, and the like) and brainpans overflowing with Marvel comics, Aurora models, and backyard G.I. Joe scenarios. This beautiful, conceptually fearless piece of all-American pulp—forget the 2001 Tim

Burton remake—remains resonant and unforgettable, but it also invokes memories of an entire decade of summers (what with its many sequels and frequent rereleases) for a lucky generation of kids, whose cerebellums are permanently branded with the image of Charlton Heston kneeling on the beach before the wrecked Statue of Liberty. Ah, to be lost on this "desert planet" once more. . . .

Butch Cassidy and the Sundance Kid (1969) The most charming outlaws of all time flee across the American West with the sun at their backs, trading quips, horse hooves kicking up dust and tumbleweeds. The combination of George Roy Hill's direction, William Goldman's witty script, and Paul Newman and Robert Redford's charisma and comic timing—all of it feather light—keeps this well-loved western feeling new. But it's the late-1960s sun flares, film-stock haze, and ironic good humor that makes it a summer movie through and through, down to the postcoital bicycle ride on a sun-drenched morning, scored by a B. J. Thomas song you've heard too many times.

Deliverance (1972) In a decade when Hollywood movies made enormous effort to faithfully render real American landscapes and weather, this controversial John Boorman–directed monster, about four men on a Georgia canoe trip that goes terribly awry, delivers an experience of the hot North American woods so authentic you can smell the pollen and feel the flies on your skin.

The Other (1972) Thomas Tryon's corn-belt Gothic thriller about a well-off 1930s country family that is plagued by twin sons (the remarkable Chris and Martin Udvarnoky), one of whom is dead (and a ghost?) and the other of whom may be crazy. A helluva yarn with a nasty taste for Grand Guignol set pieces, it's also an intensely *humid* film (thanks to director Robert Mulligan), that explores the secret spaces on a summer-scorched farm where kids dwelled in the days before Game Boys and day camps.

Chinatown (1974) The film that first reincarnated the detective-film noir, Roman Polanski's magisterial movie is all about L.A., so it's not shadowy and expressionistic—it's blistered by July sunshine, and is no less affecting for the turnabout. One of the unarguable gems of the American canon, this film can and should be seen for a variety of reasons, but the glare-and-heat seasonal mood is particularly impressive, especially in view of how the hero—Jack Nicholson's supercool private dick Jake Gittes—rather hedonistically spends his sweltering middays: hanging out and avoiding authority, kinda like a kid.

Jaws (1975) If you were there, in the theaters in the summer of 1975, you've got this movie in your DNA. This film was the last truly communal movie experiences—*everyone* saw it, *twice*, and afterward everyone had a new relationship with the beach. But put the man-eating giant monster shark aside for a moment, and you've got full-on, real-to-the-touch Atlantic beach community life, back when people listened to transistor radios in the sand and used suntan oil. The actors' clothes even seem creased with sand and salt air.

1900 **(1976)** After Italian wunderkind Bernardo Bertolucci had a couple of massive global hits with *The Conformist* (1970) and *Last Tango in Paris* (1972), he cashed in on his cachet to make this epic, which clocks in at more than five hours. (Some DVD and VHS versions are edited; find the longest-running one you can, and aim for the Italian-language version—although note that some of the film's international cast is dubbed in every version.) Robert De Niro and Gérard Depardieu are an aristocrat and a bastard peasant, respectively, born simultaneously before the turn of the century and maturing together in Italy through to the rise of fascism. Politically simplistic (or knowingly nostalgic?), this seemingly limitless pageant is chockablock with masterful set pieces and features a heartachingly beautiful score by Ennio Morricone, and its golden Mediterranean aura, which consciously reincarnates paintings by Bruegel, Millet, and Théodore Rousseau, is something special.

Phantasm **(1979)** Perhaps the only effective summertime horror film, Don Coscarelli's hallucinogenic original deals with a mysterious mortuary and the profoundly weird things going on deep inside of it—it's investigated by a lonely kid (Michael Baldwin) in the dead of deeply shadowed, suburban July nighttimes. *This* is what we'd imagined all of that staying out late during summer vacation might eventually amount to.

A Midsummer Night's Sex Comedy **(1982)** It's possible that no American movie has been as besotted with the sensual realities of summertime as this overlooked Woody Allen comedy, in which three early-century couples gather together, in a to-die-for Victorian country house, to enjoy a balmy weekend and endure various mate-swapping peccadilloes. Light on its feet, with a charming score by Felix Mendelssohn, and blessed with the effervescence of Mary Steenburgen and Julie Hagerty, Allen's movie goes for broke in terms of seasonal glamour: sunlit meadows, firefly swarms, moonlit brooks, rendezvous in the night forest, dining al fresco, daydreaming in cotton dresses, suspenders and straw hats—all of it shot with Vermeerian sublimity by Gordon Willis. Well worth repeat viewings; it's time this honey got a reappraisal.

Pauline at the Beach **(1983)** Beautiful teens and overly intellectualized adults, talking in absurd circles as they enjoy the shore in Granville. Another of Eric Rohmer's "blabby chicks on holiday" dawdles, of which some people cannot get enough. (Fortunately, he's prolific; you could watch a different Rohmer film each summer for the next two decades and never repeat a movie.)

A Room with a View **(1986)** When this Merchant-Ivory smash was first released, filmgoers didn't know what had hit them: the movie's creation of a thoroughly inhabited, semimythic, utterly buoyant Britannic universe was so enthralling that even aficionados of E. M. Forster, on whose novel the film is based, were taken aback. The movie stayed in theaters for over a solid year in this country; in England, obsessed audiences saw it every week—it became a kind of Edwardian *Rocky Horror Picture Show*. Unpredictable, eccentric, large-hearted, rhapsodic, and wildly funny, it is, indeed, gloriously worthy of repeat viewings. You can easily imagine that more than a few suicides, or at least depression-based behaviors of some regrettable stripe, were prevented in 1986 and '87 as low-feeling movie watchers returned again and again to offset the angst of their lives with essential joy. The movie's summertime vibe—in both its Florentine chapters and its idealized Surrey greenscape—is absolutely infectious. The saga of Lucy Honeychurch (Helena Bonham Carter) is, archetypally, one of repressed romance, a singsong piece of parlor-room fluff, really. But the movie itself is downright irrepressible, filthy with charming tidbits, background performances, and a generous, irreverent tone. The film is paced like a lazy afternoon, and there doesn't seem to be a limit to its ability to seduce, relax, gladden, and captivate. *A Room with a View* is the kind of film that makes you envious of anyone who is just seeing it for the first, rapturous time—although, honestly, the second, fourth, and sixteenth times are their own days in the country as well.

***Stand by Me* (1986)** The search for the dead body in the woods is merely a MacGuffin in this Stephen King–derived hit—the four tweens (Wil Wheaton, River Phoenix, Corey Feldman, and Jerry O'Connell) could just as well have been hunting for mushrooms for all it really matters. What's really at stake here is the re-creation of early-1960s childhood summers, before parents began micromanaging their kids' lives. This film reminds us that once, when summer was *summer*, not just an excuse for air-conditioning, kids could roam into the next county, along the train tracks, through the leechy swamps, into tree houses, and across mad-dog-guarded junkyards, and nobody thought twice about it.

***Summer* (1986)** Or, as Eric Rohmer originally titled it, *Le Rayon Vert*, referring to the Jules Vernian green ray that a setting sun is supposed to create at the instant of its disappearance. Rohmer's heroine here (Marie Rivière) is a secretary suddenly alone on vacation, trying different places and strategies, but maddeningly unable to enjoy herself or find fulfillment. Given such a structure, the movie can be frustrating, too, but only if you make the mistake of needing Rivière's nowhere girl to do what *you* would do. At the same time, it's a potent character portrait, a philosophical parable, and a tour of French summer choices, from Cherbourg to the Alps to the beach at Biarritz.

***Bull Durham* (1988)** This best-ever baseball movie pegs the ambience, circumstances, subculture, and ardor of this summertime sport like no other film, effortlessly grabbing the season in a headlock. (See "Opening Day," p. 99.)

***Miami Blues* (1990)** Charles Willeford's neo-noir novel gets a sharp film treatment from director George Armitage; surrounding Alec Baldwin's sociopath, Jennifer Jason

Leigh's hooker, and Fred Ward's cop is a sunburned, white-stucco, low-rent Florida
world of pawn shops, tank tops, and weary never-ending summer.

Point Break (1991) One of the few genuine camp romps of the Reagan-Bush era, this goofball, directed in high, silly style by Kathryn Bigelow, has studly FBI agent Keanu Reeves infiltrate Patrick Swayze's clan of surfin', parachutin', extreme-sports-lovin' bank robbers. Idiotic and faux philosophical, it exudes a thrill-seeking vibe that's hard to skip, especially because it's apparent—or is it?—that the stars themselves actually jumped out of airplanes.

Belle Epoque (1992) This Spanish hit has a timeworn vacation-movie story—a well-intentioned boob (Jorge Sanz) goes AWOL during the 1930s Spanish Civil War and takes shelter with a family made up of four tempestuous sisters (among them, Penélope Cruz and Y Tu Mamá También's Maribel Verdú), all of whom seem in need of a good schtupping, and their crotchety old father (Fernando Fernán Gómez). But even though it's set in the off-season, it's still Spain, and it's got the summer vibe: Mediterranean, heat-beaten stone buildings; Spanish palm trees; beautiful women in sleeveless blouses wandering around thinking about sex even when they don't think they're thinking about it. Nothing too artful, but lovely.

A Summer's Tale (1996) Another Eric Rohmer idyll for the summer months, this film traipses after a grad student on vacation and observes his various romantic crisscrosses—and his much-discussed attitudes about them.

WINTER

"What I want to know is how we're going to stay alive this winter."
—Ralph Richardson, *Doctor Zhivago*

It's too cold to go outside, isn't it? If you lean toward counteracting the months of frost with a blast of tropicalia, see the "Summer" section. But we've found that if you're hunkered down in the warmth of your home, it's all the better to punctuate the extreme weather outside—from a comfortable distance, of course.

South (1919) Forget the recent movies, IMAX and otherwise, that re-create the doomed 1914–1916 Shackleton *Endurance* expedition to the South Pole; this astonishing film was shot on the spot by one Frank Hurley, who stood there stranded on the ice with the rest of the crew, watching the ice shelves crush the ship, not knowing whether he was in fact doomed or not—and yet still filming, beautifully. All other movies about polar survival are pretenders by comparison.

The Chechahcos (1924) Amateur Alaskan filmmaker Lewis H. Moomaw's silent film is an extraordinary Klondike melodrama, shot in the northern wilderness and featuring stunning on-location glacier footage. The story is antique, but there's no denying the veracity of the on-location action. Available on a DVD set titled **Treasures from American Film Archives: 50 Preserved Films (2000)**.

S.O.S. Iceberg (1933) This early sound epic is a prime example of the 1920s–'30s specie of German adventure film known as "the mountain film," invented and primarily directed by one Dr. Arnold Fanck, and starring, primarily, one Leni Riefenstahl, who, at the time this film was made, was just a few years away from becoming the most famous director of Third Reich propaganda. The key attraction to this movie is its copious location footage—when Riefenstahl and her comrades are shown scouring the Arctic circle for lost comrades, we're not looking at a studio set. Of course, man's triumph over nature's adversities is just one shading of the *übermensch* obsession that fired the Nazis. Other terrific examples available on disc are **The White Hell of Pitz Palu (1929)** and **Storm over Mont Blanc (1930)**.

Portrait of Jennie (1948) After *Gone with the Wind*, producer David O. Selznick's career largely focused on erecting large, crazy movie-poems in honor of his beloved wife, Jennifer Jones, and this unashamedly naive phantasm might be the most lovesick. Joseph Cotten plays a struggling artist in a New York where it's nearly always snowing, and Jones is a girl that appears to him—and only to him—with a ghostly backstory of her own, inspiring him with her inner light.

Doctor Zhivago (1965) Boris Pasternak's Russian-revolution love story, done up in 1960s-epic style by grandmaster David Lean, about a good-hearted doctor-poet (Omar Sharif) swept up in a political storm he cares nothing about. In fact, he's passive about pretty much everything, including his torn love for both his gentle, devoted wife and legendary beauty Lara (Julie Christie). Set in Russia, where springtime feels like a Minnesota winter, the movie was actually shot almost entirely in sunny Spain (!); the subarctic ambience is completely fabricated out of white wax. Fake or not, the swirling flurries are relentless, and there are moments where you feel like you're watching the story unfold from inside a snow globe. *Doctor Zhivago* is overwrought and visually constipated (so much massive history, so many small rooms), but the "Zhivago and Lara stranded in the ice house" set piece has a cozy, wintry feel that's hard to beat.

McCabe & Mrs. Miller (1971) This moody, fur-bundled frontier odyssey might be the best Robert Altman film of all time. Warren Beatty plays a entrepreneurial rogue who sets up business in a muddy northwestern mining town (it looks, no kidding, as if it were shot in 1830) and eventually teams up with an opium-smoking madam (Julie Christie) who's looking to set up a whorehouse. Trouble sets in when gangsters try to squeeze out the pair and resort to authentic prairie ethics to get their way. This movie teems with life like a beehive; nobody was better than Altman at filling movies up with believable inhabitants and texture, and here the misty, greasy, snowy reality of range life is evoked like nobody's business. No chicanery here—even though the film was actually shot in Vancouver, it shows just what Rocky Mountain life without utilities was like. Even the relentless Leonard Cohen songs begin to get under your skin. The movie is also an unarguable triumph of the American New Wave—those years between 1966 and 1977 in which Hollywood went out of its way to make gritty, truthful, challenging films you could believe in.

***The Last Detail* (1973)** One of the dourest of the American New Wave's hits, this ultrareal comedy has U.S. Navy lifers Jack Nicholson and Otis Young escorting a shy newbie (Randy Quaid) across several states to prison. The boy's sentence being all out of proportion with his petty crime, the two elder servicemen take him on a fun-loving tear—which turns out to be depressing in itself. The Eastern Seaboard in February has rarely been so forbidding.

***The Dead Zone* (1983)** Director David Cronenberg keeps his wilder instincts in check with this Stephen King–based thriller about a man (Christopher Walken) gifted with second sight after waking from a coma. But perhaps no other director would've attended so fastidiously to the wintry Canadian desolation, reflective of the traumatized hero's inner wasteland, that permeates the film.

***Promised Land* (1988)** Michael Hoffman's neglected drama tracks the post-school lives of two Utah kids: Kiefer Sutherland's shy, geeky damaged goods, and Jason Gedrick's basketball star turned local sheriff. Meg Ryan costars, launching her fledgling career with her portrait of a bipolar nightmare very far from the upturned-nose sweetheart for which she became famous. The landscape is frozen, and the characters are lost.

***Archangel* (1990)** A genuine whatzit, this second feature by hermetic Canadian avantgardist Guy Maddin comes in the guise of a scratched, faded, forgotten movie circa 1930, set in the eponymous Soviet city after World War I, but quite obviously shot on cardboard sets and more believably taking place in Maddin's movie-crazed head bone. The cheapjack surrealisms and crazy non sequiturs are the joke, covered as they are in fake snow and subjected to the harshest winds fans can produce.

***Edward Scissorhands* (1990)** They have winter in Florida, too, and this lovely, melancholy Tim Burton fantasy is for you southern, snow-deprived Americans. Anyone who's had rolls of cotton wadding stapled to his or her roof as fake snow will treasure this eagleeyed film for its satiric take on postwar suburban chintz, but in the end, there's snow after all—born of misfit heartbreak and devotion.

The Russia House (1990) Adapting a John le Carré novel automatically assures you an uncommonly grown-up set of priorities, fully realized characters, and an immaculately constructed story—rarities in the Reagan-Bush era, if just as much today. Here we have Sean Connery filling out one of his best portraits—that of Barley Blair, a boozy, unsuccessful British publisher in love with Russia and fully aware of his own worthlessness. Enlisted by the English secret service to run arms-race interference for them, the great, burly Blair decides—mostly for the sake of Michelle Pfeiffer's Cold War waif, but also in an effort to rescue his own sabotaged sense of integrity—to stop the game altogether. The cold Russian locales are authentic; this is deep wool and tweed territory.

A Little Princess (1995) Quite possibly the best Hollywood film of 1995, Alfonso Cuarón's adaptation of Frances Hodgson Burnett's classic is so saturated with feeling and joy it's perpetually on the verge of bursting. Unlike the stock Shirley Temple version released in 1939, this snow-graced movie—full of Victorian orphanhood, young-girl pluck, and cosmic magical realism—is a storybook swoon of exotic images and childhood fantasies, and you have to have a world-class lawyer's hard heart to resist it. Infiltrated with lovely Indian myth imagery and visions of a Dickensian Manhattan that recalls Mark Helprin's novel *Winter's Tale*, Cuarón's film is a marvel that owes a giant debt to star Liesel Matthews, whose guileless joy, earnest intelligence, and teardrop beauty carry the movie effortlessly. The scene in which she desperately draws a protective circle around herself on the floor of the attic (in imitation of "a magic circle" drawn around a princess in her Indian myth-stories), and then curls up to sleep inside it, can wound you.

Fargo (1996) A poker-faced slalom through the icy fields of true-crime docudrama, Joel and Ethan Coen's cascade of frozen Minnesotan cops and crime is probably the loopiest based-on-fact murder drama ever made, something like *In Cold Blood* reimagined by Dave Barry. Somehow, the filmmakers tell the snowbound saga of a tumbling-dominoes permafrost bloodbath—featuring nerve-frayed scam source William H. Macy, wired hired gun Steve Buscemi, and serene pregnant policewoman Frances McDormand (who won an Oscar for her performance)—as cold realism, yet retain their trademark absurdism and larky rhythms. Having grown up in a Minneapolis suburb, the Coens know the vernacular inside and out; though it often feels like a snarky plummet down a long flight of stairs, the movie ends up being a celebration of quiet banality. By the time we reach the wood chipper, we're as thankful as McDormand's Chief Marge that there's a mittened world full of idiotic pleasantries and all-you-can-eat restaurants to go back to.

The Ice Storm (1997) At its heart, this Ang Lee adaptation of the Rick Moody novel is a humane, sane, hilarious, and rich-as-mousse dispatch on the woes, risks, and costs of the all-American family, climaxing in the very real 1973 winter storm of the title and its largely symbolic fallout. The multiple character study encompasses an affable Dad (Kevin Kline) who's equally bewildered by his affair with a trendy neighbor (Sigourney Weaver) and his slowly disintegrating family, a haunted Mom (Joan Allen) who's lost somewhere between girlhood and disillusionment, a rebellious daughter (Christina Ricci) who's experimenting with shoplifting and mock sex with the neighbor's boys (Elijah Wood and Adam Hann-Byrd), and a sweet-natured pothead son (Tobey Maguire) who's impassively grappling with puberty. But the real subject is vain, media-drunk modernity itself, and how it leaves us unprepared for the worst things in life—things that can happen at night, when everything's frozen over.

Snow Falling on Cedars (1999) It's winter 1947 in Washington State, and postwar racial animosity is sky-high. A white fisherman is found dead on his boat, and a Japanese-American neighbor is accused of his murder. The winter vibe of this dreamy adaptation of David Guterson's bestseller is virtually the film's main protagonist (Ethan Hawke's conflicted trial observer is relatively passive), from the opening scene of snow falling gently on the harbor as a lighthouse blinks its warning to the frosty breath of the Japanese citizens as they march out of town (in flashback), wearing fur-collard coats, toward the internment camps. The film was unjustly maligned and ignored when it was released; there is good acting all around, particularly by Max Von Sydow as the stalwart defense attorney, and the snow-crusted cinematography is breathtaking.

Atanarjuat: The Fast Runner (2001) The first film shot in the Inuktitut language, this nearly two-and-a-half-hour epic about Inuit love, family, and betrayal is all Arctic, all the time, shot with a wholly convincing native cast on digital video. Primal, enthralling, and very cold.

AUTUMN

"Dream I had once. I was walkin' in the woods. I don't know why. Wind came up and blew me hat off."
—Gabriel Byrne, *Miller's Crossing*

Arguably the dreamiest, most evocative of seasons, autumn is also a time of monumental transition: from the child's egocentric summertime Elysium to the social order of school days; from vacation time to orthodoxy; from near-nakedness to the altogether different heaven of jackets, sweaters, and scarves. Night comes early, college lives begin, and a green world alchemizes into the warm colors of fire, wood, blood, and rot. Worst of all, winter is visible over the horizon. Our recommendation for most of these films is to watch them *only* in the fall, when the childhood experience of standing in a world as it changes from blazing sunniness to moody portent is awakened again. (See also "Halloween," in which all of the genuine frighteners have been sequestered.)

Meet Me in St. Louis **(1944)** A film for all seasons, literally, this timeless Vincente Minnelli musical rips through an entire year, but it's the Halloween sequence that lodges in the brainpan like a dream you're not sure was sweet or scary. The preteens of the film's fin de siècle St. Louis family—eleven-year-old Joan Carroll and the still-astonishing, super-precocious seven-year-old Margaret O'Brien—enter into a suburban midnight-land of rampaging costumed kids, looming bonfires, menacing winds, and a sense of fevered menace that evokes, in economic masterstrokes, a child's view of the season's leafy coolness and evening danger. It's still a wartime musical and hardly transgressive, despite the primal behavior. (If kids today burned household furniture in the center of the street, the National Guard would be called out.) The worst that happens is O'Brien's unearthly sprite hurling flour at a neighbor's face, but the whole scene exudes the genuine buzz of self-mythologized preadolescent excitement. And the autumn nighttime—shot entirely on the MGM studio backlots—fairly shudders.

Autumn Leaves **(1956)** Most often a "man's man" hyperbolist, director Robert Aldrich did voyage occasionally into women's melodrama, here embodied by a suffering harpy (Joan Crawford) as she struggles with her bipolar hubby (Cliff Robertson). Much of the film's world is standard-issue studio scenery, with glimmers of forced seasonal atmosphere that can only be enjoyed as a memory of a pungent matinee September, when the song "The Great Pretender" was playing on the radio and Eisenhower was president. What's fading in this magnificent Freudian weepie is, of course, Crawford herself, her iron-backed 1940s masochism slowly, tensely morphing into a Grand Guignol vision of near-sociopathic Hollywood narcissism.

An Autumn Afternoon **(1962)** One of the most mature and eloquent voices in cinema, Yasujiro Ozu capped off his astoundingly consistent and insightful career with this paradigmatic masterpiece, in which traditional and contemporary Japanese values "agree to disagree" over a good-hearted widower and his grown daughter, whom he has decided must get married. Ozu was a master, and his films are surpassingly rich with humanity and respect, but although he was always patiently observant of the physical world (he pioneered the use of "still-lifes"—cutaway images of unoccupied space used as counterpoint to the quiet turmoil of the characters' lives), only *An Autumn Afternoon* has a distinctly seasonal ambience. Here the Tokyo autumn is glimpsed only in spare, koan-like tidbits—but in Ozu's sphere, the season is always as tangible a reality as the fifty flavors of heartbreak that marinate his stories.

***Sometimes a Great Notion* (1971)** Paul Newman's adaptation of Ken Kesey's novel about an Oregon logging family is thick—visually and narratively—with trees in falltime (the film was completely shot on location, using real light, as was the curious custom in Hollywood at the time). As the beach is to summer, the northern forests are to autumn, and here the quotidian of living and working amid the woodlands is altogether palpable—naturalistic, unadorned, unbeautified, respected, and run through with northwest sunlight and shadow. Sometimes retitled *Never Give an Inch*, which should never be held against it.

***Scarecrow* (1973)** The American New Wave—as the gritty, thorny, risky Hollywood movies of 1967–1977 have now been unofficially labeled—had a yen for a Middle America that previous movies had ordinarily never visited: a scrubby, weather-battered landscape of decaying industry, forgotten towns, empty interstates, aimless drifters, working-class desolation, and pockets of disenfranchised humanity surviving on the social fringes. A low-down, hyperrealistic buddy road movie, from a day when movie stars (in this case, Gene Hackman and Al Pacino) looked like real people and never exhibited the need to seem smarter or more confident than their characters, the film is set largely on the midwestern highways during a cold fall, and thanks to Vilmos Zsigmond's grainy, nondecorative cinematography, you feel every badland wind and see every distant storm head. This is a low-rent America of stained flannel, bitter junkyards, dirty windows, bad diner coffee, and ruined dreams. If you ever wanted to know what it was like to stand on an empty street corner in Michigan in the fall of 1972, this is how you find out.

***Days of Heaven* (1978)** It was director Terrence Malick's last film before his notorious twenty-year hiatus, it was moviegoers' introduction to Sam Shepard, and it's almost incontestably the most gorgeously photographed film ever made. A love saga of sorts, set in the Texas wheat fields during World War I, the movie was shot entirely at twilight—that most autumnal hour—and its visions of sunset harvests and bronze landscapes are transfixing. You've never seen a Great Plains autumn evening like this, and you never will outside of this film.

***National Lampoon's Animal House* (1978)** This film, known as little more than shorthand for a certain type of sophomoric comedy today, stands as a life-passage benchmark for at least a few generations of American men (those who attended college between 1978 and, say, 1986), and the major reason for that, let's not kid ourselves, is the legacy it spawned of frat rousters, toga parties, beer fetishism, the playing of "Shout" at weddings, and, generally, *Maxim* magazine–style pub-lad hedonism. (Virtually any single piece of the film's dialogue—"I won't go schizo, will I?"—is instantly recognizable to any man in his late thirties to early forties; try some out on a stranger some time, and you'll bond like long-separated twins.) But there's more to the picture; it might be the most evocative and resonant depiction of embarking on a college career in American film history. Never mind that it reconstituted, with the determination of James Ivory adapting E. M. Forster (the seminude sorority pillow fight notwithstanding), the details of college life circa 1963; here we have a freshman's first ferocious autumn, sweatered coeds, campus perambulating, pre-hippie teen cellar-dwelling, cafeteria chaos, and dorm camaraderie. The filmmakers don't spend much effort on September atmosphere, but because they were intent on getting the minutiae right, the movie nevertheless calls up the season and speaks to the kegmaster in all of us.

Reuben, Reuben (1983) Peter DeVries's tragicomic novel, about a thinly disguised Dylan Thomas–type poet on his last legs during an American reading tour, is a fabulous thumbnail sketch of New England hills and yardscapes in the fall. The hero's exploits are a rip, and the story—Tom Conti's weary drunk falls for a blue-blooded college lass, played by Kelly McGillis—is pure girls-in-turtleneck-sweaters melancholy, but the movie's essential purpose here is the unceremonious capture of time and place, something movies seem hardly capable of anymore.

Country (1984) Like *Sometimes a Great Notion*, a movie about family, dirt work, and the wearing of flannel. Easily the most convincing of its year's farm movies, this hard-scrabble melodrama takes great pains to muster a harvest-time ambience of sheepskin-lined denim coats, windblown curls, hard Iowa winds, rusty pickup trucks, and Sundays at home watching football in the living room.

Children of a Lesser God (1986) Here's that cuddly, romantic back-to-school vibe again. The persistent, friendly northern chill in the browning foliage (shot, as it happens, in Canada) and on the cast's rosy-cheeked faces may be the only aspects of this award winner (set, happily, in an old private school in the woods) that doesn't feel silly and dated today. But since most autumn movies tend to be either hair-raising or cynical, we offer here a snuggle-on-the-couch alternative, complete with motormouth William Hurt at his peculiar best, and a happy ending.

Miller's Crossing (1990) The Coen brothers' masterpiece one-ups Dashiell Hammett (whose novel *The Glass Key* was the film's uncredited template) with a liberal dose of rum-runner-era Midwest ambience, all overcoats and pine forests and gray skies. The story, so thick with its own weblike narrative hijinks and pearly mock patois, ropes around the conflict of nerves between two crime bosses in an unnamed midwestern city and the one man (Gabriel Byrne) trying, for his own reasons, to play both ends against the middle. Don't ask us why, but films set in Depression-era Middle America always seem to take place in either summertime (when jobless poverty is of relatively little consequence) or autumn (when, as winter approaches, it begins to matter a good deal more). Of course, the Coens aren't as concerned with actual socioeconomic conditions as much as with the movie-movie ether left lingering in the cultural forebrain, but all the same, *Miller's Crossing* lends its autumn a uniquely resonant identity. In this cockeyed world of tweed, bourbon, and northern zephyrs, being left out in the approaching cold is the sorriest fate there is.

Twin Peaks: Season 1 (1990) Protosurrealist auteur David Lynch is many things to many people, but there's no denying that he's an atmospherist—no other filmmaker is as attuned to mood and subconscious suggestion. His pioneering, wickedly absurd TV series is a triumph of autumnal vibery—the body of one Laura Palmer washes up in the woodsiest corner of the world, and Lynch (as well as his army of guest directors) frequently cuts away from the action to simply observe trees buffeting in the wind, or a nighttime traffic light presiding over a cold intersection. Centered, like Lynch's *Blue Velvet*, in a decaying lumber town, *Twin Peaks* is essentially Octoberish in nature, and thus ill-fated as a series from the get-go; had this most quixotic of network projects continued into third or fourth seasons, the story's collision with winter or summer would've seemed bizarrely inappropriate.

The Silence of the Lambs (1991) There may be too many reasons to rewatch Jonathan Demme's infamous, Oscar-reaping serial-killer chiller, even if Anthony Hopkins's saturnine whisperiness plays less convincingly now and the plot's been aped so many times it feels old hat. But Demme has always been a master at exploring the in-between places and denizens of the low-rent American landscape, and *Lambs*'s stark fall time frame and realistic posturban blight conjure a powerful sense of believable dread—an important factor in the film's success that, somehow, has eluded its many imitators. This is where the demons among us hide, right?—in the desolate no man's lands of cities' edges, those mundane, run-down places we do not visit, particularly under a gritty autumn sky.

Autumn Tale (1998) Ex–New Waver and logorrheic humanist Eric Rohmer had been creating *La Ronde*–like comedies about love and folly, in which the French filmmaker's bemused characters talk their hypereducated ways into romantic knots, for about forty years when he fashioned this climax to his Tales of the Four Seasons quartet. The gabby story centers on two middle-aged women, Isabelle (Marie Rivière) and Magali (Béatrice Romand), childhood friends of the southern wine provinces with grown children of their own, one happily married, the other stubbornly single. The ability to make us quietly bask in the rhythm and bounce of passionate friendships, platonic or otherwise, has always been Rohmer's trump card, but there's also something autumnal going on outside the film's pleasant bubble: both Rivière and Romand (each lovelier and more distinctive here than ever before) began their careers more than twenty years ago as young actresses in Rohmer films (*Perceval* and *Claire's Knee*, respectively). As always, Rohmer shoots simply, often filming long conversations in a single still take, evoking the beautiful provincial landscape around the actors without overdoing the scenery; even so, the images are lovely enough to make one notice that autumn in the south of France looks and feels a lot like summer anywhere else.

October Sky **(1999)** For a movie to be experientially potent in relation to the seasons, it helps if it is faithful to a real era and locale, and in this minihit, directed by Joe Johnston, the lucky devil who kicked off the *Honey, I Shrunk the Kids* franchise, a remarkable true story keeps everything bolted to the ground. Recounting the youth of Homer Hickam, a West Virginia coal miner's kid who bucked his upbringing and devoted himself to rocketry (he eventually worked for NASA), the film is as hardscrabble and working-class—and corny—as Hollywood movies got on the cusp of the millennium, but the low-rent Tennessee locales are convincing, and the gray sky is unmuddied by CGI enhancement.

SPRING

"Welcome to Sherwood, my lady!"
—Errol Flynn, *The Adventures of Robin Hood*

Moviewise, the difference between summer and the season that precedes it is subtle, but there is a special sense of springtime renewal in some films—a feeling of looking forward to a warmer, happier future, in much the same way that every kid gazes toward the end of the school year.

Various early-talkie *Our Gang/Little Rascals* shorts, particularly *School's Out* (1930), *Bear Shooters* (1930), and *Teacher's Pet* (1930) Sometimes the less polished the movie, the more it captures its time and place. Hal Roach's first *Our Gang* shorts that featured sound (the ones with Jackie, Wheezer, Farina, Stymie, Miss Crabtree, Mary Ann, et al.) were shot quickly and sloppily on the dirt-poor side streets and farm lots of Los Angeles County, and their portraits of sun-dappled haze, bug-thick humidity, mud-puddle whimsicality, and near-rural indolence is unsurpassed. And they're funny, too, in a way kids *still* respond to, given half a chance.

À Nous la Liberté **(1931)** There's no repressing the happy grins emerging from René Clair's classic early talkie, an anti-industrialization parable (which years later would be largely ripped off by Charlie Chaplin in *Modern Times*) that follows two escaped convicts who confront modern factory life. Spring is the season for wishing for irresponsible alternatives to maturity and duty, and this sunny, flowery, goofy film is a wish come true.

The Adventures of Robin Hood **(1938)** Errol Flynn—in color—in all of his boy-god splendor, as the famous fairy-tale bandit, bounding through green and shadowy California forests and being electrically fabulous. It's a fun romp in general, but Flynn makes it a vitamin shot.

Elvira Madigan **(1967)** The first international Swedish hit film that wasn't about sex or directed by Ingmar Bergman, Bo Widerberg's rendition of the famous (in northern Europe) Tristan-and-Isolde-ish true story of a tragic romance between an AWOL soldier and a young tightrope walker looks as though it was shot entirely on warm May mornings. Awash with sun-dappled glades and verdant glens, it may be the greenest film ever made. (It also features this unsung 1960s innovation: the realistic portrayal of young love, with all of its silly goofing, frolicking in wild fields, and spending vast amounts of time doing very little at all besides kanoodling. Movies just didn't indulge in these realities before the era's New Wave revolution.) Routinely labeled, at the time of its release, the most beautifully photographed film ever made, this movie, leavened with Mozart, is a seasonal blessing.

The Razor's Edge **(1984)** One of the strangest films of the 1980s, yet one lit up with a nutty, irrational warmth. Bill Murray, bargaining with Columbia against the inevitable success of *Ghostbusters* the same year, gained permission to cowrite this W. Somerset Maugham adaptation, and by most assessments it's a ridiculous freak: an off-balance, confusing, half-serious mess. But not so fast: filmed like a nostalgic fever dream, the path of Larry Darrell—from common American jerk to World War I vet to expatriate wandering shaman—is a promise of tedium (Tyrone Power kept him dull in the 1946 version); here, Murray's shrugging innocence and guileless irony make the arc feel powerfully human. This might be the best Larry Darrell we'll ever have: a lonely, unsettled man, defending himself from the world through reclusiveness and childish humor, yet nearing the springtime of his own existence by way of spiritual satisfaction. Little did we know that Murray himself would fulfill that promise years later, in *Rushmore*, *Lost in Translation*, and *Broken Flowers*. Director John Byrum (abetted by Jack Nitzsche, who produced a lush score) manages a powerful sense of elegy, from the pre-fireworks evening montage to Murray's Darrell pressing his cheek against the dead Sophie's lips, that could only exist in a film this unsure of itself.

A Tale of Springtime **(1990)** More Eric Rohmer, this time a gentle, matchmaking, end-of-semester pas de trois between a Parisian student, a mature philosophy teacher, and the student's bachelor father. Rohmerians need no further introduction, except perhaps the suggestion that a memorable movie-going year could be marked by quarterly viewings of Rohmer's four seasonal films—which also include *A Summer's Tale*, *Autumn Tale*, and ***A Tale of Winter*** **(1992)**—beginning in March with this inaugural honey.

The Secret Garden **(1993)** The redemptive power of spring is a common theme in literature, but it's certainly less so in movies, which tend to focus more on plot process than on seasonal transition. Agnieszka Holland's retelling of this turn-of-the-century nursery standard is so evocative of spring you can practically smell the wakening soil.

The story centers around Mary (Kate Maberly), an imperious and sullen child who is orphaned and sent to live with the husband of her late aunt at his grand English estate. Finding a locked garden as neglected as herself, Mary sets about bringing it—as well as a bedridden cousin—back to life. (More of a grouchy snipe than she is, the ten-year-old relative is convinced he's already on his deathbed.) Endless moors, swaying ivy, twittering robins, shoots struggling in the weeds, lads riding bareback—there isn't a moment of this film that doesn't feel like winter's end. Don't relegate it to the children's bin.

Emma (1996) Jane Austen's tale of a young matchmaker with social stature, a doting father, and awful instincts regarding the suitability of mates. Emma Woodhouse (Gwyneth Paltrow) takes a plain-Jane mouse under her wing and tries to plan a *shiddoch* with the insipid Reverend Elton (Alan Cumming), who actually hankers after Emma herself. From there on out, nothing goes as planned, including Emma's own relationship with the sensible Mr. Knightly, played with intelligent humor by Jeremy Northam. It's a springtime tale of love, played out in the pastoral English countryside where the ladies stroll over wooden bridges amid flocks of geese. Every scene is bathed in sunlight, crowning Paltrow's golden tresses, and the few winter scenes do not shake the overall spring-is-in-the-air feel. The soothing scenery offsets the complex machinations of Emma's faulty matchmaking, and a sweet song by Ewan McGregor is a bonus.

RAINED IN

"The wind blows so hard the ocean gets up on its hind legs and walks right across the land."
—Thomas Gomez, *Key Largo*

It might just be us, but we've always found the feeling of being safely shuttered in by inhospitable elements irresistible. Of course, rainstorms have been used and abused as symbolism by Hollywood since the beginning of movies; these particular films seem to us the most effective in making the walls close in a little tighter, and the storm outside sound a little fiercer.

Rain (1932) W. Somerset Maugham's good-versus-evil parable, as shot on the backlot by Lewis Milestone, amounts to an ideological contest between a preacher (Walter Huston) and a whore (Joan Crawford) on some rain-soaked Hawaiian atoll. An early talkie, and full of mood.

And Then There Were None **(1945)** Ominous black clouds and a stormy boat ride should have been glaring warnings to the ten strangers who are invited to a island estate by a unknown host, but the guests pay no heed; instead, they embark—and begin to get bumped off, one by one. Based on Agatha Christie's *Ten Little Indians*, this rainy-day intrigue feels claustrophobic not just because of the constant downpour spattering the windows, but also because of the paranoia that sets in when the guests realize there's no one else on the island, and one among them must be the killer. All the while, the piano plinks the nursery rhyme tune and the countdown begins. *Survivor*, indeed.

Key Largo **(1948)** The John Huston film noir based on the Maxwell Anderson play and set, imperatively, on the titular Florida island in the off-season and during a typhoon. A gaggle of gangsters (led by Edward G. Robinson's sadistic kingpin) find themselves trapped with a handful of honest victims, including Humphrey Bogart's disillusioned war vet. Claire Trevor won an Oscar as a weepy lush, and though the film is filthy with hard-boiled dialogue and character, its hothouse atmosphere is irresistible.

Seven Samurai **(1954)** Akira Kurosawa's revered samurai epic—of which the Hollywood western *The Magnificent Seven* is a tame remake—pits an ad hoc league of mercenary warriors against a bandit army, and the pivotal battle—all sword, staff, knife, forest, and mud—rolls out in the middle of a monsoon. (Speaking of remakes, the computer-animated kids' hit ***A Bug's Life*** **(1998)** played a respectful variation on the theme, with a cataclysmic rainfall in which the giant drops land like bombs.)

The Exterminating Angel **(1962)** Master surrealist Luis Buñuel's uproariously dreamlike satire has guests at a large aristocratic dinner party discovering, once dinner is over, that they cannot leave the dining room. Days, then weeks pass, farm animals come and go, social decorum collapses, lovers kill themselves, furniture is broken for a fire, yet leaving this central haven of political and economic privilege is never an option. Claustrophobia as social commentary? You could slice this soufflé any number of ways, and it'd still be pungent, funny, and inexplicable.

The Loneliness of the Long Distance Runner **(1962)** You'd be hard pressed to find grim rainy days as powerfully evoked as they are in the British films of the 1960s; these guys knew dreary and inclement weather like dogs know fleas. Here, a young con (Tom Courteney), stuck in juvenile detention, ruminates on his life while running (often in the rain), and begins to create a future for himself as a champion. The damp grayness is pervasive.

The Servant **(1963)** More British grayness, done to a T by director Joseph Losey and screenwriter Harold Pinter, in which personal butler Dirk Bogarde slowly and demonically subverts the upper-class identity of master James Fox.

Séance on a Wet Afternoon **(1964)** This grim British chiller's title says it all: the grainy black-and-white film allows not a shred of sunshine or color as we follow a guilt-ridden Richard Attenborough around London as he carries out unhinged wife Kim Stanley's plan to "borrow" a rich little girl and make everyone believe their own long-dead son has revealed to her the girl's whereabouts in an afternoon séance. Everything about this film is gray and gloomy: the boarded windows of the room where the girl is hidden, Stanley's eerie hospital-nurse pretense as she ministers to the drugged child, Attenborough's desperate unraveling as the little girl grows ill and remorse and shame overtake him. The rain dominates: windshield wipers on chauffeur-driven cars, umbrellas popping open, splashing puddles—even the music sounds like dripping water, and the raindrops on the camera lens will make you feel as if it's your window you're looking through, and that you're damned thankful to be inside.

The Spy Who Came In from the Cold **(1965)** Espionage—of the genuine, convincing, John le Carré type—has always seemed suited for rainy days, when normal people are at home and only the spooks of the Cold War must move about, mysteriously haunting the backstreets of the world's capitol cities, huddled miserably in their overcoats. This Richard Burton vehicle is a piece of clockwork so beautifully worked out that it'd be a shame to know anything about the story beforehand. We will say, however, that the overcast ambience tells a story all its own.

Murder by Death **(1976)** Generally given to writing sitcomish comedies that are sticky with bathos, Neil Simon uncorked his cellar of shtick for this murder-mystery parody, composed entirely of a character cast making easy hay of Sam Spade, Nick and Nora Charles, Miss Marple, Hercule Poirot, and Charlie Chan (not to mention blind butler Alec Guinness and deaf-mute maid Nancy Walker). The "world's greatest detectives" are locked within a booby-trapped house in a rainstorm, of course (by host Truman Capote, which is the part of the movie we still don't get), but the cast (including Peter Falk, Eileen Brennan, David Niven, Elsa Lanchester, James Coco, and Peter Sellers) are savvy pros at the top of their game, and not a campy stitch is dropped.

Nostalghia **(1983)** In Andrei Tarkovsky's oeuvre, the only place it doesn't constantly rain is in outer space; obviously, gloomy precipitation means more in his world than just weather. Made in Italy after Tarkovsky left the Soviet Union, this film involves an exiled Russian poet (Oleg Yankovsky) who longs for his wife and homeland, and the metaphysical pact he makes with an anarchist madman (Erland Josephson)—but it's really about Tarkovsky's darkling imagery and breathtaking set pieces, most of which are dripping with downpour.

SNOW DAYS

"It seems to me that the skiing up here would be fantastic."
—Jack Nicholson, *The Shining*

The great unofficial holiday of kid-dom: the snow day, that glorious "holiday" that arrives unpredictably and often without warning, canceling out the dour prospect of school on a moment's notice and at the same time offering up a dose of snow in which to spend the free day. (A fondly remembered Sayville, New York, health teacher, one Mr. Fuller, once offered up this potent description of how heroin felt: "You wake up and there's snow outside your window and your mother says there's no school; you don't have to get out of bed. Right then, the pillow feels *just right*. Your sheets, your bed, feel *just right*. Am I right? *That's* how it feels.") Of course, if the kids stay home, chances are the grown-ups can't go anywhere either. The video choices should be snowy, fanciful, and wild.

The Thing **(1951)** It's a universal assumption by now that this bouncy, matter-of-fact sci-fi thriller was actually directed by producer Howard Hawks. This accounts for its snappy patter and all-business plot stuff, but the "trapped in the Arctic with an alien" scenario comes from veteran genre scribe John W. Campbell Jr.'s story "Who Goes There?" Tight and suspenseful as hell; remade in 1982 (see below) to significantly more garish effect.

Shadows of Forgotten Ancestors **(1964)** One of the greatest art films to emerge from the Soviet Union's anti-Stalinist "Kruschev thaw," this debut feature by Georgian filmmaker Sergei Paradjanov is a realization of a Ukrainian folktale of lost love, betrayal, witchcraft, and fate. Paradjanov was a one-of-a-kind stylist, exaggerating visuals in mind-blowing ways, yet remaining faithful to the feel of traditional Ukrainian folk art. And he did it all in the Carpathian Mountains, where winter means business—the cast is clad entirely in animal skins.

War and Peace **(1967)** This massive, seven-hour Tolstoy adaptation has a crummy reputation; it's seen as a politburo-approved budget-crazy behemoth that won an Oscar while Soviet authorities censored scores of more personal films and exiled more inventive filmmakers. It *is* the largest and most expensive movie ever made, involving more than a quarter-million extras and eating up resources enough to support a small nation (in today's economy, the movie would cost close to *one billion dollars* to make). Whatever; it's passionate and visually stirring, it's good for an entire day of movie-watching, and the snowy Russian landscapes are grand.

Murder on the Orient Express **(1974)** It'd be hard to do better than to hunker down with this gleefully professional, completely confident all-star cast, on an aristocratic-age luxury train, on a day when the snow piles up outside just like it piles up around the train, stuck as it is in a Yugoslavian mountain drift while one of its passengers (Richard Widmark) is murdered in his private berth. Agatha Christie stalwart Hercule Poirot (Albert Finney, slicing his lean ham so nicely) interviews the suspects, twirling his trademarked moustache, and decades of celebrities parade before us, acting up snowstorms. Ah, the lost days when murder was fun, train travel was elegant, and royalty were to be pitied their vanished empires. An Oscar went to Ingrid Bergman for her one scene because, well, she's Ingrid Bergman.

The Shining (1980) Jack Nicholson, a telepathic boy, an empty hotel, an axe. And oh, so much more—Stanley Kubrick's landmark boo-fest rewards repeat viewings like a slot machine, from the awful sound of the kid's Big Wheel on those silent corridor carpets to the beautiful naked ghost in the bathtub to Lloyd the saturnine bartender, fueling the animal for a night of mad havoc. It's as much a hair-raising exploration of writer's block, wintertime claustrophobia, and paternal impatience as it is a whacked-out horror flick—and it does run amuck in its own ozone. If little else, it'll surely cure you of the notion that getting genuinely snowed in within a cavernous resort hotel might be fun or restorative, but being trapped at home with this dilly can electrify a cold, dull afternoon. If you can't already quote at least half a dozen lines ("Give me the bat, Wendy . . ."), you need to catch up with the rest of America. All work and no play, indeed.

Reds (1981) A film for all seasons, it would appear, but Warren Beatty's gargantuan, passionate, inventive biopic of journalists/socialist activists John Reed and Louise Bryant (Beatty and Diane Keaton) is poundingly eloquent when it comes to the famed lovers' time in Revolutionary Russia (the film was shot, for the most part, in Finland). But there's more: It's possibly the best historical film ever made in America, it's an exhausting and involving romantic tragedy, and it's a deft primer on socialist thought (in a Hollywood movie!), the embattled legacy of unionism, and the inherent, decid-edly nonsocialist madness of the post-Bolshevik Soviet system. And it's got Beatty, Keaton, and Jack Nicholson (as a booze-hardened Eugene O'Neill) in their prime, and dozens of "witnesses" long past theirs (including Rebecca West, Will Durant, Henry Miller, Georges Seldes, Roger Baldwin, and George Jessel), eloquently speaking of their post–World War I memories. Besides, if you can't go out, you've got time for all of the film's 194 minutes.

The Thing (1982) John Carpenter's explosively gruesome remake of the 1951 suspense flick was reviled upon its release, and today it's remembered most for its hellish, syrupy animatronic special effects. (They're pretty foul in spots, but in other scenes they're absolutely unforgettable.) Look at it with fresh eyes, though, and you see an expertly crafted redo of John Ford's *The Lost Patrol*. Here, a shape-shifting alien besieges an arctic science station, which is entertainingly populated by Kurt Russell and a crew of eleven great character actors (including Wilford Brimley, Donald Moffat, Richard Masur, Keith David, Charles Hallahan, and T. K. Carter). Carpenter knew what he was doing here, for a change.

Smilla's Sense of Snow **(1997)** An avalanche tumbles across the screen, blinding white and burying everything in its path, and the next thing we know, years have passed, and a six-year-old boy is dead on a snowy Copenhagen sidewalk, having fallen from the roof. Friend and neighbor of the neglected boy, Smilla Jasperson (Julia Ormond), is convinced he's been murdered and investigates. As created by novelist Peter Hoeg, Smilla is a great character, full of depth and edginess, and this is an unparalleled snow-day movie—more than just a steady supply of flurries, there are glaciers, arctic caves, and the frosty expanses of Greenland. A great mystery for the kind of shut-in day when there's no point in shoveling because the snow is coming down too hard.

Werckmeister Harmonies **(2000)** Glacial Euro-art cinema by Hungarian Bela Tarr, casting a very cold eye on a frozen post-Communist village that's visited, for unknown reasons, by a traveling exhibit of a giant, taxidermied whale. Other mysteries proliferate, none of them solvable. Spectacularly grim.

OPENING DAY

"I believe in the Church of Baseball."
—Susan Sarandon, *Bull Durham*

It's coming, sure as April, death, and taxes: the only first day in sports that's celebrated like a holy occasion. The people of Cincinnati, home of the first pro baseball team, still take the day off, but in the meantime, before the games begin, the anticipation can get heady—and baseball movies, a great American subgenre, are a natural remedy.

Casey at the Bat **(1927)** A rarely seen silent version of the Ernest Lawrence Thayer poem, with Wallace Beery as the batting champ in question. Minor, but superior to Disney's rather cloying Jerry Colonna–narrated cartoon from 1947.

The Pride of the Yankees **(1942)** There may be people who love this weepiest of sports-legend biopics simply because they're fans of Gary Cooper, or because they're hard-core Yankee fans who'll see any movie with the team's name in the title, but let's face it: most of us still get a lump in the throat at the sound of Lou Gehrig (or Cooper doing

Gehrig), intoning into the ballpark's vast echo, "Today-ay-ay, I consider myself-elf-elf the luckiest man-man-man on the face of the Earth-Earth-Earth." Most of us heard Cooper say it before we'd heard Gehrig (if we've heard Gehrig at all), and if the Iron Horse is still a universally beloved ballplayer, this movie has fostered that worship. Because it's baseball, and it's the movies, it's not surprising that the legend supplants the original in the public consciousness. Cooper portrays Gehrig as a lovable, innocent bumbler: witness the earnest clumsiness as he wipes out on a pile of bats; the missed ball when wife-to-be Eleanor (the still underappreciated Teresa Wright) bestows a smile upon him; the aw-shucks waves to the roaring crowd. For millions of Americans, in the war years and after, this movie was a collective dream of baseball, in which a poor immigrant's son can triumph and live a heroic life in the most democratic of sports. The movie leaves Gehrig at his final field appearance, sparing us the trial of his struggle with amyotrophic lateral sclerosis. Who'd argue that this isn't as it should be? Does the film depict Gehrig as he really was? Of course not. Baseball fans love the game's stories, names, stats, and legacies, and this is their Achilles tale, their Greek tragedy. Those same fans know, too, that this film offers opportunities to witness once-living legends Babe Ruth, Bill Dickey, Mark Koenig, Bob Meusel, and announcer Bill Stern playing themselves.

Take Me Out to the Ball Game (1949) Musical hokum that looks back to the game's early days, but is actually fluent in the pop-culture fun and games of 1949, with Frank Sinatra (as a hoofin', singin' second baseman!) and Gene Kelly both wooing new team owner Esther Williams. Cute as a bug.

The Jackie Robinson Story (1950) The first African American player in the modern major leagues, Robinson also played himself in his very own Hollywood biopic—while in his third year with the Dodgers. It must've been a surreal experience for the man, amid his seasons of play, publicity, and endurance of racist vitriol, to have made this film, with Ruby Dee starring as his wife and industry stalwart Louise Beavers playing his mother. It was a low-budget affair, and Robinson wasn't an actor—but the project has the glow of history about it.

The Pride of St. Louis (1952) A strictly OK biopic of pitching great/ex–Gashouse Gang member Dizzy Dean, whose stubborn, egomaniacal style made him a hot commodity but also ended his career early (due to an unaddressed injury); this film, starring Dan Dailey, finds a triumphant capstone to the Diz story in Dean's subsequent career as a malapropism-spewing sports broadcaster.

Damn Yankees (1958) Completely subtlety-free, this adaptation of the Broadway hit musical tells you a lot more about Broadway musicals than it does about baseball. A Washington Senators fan literally sells his soul to the devil to be a young baseball hotshot but can't seem to forget the middle-aged, loyal wife he abandoned for fame and glory. Gwen Verdon vamps it up as best she can, but this creaker will appeal to a pretty narrow demographic: indiscriminate fans of both baseball and old-school musicals.

***Bang the Drum Slowly* (1973)** Could this be the saddest baseball movie ever? Coming from a 1955 novel, this subdued, grown-up drama simply waits out the last season of a low-IQ MLB catcher (Robert De Niro), who learns at the outset that he has a fatal disease. Emphasis is placed less on mortality or the game, and more on the day-to-day traveling life of pro players in the days before bazillion-dollar contracts and steroids. Viewers who were moved when this movie came out—and it's tough not to be when the catcher, in his last game, looks for a fly ball that's no longer there—keep it close to their hearts.

***The Bad News Bears* (1976)** Besides being possibly the least condescending Hollywood film ever made about kids, as well as a scabrous mockery of American suburbia and so many of the life principles our middle class holds dear, this Little League satire (which spawned a deplorable remake in 2005) remains a paradigm of 1970s realism—the dusty fields, arid sprawl, parking lots, beer in the dugout, and glaring noon light will reignite anyone's memories of small-town ball, organized by annoying adults but played in the heat by kids.

***The Bingo Long Traveling All-Stars and Motor Kings* (1976)** A rather weak-kneed attempt to tell an all-American story (that's still waiting to be retold) about the Negro League baseball players who barnstormed around the Midwest in the 1930s, where they faced exploitation and discrimination but played for the love of the game. Richard Pryor, James Earl Jones, and Billy Dee Williams star. Despite its release date (the 1970s were crazed with Depression nostalgia), the movie's feel for the 1930s heartland is only half baked.

***The Natural* (1984)** Baseball is already drunk on mythology, but this lush saga, based on the novel by Bernard Malamud, reeks of legend, destiny, and symbolism. Robert Redford and Glenn Close were both already a little long in the tooth to get away with playing youthful lovers (and Redford was even a little too old to be playing a past-his-prime slugger), but that doesn't bother most baseball fans, who tend to love the game with a child's ingenuousness. From the "bat of destiny" carved from a lightning-struck tree, to Randy Newman's heraldic score, this film—like the idea of the Cubs winning a World Series—is an overripe fairy tale only a fan could buy.

***Bull Durham* (1988)** There's no other sport that inspires more emotion, rumination, and heartfelt worship than baseball, and Ron Shelton's signature movie embodies all of these in one perfect, life-loving swoop. This slice of minor-league life remains lovable because there are no big-headed major-league egos around—just the fervent hoping to get there. No underdog triumphs, no sentimental formulas, and no baloney to be found—from Tim Robbins's talented jerk to Susan Sarandon's small-town groupie who's dizzy with big-city ideas to Kevin Costner's career-anchoring performance as the aging catcher who shoulders the responsibility of molding the uncontrollable pitcher into a star even as his own dreams of the majors sail further out of reach. The script crackles with educated wit, the minor characters are just as funny and original as the main players, and the homage to baseball is everything it should be: heartbreaking in some ways, but crazy for the game, for summer evenings, and for retaining a fiery sliver of youth deep into the middle years.

Eight Men Out **(1988)** The story of the 1919 Black Sox scandal, in which the Chicago White Sox conspired with gamblers to throw the game, brought to you in historical broad strokes by staunch unionist writer-director John Sayles. So here the players (including John Cusack, Charlie Sheen, David Straithairn, and, as the famous "Shoeless" Joe Jackson, D. B. Sweeney) are driven to cheat by the stinginess of owner Charlie "Commie" Comiskey (Clifton James), who routinely reneged on promises and bonuses alike. Sayles's take is hoary baseball-fan optimism, but of course we all want to believe the best of our heroes—that Pete Rose didn't gamble, that Barry Bonds never took 'roids, that the illiterate Jackson didn't understand what he was doing or even the import of the confession that he signed. No one can say for sure—but as long as the stats are accurate, we're willing to think it *might've* gone down this way.

The Life and Times of Hank Greenberg **(1999)** A simple and affectionate tribute to the first Jew to ever gain fame in major league baseball, Aviva Kempner's utterly conventional documentary plays like a deleted chapter from Ken Burns's *Baseball* miniseries. A strapping, good-natured, six-foot-four Bronx-born lad, Greenberg was one of the league's best hitters, and he became a local Detroit monument and a national symbol for Jews all over the country. (For interviewee Walter Matthau, Greenberg's success meant the possibility of "not having to be a cutter or salesman in the garment business," while Alan Dershowitz entertained fantasies of Greenberg being the first Jewish president.) The details are winning, including an account of how the Tigers would lose crucial games on Yom Kippur because Greenberg wasn't playing.

Fastpitch **(2000)** Jeremy Spear and Juliet Weber's documentary portrays a neglected subculture that inhabits the vast badlands between American cities: fast-pitch softball, a rough game that challenges the batter with shorter mount-to-plate pitch visibility than in pro baseball, and attracts a thriving regional fan base. An ex-Yale ballplayer and artist pursuing athletic glory for the last time, Spear encounters all manner of titans in his season in the sun, including a Ojibway pitching menace and a Maori home-run champ, both of whom, like all of the players, are neither pros nor obsessives, just working stiffs with a passion.

61* **(2001)** There are a few years that mean only one thing to baseball fans; ask a true aficionado what historic event happened in 1941, and instead of talking about Pearl Harbor, he or she will tell you that that's the year DiMaggio hit in fifty-six consecutive games, a feat that's never been surpassed or even matched. Likewise, 1961 conjures immediately the home-run race between Yankees legends Mickey Mantle and Roger Maris, both chasing Babe Ruth's record of sixty home runs in a single season. Still, this HBO movie, directed by Billy Crystal, is no idealized view—Mantle (Thomas Jane) is a tremendous talent, but also a womanizing drunk; the animosity toward Maris (Barry Pepper) is laid bare for us as well. It's not a great movie, but c'mon, baseball movies aren't about great cinema, they're about *baseball*. Pepper and Jane are both fine in two pairs of big shoes, but who would have thought we'd ever see Anthony Michael Hall, the skinny nerd from *Sixteen Candles*, as Yankees pitching great Whitey Ford? Baseball fans will love the movie's real footage of a time when athletes didn't rely on artificial means to gain glory—just talent, dignity, hard work, and luck.

***The Rookie* (2002)** The true tale of Jim Morris, a middle-aged high school science teacher who loses a bet with his students, tries out for the majors, and makes it. Though it was advertised as a kids' movie, the script never condescends or collapses into silliness, and Morris's tale is genuinely warming. Americans love the triumph of the underdog against all odds (and what's more intimidating than growing old?), and *The Rookie* doesn't disappoint in this regard: who would believe that a thirty-five-year-old rookie could throw a hundred miles per hour?

KICKOFF

"You take your football down here real serious, don't you?"
—Burt Reynolds, *The Longest Yard* (1974)

Antsy gridiron fans, slogging out the summer months before their season starts, have known to resort to even the cheesiest football movie to tide them over. These are the best of a sketchy lot.

***The Kickoff* (1931), *Washee Ironee* (1934), and/or *The Pigskin Palooka* (1937)** These *Our Gang/Little Rascals* shorts show football as it should be played—by pugnacious tykes in moth-eaten sweaters, in empty lots, with dogs involved in play and bubble gum on the ball.

***Horse Feathers* (1932)** The Marx Brothers attack college life, a life-brightening process that climaxes, more or less, with a crucial football match, between universities Darwin and Huxley, that is itself reduced to slapstick chicanery. (See "College Days," p. 303.)

That's My Boy **(1932)** A rather peculiar melodrama about college football stars becoming embroiled in dodgy bond-selling, but it features old-fashioned pigskin played by actual USC footballers, including John Wayne, plus Olympian Buster Crabbe.

Knute Rockne: All American **(1940)** The film that established college sports—and the sniffly, tear-jerking sports movie—as pillars of American life, this film lionizes the grid-iron legacy of Notre Dame, its famous coach Rockne (Pat O'Brien), and the doomed team martyr George "The Gipper" Gipp, played with boyish likability by Ronald Reagan. If you are a devotee of college ball, quote Rockne's climactic speech when tipsy ("win just one . . ."), or found Reagan adorable even as president, this is a DVD worth buying. Just don't bring it to our house.

M*A*S*H **(1971)** As if to summon the spirit of Harpo Marx and *Horse Feathers*, this kudo-ed, possibly overrated Robert Altman war comedy self-consciously climaxes with a long and utterly ridiculous football game, shot with Altman's trademarked, focal-plane-neurotic realism, but edited as if it were a gag reel.

The Longest Yard **(1974)** Too fondly remembered by mucho-macho ball fans, this low-brow Burt Reynolds yarn is about a ex-quarterback convict stuck in a Georgia penitentiary who's coerced into leading prisoners in a football game against the guards. Neck-breaking brawl stuff ensues, among a crowd of rough-and-tumble character actors that include several real NFL players. The 2005 remake, starring Adam Sandler, drained the property of its sole resource: hardscrabble authenticity.

Semi-Tough **(1977)** Michael Ritchie, making his short-lived claim as a premier American satirist, directed this adaptation of Dan Jenkins's comic novel about two pro footballers (Burt Reynolds and Kris Kristofferson) caught in a triangle with their best friend—team owner's daughter Jill Clayburgh. The farce turns sharpest when steered toward the new-age fads that dominated California society at the time.

North Dallas Forty **(1979)** The first sports movie written by a genuine pro athlete (Dallas Cowboys alum Peter Gent) about his own experiences, this comedy cries foul at the business end of the game (owners, coaches, and so forth) while paying homage to players (Nick Nolte, country singer Mac Davis, and NFL vet John Matuszak) who struggle to just be boys. Authentic to a degree (just listen to Nolte's bones creak in the morning), but hampered by mediocre sitcom-style direction and ex-model Dayle Haddon's woodenness as the love interest.

Any Given Sunday **(1999)** Oliver Stone's attempt at the definitive late-century pro football saga is as thunderous and abusive a film as you could hope for—albeit at some cost to narrative, character, and visual space. The movie manages to moralize about America's favorite pituitary-fueled blood sport—the film doesn't shy away from showing us the game's harrowing physical costs, social damage, false dreams of individual glory, and commercial soullessness—and love the testosterone-heavy warfare all the same. The story hits every point: the primary (fictional) team is coached by an aging, exhausted vet (a truly haggard Al Pacino), managed by the fiery, greedy daughter of the original owner (Cameron Diaz), quarterbacked by a past-his-prime, drug-pumped all-star (Dennis Quaid), and ostensibly rescued by a hotshot (Jamie Foxx) with a race-card chip on his shoulder and an ego that, soon enough, gets him into big trouble with his own defensemen. Stone's freeway-pileup style of filmmaking tries for nothing but unleashed energy, so this might best be enjoyed in a testosterone-amped home theater on Super Bowl Sunday—before the game, but after the drinking has begun.

Jim Brown: All-American (2002) Spike Lee's long, worshipful documentary about the football player/movie star/domestic-abuse felon may end up being the only nonfiction feature ever made about a midcentury football star.

Friday Night Lights (2004) Something of a Rorschach blot among football sagas, this Peter Berg–directed vision of poor small-town Texas and its veins-in-the-teeth devotion to high school ball is, on one hand, an incisive poison-pen letter excoriating empty-headed hypocrisies and oppressive social madness; on the other hand, it strives to celebrate the rush of the game—the germ of the problem—with every shaky-cam moment of field play. Take from it what you will.

BASKETBALL SEASON

"You either smoke or you get smoked, and you got smoked."
—Wesley Snipes, *White Men Can't Jump*

Devoted b-ball fanatics have months to wait between seasons, and fewer movies to pick from than fans of the other big sports. (It is, it seems, a less cinematic game, and it's less dramatically structured.)

Hoosiers (1986) Indiana in the 1950s finds Gene Hackman as the unwelcome outsider who comes to turn around the hometown high school basketball team with novel methods (read: harassment). The story is predictable, but there's an abundance of court time, which is suspenseful and convincing even to those who aren't fans of the game; devotees already know the movie by heart.

White Men Can't Jump (1992) Hollywood sports maven Ron Shelton takes aim at pickup-game basketball, with Wesley Snipes and Woody Harrelson as a pair of b-ball hustlers who unite to exploit Harrelson's whiteness and eventually fall afoul of mobsters. Shot partially in Watts, the movie has a distinctive truth to it, and, as you'd expect, the sports talk is 100 percent genuine (or was in 1992).

Blue Chips (1994) A cool, ballsy, bracingly cynical exploration of the all-too-easily corruptible world of college basketball, this Ron Shelton–scripted movie centers on Nick Nolte as a loudmouthed coach caught in the tug-of-war of enlisting the best new prospects for his school while trying to resist payoffs, kickbacks, and player elitism. He fails, of course, allowing his college's alumni faction to provide the kids with anything they want, and the ethical downside is as traumatic as the team's success is exultant. The players are all NBA pros, nothing is faked, and the on-court action (shot as real, improvised games and later edited) is exciting and tough without being calculated. Winning the big game isn't the issue here; the important thing is *how* you win, and the film takes serious, all-business swipes at the college farm system on all levels while maintaining a sense of the game's immediate appeal.

Hoop Dreams (1994) A crowd-dazzling, nearly-three-hour documentary about two Chicago kids who think, or hope, they've got the goods to make it as pro leaguers. Filmmaker Steve James follows them for five years, from the blooming of their teenage dreams to the crystallized moment of either doom or success, and the upshot is not only a grand social portrait, but also a chilling indictment of the modern American dream, sold day and night on TV but, in fact, as empty for most of us as discarded Coke cans.

HOCKEY SEASON

"One hundred bucks of my own money for the first of my men who really creams that guy."
—Paul Newman, *Slap Shot*

You could name the decent hockey movies on one hand, and they graduate from memorably scabrous 1970s comedy to treacly triumphalist nostalgia *for* the 1970s. It says loads about Hollywood's evolution, if not much for our love of the game.

Slap Shot (1977) The first and probably only genuine American satire about hockey, this black-eyed hoot in the Michael Ritchie style (think *Smile, The Bad News Bears,* and *Semi-Tough*) has Paul Newman playing an aging sub-league coach/captain determined to make his small town's scruffy franchise profitable, even if it means breaking every rule and premeditating assault. Written by veteran radical comedy ace Nancy Dowd, the unglamorous film was a modest success upon its release, but its fame and cult esteem have grown exponentially in the years since. If you can't quote from it, you've gotten yourself left behind.

The Mighty Ducks (1992) Essentially *The Bad News Bears on Ice,* this formulaic story of a self-centered lawyer (Emilio Estevez) who finds redemption coaching a klutzy pee-wee hockey team garnered enough box office draw and wholeheartedly devoted fans to warrant two sequels, a TV series, and a video game. For the prepuberty leagues only, the film certainly pounds home the importance of teamwork—and the potential amorality of rich lawyers.

Mystery, Alaska (1999) This is a hockey movie for people who *play* hockey as well as for those who just watch it. The local hockey team is the focal point of this small Alaskan town, in which the greatest ambition and honor is to skate in the Saturday Game—a weekly event that entails skating out of a log-cabin locker room to the cheers of the town's populace and playing on frozen ponds circled by towering firs and ice-capped mountains (this is a place where snowmobiles and ice skates are used for transportation, not recreation). Of course, plot-wise, the big-city types invade with a deal to play a show game with the New York Rangers. It's heartwarming underdog schmaltz without being smarmy, and true fans will appreciate such quirkiness as warming skates with hot potatoes and being forced to slide, bare-assed, across the ice as punishment for transgressions against teammates. Ranger fans will be put off, though: their team are depicted as overpaid, spoiled princes who can only play in heated rinks.

Miracle (2004) It's nearly impossible to make a sports movie these days that isn't over-the-top, fists-in-the-air hypersentimental and "inspiring," and most of these recent offerings are deplorable. This one may be the best of the lineup, thanks to its period story (the underdog U.S. hockey team besting the Soviet *übermensch* in the 1980 Winter Games) and Kurt Russell, as the coach, in an outrageous hair-helmet wig.

HITTING THE LINKS

"Do you know what gophers can do to a golf course?"
—Ted Knight, *Caddyshack*

Golfers are intimate with a special sub-subgenre of movie—the golf movie, which, in essence, includes virtually any film with a single use of a club or a single shot of a green. (*Bringing Up Baby* is a classic example, as is *The Aviator*.) But we're including in this category only all-out chip-and-putt movies, which are all comedies (naturally, given the lightness of the game), except for the last, endearing but typically self-serious recent entry. So much that was once deemed fit only for lowdown yucks seems now, in the new millennium, appropriate for sniffly melodrama.

The Idle Class (1921) This vintage Charlie Chaplin two-reeler (amounting to about thirty minutes) is the first notable golf comedy: Chaplin's Tramp infiltrates an aristocratic golf club and shows up the snobs. The brilliant pratfall gags are so concise you'd think they were digitally timed.

The Golf Specialist (1930) Always a master juggler, W. C. Fields worked up entire vaude-ville routines about billiards, golf, and various pieces of furniture; in this short, made on the cusp of America's affair with the game and at the onset of many instructional shorts routinely shown in movie theaters, Fields's putting game gets the exasperated runaround.

Divot Diggers (1936) In this superb two-reel *Our Gang/Little Rascals* short, Alfalfa, Spanky, Porky, and Buckwheat takes jobs as caddies, and snot-nosed slapstick ensues. Priceless for a particular generation of player who were raised on *Little Rascals* reruns.

My Bunny Lies Over the Sea (1948) Bugs Bunny mistakenly tunnels to Scotland, crosses a kilted Scot, and takes him up on what turns out to be an outrageously cheat-ridden grudge game of golf. Seven minutes of typical fabulousness.

Pat and Mike (1952) Katharine Hepburn is a pro golfer, Spencer Tracy is her promoter, and Garson Kanin and Ruth Gordon's screenplay gives them helping after helping of gender-combat banter, on and off the course (we're treated to the sight of Hepburn herself, in a championship game, hitting against legendary real-life pro Babe Didrikson Zaharias, who was the subject of the 1975 TV movie *Babe*). This is perhaps the best of the Hepburn-Tracy comedies—because here, Tracy doesn't always get the upper hand.

The Caddy (1953) Lewis and Martin assault a country club golf tournament, by way of a hokey plot, and with the help of pros Sam Snead and Ben Hogan. As always, your taste for Jerry Lewis's special brand of infantile shtick dictates your reaction, but the slapstick on the fairway is at least energetic.

Caddyshack (1980) The pivotal *National Lampoon/Saturday Night Live*–era comedy, cowritten and directed by Harold Ramis, in which gophers run amok, Chevy Chase hits droll notes (this was back when he was funny), Bill Murray invents Carl the groundskeeper, Ted Knight bursts a blood vessel, and Rodney Dangerfield asks who, in fact, stepped on a duck. There's more. It's a bit of a mess, but golfers can't go wrong with this film, especially if they're loaded.

Happy Gilmore **(1996)** Adam Sandler, in his ascendancy as America's mascot dolt, plays a booted hockey player taking his skills to the links for the sake of saving his grandmother's house from foreclosure. Very popular with a certain type of quasi-jock, as well as a narrow slice of serious golfers.

Tin Cup **(1996)** Ron Shelton's making his incisive way through the major sports (let's hope he hasn't given up before getting to boccie), and here he rampages across the green with Kevin Costner's gone-to-seed golf rogue, who's trying to qualify for the U.S. Open in order to impress Rene Russo. Because it's Shelton, this is probably the most faithful movie ever made about the game, even if it's too long and Costner's aging rapscallion pales after a while.

The Greatest Game Ever Played **(2005)** A serious, heartwarming, inspirational golf film? What's happened to the world? The true story of the 1913 U.S. Open, in which twenty-year-old caddy and amateur player Francis Ouimet (Shia LaBeouf) defeated reigning champion Harry Vardon (Stephen Dillane) out of nowhere, is terrific stuff, and actor-turned-director Bill Paxton whips up quite a period flavor. Penned, oddly enough, by former David Lynch collaborator Mark Frost.

THE TRIPLE CROWN

"Marry me and I'll never look at any other horse!"
—Groucho Marx, *A Day at the Races*

The most seductive aspect of horse racing is its perennial nature—it's an age-old tradition, full of lore, and most of the movies that target its appeal reek of yesteryear. But if you're a true fan, not just a bettor, any interface with the sport will do.

A Day at the Races **(1937)** The Marx Brothers do the horse track—which is to say that this film has very little to do with racing at all. Unfortunately, it's one of the brotherhood's later films, for MGM, which despite hearty servings of Marxian wackiness are overrun with romantic subplots and unfunny musical numbers. Still, if you're having juleps, this is your best bet.

National Velvet **(1944)** A hallmark family film that is less about a girl's relationship to her horse than it is about her relationship to her family, her determination, and her adolescence. It's based on a bestselling Enid Bagnold novel, and features 1940s Technicolor, but none of that is as bewitching as a twelve-year-old Elizabeth Taylor, whose earnest zest for competition lights her from the inside. Well-turned-out performances all around, and with more subtle, genuine moments than fluff, thanks to the good humor of the script and the Oscar-winning performance of Anne Revere as the wise mother.

The Black Stallion (1979) Probably the greatest horse-love film that will ever be made, Carroll Ballard's entrancing take on the Walter Farley children's book is rich in atmosphere, light on unnecessary chitchat (the grand middle passage, set on a desert island populated only by a boy and a wild horse, is essentially dialogue free), and visually so beautiful it can stop your brain from working. From the shipboard opening (with an enigmatic poker game and a traumatic storm) to the stranded courting of horse by kid (Kelly Reno is fabulous) and beyond, it's a deeply mysterious film—clear, but hinting at deeper ravishments. As a result, it may also be one of the best evocations of the ecstatic currents flowing through childhood.

Seabiscuit (2003) In 1938, an undersized thoroughbred snagged the attention of the entire country with his dominating speed, and in 2001, an unknown author with chronic fatigue syndrome made the bestseller list with her book about this rather ungainly horse. The ugly duckling syndrome plays out as well for one-eyed jockey Red Pollard (Tobey Maguire), and the whole package is pumped with inspirational juice by screenwriter-director Gary Ross. The period track milieu is authentic and omnipresent, and the story still hums.

Dreamer: Inspired by a True Story (2005) A movie that supports the theory that animals provide us both a means to connect with one another and inspiration for us to succeed against impossible odds. The horse in this case is Sonador, and the broken family are the Cranes, who own a Kentucky horse farm devoid of horses. Dakota Fanning gives father Kurt Russell her best puppy-dog eyes, and Sonador is immediately ensconced at the Crane homestead for rehabilitation and a second chance at racing, mending the Cranes' hearts while they mend her leg. You've seen it before, but it's serious, and the well-seasoned Russell supplies gravitas.

GRAND PRIX/LE MANS/INDY 500

"When you're racing, it's life."
—Steve McQueen, *Le Mans*

Car chases—what's more movie-movie? Except that pro racing is often about going in circles, a nut filmmakers try to crack on occasion but, arguably, have yet to do. At the same time, dangerous circular speed-freak compulsion has served well as a kind of live-fast existential metaphor for Humphrey Bogart–style masculinity. Whatever; it's cars, moving fast.

Genevieve **(1953)** A consummate English comedy, less fondly held to the bosom here than in the United Kingdom, in which two obsessive antique-car-racing buddies (John Gregson and Kenneth More) get their competitive blood up and wager on who'll win in a drive from Brighton to London and back. Virtually a P. G. Wodehouse novel come to life (at least in terms of the abundance of superbly turned, super-dry Brit banter), the film is essentially stolen by Kay Kendall and Dinah Sheridan, as the women dragged along for the ride.

Roar of the Crowd **(1953)** A notable postwar indie, made for Monogram Studios by hack William Beaudine, in which racing hotshot Howard Duff must choose between marriage and a winning career. Shot at L.A.'s Ascot Park Speedway, with real-life drivers Johnnie Parsons, Duke Nalon, Manuel Ayulo, and Henry Banks playing themselves.

Grand Prix **(1966)** International car racing became big cultural noise in the 1960s, so Hollywood let loose with a stream of big-budget potboilers, often made at the behest of their racing-infatuated stars, set on and around the racetrack. The first, this widescreen John Frankenheimer hit, pits American driver James Garner against French rival Yves Montand; also featured are romance, intrigue, and burning asphalt. (There's only so much you can do plot-wise with this sport; Paul Newman's pet racing film, *Winning* **(1969)**, and Steve McQueen's baby, *Le Mans* **(1971)**, cover essentially the same territory. Neither hit the road with Frankenheimer's visual panache.)

The Last American Hero **(1973)** This post–*Easy Rider* nitty-gritty flick is based on Tom Wolfe's hyperbolic *Esquire* article about Ozark roadrunner Junior Jackson, here personified by Jeff Bridges as a moonshiner hick who's making his way up the stock-car circuit and burying anyone in his path. The era's jones for the reality of the dusty, poor South is in full bloom, photographed like it'd never been before and never will be again.

Bobby Deerfield **(1977)** A now-forgotten Hollywood turkey from director Sydney Pollack, who misguidedly adapted Erich Maria Remarque's novel about a pro racer (a comatose Al Pacino) who falls in love with a terminal Euro babe (Marthe Keller). Esteemed critic David Thomson was apparently fascinated by this film, but he's all alone in that.

Greased Lightning **(1977)** More Southern color, laced with racial combat, surrounding Richard Pryor as real-life racer Wendell Scott, the only black NASCAR champion ever and, for most of his career (which spanned the 1950s and '60s), the only man of color on the circuit. Directed by Michael Schultz, one of the first black men to make a directorial career for himself in Hollywood.

Fast Company (1979) David Cronenberg, early in his career, indulges himself with a racing drama, in which good-guy drag racer William Smith tries to outdrive the bad guys. Surprisingly limp and simplistic, coming from this filmmaker, but it's got B-movie duchess Claudia Jennings.

Heart Like a Wheel (1983) Channeling the spirit of *Greased Lightning*, this peppy biopic chronicles the triumphs and travails of racing's "First Lady," Shirley Muldowney, battling man's-world prejudices and winning hot road races up until the early 1980s. Directed by pulpster Jonathan Kaplan, and starring an effervescent Bonnie Bedelia.

Talladega Nights: The Ballad of Ricky Bobby (2006) It had to happen, eventually, if only for the marketing synergy: a Will Ferrell comedy about NASCAR. However dominated by Sacha Baron Cohen's gay French rival (a theme that hearkens back to *Grand Prix*), the movie burps up some proportional yucks—the more you love NASCAR, the more you'll get a kick out of this film.

II

OLYMPIAD

"Run them off their feet!"
—Ben Cross, *Chariots of Fire*

Every few years, the summer or winter Olympics toss up scores of potential dramatic stories to the world, and some of the best movies that have used the Olympics as context are, in fact, based on true stories. Either that matters to you or you just simply love the international-competition vibe of these films.

Charlie Chan at the Olympics (1937) The title of this film, a latecomer in the famous series, pretty much says it all. With the help of the U.S. swim team, Warner Oland's Chinese sleuth foils Nazi spies during the 1936 Berlin games. With news footage of the real Berlin Olympics.

Olympia (1938) Nazi propagandist Leni Riefenstahl (who, at the age of 101, died sixty-five years after directing this documentary, still denying culpability for her films) shot this record of the Berlin competition at behest of the führer. Historically it's invaluable, and visually it's lovely. As Aryan propaganda, it isn't terribly effective (insofar as we can measure such things), since the Third Reich's greatest athletes are left in the dust by none other than a "Negro American," Jesse Owens. Hitler does not look pleased.

Tokyo Olympiad (1965) Twenty-seven years after *Olympia*, Japanese director Kon Ichikawa was commissioned by the International Olympic Committee to document the 1964 games with a loving CinemaScope eye, a spectacular sense of visual space, and a fondness for the lyricism of losing as well as of winning. More of an epic avant-gardism, full of abstracted details rather than athletic achievements.

Walk, Don't Run (1966) A rather dated sex-love farce, based on 1943's *The More the Merrier* and set around the 1964 Tokyo Olympics, wherein elder Cary Grant plays matchmaker between Samantha Eggar and Jim Hutton. Shot in Tokyo after the games, the film contains no authentic Olympic footage to speak of.

Visions of Eight (1973) The last international Olympic documentary to date, in which eight directors were assigned to chronicle the 1972 Summer Olympics in Munich: Japanese Olympic veteran Kon Ichikawa, Czech humanist Milos Forman, French mush-head Claude Lelouch, American New Waver Arthur Penn, British Oscar-winner John Schlesinger, Swedish feminist Mai Zetterling, German hack Michael Pfleghar, and Russian epic-maker Yuri Ozerov. Actually, the episodes aren't terribly varied, and all owe their poetry to *Tokyo Olympiad*.

Babe (1975) A TV movie, back in the day when network-produced feature films could actually be ambitious and/or inventive, about track star Mildred "Babe" Didrikson Zaharias, who won two gold medals at the 1932 games, struggled against the all-male sports world at home to become a champ pro golfer, and succumbed, tragically, to cancer. Susan Clark, peppy but forgotten semistar of the decade, did her best work in this loving tribute, winning an Emmy for her efforts.

Chariots of Fire (1981) "More cavalier!" someone says in this Oscar winner—it's a reference to the British participation in the 1924 Olympics in Paris, but it sums up the movie, which follows two hard-nosed runners (Ben Cross's angry Jew, Harold Abrahams; and Ian Charleson's pious preacher, Eric Liddell) as they attempt to outrun everyone (except each other) as a matter of principle. A lovely ode, made hypnotic by Vangelis's electronic score.

Cool Runnings (1993) Everyone enjoys rooting for the underdog, and there can't be anyone more disadvantaged than a bobsled team training in the tropics. A lighthearted and often childish tale of Olympic trials and tribulations, bizarrely based on the true story of the Jamaican team's history-making appearance at the 1988 games in Calgary, with the late John Candy as, unbelievably, the straight man (the down-on-his-luck coach) to the cast of youngsters and canines.

Without Limits (1998) The second of the late 1990s biopics of James Dean–ish track star Steve Prefontaine, made by impassioned screenwriter Robert Towne and starring Billy Crudup as the golden boy who broke loads of records but failed to win any medal at the 1972 Munich Olympics, and died tragically in a highway wreck at age twenty-four. Towne tries to wax philosophical, imagining the debate between coach Bill Bowerman (Donald Sutherland) and Prefontaine to be a struggle between goal-oriented reason (*win*) and Ayn Rand–ish individualism (*run*), but the cloud of preordained doom hangs heavily over the action. What makes Prefontaine a worthy subject is somewhat mysterious; he didn't place at the Olympics (somehow, the kidnapping of the Israeli track team is supposed to have spoiled his chances), and when all the eulogies are said and done, you can't be blamed for thinking that all that time and energy would've been more fruitfully spent tracking the travails of the Finnish cop who *did* win.

Endurance (1999) A portrait of Ethiopian runner Haile Gabrsellasie, who won the gold in Atlanta in 1996, that is both documentary and biopic—Gabrsellasie plays himself (just as Jackie Robinson and Muhammad Ali did in their own biodocs), in present-day footage and in flashbacks, among other nonprofessional actors who play his relatives. Powerful but not manipulative—in fact, it's rather distancing and mysterious. Codirected by nonfiction vet Leslie Woodhead and Olympics documenter Bud Greenspan.

Southpaw (1999) Liam McGrath's documentary hones in on light-welter Irish boxer Francis Barrett, the piercingly modest Galway teen who, at nineteen, qualified for the Olympics and fought in Atlanta in 1996. Francis's handicaps are formidable: not only is he diminutive and short-armed (the opponents in his weight class often loom over him), but he's also a Traveller who grew up in a trailer park with no electricity or plumbing, and carries the stigma of belonging to what is apparently the most loathed minority in Ireland. Barrett does feel some ambivalence about carrying the Irish flag in the Atlanta ceremonies for, as an Irish journalist puts it, "the only country in the world that would discriminate against him."

CHAMPIONSHIP BOXING

"I never went down, Ray."
—Robert De Niro, *Raging Bull*

The simplest, and most dramatic, of all sports, because it so fundamentally resembles plain old-fashioned hand-to-hand combat. The boxing subgenre is rich with films that either use the sport as a plot device or actually glamorize the biographies of well-remembered fighters who stand alone, practically naked in the public eye, as few other competitors do. Still, starting so close to the gutter, it's not a subgenre that's overcome with nobility.

Battling Butler **(1926)** Buster Keaton enters the ring, maintaining a masquerade as a championship fighter so as to impress a mountain girl's father. A medium stab among Keaton's features, probably because boxing, as Chaplin and the Three Stooges would later discover, isn't very comical.

Gentleman Jim **(1942)** A Warner Brothers star machine that has little or nothing to do with real-life boxer Jim Corbett, but it's one of its decade's most intensely likable ventures, with director Raoul Walsh emphasizing comedic relationships over drama or action, and a boisterous cast, led by Errol Flynn, having too much fun at their day jobs. (Ward Bond, as John L. Sullivan, is a casting agent's dream.) For what it's worth, though, the film might have the least convincing boxing matches ever filmed.

The Great John L. **(1945)** A rather skimpy biopic on the famed John L. Sullivan, played—forgettably—by Greg McClure. For completists only, and a true tale that deserves a remake.

Body and Soul **(1947)** Robert Rossen's meat-and-potatoes boxing melodrama, written by Abraham Polonsky and starring John Garfield, was the beginning of the end for all three men, as the House Un-American Activities Committee loomed. Actually, it's a fairly familiar tale, not all that different from *City for Conquest*, but the integrity and passion brought to the table (and the ring) is still redoubtable.

Champion **(1949)** Boxing movies must, on some level, decide on the psychological underpinnings of their heroes—why does anyone put himself through this? In reality, and in the movies, it's often poverty—but as this Kirk Douglas saga was the first film to demonstrate, the instincts and abilities that make a man good at beating others into unconsciousness sometimes also produce a rabid ego and lust for glory. This film is the flip side of *Body and Soul*, in which the fighter is surrounded by bottom-feeders; here, Douglas's meat-eating protogangster is the heel, and everyone else must get out of his way. So, of course, he gets his in the end.

The Set-Up **(1949)** The only Hollywood film ever "adapted from" a contemporary poem, by Joseph Moncure March, ex-editor of *The New Yorker*. Robert Wise's film has an iambic cadence to it, but mostly it's a great, brooding, stylized noir about a has-been boxer determined to face up to one more shot at the big time. The presence of Robert Ryan, one of the midcentury's greatest movie actors, gives the perhaps unoriginal material an immediate emotional force.

Somebody Up There Likes Me **(1956)** Paul Newman's true debut film (if everyone could just forget *The Silver Chalice*), in which he plays Rocky Graziano—New York son, crook, convict, and eventual middleweight champion. Overwrought and full of heavy *dee*s and *dum*s, but memorably inspirational, in that postwar, TV-drama kind of way. The boxing isn't thrilling, despite the presence of real industry figures (including ex-fighter and ref Dynamite Jackson). The first film for Steve McQueen and Robert Loggia.

The Great White Hope (1970) A very stagy rendition of Howard Sackler's play based on the life of Jack Johnson, the first black heavyweight world champion (1908–1915). The drama is, of course, racially based, as James Earl Jones's righteous fighter faces down racism in the industry and in society, in part because of his relationship with a white woman (Jane Alexander). (Johnson himself would go on to have three white wives.) Both stars reproduced their acclaimed stage performances, and both were nominated for Oscars.

Rocky (1976) Don't blame this lovely, innocent, gritty little 1970s smash hit for the many sequels, rip-offs, and influences that it has inadvertently cast into the world over the last thirty years; just watch the movie. It's dated, but often in a good way—can you imagine a Hollywood film today paying such close attention to city neighborhoods, poor ethnic families, and the emotional lives of the uneducated? Sylvester Stallone deserves a handshake, both for his (rather unglamorous) performance in the starring role and for the screenplay, which triumphs, in the end, not with the championship bout, but with a simple schoolkid romance.

Raging Bull (1980) What can be said? It's the definitive and most realistic boxing film ever made, the career acme for Robert De Niro (who displayed the self-sacrifice of a penitent in his bodily abuses), and quite possibly the best American film of the 1980s (as it was voted by critics and filmmakers once the decade ended). Director Martin Scorsese earned a place in heaven with this very difficult, very unpleasant trip through the pathetic life of monstrous middleweight champ Jake LaMotta; it's filmmaking as aria. In fact, the film has been something of a puzzle to many: why lavish such gorgeous, devotional, arresting art on the life of such a miscreant? The climactic Bible quotes are a hint: made at a crisis time in Scorsese's life, Raging Bull could be said to be itself an act of contrition and a struggle toward Christian sanctity, where even this abusive, malevolent hump is deserving of a heartrending biopic. Even *him*, among the martyrs and saviors and heroes of pop culture.

The Great White Hype (1996) Ron Shelton (*again* with the sports movies) cowrote this ludicrous comedy about a Don King–style boxing promoter (Samuel L. Jackson) ramping up his profits by pitting his lazy champ (Damon Wayans) against an unknown white boy (Peter Berg). Broad as a Swedish barn, it's great fun, if a little self-satisfied, but in the end we're left without a punch line. (Frankly, Wayans's obviously prosthetic paunch in the final bout takes the fight right out of this baby.)

When We Were Kings (1996) A riveting, spectacularly entertaining documentary about the 1974 Ali-Foreman "Rumble in the Jungle" fight in the new nation of Zaire. Leon Gast's film was long in the making: it was shot on location at the time of the fight, with the assumption the film's postproduction would be financed by the proceeds from the accompanying music concert (featuring B. B. King and James Brown, among others). However, due to a minor cut on George Foreman's eye (incurred during training), the fight was postponed for six weeks; by then, the event's cachet had disappeared, and the musical acts performed pretty much to an empty stadium. Gast's film footage sat on a shelf for decades, acquiring the luster of recent pop culture history—a forgotten chapter in the duel between sports and publicity, between Ali and the white establishment he discontentedly served, and between America and postcolonialist Africa. It's a complex sociopolitical portrait, with racial conundrums lurking in every corner, but dominating it all (including the 1990s interviews with Norman Mailer and George Plimpton) is Ali, who is clearly the most engaging and magnetic presence ever to master a press conference in the history of televised news. Whether literally sparring with the camera, wisecracking at reporters ("Just the other day, I killed a rock!"), or expressing genuine and eloquent concern for race relations back home, Ali was the real Elvis, our modern culture's truest cult of personality. We will never see the likes of him again.

Ali **(2001)** The biopic of the Greatest, slickly and vividly produced by director Michael Mann, is a clarified reminder of exactly how genuinely committed this loudmouthed boxer was to the ideas of civil rights and public progress. Still, the cool, thin-boned, low-key Will Smith is no Ali. (Jamie Foxx, terrific as Ali's helpmate Bundini Brown, would've been a more sensible choice.) After seeing *When We Were Kings*, this Hollywood routine feels distinctly unnecessary.

Million Dollar Baby **(2004)** Clint Eastwood's Oscar-winning melodrama has a regal, autumnal edge to it, but the material is a little hackneyed; the story desperately needed the tragic twist that screenwriter Paul Haggis gives us in the final third of the movie. As the boxer in question, Hilary Swank is mean, lean, and earnest.

THE OSCARS

"A glitterin' stah in da cinema fuhmament."
—Jean Hagen, *Singin' in the Rain*

Truly, it seems that "Oscar movie" has become a subgenre all its own—consisting mostly of giant epics that spell out, in no uncertain terms, Hollywood's greatest ambitions for itself, and movies that personify "star power" or "old-fashioned showbiz." In other words, to appreciate them, you have to have the mindset of the movie-industry community, not one of its customers. But if you just don't think there's already enough Oscar hoopla before the annual Academy Awards show, check out these best bets for preceremony programming.

It Happened One Night **(1934)** The first Oscar winner that everyone still remembers fondly (sit through the previous year's best-picture winner, *Cavalcade*, if you don't believe us), this Frank Capra screwball comedy simply gave Clark Gable and Claudette Colbert lots of prideful spite in which to couch their lovey-dovey yearnings, and it was a formula Hollywood would use for decades. Gable, in particular, is clearly captured in the very moment that it became apparent to all eyes that he was the stuff of stardom. Perversely, very few romantic comedies have garnered subsequent best-picture Oscars; instead, the film industry began to favor epics, snooty biopics, and topical melodramas.

Stand-In **(1937)** Not an Academy Award winner, but a salty, gimlet-eyed farce about Hollywood in the 1930s, in which East Coast efficiency expert and accountant Leslie Howard investigates a failing studio and finds out that the movie business is a psychotic endeavor run by fools, drunks, and schemers. Humphrey Bogart gets a plum comic role as a runaway producer, and Joan Blondell handles the foreground as Howard's enlisted gal Friday.

Gone with the Wind **(1939)** No movie has more Hollywood stories and myths surrounding it than this Civil War epic and women's film odyssey. The public long ago stopped thinking of it merely as a movie about a tempestuous Southern belle (Vivien Leigh, grabbing a gimme Oscar); it's come to be considered a movie about its own size and glory, about Hollywood's golden age, about producer David O. Selznick's Napoleonic machinations, and about the twin offscreen marriages, both doomed, of Leigh and Laurence Olivier, and star Clark Gable and Carole Lombard. It's entirely possible to plan a full-day Oscar fete with no other movie on the menu; after all, you've got the length of the film itself (which runs close to four hours), the unavoidable DVD supplements, and all the controversy and legends to sort out: Did Selznick really discover Leigh partway through production, on the burning set of Atlanta? Should Olivia de Havilland have received the Oscar that year instead of Hattie McDaniel? And what about Clark Gable, who lost out on the Best Actor award to Robert Donat for *Goodbye Mr. Chips*? *GWTW* is flawed as hell and, of course, outrageous in its apologies for slavery, racism, and plantation society. But it's the event-movie that established the Oscars as an event in and of themselves.

All About Eve **(1950)** This Joseph L. Mankiewicz satire is about the backbiting cynics and fame-hungry scabs of the theater world—Bette Davis and George Sanders purr savage quips at the rest of the cast—but it's just as much a statement about Hollywood. The film took home the prize for Best Picture, beating out *Sunset Boulevard*.

Sunset Boulevard **(1950)** Other "Hollywood on Hollywood" movies are love letters compared to this bitter pill, a requiem for the early years of the business. Written and directed by Billy Wilder, the story tracks the last, fusty, shut-in days of a once-reigning, now deranged matinee queen (Gloria Swanson) and her uncomfortable sexual relationship with a self-hating writer (William Holden). Inhabited by has-beens (including Buster Keaton, Erich von Stroheim, Anna Q. Nilsson, and H. B. Warner), sick with perverted narcissism, and narrated by a drowned corpse, it's a remarkably cynical statement that's perfectly geared toward the Oscar cynics in the crowd.

The Bad and the Beautiful (1952) More "Hollywood as snake pit" cynicism, from Vincente Minnelli and underappreciated screenwriter Charles Schnee. Kirk Douglas's reptilian producer screws over everyone within ten yards of him, including his screenwriter (Dick Powell), his leading lady (Lana Turner), and his director (Barry Sullivan). The movie flows with wickedly sarcastic, noirish repartee, and Gloria Grahame won a deserved Best Supporting Actress Oscar for her performance. Many industry figureheads saw themselves in Douglas's wolverine, but the commonly held belief today is that the character is based on David O. Selznick.

Singin' in the Rain (1952) Truly needing no introduction, this hallowed cotton-candy musical might be terrific Oscar-night viewing because it simultaneously honors and satirizes the very period—1927–28—in which the Academy Awards were born. It won zilch in its day, however, even losing for best musical score to *With a Song in My Heart*, a forgotten Susan Hayward melodrama.

On the Waterfront (1954) In the postwar years, Oscars began casting a favorable eye toward "problem pictures"—films that dealt with pressing social issues in a hard-bitten manner—and this is the most beloved of the lot: an Elia Kazan–helmed voyage to the New York docks that was shot (on location, during cold, gray days) and acted (by Marlon Brando, Rod Steiger, Lee J. Cobb, and Karl Malden) in a more realistic style than American audiences were certainly used to. It's an enthralling film, even if it comes off as a bit too certain about the notion that it's the unions, not the companies, that are the demons. If the film's politics seem odd coming from Hollywood (a town awash with craft unionism even in 1954), remember that Kazan and screenwriter Budd Schulberg were both notorious rats for the House Un-American Activities Committee.

The Bridge on the River Kwai (1957) David Lean's first serious international hit, a morally ambiguous World War II epic about a Japanese POW camp in Burma, the railroad bridge the British prisoners agree to build while demanding adherence to the Geneva Conventions, and the Allied efforts to blow the baby up. As the ramrod Brit officer in charge, Alec Guinness netted an Oscar, but just as memorable is William Holden, as an opportunistic American soldier who's talked into handling the bombing mission. Shot in the Sri Lankan jungles; as usual with Lean, everything about this film feels vastly real.

Lawrence of Arabia (1962) Perhaps the only behemoth of the 1950s and '60s that fully lives up to its extraordinary reputation, this David Lean–directed corker is a veritable shrine to the days when visual spectacle meant the staging of huge events in extraordinary places—stuff you can't fake with a computer. It's also a more fabulous, ambiguous launch into historical psychodrama than it's ever been given credit for, with easily the most perverse and original hero in epic-film history. Opportunist and moralist, sadist and masochist, exotica-entranced English fart and effeminate tribal godling, Peter O'Toole's T. E. Lawrence is such a freak, all that's clear about him by the film's end is that the only place he truly belongs is on the absurd mantle of posthumous myth.

The Godfather (1972) There was no Oscar mystery this year; rarely before had a film come along that so confidently commanded everyone's attention, demanded virtually every award, broke every box-office record, and entered the cultural consciousness like an unstoppable siege of Huns. *Of course* it won—not because it was the best the year had to offer (one of us, at least, would've voted for *Deliverance* or *The Discreet Charm of the Bourgeosie*), but because it redefined filmgoers' expectations regarding American movies, and therefore became, like *Casablanca*, not just "a movie" but the Movies.

Annie Hall (1977) Most Academy Awards presentations come and go, fading from the memory almost as quickly as they are made—who remembers, or cares to remember, the award for Best Picture going to *Patton*, or *The Last Emperor*, or *The English Patient*? But this beautiful Woody Allen comedy was the film entire swatches of America were waiting for in 1977, and its multiple wins—in an awards system that rarely compliments either romantic comedies or projects by New York–based filmmakers—was a stirring instance of cultural justice.

Out of Africa (1985) Movies that grab the Best Picture Oscar are generally not small in scope, which is as it should be, but the winner should have some balance to it. It shouldn't tip the dramatic scales so far as to be seen as rather ridiculous in hindsight, and hindsight sometimes comes quickly—say, while the Oscar-winning producers are still thanking their mothers (think *Titanic*). *Out of Africa* found that balance: it's a meaty love story (between real-life author Isak Dinesen—known, at the time of the events depicted, as Karen Blixen—and famous colonialism-era big-game adventurer Denys Finch Hatton, played respectively by Meryl Streep and Robert Redford), told with grace and humor and respect for everything: the characters, the landscape, the natives, even the rights and wrongs of the politics of colonization. Only Redford feels out of place, occasionally spouting ponderous homilies as if he'd stepped, squinting, into the wrong film. But the rest of the movie more than makes up for his performance with sweep, sub-equatorial exotica, and beautiful prose (lifted straight from Dinesen's memoir). If the current Oscar choices disappoint, you'll always find this winner reliable and deserving.

Unforgiven (1992) Arguably, this was the last film to have both deserved and won a Best Picture Oscar, and the first since *The Deer Hunter* in 1978. Clint Eastwood's masterful study in western violence is such a powerful, poignant experience, however, that whatever happens to be up for statuettes on subsequent Oscar nights is bound to pale by comparison. Still, any occasion, including the Oscars, will do as an excuse to revisit this melancholy saga.

For Your Consideration (2006) Not many films—at least, not many good ones—dare to utilize the Academy Awards as a story point, but Christopher Guest paints small-time Hollywood all kinds of goofy colors in this ensemble piece, in which the cast and crew of a deplorable indie get infected with could-be Oscar buzz. An ebb in Guest's very special career project, but undemanding and worth the detour.

I   II   **III**   IV   V   VI

THE TIME OF THEIR LIVES

BIRTHDAY

"What do you get for the man who has . . . everything?"
— Sean Penn, *The Game*

Few of us should waste a birthday—ours or someone else's—by watching a movie, but in case you view movies as emotional repair or wicked augmentation, these birthday-pivotal not-so-classics offer up what are bound to be alternative scenarios.

The Birthday Party **(1968)** Not really about a birthday at all, this William Friedkin–directed film, based on Harold Pinter's play, is about a nowhere man (Robert Shaw) besieged by two shady characters who want something unspecified from him, and who say they want to bring him to the titular fete, though it's no one's birthday that we know of. Modern absurdist theater, best taken as gag viewing.

Sixteen Candles **(1984)** Milestone birthdays should have memorable celebrations, but in this successful, and catastrophically influential, John Hughes high school romp, Molly Ringwald's sixteenth is lost in a sea of other events: her sister's wedding, the high school dance, her crush on an oblivious jock, and some machinations involving the school nerd and her own panties. Anthony Michael Hall is unforgettable as the jittery Geek.

Madadayo **(1993)** One of film history's grand old giants, Akira Kurosawa died (at age eighty-eight) a few years after finishing this swan song, which is a film only an old man could've made: it's an effort, after a stormy and celebrated career, at under-standing—a reconciliation with and appreciation of life's raw pleasures. Starting in 1943 Tokyo, we track the life of a student-worshipped, sardonic professor of German, Uchida (Tatsuo Matsumura), who, at age sixty, announces his retirement. Hard as it might be to fathom in the West, where teachers are held in something less than high esteem, Uchida is perpetually surrounded by his former students, a gaggle of middle-aged men who honor and celebrate the grumpy geezer at every opportunity. Their relationship is the movie's spine: as Kurosawa graduates from the war years to the reconstructive boon years to follow, Uchida diffidently enjoys one birthday cele-bration after another, until the bacchanals fill an entire banquet hall. Aping a childhood call-response rhyme that Kurosawa uses as a beautiful coda, the students always ask Uchida if he's ready to pass into the next world, and his answer is a ceremo-nious "Madadayo!"—"No, not yet!" It's a film of effusive affection, contemplative moments, and kind deeds done in private.

The Game **(1997)** Luxuriously overshot by David Fincher, this puzzle box of a movie offers up the most troublesome birthday gift in Hollywood history: an introverted, control-freak millionaire banker (Michael Douglas) is invited to play, by his disreputable

brother (Sean Penn), a "game" run by a mysterious corporation. No one will tell the
man with everything, yet with nothing, what the game is, but once he's in, he can't
seem to get out. He's baited, humiliated, fooled, and fleeced, and every step he takes
to stop the game or involve the law is stymied. Eventually, the manipulations get
more serious, until Douglas is convinced that the entire enterprise is an elaborate con
devised to clean him out of some six hundred million dollars and push him off the
grid for good. It's kind of like a dead-serious version of the Dan Aykroyd half of *Trading Places*: in one set piece after another, Douglas's epitome of cowardly affluence is
run through the ringer. Viewed in those terms, the film could be seen as a pleasant,
if repetitive, late-capitalist fantasy. But, of course, "the game" turns out to be something else altogether. What are brothers for?

HIGH SCHOOL GRADUATION

"An overwhelming sense of ickiness had set over first period."
—Alicia Silverstone, *Clueless*

All high schoolers think they are living in the only "now," and that their teen experiences are absolutely the most vital and epochal in the history of mankind. Since
every movie that nails that life moment down is inevitably about "back then," these
films run the risk of being overlooked by the demographic that could benefit from
them the most—the jacked-in, earPod-stuffed, nose-ringed teen of today. Consider
what an eye-opener these blasts from the past could be for the right adolescent.

American Graffiti (1973) The first coming-of-age ensemble comedy in American movies?
George Lucas's sublime evocation of a midwestern 1962 of cars, rock 'n' roll radio, and
lost subadults certainly established the timeless stereotypes of that post-graduation
summer night that everyone experiences, from the high school sweethearts (Ron Howard and Cindy Williams) confronting college and separation, to the itchy smart kid (Richard Dreyfuss) who doesn't know if college is what he wants, to the hopeless dweeb
(Charles Martin Smith) looking only to score, to the cool dropout hood (Paul LeMat) who
cannot adjust to the real world. Roaringly funny and bittersweet.

Fast Times at Ridgemont High (1982) Amy Heckerling's overrated and rosily remembered
high school farce, based on the book Cameron Crowe wrote after *he* went undercover
in an American high school for *Rolling Stone*, does etch out various familiar social
species (geeks, freaks, hotties, jocks, and the semiforgotten loser among them), and

the performances (particularly those of Sean Penn, Jennifer Jason Leigh, and Phoebe Cates) are genuinely felt.

***Say Anything…* (1989)** Remember when you spent all your years of high school yearning after that one person, despairing of ever having him or her realize you exist? That's just what happens to Lloyd Dobler (John Cusack). Fortunately, after graduation, she does notice him, and they spend the summer dancing around the possibility of falling deeply in love. This Cameron Crowe movie goes a long way just on charm, from Cusack's diffident-yet-deeply-ethical everyman quality to Lili Taylor's awful guitar-strummed songs about lost love, to the pack of nowhere boys (including Jeremy Piven) hanging out at the local Gas 'n Sip and philosophizing about women they know nothing about. Ignore the secondary plot, about Diane's possibly shady father, and savor the whiff of teenage desires anxiously fulfilled.

***Dazed and Confused* (1993)** This is what the beginning of summer, with school already a fading memory just a day after it's ended, felt like for director Richard Linklater, whose milieu here was Texas in the late 1970s. Trailing after a dozen or more recently freed high schoolers as they search for a party, contemplate their dubious roles in the social order, and inflict or escape from the hazing rituals that may be particular to suburban Austin schools, the film is dense with detail, one-liners, deft performances, and astutely observed reality—though it may take two viewings to mesh with the movie's unique rhythms. It's also something of *The Outsiders* of its generation, more or less introducing the world to future stars including Matthew McConaughey, Ben Affleck, Nicky Katt, Rory Cochrane, Joey Lauren Adams, and Parker Posey.

***Clueless* (1995)** Jane Austen's *Emma* recast as a 1990s Beverly Hills teenager who rules the high school roost, negotiates grades with teachers, and creates a social pecking order based on good looks and fashion savvy. Surprisingly witty, it's definitely one of the best in the "updated great lit for teens" subgenre.

***Can't Hardly Wait* (1998)** An overlooked gem among a hundred cretinous teen-party comedies, in which another dozen or so easily recognizable high school types flounder their way through a single night of epiphany, melodrama, humiliation, socialization, and beer. The film's pulsing, forgiving heart and sharp ear (courtesy of writer/director team Deborah Kaplan and Harry Elfont) are responsible for the movie's distinction; the joyous chaos of teenage parties is not easy to depict, but this movie gets it—and celebrates it, with a title from an old Replacements song, no less. Jennifer Love Hewitt and Ethan Embry are the mismatched hottie and nerd, but funnier and more believable are Lauren Ambrose's quasi-Goth cynic, Peter Facinelli's monster jock, and Charlie Korsmo's ultrageek.

***Rushmore* (1998)** A giddily unpredictable comedy that, among other things, harbors an Oscar-ready supporting performance by Bill Murray as an exhausted, self-destructive businessman. Rushmore, both the movie and the prep academy it's named for, centers around the unforgettable Max Fischer (Jason Schwartzman), a fifteen-year-old genius who can't be bothered with schoolwork, but who instead devotes himself to a kingdom of extracurricular activity. Overly cultured and beneficently power mad, Max meets his first real challenge in the tenth grade: that of wooing the new kindergarten teacher (Olivia Williams). But there's no describing how *Rushmore* does what it does; coscripted by Owen Wilson, the movie's comedy is so subtle, organic, and eccentric that it could fly in under your radar. In fact, scene for scene, the story has the loopy, unreasonable feel of life zooming right by you. We're never told how to judge any of the characters; however whimsical, they carry the same possibilities that real people do. (The smart kids aren't smart all the way through; the bullies don't stay bullies; and so on.) The performances, which are just as unsettling and original, are uniformly fine, but Murray, as the sad-sack 'Nam vet whose moneyed suburban hell makes him cannonball into his pool and float underwater for peace, is flat-out great.

American Pie (1999) Four friends make a pact to get laid by prom night—as if teenage boys need more motivation than they've already got. Raunchy, sophomoric, and a smash hit with teenagers—for real and undeniable reasons.

Ghost World (2001) The pioneering film portrait of a distinctive, universal, and heretofore ignored teenage social class: the bitter, frumpy, snobbish, willfully unpopular "weirdos," self-defined only in their disdainful opposition to their peers. It's a state that often provides for a certain amount of lostness after graduation, which is what the heroines of Daniel Clowes's graphic novel and Terry Zwigoff's acerbic movie struggle with: the vacuum left once they're left to their own devices. Thora Birch and Scarlett Johansson are pitch perfect in what amounts to an act of modern anthropology—the rescuing of a lovable misfit-teen type from obscurity.

Elephant (2003) Gus Van Sant looks sideways at the Columbine High School massacre, tracing and retracing the paths of several high schoolers as they wander through a largely empty high school, looking for . . . salvation?, before the shootings unexpectedly begin. Every shot is a question —why?—and every detail is potent.

Napoleon Dynamite (2004) The ultimate geekhood high school comedy, made in Idaho for chump change and so infectiously hilarious that it's earned a massive cultural ardor from an entire generation of American kids who don't even get the jokes or understand the horrors of adolescence. Jon Heder's titular hero is an outrageous creation, even if he seems to be a cruel mockery of an already outcast type of American kid.

COLLEGE GRADUATION

"What I used to pass off as just another bad summer could now potentially turn into a bad life."
—Chris Eigeman, *Kicking and Screaming*

College graduation is a rueful, emotionally loaded, terrifying time—the brink of the
no-more-screwing-around real world, and then the plunge into the abyss. Naturally, movies tend to look on this momentous event with a mixture of ghastly humor
and quiet, neurotic angst.

The Graduate **(1967)** A generational emblem more than a movie, this Mike Nichols classic captures the essence of alienation and social incompleteness as only films made
in the late 1960s and early 1970s can. Dustin Hoffman became a star in the unlikeliest
of circumstances: as an aimless college grad who cannot get a fix on what he wants
out of life. He is seduced by a family friend (Anne Bancroft), and is then pressured
into dating her daughter (Katharine Ross); as life gets more complicated, he searches
madly for any reason at all to choose one destiny over another. Credit is due to 1967
audiences, who saw themselves in this ambivalent portrait, and who dared to ask big
questions of themselves and their movies. Picture, if you can, the new millennium's
freshly graduated degree-holders facing the same choice.

Fandango **(1985)** A narrow but rueful valentine to the college grads of the 'Nam era, this
is the film that introduced Kevin Costner to the world. Here he plays the larky leader of
a motley gang of sullen jerks, each of whom is engaged in either embracing the war,
running from the draft, getting married, or merely remaining drunkenly unconscious.
Costner's energy keeps the film afloat.

Reality Bites **(1994)** Nobody college grad Helen Childress penned this magnifying-
glass comedy about postgraduation aimlessness and slackdom, and with a great
cast (including Winona Ryder, Ethan Hawke, Janeane Garofalo, Steve Zahn, and Ben
Stiller) it lands on a facet of modern reality rarely seen on film: the way twentysomethings can talk in comic code to each other and to themselves, aggrandizing their
nothingness and elevating childhood pop culture to the status of idolhood.

Kicking and Screaming **(1995)** Here was the late twentieth century's generational anthem
film, except no one seemed terribly interested in identifying with it. Writer-director
Noah Baumbach's debut, the movie is a rueful portrait of four preppy, Ivy League–ish
friends. Living off campus, they're suddenly left in the weird afterworld in which
graduation has marked them as grown-ups, but the indulgent, trivia-obsessed allure
of college life maintains its grip. Baumbach poured a hundred college careers' worth
of ironic humor into the script, and Chris Eigeman, Josh Hamilton, and Carlos Jacott

are a dry riot. Eric Stoltz almost steals the movie in an improvised role as a philosophi-cal bartender, but it's hard not to fall for Olivia d'Abo as an impulsive creative-writing major who's a tad self-conscious about her braces.

Road Trip (2000) Post–*American Pie* shenanigans involving a missent videotape and four college buddies, launching out onto the road with a mission and a tendency toward foolishness. As E.L., Seann William Scott confirms his status as the savior of the turn-of-the-century teen farce.

DATING

"We control our thoughts, which mean nothing, and not our emotions, which mean everything."
—Jean-Pierre Léaud, *Masculin Feminin*

Ah, which movie to watch, for which relationship, on which date? There are a mil-lion possible combinations; the movies talked up here are simply reliable dating workhorses, agreeable to both men and women in the full flush of mating season, but also tasteful, witty, and a little sex-minded. One must never neglect the power that the right movie, seen by the right couple, at the right stage in their courtship, can have—not merely on the current state of that relationship, but also on its course in years hence—any of these could become an "our movie," like an "our song," and fuel passionate allegiance for a lifetime. Or, if you're just dating, they're simply dynamite movies that happened to have men, women, and love stuff in them.

Shanghai Express (1932) Movies are make-believe, but some are more make-believe than others: this Josef von Sternberg daydream, ostensibly set on the title train but really unfurling in the misty, voguing netherworld of romantic heat, where Marlene Dietrich reigns supreme.

Zoo in Budapest (1933) One of the strangest films of the early '30s, and a storybook beauty, set entirely in a Hungarian zoo (!), where a zookeeping Dolittle-like man-child (!!) played by Gene Raymond courts Loretta Young's refugee from "the orphan asy-lum" (!!!) overnight amid the animals, which eventually escape and rampage—lions, elephants, monkeys and . . . porcupines (!!!!). Beguiling and naive (especially about animals), it's absolutely unique.

The More the Merrier (1943) A wartime sparkler in which Jean Arthur, she of the famous cashmere croak, possibly the most distinctive voice of any Golden Era actress, must live out the D.C. housing shortage with Army researcher Joel McCrea and avuncular businessman Charles Coburn, who does his best to play Cupid.

Jules and Jim (1961) Two French fellas (Oskar Werner and Henri Serre) and Jeanne Moreau, as a whimsical fin de siècle Paris tart who loves them both, initiating not a dramatic battle between rivals but a cooperative menage a trois, stretching for several decades. François Truffaut's lively and lovable New Wave classic is one of the movies that commonly strikes a person's life like lightning, leaving a mark.

Masculin Feminin (1966) Whatever else they have been, the French New Wavers were lavish romantics—and that includes Jean-Luc Godard, who takes on the gender gap as it manifested in 1960s Paris: a budding Communist (Jean-Pierre Léaud), his pop-singer girlfriend (Chantal Goya), their circle of friends and acquaintances, and the city itself strain between the buzz of Coca-Cola commercialism and the Marx-tinged resistance to the war in Vietnam.

III

My Night at Maud's (1969) Probably New Waver Eric Rohmer's masterwork, which pits Catholic piety against laissez-faire hedonism. It's set in a Clermont-Ferrand bedroom that's warmed by a single vivacious woman. Jean-Louis Trintignant is the hero in trouble; Françoise Fabian is the calm defender of pleasure and happiness.

Witness (1985) Dating movies don't often come this well stocked: for the guys, there's Harrison Ford as a cop in a suspense-rigged thriller; for the gals, there's Harrison Ford, as a fish out of water in an amorous tango (in Amish country, no less). Sexual tension is high, but it's consummated only with gunfire.

The Abyss (1989) James Cameron goes all action-movie sci-fi on underwater technology and alien life, with plenty of vein-bulging special-effects action for the fellas, and for the ladies, a surprisingly passionate story of eternal love at its hot center.

Defending Your Life (1991) Once, Albert Brooks was the ultimate everyman schlemiel; here that schlemiel dies, and he's uncomfortable even in the afterlife. This is a date movie? Well, he meets Meryl Streep, the only other recently deceased person under seventy, and as they each attend hearings before a purgatorial tribunal to examine their lives and determine if they have exhibited enough courage to "move forward" (think of it as Beverly Hills Buddhism), they fall in love, even though there's no hope that they can ever be together. This is an especially appropriate film for nascent relationships—it's funny but not raunchy, cute but not sticky. It's probably best to plan for a dinner afterward; one of the clear benefits of spending time in Judgment City (which looks remarkably like Southern California) is that you can eat as much as you want and never gain weight, so there's plenty of moaning over mounds of shrimp and piles of pasta.

The Last of the Mohicans **(1992)** Frontier life plus action, lust, history, warfare, heroism, and cosmic romance, all rolled into one leatherstocking package by director Michael Mann. This version is based more on a 1936 Hollywood screenplay than on James Fenimore Cooper's tome (which had no love story in it at all). (See "Independence Day," p. 24.)

Before Sunrise **(1995)** Jesse and Celine (Ethan Hawke and Julie Delpy), each alone and separately heartsick, meet on an aimless train ride through Austria, and decide to disembark and spend a day talking. That's all there is to it—or almost all—and yet this impossibly brilliant, moving film is a perfect date movie. Actually, it might be *too* perfect—does it raise expectations too high regarding just-met sparkling conversation, witty sex appeal, and intelligent soul sharing? Jesse and Celine seem preposterously and blissfully well suited for each other, no matter how messily realistic Richard Linklater's screenplay is about emotional exchange—could their ease and confidence intimidate the naturally nervous dater? Perhaps—or maybe it'd help boil the water and get the gears greased. The socially handicapped might consider it a form of basic training to view this movie on (or even *before*) a date. Pay attention, pilgrims: this is how it is done.

Get Shorty **(1995)** An adaptation of an Elmore Leonard novel is a gift from the gods—*everyone* involved looks like a witty pro. Here, hijinks ensue when gangsters get involved in the movie biz; Leonard's trademarked ping-pong matches are this time played by John Travolta, Rene Russo, Gene Hackman, and Danny DeVito.

Jerry Maguire **(1996)** A romantic comedy about a sports agent is, in concept, kind of like a musical about an arms dealer, but Cameron Crowe's hit remains refreshingly witty, sharp, affecting, and—glory of glories—slick without being trite. A pleasurably humane and light-footed stroll through familiar territory, the movie at times smacks of a Ron Shelton or Paddy Chayefsky satire on the agenting industry, but in the end it's too starry-eyed by half for that. Let's face it: Tom Cruise is usually too good-looking and supercilious to be convincing as a normal, modest human being, but here, as a go-getter agent whose bread and butter are his empty smile and his spiel, he's superb—suddenly, all of that self-love and amoral charm makes perfect sense. The dramatic crux is the hero's midcareer crisis of integrity—a fit of self-loathing impels Maguire to write a "more heart, less profit" memo and distribute it around his bustling agency's office. Of course, he's summarily fired, but he manages to convince single-mom accountant Dorothy (Renee Zellweger) to come with him to help start up his own business. All of his clients drop him; all but one, that is—showboat Rod Tidwell (Cuba Gooding Jr.), a wide receiver with more attitude than talent. *Jerry Maguire* may be the most femme-friendly sports movie ever made, and it manages that feat without resorting to bathos.

Out of Sight **(1998)** This might well be the best date movie ever made. You could watch this Elmore Leonard adaptation, in which George Clooney and Jennifer Lopez flirt like they're in heaven together, again and again; it's a perennial, and it's inexhaustibly brimming with character bits, witty dialogue, and narrative invention. Crooks, cops, heists, and so on abound—but this movie is less about the plot than it is about the people—and that's what dating's about, really, isn't it?

Fever Pitch **(2005)** Perhaps date movies shouldn't be about people who are dating at all, since films that focus on relationship strife provoke questions of rights and wrongs, guilt and innocence that viewers on a date might not want to get into. At least *Fever Pitch* (which is based on a much more cynical Nick Hornby novel that revolves around English football, not baseball) is relatively innocuous in this regard, if only because the main characters are both so adorable: *Saturday Night Live* vet Jimmy Fallon is Ben, a humble schoolteacher who loves his job and the Boston Red Sox; Drew Barrymore is Lindsey, a high-powered business genius who's looking for something better than the shallow corporate climbers she usually dates. Trouble occurs when she starts realizing that Ben just might not consider her as important as a bunch of overpaid jocks. (Note to male viewers: the correct response to this realization is not, "Yeah, so?") The movie includes cameos by some of the 2004 Sox—who beat the odds and earned Boston a World Series victory for the first time in eighty-six years. (The last scenes of the film were rewritten and shot during the series to capitalize on this amazing turn of events—who coulda thunk it?) In the end, though, *Fever Pitch* is a dimple-deep mushfest.

ENGAGEMENT

"People get married and then they do the most hideous, unbelievable things to each other."
—Nicolas Cage, *Honeymoon in Vegas*

Few other passages in our modern lives are as primed for related cinematic fare—engagements can last for two years or more, the whiplash of lifelong commitment can be bruising, in-laws become a psychotic element in the engaged couple's lives, and the madness and frustrations that go into planning a wedding that has fed scores of movies' fuel tanks can also destroy your sanity. The solace and vindication of experiencing engagements and wedding build-ups far more bizarre, comical, and painful than yours, and yet not so different, can be substantial.

***The Wedding March* (1928)** The next-to-last-straw that broke the back of Erich von Stroheim's remarkable directorial career, this social satire about an arranged marriage among ruinous aristocratic clans in pre–World War I Vienna survives as a dazzling fragment; production was halted after von Stroheim dragged out filming for nine months. It does, in any case, throw a painstakingly detailed light on how chaotically garish and complex weddings *used* to be, in certain circles.

***The Philadelphia Story* (1940)** A famous prenup crash and burn: Katharine Hepburn is the proud, self-righteous bride to be who wants to be knocked down from her pedestal ("I don't want to be worshipped; I want to be loved"); Cary Grant is the sarcastic ex who's determined to make her feel guilty and stop the wedding; Jimmy Stewart is the class-conscious society reporter thrust into the maelstrom. General wedding-planning tizziness abounds. The comedy is high, and the racehorses in this stable all run in peak form—even if the thrust of the movie seems to be that women should forgive men their boyish faults, whether they include drinking, adultery, or just the pinching fingers of the slightly creepy Uncle Willie (Roland Young). Though overrated, this may be a good movie to watch before making or accepting a marriage proposal, if only because it stirs up every doubt and second thought you *should* have before tying the knot.

***The Forgotten Man* (1941)** The old jokes about the bride's father being milked dry, ignored, and sidelined throughout the protracted wedding-preparation process began here, in this vintage Robert Benchley short. No one did, or has ever done, befuddled paternalism as well as Benchley. Find this flick, along with several other short films, on the Kino DVD ***Robert Benchley and the Knights of the Algonquin* (2006)**.

***Father of the Bride* (1950)** The granddad of all Hollywood wedding comedies, this story begins at the end: an exhausted father, in the aftermath of his only daughter's wedding, sits among the wreckage of his home, rubbing his aching tootsies. If you're contemplating a simple home wedding, this movie will give you pause—there's nothing simple about the prospect, and you'll be left cleaning up after the newlyweds have hopped their plane to Bermuda. Spencer Tracy, at his comical best as the ineffectual dad, will make you glad if you're the father of the groom, who seems to get a free ride. Then again, the costs Tracy incurs seem a bargain in comparison with today's wedding price tag ($3.75 a head? If only!).

***Seven Brides for Seven Brothers* (1954)** Big, brash, cartwheeling musical (based on a Stephen Vincent Benet story!) about lumberjack brothers who shanghai townie girls into being their wives, in an 1850 Oregon Territory that looks plainly like a backdrop set on the MGM lot. Boisterous, if dim-witted and more than a little misogynistic.

***Cousin, Cousine* (1975)** Bubbly French romantic comedy: two cousins (related as the result of a recent marriage between their families), already unhappily wed to sluts, link up and have an affair, which causes problems at subsequent family gatherings.

Sexy and light, with Marie-Christine Barrault holding it together with the easiness of her smile and the lilt in her voice.

Moonstruck **(1987)** Romance and *Italiante* comedy abound in a kind of dreamy, magical hunk of brownstone Brooklyn, with Cher's widowed frump dubiously accepting the proposal of Danny Aiello's dumb mama's boy, then falling for his troubled, one-handed brother (Nicolas Cage). Luckily, the margins of the movie are filled to the brim with witty character actors, slabs of comedic nonsense, behavioral detail, and a sense of warmheartedness in regard to the follies of humankind. Screenwriter John Patrick Shanley captured a cartoon-*paisan* flavor; though it seems somewhat dated now, it's a far better submersion in Mediterranean-emigré boisterousness than *My Big Fat Greek Wedding* (see below).

The Princess Bride **(1987)** A fractured fairy tale, courtesy of William Goldman and Rob Reiner, in which one Princess Buttercup (Robin Wright) grieves so deeply over the death of her true love, Westley (Cary Elwes), that she agrees to marry the loathsome Prince Humperdinck (Chris Sarandon)—but Westley isn't really dead. Goldman manhandles Grimm-style fable elements into a self-mocking pastiche that never collapses into all-out Mel Brooks–style parody. (This is, in fact, the movie that *Shrek* tried to be.) The milieu offers an inspired cast (including Billy Crystal, Christopher Guest, Andre the Giant, and Carol Kane) lots of opportunities for hijinks, and the results are pleasantly Borscht Belty. The supreme example of the film's attitude may be its casting of the lisping, stumpy Wallace Shawn as a much-feared evil genius—a *Sicilian* evil genius.

Cousins **(1989)** An American remake of *Cousin, Cousine*, it's definitely not as sexy as the original, natch, but you can appreciate Isabella Rossellini's natural glow and the sardonic chutzpah required to have a young couple's choice of wedding song be U2's "With or Without You."

True Love **(1989)** Nuptial planning, Bronx-Italian style, including tacky, rainbow-colored bridesmaid gowns, tawdry wedding halls that serve mashed potatoes dyed to match the color of the gowns, opinionated friends, interfering relatives, and a bride and groom who are swept along with the idea of marriage as something you ought to do, and so convince themselves that they *want* to do it. Ron Eldard's groom is hopelessly immature and unromantic; Annabella Sciorra's bride ignores the fact that her marriage is doomed before it starts (she can't help it—she's too busy wiping fingerprints off her back). You'll probably find this movie a lot funnier if you've witnessed this type of New Yawk behavior up close; otherwise, it may all just seem completely crazy.

Father of the Bride **(1991)** Remake the 1950 Spencer Tracy hokiness with Steve Martin? It was a hit anyway (and it spawned a new generation of wedding comedies), though the boat is kept afloat only by Diane Keaton as the calming, ironic mom, and Martin Short as an outrageously queeny wedding planner.

***Honeymoon in Vegas* (1992)** Commitment-phobe Nicolas Cage loses a Vegas poker game to a cunning gambler (James Caan) who offers a devil's bargain: the debt is forgiven in exchange for a weekend with the loser's fiancée (Sarah Jessica Parker). Nicolas Cage is at his frenetic best as the desperate bridegroom trying to win back the girl, if only he can find her—and be on the lookout for Peter Boyle in a hilarious cameo. Deftly written and directed by Andrew (*The In-Laws*) Bergman, this is for anyone who chooses to skip the traditional wedding in favor of the quickie hitch at the Elvis Chapel of Love.

***Four Weddings and a Funeral* (1994)** A band of single friends, led by the shyly charming Hugh Grant, chase each other around England, attending weddings in various states of disarray and embarrassment. Star-crossed *amour* and funny wedding mishaps abound, but this international smash sucked in both its audience and an Oscar nomination with the grace of its execution, a brilliantly witty screenplay—perfectly staged and acted—and a pervasive fondness for even the bit characters and background extras.

***Muriel's Wedding* (1994)** An Australian pariah (Toni Collette) hides in her bedroom from her bullying father, escaping her grim reality with heavy doses of ABBA and dreams of getting married. Embarrassing and funny (because you've been there, to some degree), this bust-out P. J. Hogan comedy ends with a triumphant emotional release that beats out its heroine's dreams of being a newlywed "Dancing Queen" at her own posh nuptials.

***Miami Rhapsody* (1995)** This effervescent, if very Woody Allen–like, comedy from writer-director David Frankel (who would go on to make 2006's *The Devil Wears Prada*) poses a particular quandary for its east-coast-Florida-Jewish heroine (Sarah Jessica Parker): how to be ecstatic about getting engaged when everyone around you is cheating. Each of her parents (Mia Farrow and Paul Mazursky) is embroiled with someone else; her newly married sister (Carla Gugino), desperate for the attention she doesn't get from her jock husband, beds an old boyfriend, while her brother (Kevin Pollack) cheats on his very pregnant wife. Is there something wrong with the Florida water, other than sulfur and chlorine? The incisive jokes and deliveries (Parker has never been so good, before or since) make a good case for remaining uncommitted, so anyone whose toes are getting a little frosty should be careful.

***Walking and Talking* (1996)** Nicole Holofcener's sparkling feature debut studies the interpersonal tremors emanating from two lifelong friends (Catherine Keener and Anne Heche) as one prepares for matrimony and the other struggles with a dead-end love life. (See "Girls' Night Out," p. 247.)

***My Best Friend's Wedding* (1997)** The question of whether or not men and women can be true friends without being romantically involved is put to the test when Dermot Mulroney tells best friend Julia Roberts that he's getting married—and, by the way, it's this weekend, so please fly out to celebrate the nuptials. Nothing ever looks so good as it does after it's slipped from your grasp, so our heroine pulls out the underhanded stops to try to win him. Eccentric and campy, the fete includes Cameron Diaz, in full bloom, and the irrepressible Rupert Everett rescuing the day more than once.

Black Cat, White Cat (1998) Those who are familiar with the films of Sarajevo-born Emir Kusturica knows what they're in for with this unrestrained absurdism, about the inhabitants of a Romany enclave (a festering nest of stray animals, sniping neighbors, grifters, crooks, and layabouts) on the banks of the Danube as they prepare for a particularly troublesome wedding. What with the car-eating pigs, humping dogs, begging gypsies, dwarf brides, gold-toothed paraplegic mobsters, and hidden corpses, it's a safe bet that you'll never be bored. Kusturica's stories (this movie could hardly function with just one) don't always work, and his humor is often crude, but his films intend to be filthy, hungry parades of life, and they succeed. It can get exhausting—imagine a more-than-two-hours-long Serbian Little Caesars commercial—but who's going to complain that a movie has *too much* stuff in it?

Meet the Parents (2000) This brutally comic hit found the lurking fears of all young lovers who are meeting their prospective in-laws for the first time—and lit them up good. Ben Stiller is just, well, Ben Stiller, but Robert De Niro, as the fiancée's father, shines: much more than just a controlling, disapproving patriarch, he's actually a semiretired CIA ramrod, with only his little girl now to serve and protect. Every step Stiller makes is the wrong step; every action is scrutinized mercilessly. Stiller's anxious gaze of disbelief as each new mishap befalls him is a wonder, and De Niro flexes all of his dead-eyed menace.

My Big Fat Greek Wedding (2002) The ugly duckling story of a shy plain Jane who finds success, love, and happiness as soon as she gets contact lenses, a decent hairstyle, and clothes that accentuate her voluptuousness. It's an old story, but this blockbuster comedy tapped into millions of Americans' memories and anxieties about their own loud, crazy ethnic families (Italian, Jewish, Greek—it hardly makes any difference), which were always at their loudest and craziest during public rituals. As both the film's screenwriter and its star, Nia Vardalos leaves no cliche unused, and her narration is peppered with annoying one-liners, but the popularity of this movie makes it impossible to ignore. There's this much: Vardalos and befuddled hunk John Corbett are unglam enough to resemble people you might actually know.

The Groomsmen (2006) Possibly Edward Burns's most accomplished feature (which says only so much), about five Long Island buddies reuniting for a wedding. Jay Mohr and Matthew Lillard make this flick worthwhile.

BACHELOR PARTY

"Let's have a bachelor party with chicks and guns and fire trucks and hookers and drugs and booze!"
—Barry Diamond, *Bachelor Party*

No, do not watch any of these movies *during* or *as a substitute for* a bachelor party—God knows, your docket should have livelier things lined up, whether you're the groom, a groomsman, or just a buddy along for the ride. But if you want to gear up for the festivities, you might check out one of these films.

***Bachelor Party* (1984)** Once upon a time, Tom Hanks was an infectiously comic performer, and this lowdown yuckfest, shot before 1984's *Splash* made him a star, is rude, crude, and full of silly energy. It may be the only truly funny, truly upbeat bachelor party film ever made, even with its 1980s hair and Adrian Zmed.

***Very Bad Things* (1998)** Think *Deliverance* in 1990s suburbia: Peter Berg's hair-raising exercise in audience discomfiture watches patiently as a pack of ordinary, if highstrung, schmoes (Christian Slater, Daniel Stern, Jeremy Piven, and Leland Orser) take a buddy (Jon Favreau) to Vegas for a rockin' bachelor party, which quickly degenerates from your run-of-the-mill coke-and-scotch-infused hotel trashing to a full-on panic attack when Piven accidentally kills the requisite stripper/whore in mid-rut. The decision to bury the body in the desert is just their first mistake; mucking up manic bride-to-be Cameron Diaz's plans for the perfect wedding might be their worst.

***American Wedding* (2003)** For desperate *American Pie* fans only; it's the third in the series, and Jason Biggs's schmo is headed for the altar. Naturally, ceremonial baked items are defiled, and everyone's best-laid plans go clumsily awry.

***Wedding Crashers* (2005)** Despite the title, there isn't much wedding stuff in this hit—at least not after the opening blitzkrieg, anyway, in which Vince Vaughn and Owen Wilson's libertines attack the receptions of others as if it were a sport, complete with a season, rules, and an end game: free food, booze, and, most of all, booty. It's a goofy character farce that attends to the duo's infiltration of a rich congressman's family over a long weekend. The boys might be hosers, but the movie's affection for the rituals of weddings is real.

NEWLYWEDS

"I say, marriage with Max is not exactly a bed of roses, is it?"
—George Sanders, *Rebecca*

Now you've done it—and life as a couple comes at you like a tidal wave. How much do you actually know about your spouse (not to mention your new family)? Who is this person with bed head and death breath? You're living *where*? Why didn't someone tell you about all this *stuff* you have to put up with?

Made for Each Other (1939) Merely a formulaic studio product from back in the day, but Carole Lombard and James Stewart, as newlyweds beset by money problems, in-laws, and a sick baby, are luminous.

Rebecca (1940) Alfred Hitchcock's unassailable Gothic classic is merely the first of his many biopsies on marriage and the secret poisoning within them. Filled with superb set pieces and supporting performances, it all boils down to Joan Fontaine's name-less heroine, nervously thrust into both an aristocratic milieu and an incommunicative union she has no business occupying. Reportedly, Hitchcock (with the help of costar Laurence Olivier) subtly abused Fontaine on the set, a ploy that not only made her performance realer than real, but made the entire film, inside and out, a working metaphor for a dysfunctional marriage.

I Married a Witch (1942) You think you know what you'll get, but sometimes you don't—in this René Clair comedy, Fredric March is surprised to discover, on the eve of his power marriage, that he's instead in love with Veronica Lake, a spell-casting witch.

I Married a Monster from Outer Space (1958) Every suspicion and lurking phobia a woman can have about her new husband is metaphorically crystallized in this pulpy genre riff from the Cold War 1950s. Poor Gloria Talbott slowly realizes that hubby Tom Tryon is an alien looking to populate Earth with his cold, tentacled kind, and wives everywhere know how she feels. Whether this lesson in anxiety works as a cathartic for your marital doubts, exacerbates them, or creates a few where none had been before, it's clearly a movie that can try the tensile strength of any new marriage.

Barefoot in the Park (1967) One of the first adaptations of a Neil Simon play, this dated bonbon features exuberant drama queen Jane Fonda and staid pragmatist Robert Redford as fresh-faced newlyweds who can't keep their hands off each other (goos-ing bottoms in elevators, hanging "do not disturb" signs on hotel doorknobs for days on end, and so on). But the honeymoon ends, and the comedy ostensibly begins, when they move into a tiny, five-flight Manhattan walk-up (which is refreshingly—and realistically—tiny compared to the bountiful dwellings shown in *Friends* and *Seinfeld*). The film has no other relation at all to reality, but it's cute as a button.

Mississippi Mermaid (1969) François Truffaut takes on another hard-boiled noir (Cornell Woolrich's Waltz into Darkness), transposing the action to exotic Reunion Island, where tobacco magnate Jean-Paul Belmondo receives a mail-order bride (Catherine Deneuve) who doesn't match the photos he was sent. He understandably marries her anyway, and the scam/betrayal begins. Remade—badly, with Angelina Jolie—as Original Sin (2001).

The Heartbreak Kid (1972) Why has this scary Neil Simon comedy been forgotten? Newlyweds Lenny (the peerlessly dry Charles Grodin) and Lila (the counteractively brash Jeannie Berlin) are honeymooning in Miami when Lenny meets blonde shiksa goddess Cybill Shepherd and decides that she's the one he can't live without. Director Elaine May keeps the farce so deadpan it becomes chilling.

So I Married an Axe Murderer (1993) Mike Myers's big solo-star debut, in multiple roles, one of which marries Nancy Travis, whom he slowly begins to suspect is a homicidal maniac. A cheesy riff on a well-worn, even reflexive, theme.

Sleep with Me (1994) A fabulously textured comedy that centers on how sensitive guy Frank (Craig Sheffer) deals with buddy Joe's (Eric Stoltz) marriage to Frank's secret true love, Sarah (Meg Tilly). Director Rory Kelly divvied up the screenplay into six chunks, to six different screenwriters (including himself), and as a result it's the social whorl of characters around the tense triangle that sings: Dean Cameron's testy paraplegic, Todd Field's laconic screenwriter, and Thomas Gibson's amused Brit are particularly memorable, plus there are fiery bit performances by Quentin Tarantino, Parker Posey, Joey Lauren Adams, June Lockhart, Susan Traylor, and Adrienne Shelly. Criminally overlooked.

I Married a Strange Person! (1997) Bill Plympton, an idiosyncratic cartoonist whose pregnant-pause, restless-color-pencil style is instantly recognizable from years of seeing MTV tidbits and frequently cablecast short films, fashioned this feature entirely by hand. He is peerless at bending, twisting, folding, inside-outing, and generally mauling the human form (usually, the human form of a pudgy, balding, barely cognizant middle-aged man), and here the dam breaks on a flood of mutilation, decimation, and incineration gags. The plot involves a newlywed man being subject to special powers after a stray laser (or something like that, anyway) hits him. The film's money scene is that of the marriage's consummation—it's a lengthy, all-penciled sexcapade in which the wife is objectified into a hundred absurd dream identities (including, finally, a huge pair of expanding, house-bursting breasts) as every inanimate object in the room telekinetically mimes the old in-out. Needless to say, the movie asks (however absurdly) what we think we're getting into when we marry; Plympton's explosive nonsense could easily be seen as a husband or wife's interior experience of a married life spiraling out of control.

The Secret Lives of Dentists **(2002)** A delicate indie, based on Jane Smiley's novel *The Age of Grief*, about a mild-mannered dentist (Campbell Scott) whose growing suspicions surrounding his wife (Hope Davis) begin to poison his life. Funny, but not really a comedy.

PREGNANCY

"I'm pregnant. Can you pass the turnips?"
—Molly Ringwald, *For Keeps*

Here's a devastating, intensely private moment that few movies have tried to do justice to: the discovery that you will, within three-quarters of a year, be a parent. After you've calmed down, you might want a little cinematic company. Unfortunately, the pickings are slim.

The Miracle of Morgan's Creek **(1944)** Arguably comic maestro Preston Sturges's densest, craziest comedy. After enjoying the send-off bash of a now-absent soldier (whose name is something like "Ratzkywatzky"), Trudy Kockenlocker (Betty Hutton) wakes up, hung over and thinking that she may have married the guy. One thing she knows for sure, soon enough, is that she's pregnant. She enlists town nerd Norval Jones (Eddie Bracken) to lie about it being *his* baby, which ignites a blitzkrieg of lies, misunderstandings, and overall lunacy. Watching this movie is like attending a well-liquored party of hyperactives.

For Keeps **(1988)** One of the last hurrahs in Molly Ringwald's brief and peculiar snatch of stardom, in which she plays a high schooler pushed into marriage by an unplanned baby. The film goes for serious, but barely qualifies.

She's Having a Baby **(1988)** This John Hughes movie ostensibly follows a young couple's long journey to maturity and parenthood—in truth, the supposedly "comically" immature male half (Kevin Bacon) seems scarcely able to adjust to puberty, let alone marriage and fatherhood. As unsubtle as it is unrealistic, especially when it comes to Elizabeth McGovern's labor.

The Snapper **(1993)** Another unwanted pregnancy, but here it belongs to the stubborn eldest daughter of a splenetic Dublin family. Colm Meaney gives a giant-sized performance as the family patriarch, a working-class knucklehead who runs the scale of emotional reactions when he's told that, come hell or high water, he's going to have a grandkid. Written by novelist Roddy Doyle, this is the one movie that pungently gives life to his working-class Irish singsong.

CHILDBIRTH

"I don't care what I see outside. My vision is within! Here is where the birds sing!"
—Denholm Elliott, *A Room with a View*

As you may or may not know, pregnancy labor is a fickle master—it might last one hour or fifty. If you're on the business end of that scale, you've got a lot of time to kill (sleeping isn't a dependable option), and you may want a distraction from the thunderous agony that's hitting you, like ocean waves, with accelerating regularity. A movie just might be what the doctor ordered. But what kind? It cannot be anything very demanding—no art films, no subtitles, no heavy metaphors—and it cannot be violent, irrational, "pulpy," silly, or inordinately dull. It also cannot be very masculine in nature: it's because of *him* that you're in this hellish predicament to begin with; you don't need a movie that glorifies guns, sports, stoicism, war, or bathroom humor. It also cannot contain sex scenes, for much the same reason. In addition—and this is important—the movie cannot be *about* pregnancy or labor. That'd be like watching *Marathon Man* while you're at the dentist. The answer: literary costume dramas. These movies, when done well, are cinematic lithium. A good period melodrama is quiet, polite, luxurious, quaintly scored, and filled with antiques and pristine woodwork, and you know that the worst that can happen is that a heroine might get dissed at a ball. It's as if they all understand that *you* have bigger problems just now (like the fact that, as far as your body is concerned, you're getting run down by a Ford Expedition every two-and-a-half minutes). Word of caution: choose carefully, because the film you watch to help get you through this may thereafter be cursed with hip-splitting associations from that day forward.

***Pride and Prejudice* (1940)** Certainly the most enjoyable of classic-lit adaptations made during Hollywood's Golden Era, before producers understood the addictive power of authentic architecture and the real English countryside. Greer Garson and Laurence Olivier, at their most gloriously vibrant, do a smartly condensed version of Jane Austen's novel that retains all the good jokes.

A Room with a View (1986) The film that started the modern wave of crinoline-and-mahogany costume dramas, and a high-end getaway-weekend movie if there ever was one. Depending on your labor experience, this rangy, high-spirited Merchant-Ivory landmark may be *too* wacky and eccentric. Then again, it may not be, and it certainly won't if you've already seen it, which you certainly should have by now.

Howards End (1992) This Merchant-Ivory entry offers more than just gentle suffering and witticisms; there's also a bit of drama about Victorian class struggle and the wealthy, landed elite who don't want to suffer the company of either the crass workers or the intellectual bourgeois. The E. M. Forster–based script is well written, and it will keep you distracted during your deep-and-slow-breathing phase (before the "hee hee hoo hoo" phase of counting pants, when no movie can help you).

The Age of Innocence (1993) Swirling dresses, shining spats, obsessively appointed period interiors, and anguish-filled eyes are the stuff of Martin Scorsese's adaptation of the Edith Wharton novel. At the heart of the story is the struggle between social machinations and the vagaries of the human heart, with demure little Winona Ryder occupying the fringes of the drama until she emerges as the tale's secret weapon. If that doesn't sound soothing enough, how about a wall-to-wall narration, read in Joanne Woodward's gentle tones? If she could only narrate everyone's life, surely the world would be a more serene place.

Sense and Sensibility (1995) Ang Lee's lovely adaptation of this classic novel is perfect for a long labor. Jane Austen's plot revolves around misunderstandings and unexpressed longings—your blood pressure falls just thinking about it. The movie is scrupulously intelligent yet modest, perfectly acted yet underplayed, and filled with women bonding with other women—it's like they're surrounding you in the birthing tent in Africa. Hugh Grant is dashing and bashful, and Emma Thompson (who also wrote the screenplay) is long-suffering but also whip-smart and witty—who else would you rather spend your time with? And the Devon countryside is heaven on Earth, with nary a phone wire, strip mall, or sports bar in sight.

The Last September (1999) First-time filmmaker Deborah Warner's adaptation of Elizabeth Bowen's novel is a lovely, transporting piece of work, as sure-handed in its balance of comedy and tragedy as it is in evoking a burnished visual tone poem to Ireland, adolescence, and a dead way of life. Falling into the Chekhovian subgenre of elegies to the end of aristocracy, the film is largely about mood and manners. The setting is 1920 County Cork, on the estate of Sir Richard (Michael Gambon) and his wife, Lady Myra (Maggie Smith), two broken-down Anglo-Irish who are quite baffled by the Catholic-British-Protestant warring that's all too quickly closing in on their manor. Visiting are diffident Brit couple Hugo and Francie (Lambert Wilson and Jane Birkin), sarcastic, worldly "vamp" Marda (Fiona Shaw), and, central to the film, Lois (Keeley Hawes), Sir Richard's lovely, winsome (and, for all intents and purposes, orphaned) young niece, around whose viewpoint the film revolves. Lois doesn't know exactly what she wants, and her daydreamy contemplation of her options and destiny is what the film is really about. Cinematographer Slawomir Idziak achieves Gustave Moreau–like depth, richness, and reflective resonance in the imagery that is utterly breathtaking; it's as if he had equipment—and knowledge—that other, mortal cameramen don't.

NEW PARENTHOOD

"These were the happy days, the salad days as they say, and Ed felt that havin' a critter was the next logical step."
—Nicolas Cage, *Raising Arizona*

You're not watching many movies now—not in their entirety, anyway. You have a baby to take care of. Has anyone else ever undergone this bizarre, exhausting, cosmic experience? Not with *this* baby, right? Few of the movies below deal authentically with the pressures of new parenthood—how could they do it justice?—preferring instead to either squeeze comic juice out of the scenario (which is always funnier to watch than it is to endure), or push your newly sensitive baby-love buttons.

Various *Our Gang/Little Rascals* shorts (1929–1934) Here's a crash course in the art of being a baby. These well-known Hal Roach shorts—we're talking here about the early ones, before Spanky McFarland reached a chubby preadolescence—are so reckless and impulsive, they're virtually comic films made *by* toddlers. The under-six set is represented in all of its surreal glory and destructive messiness as it is in no other cinematic experience. Food, housewares, diapers, farm animals, plumbing, mud puddles—it's all fodder for fresh human chaos. Long live Weezer!

***3 Godfathers* (1948)** The template for the "bachelors find themselves raising an infant" comedies of later years, this John Ford western is actually pretty emotional and defiant of expectations, what with John Wayne as a self-pitying leader of a band of bank robbers (which also includes Pedro Armendariz and Harry Carey Jr.), the last act's desert walk of death, and Ward Bond's humane lawman. Made a decade after *Stella Dallas*, that ode to maternal martyrdom, this might well be the first American film that's centered on the *paternal* sacrifice for the future of a gurgling newborn. Ignore the canned New Testament parallels and invocations if you can.

Cheaper by the Dozen **(1950)** The hokey, blushing original comedy based on Frank B. Gilbreth Jr.'s memoir about being one of twelve children belonging to Frank B. Gilbreth Sr. (Clifton Webb), a real-life efficiency expert who struggled to maintain his household in scientific order. Myrna Loy, who hardly looks like the mother of twelve, suffers quietly, except when she's made to speechify about the evils of birth control.

Z.P.G. **(1971)** Provocative if cheap British sci-fi diatribe about a polluted, overpopulated future in which pregnancies are outlawed; brainwashing and robotic baby substitutes are the wholly inadequate replacements offered. Somehow, one couple (Oliver Reed and Geraldine Chaplin) manages to slide under the tense social radar and have a baby. Rather inept in most departments, except when another couple learns the protagonists' secret and blackmails them for a chance to spend some time with the infant, which is a queasy yen every parent can understand.

Raising Arizona **(1987)** Joel and Ethan Coen's second film, and a wild-eyed, Rube Goldberg white-trash riot, as Southern-fool marrieds Nicolas Cage and Holly Hunter, unable to have babies of their own ("Her insides were a rocky place," Cage's dopey felon bemoans in an unforgettable narration, "where my seed could find no purchase"), kidnap one from a set of quintuplets. From there, it's a veritable Road Runner cartoon revolving around the infant's essentially irresistible baby-ness, and there are enough character-rich hee-haws for ten movies. The urgent matter of getting your hands on some Huggies in the worst of circumstances was never made so thrilling.

Flirting with Disaster **(1996)** A devilishly rich character comedy about how being a new parent compels one to explore one's own roots, David O. Russell's high-concept rip is packed with unpredictable rhythms, dead-perfect line readings, and hilarious peripheral characters. New dad/adopted schlemiel Ben Stiller decides he wants to find out who his biological parents are; a cross-country journey ensues, in which viewers are treated to frustrated wife Patricia Arquette, chain-smoking social worker Téa Leoni, gay cop couples, a raft of mistaken identities, inadvertent LSD consumption, armpit sex, and the meddlesome hell of Jewish parents Mary Tyler Moore and George Segal. The baby is somewhat secondary to the mind frames of the neurotic father, but the states of parenthood and familial belonging have never been so hilariously besieged. From Leoni's look of exhausted awe when LSD manufacturer Alan Alda tells her as he wrestles a tripping-out-of-his-mind dinner guest—that, sorry, it's a nonsmoking house ("I guess it's just one of those ex-felon, pro-acid type of nonsmoking houses," she moans) to the moment when Stiller walks in on bisexual stud Josh Brolin tonguing Arquette's armpit (the shiveriest moment of marital violation in modern movies), Russell's movie melts like butter. One viewing won't cut it.

Wonderland **(1999)** Eclectic virtuoso Michael Winterbottom knocked out this hyperreal drama between much more newsworthy projects, but it's splendid. Three working-class London sisters (lonely girl Gina McKee, pregnant wife Molly Parker, and belligerent floozy Shirley Henderson) suffer the inadequacies of men (Ian Hart and Stuart Townsend among them); the movie climaxes in a poetic redemption-by-childbirth.

Little Otik **(2000)** Few films express parental anxiety better than this wicked lark by Czech filmmaker/animator Jan Švankmajer: riffing on an ancient folktale, the movie has an impatient husband of a childless woman carve her a baby out of a hunk of tree root. Naturally, the nurtured baby comes to life and begins eating—and eating, turning the life of the new parents into a bloody fiasco. Not for the faint of sensibility, it's a cold cackle of a movie, seemingly intent on both mocking and venting parents' feelings of helplessness in the face of infantile hunger and neediness.

PARENTING TWEENS AND TEENS

"All we want is to be treated like human beings, not to be experimented on like guinea pigs or patronized like bunny rabbits."
—Winona Ryder, *Heathers*

You have kids, you feed them, and they grow. Then, somewhere on the road to fully maturing and moving out, they become nasty aliens, visiting Earth on a mission to drive you out of your mind. But what's really happened is that *you've* changed, too. There's nothing like parenthood to make you forget what it was like to be a teenager: uppity, tetchy, exhilarated with rebellion, horny (!), fixated on *now*, driven berserk by peer pressure and school conformity, dizzy with hormones, and inherently repulsed by everything grown-up. The movies listed here run the gamut from masterfully observed, potentially instructive reacquaintances with the preadult sensibility (know thine enemy); to lurid pulp that's sympathetic to the parent's plight; to peripheral films that nevertheless have something rich to say about being a kid, a parent, or both.

Zéro de Conduite **(1933)** Son of an anarchist and a consumptive art-film martyr who died at age twenty-nine, leaving less than three hours of film behind him, Jean Vigo remains one of cinema's preeminent artists, and this joyful schoolyard revolution focuses on one of the twentieth century's great cultural concepts: the dreamy exaltation of adolescent rebellion, personified here by a gaggle of students in a chaotic, pompous, and repressive school who decide, impulsively, to fight back. The shock waves of this rough-hewn, homemade hand grenade (shot without sound, which was added later, and as unpolished as freshly dug shale) are still rippling across adolescent brainpans everywhere. No film has ever spoken to the reckless hearts of boys with the same sympathy, and it might be the first unsung glint of the spirit of rock 'n' roll.

Rebel Without a Cause (1955) The roundly famous movie that made a totem saint out of James Dean, this spectacular Nicholas Ray melodrama functioned in the 1950s as the war chant of a new generation—and it still conveys the hot anger and lost self-pity of every misunderstood teen. This film can get under your skin, and make you glad you're no longer seventeen.

The 400 Blows (1959) The turn of the key that started the engine of the French New Wave's international buzz, François Truffaut's debut masterpiece is a rough-and-ready document of a young teen (Jean-Pierre Léaud), ill-raised by self-obsessed parents, restlessly rebelling against school, and slowly veering, as Truffaut himself had, into petty crime and the jaws of juvenile detention. Essential viewing all around, it's an uninflected, true-hearted experience as seen exclusively from a fourteen-year-old's point of view. As fresh as the day it was made.

Village of the Damned (1960) A grand nail-biting launch of quiet Brit sci-fi, in which telepathic super-schoolkids plan to take over the world. George Sanders, that most cutely intolerant of actors, is the only man who can help.

Lord of the Flies (1963) Have no doubt: your preadolescent boys will happily revert to bloodletting barbarism if given half a chance. It's a dynamic that's demonstrated with cold-blooded efficiency by William Golding's never-out-of-print novel and Peter Brook's chilly, black-and-white film rendition. It's a very literal film, however—so perhaps it'll just make you wary of *British* schoolboys.

If . . . (1968) British critic-turned-director Lindsay Anderson made his mark with this boarding-school diatribe. Something of a remake of *Zéro de Conduite* (right down to the rooftop climax), but this version cuts the English disciplinarian education system to ribbons. It was, also, a generational anthem film, ill-mannered and furious, and it made Malcolm McDowell enough of a key figure for Stanley Kubrick to consider him the inevitable choice to star in 1971's *A Clockwork Orange*.

Badlands (1973) The prototypical realist outlaw road movie of the Nixon days, Terrence Malick's first film is a fictionalized account of the Charlie Starkweather–Caril Ann Fugate Midwest murder spree of the late 1950s. Gorgeous and scary, it's a lyrical film about the banality of evil in which the teen killers, played with mesmerizing vacancy by Martin Sheen and Sissy Spacek, never seem to care what happens or why. It's a riveting portrait of young sociopaths in action, as well as of the postwar, movie-soaked culture from which they sprang. "He looked just like James Dean," Spacek's Holly explains in her hick, *True Confessions*–type narration, which presents the film's whole landscape through the rose-colored squint of a teenage mind overfed on cheap magazines. Parents of puberty-pounded teenage nihilists everywhere will feel this movie sing in their dreams.

Small Change **(1976)** Truffaut returns to early adolescence, in a tapestry film that depicts an array of suburban French children who overcome ordinary adversities and embrace life's simple glories in ways that are alien to grown-ups. Invigorating and hopeful.

Who Are the DeBolts? (And Where Did They Get Nineteen Kids?) **(1977)** Sure, this is nothing more than a preachy, feel-good documentary about a tirelessly sacrificial family who began adopting war orphans and handicapped children, and didn't stop until they had accumulated nineteen kids. But you'd have to be made of glacier ice to not have this award-reaper render you speechless and, chances are, more than a little shamed by your life complaints and complacencies. When the film was shot, most of the DeBolt kids were between the ages of eight and sixteen, and most of them required prosthetics. It's a convincing portrait of a happy household in which teenage persnicketiness is a wasteful luxury.

À Nos Amours **(1983)** This little-seen French movie, from misanthropic director Maurice Pialat, is a troubled, unsettled, inconclusive portrait of a dysfunctional middle-class family pushed over the edge into savagery by the promiscuous self-possession of the fifteen-year-old daughter. As the infinitely complex but wholly unself-conscious girl, Sandrine Bonnaire became a generational icon—had she died young (thankfully, she's still very much alive), she'd have been the French James Dean.

Rumble Fish **(1983)** Francis Ford Coppola's lurid, expressionist view of teenage angst by way of the S. E. Hinton book. Fascinating to look at, but does it in fact grab hold of something self-dramatic and apocalyptic about being seventeen, on the loose, under-parented, and gang prone? You tell us.

Heathers **(1989)** A movie made, it seems, specifically to express the rancorous sarcasm of the modern teen (see "Remembering High School," p. 302), so it may be instructive as an object lesson for struggling parents. The film demonstrates what's mordantly funny and fiercely scary about high school life better than many well-meaning "serious" films.

Parenthood **(1989)** This Ron Howard movie is reflective of the late-1980s assumptions that every adult is in therapy and that there's no shame in admitting you're a lousy parent because *everyone* is, by definition. In a seemingly new way, the era presented parents as overwhelmed, harried, and imperfect; the notion that the kids were also imperfect, with their own emotional problems, destructive behaviors, and immature conceptions about life, was seen as a let-our-hair-down revelation. Here, the generations of screwups begin with neglectful patriarch Jason Robards and spiral down to earnest but inept dad Steve Martin and the layabout kids of his single-mom sister Dianne Wiest. Full of Talking Heads–type "How did I get here?" moments (Wiest, upon viewing glossies of her daughter in flagrante delicto: "I was at Woodstock, for Chrissake!"); the dynamic may be Hollywoodized to the hilt, but it's nevertheless sometimes painful to watch.

***Welcome to the Dollhouse* (1995)** Todd Solondz's horrifying film focuses on Dawn Weiner (Heather Matarazzo), a homely junior high schooler trapped in a nerd-suburban Inferno, a real and desolate New Jersey no man's land that Solondz hammers to the wall for all time, down to the paneling in the family TV room. Everything-impaired and far from smart, Dawn quietly endures the trickle-down barbarity of bullies, the raw purgatory of the seventh grade (a terrifying moment is spent standing at the blackboard staring at math problems), and her own stunted self-image. All of which might make *Dollhouse* sound merely like an ordeal, but it's an ordeal by joy buzzer; Solondz's style is split-ranch absurdism. Carrying the whole movie on her folded little shoulders, Matarazzo is astonishingly sharp, vulnerable, and authentic, a portrait of pubescent gracelessness under pressure.

***Comedy of Innocence* (2000)** Isabelle Huppert is the devoted mother of a young boy (Nils Hugon) who, on the occasion of his ninth birthday, tells her—in all seriousness and with some amount of irritation—that now he wants to go to his "real home" and his "real mother." Raúl Ruiz's movie takes this world-rocking idea to the psychological mat; it's all about Huppert's fundamental identity as a mother being questioned, and indeed denied.

***All About Lily Chou-Chou* (2001)** Shot on beautiful digital video, this neglected film fashions an epic pop-culture ballad out of Japanese adolescent angst, in which teens can communicate only by way of celeb-worshipping chat rooms and, more habitually, by joining the pop-music "ether" they experience alone on their headphones.

***Fat Girl* (2001)** Catherine Breillat's extremely uncomfortable film observes two unhappy sisters—one, a saucy fifteen-year-old (Roxane Mesquida); the second, an obese twelve-year-old (Anaïs Reboux) who must abet and observe her sister's ill-advised sexual adventures. Breillat is a radical grenade thrower, and, like her graphic-sex-filled *Romance* (1999), this movie probes our raw nerve endings on its way to just cutting us wide open.

***Brick* (2005)** A deeply odd independently made stunt that ends up revealing teenage emotional terrain that no other film has. Rian Johnson's debut movie is a meta-noir: it revolves around a dead girl, a drug dealer, and a lost brick of dope, and it offers up angsty high schoolers who all talk in crime-fiction patois and think in dog-eat-dog cliches. The obligatory criminal syndicate is now an exclusive social clique; the mysterious Mr. Big is a young coke kingpin; the play-ball detective trying to get the lonely hero (Joseph Gordon-Levitt) to aid the law is his school's assistant vice principal (Richard

Roundtree); and parents are virtually absent (like in *Peanuts*!). It sounds gimmicky, but everyone involved means business every minute, and the result is a moving portrait of teenage self-seriousness.

ANNIVERSARY

"If you had it all to do over again, would you've married me?"
—Carole Lombard, *Mr. & Mrs. Smith*

The answer to that question is yes—if not, you should be looking for another category and another bunch of movies. Here is where the great, risky, important, *long-term* romantic movies lurk, free from the pressures of dating, Valentine's Day, wedding planning, and so on. As things shook out, our favorites all turned out to be old-school.

III

Sunrise **(1927)** The supreme silent melodrama, and the last film by German emigré F. W. Murnau before he died in a car wreck, this abstracted tone poem is one of the most beautiful films ever made, and it stands as exhibit A for the case that silent cinema might've achieved untold sublimities if sound hadn't come in for another few years. There's a Man, a Woman, and the Other Woman, and an entire arc of middle-life frustration, crisis, resolution, and loss plays out in a single day, on Hollywood's most beautifully photographed soundstages.

Queen Christina **(1933)** Arguably the definitive Greta Garbo film—the epitome of her lush melodramas, made by inventive visual artist Rouben Mamoulian and costarring John Gilbert, Garbo's old love, whose floundering talkie career Garbo tried to boost. The couple's rueful circumstances alone make this a swoon-worthy prize (Gilbert, an alcoholic whom Garbo had left literally standing at the altar years before, died of heart failure three years after making this film). But the story is a tragic daydream version of the eponymous Swedish monarch, resisting arranged international marriage and falling for Gilbert's Spanish emissary. Surprisingly sexy, poetic, and, in the end, devastating.

The Thin Man **(1934)** An eccentric inventor disappears and there's no shortage of suspects, from his tawdry girlfriend to his ex-wife's deadbeat husband. There's a Dashiell Hammett mystery at the bottom of this movie, but it's inconsequential—what this dishy lark is really about is the enthralling banter between the most debonair, comfortably droll, mutually secure movie couple of all time, Nick and Nora Charles (William Powell and, in a career-making turn, the delectable Myrna Loy). This is an anniversary movie for those who don't want romance and sentiment; these two are past that stage, and instead they make marriage look *fun*, from Loy's dismissive nose shrug to Powell, hungover, shooting at Christmas ornaments while reclined on the sofa ("Best Christmas present I ever got!") to fur-trimmed dressing gowns and flowing martinis. Movies haven't dared to portray this kind of grown-up relationship too often, and this one made stars of its leads. But the secret of it is that this *is* romance, too—there are no moony gazes or clinches, but it's evident to the blind that the Charleses, however they may snipe and gripe, are terribly, splendidly in love, and that they enjoy each other like sunny days.

My Man Godfrey **(1936)** For pure life force, guileless invention, brilliant sexual energy, a sense of humor so sharp it could split a hair, and beauty so dazzling it could make you forget the movie that surrounds her, there's no actress on Earth who can or could touch Carole Lombard. Undoubtedly, the fact that she died so tragically young (at thirty-three, in a 1942 airplane crash, while selling war bonds) furnishes our memory of her with an extra layer of luster—never had a movie star seemed so *alive*. Once you're hooked on this woman's lightning-like beauty, brown-sugar-and-cinnamon voice, babbling-brook line readings, and overall unearthly nerve, you're sold for life. This Gregory La Cava–directed screwball is her masterpiece; in it, she plays a loopy, dim-witted heiress who, in a scavenger hunt, hauls "forgotten man" William Powell off a rubbish heap and hires him as her wildly eccentric family's butler. Powell is, as he was in the contemporaneous *Thin Man* films, a dry martini of an actor, sharp and subtle and capable of comebacks so smooth you can skate on them. But Lombard's the whole show—the fiery, happy essence of movie liveliness personified. It says scads that Lombard and Powell had already married and divorced by the time they made *Godfrey*—it didn't stop them from having the time of their lives making it, or from enjoying each other like fizzy cocktails. It's partnership as *joie de vivre*.

The Awful Truth **(1937)** A movie about a couple in the midst of a divorce may seem an odd choice for an anniversary movie, but this is the antiromantic romance, marriage as ping-pong, and one of the preeminent screwball comedies. Director Leo McCarey and timeless stars Cary Grant and Irene Dunne are virtually without peer in handling sparkling dialogue. Even when they're actively destroying each other's lives in bouts of schadenfreude, they're entertaining—and the characters (embodying 1930s Hollywood's excellent idea of a healthy marriage) are just as addictively entertaining to each other, as well. This isn't the choice for couples who want to moon at each other over candlelight, but if you've seen enough road to find laughs at each other's expense, it's essential viewing.

The Prisoner of Zenda **(1937)** Based on the fin de siècle swashbuckler by Anthony Hope, this is a stirring tale of adventure, old-world intrigue, and love. Our hero is Rudolf Rassendyll (Ronald Colman, at his Colmanest), a cheerful Englishman on a fishing holiday in the fictional kingdom of Ruritania, where he encounters the king, to whom he bears an uncanny resemblance, the evening before the coronation. The king is kidnapped by his evil half brother, Black Michael, (played with perfect malevolence by just whom you'd expect, Raymond Massey) and Rudolf is pressed into nobly masquerading as the king to prevent Michael from taking the throne. The good news is the king is engaged to marry the flawless beauty Princess Flavia (Madeleine Carroll); the bad news is she hates the king—until now. It's amazing how the filmmakers managed to make Colman shake hands with himself in low-tech 1937, but even so, the whole ornate shebang is almost stolen by Douglas Fairbanks Jr. as the most irrepressible henchman of all time, Rupert of Hentzau. Swordplay *and* love scenes, spry villain banter *and* heartbreaking true love. Watch with wine.

My Favorite Wife **(1940)** Cary Grant, Irene Dunne, and Leo McCarey again (he cowrote the original story), contemplating the fact that in all but the newest of marriages, there comes a time when you will likely contemplate losing your spouse to tragedy and having to find a replacement. Imagine, for example, that your wife is lost at sea in a shipwreck and presumed dead. Now, years later, you've just married the trophy wife you've always longed for—only to discover that wife number one had been stranded on a desert island all this time and is very much alive. Of course it all comes out in the wash, because it's Grant and Dunne, and it's painfully clear that no matter how much they lie, connive, and needle each other, any other spouse is a poor second choice.

Mr. & Mrs. Smith **(1941)** Every pair of married lovebirds has to ask: if you had to do it all over, would you get married again? The luminescent Carole Lombard asks Robert Montgomery that very question and he responds "no," leaving us all to wonder if his eyes, brain, and loins are still in functioning order. It turns out that a paperwork glitch grants him his wish—they're not legally wed after all, and Carole hands him his hat in high dudgeon, giving him no choice but to woo her back. It certainly seems improbable that this marital conundrum is brought to you by cynical master Alfred Hitchcock, but we should be so lucky as to still have romantic comedies like this: you haven't seen anything until you've seen Montgomery try to punch himself in the nose, or Lombard handle acres of prime slapstick dialogue with the fierce energy of a tornado. A caveat: this is an anniversary movie only for those who would answer that question—"Would you marry me all over again?"—with an emphatic *yes*. Otherwise, your yearly celebration of conjugal bliss might end in separate bedroom assignments.

The Enchanted Cottage **(1945)** The second film version of Arthur Pinero's Victorian play about a plain-Jane maid (Dorothy McGuire) and a scarred World War I vet (Robert Young) who meet and bond in a fairy-tale villa, growing more beautiful to each other while remaining ugly to the world. Cornball with a capital C, so let your guard down.

The Ghost and Mrs. Muir **(1947)** Gene Tierney, that most self-possessed and honey-voiced of 1940s stars, buys an old house and discovers that it's haunted by Rex

Harrison's dead old sea captain. Decades of respectful, loving repartee ensue—no Hollywood film makes a sweeter case for growing old in good company.

FAMILY REUNION

"You gotta laugh, ain't ya, sweetheart? Else you'd cry."
—Brenda Blethyn, *Secrets & Lies*

There's no summarizing this chaotic occasion; each get-together is as daffy, eccentric, infantile, maddening, surreal, and full of misunderstandings and resentments as the particular family involved—only times ten, because everybody's trapped in one place together. Insofar as a movie can help, you'll probably need all the sympathy and corroboration you can get.

III

***You Can't Take It with You* (1938)** Imagine if *all* your relations were complete eccentrics—and you had to mix them with your beloved's stuffy clan, like combustible substances meeting over dinner. George S. Kaufman and Moss Hart's supremely larky play won a Pulitzer, and Frank Capra's film won a Best Picture Oscar, but something tells us you had to be there, in the 1930s, to appreciate this stagy, singsong fluff. Still, the cast is rich stuff, beginning with James Stewart and Jean Arthur as the kids in love; Lionel Barrymore, Spring Byington, Ann Miller, Mischa Auer, Dub Taylor, and Samuel S. Hinds fill out the tax-evading, semidelusional, near-anarchist Sycamore tribe.

***Fists in the Pocket* (1965)** Marco Bellocchio's famous first film—about an Italian family self-cannibalized by psychosis, epilepsy, decaying aristocratic privilege, and murder—could make anyone's family look even-tempered and loving. As the "hero" plagued by manic-depression and homicidal quirkiness, Lou Castel is unforgettable.

***Secrets & Lies* (1996)** Englishman Mike Leigh's films, though often comedies, are never optimistic about the amount of emotional damage families can and will inflict on themselves, and this Oscar-nominated mini-epic might be his definitive statement on the matter. A portrait of a decimated British working-class family on its way down the crapper, the movie revolves around a well-off portrait photographer (Timothy Spall), and his middle-aged sister Cynthia (the incendiary Brenda Blethyn), the family's crucible, and an aging, dim-witted slut with a grown daughter no one's sure who fathered (Claire Rushbrook). The dung starts hitting the proverbial fan when a modest, intelligent young black woman (Marianne Jean-Baptiste) discovers through an adoption agency that Cynthia is her birth mother, and contacts her. The characters are genuine, and so sharply realized they cut like knives. People in Leigh's films simply don't behave like other movie characters—they are, only and completely, themselves, not types or ideas created to serve the story. (Leigh notoriously begins his moviemaking process with the actors and characters, and then develops a script.) You can't not find them convincing, and you'll have to admit that your family is at least in better shape than this crew.

The Celebration (1998) The first true "Dogme 95" movie—which means it was made according to the Danish filmmaker cabal's rules of production "chastity," including being shot with handheld cameras, with fidelity to the location, and with natural light, and without unrealistic indulgences like sets, soundtrack music, and postproduction tinkering—Thomas Vinterberg's Scanda-Gothic seems to have been filmed by a stoned documentary camera crew, and the effect borders on the queasily threatening. When you can make out the characters in the underlit video haze, they're a riveting crew, a large and wealthy Dutch hotel family attending an annual party for the patriarch's birthday. Of course, the closets are opened, the vicious family secrets come tumbling out, ghosts are detected, and roles are switched, and it's all supremely hilarious, appalling, and alarming.

The Family Stone (2005) Bringing your partner home to meet your parents is intimidating enough without the newbie being as high-strung and bigmouthed as Sarah Jessica Parker (who wears stiff buns and sensible suits to let you know how uptight she is), and without your large clan being as relentlessly sarcastic, tough-skinned, and scriptwriter-clever as this one. Tragedy eventually strikes, too, as if Parker's performance wasn't enough. But irate prodigal Dermot Mulroney, the faintly crispy Luke Wilson, and matriarch Diane Keaton are fine.

Junebug (2005) An impeccable and eccentric indie for anyone who's fled small-town life. Going home is often fraught with land mines; here, Alessandro Nivola goes home to his North Carolinian white-trash family, with his new, British art-dealer wife (Embeth Davidtz) in tow. The point of view is hers, however, and the cheap notion that small-town folks are simple doesn't play here: relationships are complicated and much is left unsaid. Dry and charming, the film is lit at its center by Amy Adams, as the huge-hearted pregnant sister-in-law, whose performance netted her an Oscar nomination.

NEW HOUSE

"I refuse to endanger the health of my children in a house with less than three bathrooms."
—Myrna Loy, *Mr. Blandings Builds His Dream House*

Another milestone on most of our American pathways: the insane spend-orgy and debt-nightmare of purchasing a home. The cocktail of dread and elation can be dizzying, and the movies know it.

The Uninvited **(1944)** Discovering that you've bought a haunted house is rotten luck, especially when it's this kind of wonderful, a British manse on a seaside cliff with windows and trim to die for. Ray Milland and Ruth Hussey are the brother-sister owners (was this not unusual in the '40s?), and Gail Russell is the neighbor girl/daughter of the old owners, who seems to be quite haunted herself. If your new pipes rattle in the night, remember: it's still better than a weeping disembodied voice.

Mr. Blandings Builds His Dream House **(1948)** This movie examines a postwar experience that was common to a large class of Americans—the swapping out of a cramped city apartment for the creation of a modern home from scratch. (That particular concept had never been seen as the viable basis for a comedy before the vets came home.) The glory of the film is all in the details—the lally columns and lintels and cement and water purifiers; Cary Grant suffering like a city boy in the wilderness; Myrna Loy providing balance and succor; and Melvyn Douglas chipping in with color commentary.

The Amityville Horror **(1979)** The infamous schlockfest, multisequeled and already remade for the new millennium, may be the ultimate new-house bad dream: you move in, clouds of flies invade, red-eyed pigs peer out of second-floor windows, Rod Steiger overacts as a priest, and Daddy (James Brolin) slowly becomes a little too fond of his ax. There's a happy ending; it's all complete hogwash, and not even very scary.

The Money Pit **(1986)** Essentially a remake of *Mr. Blandings Builds His Dream House*, but with Tom Hanks, a bigger budget, and a deeper hunger for pratfalls and unbelievable happenstance.

Beetlejuice **(1988)** Tim Burton's breakout film, but it's Michael Keaton's as well; his indecipherable, foul-minded minighost is a bizarre creation that never gets old. And it's all keyed to the love of a particular *This Old House*–ish Victorian, which ardent owners Geena Davis and Alec Baldwin lavish with attention until they die—and after. The now-ghostly couple takes up residence in the attic to try to fend off the pretentious new owners, with the help of Keaton's otherworldly lowlife.

The 'Burbs (1989) In this goosey Joe Dante comedy, the new home owners are the secret, creepy, seemingly devolved family on the suburban block, of whom everyone, including vacationing stress case Tom Hanks, is alarmingly suspicious. A view from the other side, ramped up like a silly campfire story.

Howards End (1992) This Merchant-Ivory melodrama, based on E. M. Forster's novel, involves itself grandly with love and class and fate, but a lot of it is about *that house*, a modest English cottage that the characters cannot stop talking about, wrestling over, and betraying each other for. It doesn't look like much, but it generates a lot of feeling.

SATURDAY EVENING WITH NO BABYSITTER

"Pay no attention to that man behind the curtain."
—Frank Morgan, *The Wizard of Oz*

It's a common dilemma: what to rent that would captivate kids without nauseating (or at least anesthetizing) parents? When you're done with the Pixar catalog, these semiforgotten stalwarts can repair a collapsing weekend.

Sherlock Jr. (1924) This majestic masterwork—all of forty-four minutes—abounds with buoyant resilience and forward-looking esprit. Simply put, Buster Keaton is a lovelorn projectionist who dreams himself, as a master detective, into the film he's showing. There's no *not* being seduced by Keaton's laconic shenanigans and eye-popping stunts. But this film has also been roundly acclaimed as one of the wisest and savviest ever made about our relationship with movies. There isn't a wasted minute, an unfunny gag, or an ounce of fat.

The Gold Rush (1925) Even to Keatonians like us, this is perhaps Charlie Chaplin's greatest claim to posterity—a streamlined (and relatively unmawkish) litany of classic gags, all centered in the precivilized Yukon.

The Gaucho (1927) Herein we have the infectious, bounding élan of Douglas Fairbanks, cinema's first embodiment of an all-male life force: tireless, lusty, irreverent, peerlessly athletic, and bursting with robust happiness. No wonder he was a star in movie's infancy, for the young and old and in-between—who *wouldn't* want to be Doug Fairbanks? (Except, of course, those who just wanted him, period.) This silly adventure movie, in which Fairbanks plays a lovable outlaw battling evil colonial forces in Argentina, is more or less identical to most of his other films; the other home runs are *Robin Hood* (1922), *Don Q, Son of Zorro* (1925), and *The Black Pirate* (1926).

Our Gang/Little Rascals shorts (1929–1938) Rough-hewn but brilliantly funny and captivatingly spontaneous, these seminal Hal Roach comedies will be a rapturous flashback for parents who remember seeing them rerun on local TV in the 1970s and early '80s, but anyone, regardless of age, will find them irresistible. The year span noted here is not arbitrary—after 1938, Spanky McFarland got too close to puberty, and the 1940s shorts were just not in the same class.

David Copperfield (1935) Dickens done by early Hollywood, and the results are rickety but, thanks to the best character actors money could buy at the time, enthralling all around, from Freddie Bartholomew's David to Basil Rathbone's Murdstone, Edna May Oliver's Aunt Betsy, Lionel Barrymore's Dan Peggotty, and Roland Young's Uriah Heep to W. C. Fields's magnificent Micawber. Might just get vulnerable grade-schoolers reading.

Captains Courageous (1937) Today's overindulged children may have a little too much in common with Freddie Bartholomew's Harvey, the intolerable tycoon's son who irresponsibly falls overboard and is rescued by fisherman Spencer Tracy, wearing a Harpo-style 'do and spouting sea-related homilies in a mockable Portuguese accent. Those details are easy to overlook, though, once you're in the grip of the enthralling Rudyard Kipling tale (which, incidentally, seeks to entertain far more than preach). Although Tracy won a Best Actor Oscar, the film is really an ensemble piece (with Melvyn Douglas, John Carradine, and a young Mickey Rooney) that's almost stolen by the great gruff Lionel Barrymore.

Gulliver's Travels (1939) Dave and Max Fleischer, masters of Popeye and Betty Boop, attempted to rival Walt Disney by animating only one branch of Jonathan Swift's political satire: Gulliver's awakening and adventure in Lilliput. The satire was discarded, and a simplistic romance and parental feud story took its place: the kingdoms of Lilliput and Blefuscu wage war over the choice of a wedding song. The animation is easy to appreciate for its very distinct Fleischer style—crazier and more surreal than Disney's—that hero includes a fully rotoscoped Gulliver, who swats away Lilliputian arrows with a gentle sweep. An effective antiwar statement on top of it all, the film will certainly add to a child's cultural knowledge in ways that *The Lion King* never will.

The Wizard of Oz (1939) No introduction needed, except to say that this gorgeous, emotional standard text used to be an annual television ritual, but now might need to be discovered by a new generation of kids otherwise bedazzled only by the likes of SpongeBob and Pokémon.

The Blue Bird (1940) Perhaps this big-budget Hollywood adaptation of Maurice Maeterlinck's play *was* only an effort to ride the projected box-office wake of 1939's much-anticipated *The Wizard of Oz* (itself an attempt to cash in on the success of Disney's 1937 *Snow White and the Seven Dwarfs*), using a near-puberty Shirley Temple after she lost the role of Dorothy. But it's a vivid, strange, underrated fairy-tale journey, climaxing in a geyser of tears with the Land of the Unborn, in the Kingdom of the Future. The silent 1918 version is fine, too, in a creaky, musty way, but the modernized, Technicolor world created in this angsty Twentieth Century Fox production will keep the kids agog.

Meet Me in St. Louis (1944) This sly, sweet, intoxicating classic runs through an entire year, from summer to an atmospheric fall to a heartbreaking Christmas to a rejuvenating springtime, making Vincente Minnelli's musical version of Sally Benson's bestseller an endlessly rewatchable experience. Possibly the most likable family musical in Hollywood's annals, and one with enough character, comedy, and bounce to keep everyone glued to the screen.

Singin' in the Rain (1952) This well-worn musical has become an American favorite (although it won no Oscars and enjoyed only limited success when it was first released). It runs on a full tank of petrol from beginning to end, and the humor and energy (or mugging and hyperactivity, depending on your sensibility) spans the generations better than most films from that era. The Hollywood satire will fly past the young 'uns, but Donald O'Connor and Jean Hagen, overcooking their roles with tireless zest, will not.

The 5,000 Fingers of Dr. T (1953) A rare piece of out-and-out Hollywood dadaism, adapted from Dr. Seuss and seething with abstract craziness and menace as seen from a kid's point of view. Children will identify with the story, about a boy's hyperactive, imaginative dread of his evil piano teacher (Hans Conried), while adults will gasp incredulously at the movie's symbolic excesses.

Shane (1953) The one western that will still hypnotize any eight-year-old, this film has a narrative gravity and iconic simplicity to it that grown-ups can interpret as either mythic or pretentious; the choice is theirs. The tale of good and evil features laconic Alan Ladd, perky brat Brandon De Wilde, and ultravillain Jack Palance. And visually it's a feast.

20,000 Leagues Under the Sea (1954) This blubbery Disney version of the Jules Verne phantasm is equal parts matinee rowdiness and knowing camp. If the mock-ups of Captain Nemo's submarine, the *Nautilus*, and a wild giant squid don't do it for you, Kirk Douglas's singing might.

Star Wars (1977) We know, no one needs to be reminded that children love this movie. If your own kids haven't yet experienced it, go ahead and show it to them; they will be ridiculously grateful. Just keep in mind that you'll start an avalanche you may not want to endure yourself: the first sequel, *The Empire Strikes Back* (1980), is rousing and fun, but the next four movies are slogs.

The Black Stallion (1979) Horses are just the MacGuffin here; the real subjects are boyhood, nature, and memory. More grandeur per foot of film than any other five G-rated films put together. (See "The Triple Crown," p. 108.)

Time Bandits (1981) Ex–Monty Pythonite Terry Gilliam's second solo feature is a nutty, sui generis fantasy-comedy crack-up about a rebel band of time-traveling dwarves bouncing through history (both documented and completely nonsensical). The rambunctious journey is made possible by a certain time-portal map desired by both the underworldly Evil Genius (David Warner) and the beneficent Supreme Being (Ralph Richardson). With tons of in-jokes, pratfalls, cameos, wondrous fantasy ideas, and Pythonesque surrealism, it's quite lovable and inventive in ways that Gilliam's subsequent films haven't managed; kudos to John Cleese as a clueless Robin Hood, and David Rappaport as the leader of the pint-sized insurrectionists.

The Secret of NIMH (1982) A proto-Disney cartoon fable that's many times nastier and more imaginative than any Disney film, this darkling tale involves a mother mouse trying to save her sick, unmovable child before the reaping machines come. She nervously seeks counsel from a great horned owl (voiced, unforgettably, by John Carradine) and eventually enlists the aid of a secret race of intelligent rats, mutated from experiments conducted at the titular research institution. Entwined narratively and visually with the anxious work of the season, the movie manages epic melodrama on a minuscule scale.

Who Framed Roger Rabbit (1988) Nobody remembers or remarks on this hybrid blockbuster much anymore, but its deranged conceit—that in a noirish version of reality, the cartoon characters we've come to know and love (including those of Disney, Warner Brothers, and other animation studios) all work as exploited Hollywood talent and occupy a scary ghetto on the edge of town, where virtually anything can happen—remains fascinating. Bob Hoskins is the shamus tracking a criminal plot, and Kathleen Turner voices a voluptuous animated vamp.

Dick Tracy (1990) Warren Beatty directed this big-budget version of the Chester Gould comic strip as a run-amuck circus, a neon-hued hyper-comic (much more hyperbolic than Gould's originals) in which the busy cast (including Al Pacino, Madonna, Dustin Hoffman, and virtually every character actor Beatty has worked with in his entire career) and the whole-hog cinematography and design crews vie for the Most Over the Top trophy.

The Iron Giant (1999) Adapted from the fantasy tale that poet Ted Hughes wrote for his children after their mother, Sylvia Plath, killed herself, this splendid Brad Bird feature is as visually arresting as it is a potent skewer through 1950s Cold War anxieties and arms-race paranoia. The climax, involving an errant nuclear missile, the naive alien robot of the title, and a single inspiring memory of *Superman* comic books, is a throat-catching marvel.

Looney Tunes: Back in Action (2003) Kids always appreciate seeing cartoon characters mingle with humans (in this case, Brendan Fraser and Jenna Elfman), but for the adults, this Joe Dante film is a torpedo of in-jokes, film-geek allusions, and double entendres. Dante's the only man standing who had the history and the true cartoon sensibility to revivify Daffy, Bugs, and the rest of the gang in the old style—albeit without the voice talent of the late Mel Blanc, of course. (It's also a breath of fresh air to see a road trip movie that features, not a vintage Caddy, but a humble, ailing Gremlin.) Unfortunately, this film bombed at the box office, and the planned production on a new line of Looney Tunes cartoons was canceled.

Harry Potter and the Prisoner of Azkaban (2004) It's impossible to talk about movies that bridge the parent-child gap without mentioning the Harry Potter epics, which are, of course, first and foremost a literary phenomenon. Appealing to parents almost as much as to kids, the books—and their subsequent movie adaptations—have given the generations something to obsess about together. The best of the four movies to date is Alfonso Cuarón's *Harry Potter and the Prisoner of Azkaban,* which evokes a truly sinister atmosphere and features plenty of Mike Leigh alums (among them Gary Oldman and David Thewlis). In case you've been marooned on a desert island since 1998, Harry Potter is a British orphan who discovers he's a wizard, and attends Hogwarts School of Witchcraft and Wizardry to learn how to do magic properly and to overthrow the evil Lord Voldemort. **Harry Potter and the Sorcerer's Stone (2001)** was the introductory cinematic glimpse into J. K. Rowling's universe; although it's something of a lumbering blockbuster, there's a certain amount of, well, magic to it, particularly in the first third of the film. The second installment, **Harry Potter and The Chamber of Secrets (2002)**, and the fourth, **Harry Potter and the Goblet of Fire (2005)** are reflexive choices, too, if you and your offspring are fans of the books. Don't be misled by the marketing, though; even *Chamber of Secrets,* the silliest in the series, is not meant for the kindergarten set. (Be forewarned, in particular, that *Sorcerer's Stone* contains the single creepiest image found in any of these four films; you should definitely judge your child's "scare factor" before you pop it in.)

GETTING A PET

"Some animals are more equal than others."
—Patrick Stewart, *Animal Farm* (1999)

Look no further than the movies for affirmation that a pet—be it a dog, cat, anaconda, or hermit crab—can be a crucial matter of happiness, childhood, personal peace, and, sometimes, life and death.

III

Lassie Come Home **(1943)** The first of countless movies and TV series starring the world's most famous and faithful collie, who refuses to miss her four o'clock appointment at the school yard to meet her Yorkshire lad (Roddy McDowall), no matter how many fences, hills, rivers, or miles separate them. Surely the greatest testimony ever to the devotion of dogs, this is a family movie that makes you wish Hollywood still made them like this: no wisecracking kids, no bathroom humor, no cursing to draw in the older set. Yet even today's kids will be sucked in. The toughest con on Rikers Island would be unable to stem a rolling tear at the end, as Lassie limps her way home to her beloved boy.

Lady and the Tramp **(1955)** No other animal has evidenced such loyalty to people as a dog, who will eagerly wait for you to get home from the minute you take your first step toward the door to leave. No wonder *Lady and the Tramp* has found a soft spot in the hearts of Americans—especially the grown-ups who remember seeing it in air-conditioned movie theaters as a summer matinee. The movements of the film's canine characters are superbly observed in ways that anthropomorphized cartoons have long forgotten, and their vivid personalities, especially those of the residents of the dog pound, are memorable. Someone in our house has, ahem, been waiting twenty years and twenty Christmases for a hatbox with a puppy inside; annual viewings of this, the most endearing and mature of all Disney films, have had to suffice.

101 Dalmatians **(1961)** In this, Disney's biggest ticket-seller ever, dalmatians and people live in peaceful coexistence in a heaven-sent cartoon England, a covert society of domesticated animals secretly acts to save kidnapped puppies, and the most memorable human is the strident, tobacco-hoarse, floridly decadent dog-skinner Cruella De Vil. Physiologically, the antics of the puppies are on the money: look at the way these hounds move, then compare that to something more recent, like 1988's *Oliver and Company,* in which dogs magically spring onto the tops of taxicabs. The 1996 live-action remake of this film, in which the real doggies have no voices, is a poor substitute.

Doctor Dolittle **(1967)** Possibly the most ridiculous Best Picture Oscar nomination ever, this family film is clogged with barely trained wildlife that crowds obliviously around

Rex Harrison, as the doctor who *says* he can speak the language of beasts, whom we never hear talk back. If you consider the possibility that he's delusional, and that this virtually plotless musical is secretly a kind of schizo comedy, it might be fun.

***The Black Stallion* (1979)** A boy, a horse, and a desert island, breathtakingly photographed. (See "The Triple Crown," p. 108.)

***Cujo* (1983)** Saint Bernards are scary in real life because of their size, but on film? This 1980s thriller is more reflective of an ardent pet owner's point of view—the monster of a cuddly pooch appears huggable to us even as it's obviously a rabid behemoth to the movie's cast (led by Dee Wallace).

***Max Mon Amour* (1986)** A transgressive semicomedy in which a diplomat's wife (Charlotte Rampling) takes a lover, which is only the smallest hurdle for distraught hubby Anthony Higgins, because the *amour* in question is a full-grown chimpanzee. (The animatronic makeup is surreal.) Bestiality eventually becomes a secondary issue as well; it's all about intimacy and estrangement. Directed by Japanese troublemaker Nagisa Oshima, the man who made the first art film that featured graphic sex, 1976's *In the Realm of the Senses*. *Max* has none, thank goodness.

***Ace Ventura: Pet Detective* (1994)** The Book of Exodus movie of modern pet obsession, complete with a Moses: Jim Carrey's otherworldly, Dolittle-like animal shamus, conceived as a fully formed textual glitch thrust into the center of an otherwise normal movie world. Inhabiting a silly plot in which he must investigate the kidnapping of the Miami Dolphins' mascot dolphin, the TV-distorted Carrey suggests a well-scrubbed sportscaster possessed by Daffy Duck. In any case, the movie's a passionate paean to pet-ness.

***Babe* (1995)** Conforming to the dog lover's premise that dogs are the only *real* pets and all others are just "practice," this wacky Aussie fairy tale features a good-hearted piglet who goes canine as he strives to become useful. It's a concept that makes for a gentler admonishment of the unfairness of class systems than that espoused in *Animal Farm*, but it's certainly a much more humorous one. A completely endearing movie, *Babe* was the sleeper hit of 1995, garnering seven Academy Award nominations (including one for Best Picture—think on that for a moment) and winning the Oscar for Best Visual Effects (a mix of digitals and Jim Henson's Creature Shop animatronics).

***Balto* (1995)** The story of the first Iditarod, which of course in 1925 wasn't a race but a cross-country run, made by dogsled, to deliver diphtheria serum to patients in Nome, Alaska. Actually, this cartoon extrapolates a cockamamie fairy tale in which the heroic team-leader dog of the title is sabotaged by another dog and ends up delivering the medicine all by himself, climbing out of canyons, and so forth. That the animals talk doesn't help. Still, it's a stirring story, with a lovely live-actor coda.

***Dr. Dolittle* (1998)** Eddie Murphy modernizes the limp Disney staple, as a vet who can hear the chitchat of the beasts. We hear them, too: Norm MacDonald's mutt, John Leguizamo's rat, Albert Brooks's tiger, Gilbert Gottfried's OCD-afflicted hound, Chris Rock's guinea pig, and others snap quips and revel in excrement jokes.

***Animal Farm* (1999)** This Turner Network Television production of George Orwell's ubiquitous Stalinist parable is something of a world-beater: using both real farm animals and the Jim Henson's Creature Shop trickery employed in 1995's *Babe*, it easily beats out the lame 1955 cartoon version (which may owe its dire state to the recently reported fact that it was actually secretly produced by the CIA—no kidding!—which watered down its anticapitalist statements). Unfortunately, it comes with a glorifying procapitalism ending that Orwell surely would've choked on.

***Best in Show* (2000)** Directing in mock-documentary mode and allowing his handpicked cast to improvise the script, director Christopher Guest rakes through the absurdities of dog show culture. There's no shortage of hilarious caricatures of obsessive dog nuts (portrayed by the dazzling likes of Guest, Eugene Levy, Catherine O'Hara, Parker Posey, John Michael Higgins, and Jane Lynch, among others), and the filmmaker lashes the inhabitants of this peculiar world with their own self-absorbed idiocies—but there's also a strong feeling for the human-pet bond. Fred Willard, as a Joe Garagiola–style announcer who knows little about dog shows, virtually steals the movie.

***Cats & Dogs* (2001)** In the vein of *Toy Story*, this CGI-abetted fantasy suggests that under our oblivious noses, the world's dogs and cats have been waging an age-old covert war against each other, complete with secret cave headquarters, laser technology, espionage, air attacks, and parachuting ninja cats in night-vision goggles. Rather clumsily handled, it's nevertheless ridiculously inventive, and it puts a clever twist on the *Dolittle* template: we may *imagine* we know what our pets are thinking when they look at us, but the truth is that they are actually keeping huge, menacing secrets.

***Willard* (2003)** An underrated nasty-giggle-fest, this remake of the awful 1971 hit presents the worst-possible-scenario case for getting too intimate with your animals (here, rats), and training them to do your enemies ill.

***Lassie* (2005)** This remake of the 1943 heart-tugger *Lassie Come Home* (see above), which revolves around a dog's fierce loyalty to her boy, provides the same ironclad guarantee to knead your tear ducts. Fairly faithful to the original story, but with a few revved-up liberties regarding Lassie's homecoming—which makes it a tad disappointing for those of us who know the *real* story.

***Wallace & Gromit: The Curse of the Were-Rabbit* (2005)** The all-Brit Aardman Animations boys hit a home run with this feature-length comedy, in which absentminded, cheese-loving inventor Wallace and his faithful, sensible dog Gromit endeavor to battle a local rabbit problem, with explodingly dreadful results. Directors Nick Park and Steve Box have superb timing, and the milieu is a gentle parody of rose-garden-and-manor England. Ralph Fiennes as a sniveling jerk of a hunter is the funniest voice-to-figure match in years. But it's Gromit, modern cinema's most heroic pooch, that shines.

NEW JOB

"I can sit here and do nothing as good as anybody."
—Parker Posey, *Clockwatchers*

Entering a place of employment for the first time can be scary, but fear is usually overruled by starry-eyed, "this job is gonna be great" optimism. The Movies say, *watch out*. Don't underestimate the jungle law at work.

III

The Bank Dick (1940) Perhaps W. C. Fields's masterwork, in which the unfocused, red-nosed layabout takes a job as a bank guard; the structural demands of employment only add to the Fields persona's already looming mountain of agitations. Brutally hilarious, especially if you, too, are pickled (on the job?!). Fields was easily the most despicable comic figure in Hollywood history, making dour jokes about his own alcoholic ruin, but that doesn't mean he didn't know what was funny.

The Man in the Gray Flannel Suit (1956) After World War II, Hollywood struggled—and only occasionally succeeded—to bring films down to earth for the exhausted and traumatized postwar audience. In this bestseller-derived drama, Gregory Peck plays a memory-haunted vet who returns to his suburban life and a new media PR job, only to struggle with the banality of corporate striving, with the ghosts of the war still impinging on his consciousness. It may be the first film to seriously weigh the difference between leading a happy life and succeeding in the business world—a common, if not easily dramatized, modern dilemma. Fredric March plays the hard-charging boss as if he's imagining the saddest future possible for *his* bank-exec vet character in 1946's *The Best Years of Our Lives*.

Blue Collar (1978) After establishing his credibility among the American disenfranchised with the screenplay for 1976's *Taxi Driver*, Paul Schrader directed this gritty, dyspeptic working-class ode about three poor autoworkers (Richard Pryor, Harvey Keitel, and Yaphet Kotto) who decide to rob their own corrupt union. Nothing good can come of the plan, of course. The 1970s recession looms over the story, reminding us of socioeconomic hardship in a way that is no longer allowed in Hollywood.

Wall Street (1987) Oliver Stone's strenuous depiction of the fast-paced stockbroker lifestyle is equal amounts pungent Reagan-era commentary and pure applesauce. In any case, it gets your blood pumping (in a "career as food chain" kind of way); just ignore a full 50 percent of the dialogue that Charlie Sheen is forced to utter, and 100 percent of Daryl Hannah's. Michael Douglas gets the best of Stone's dialogue; he landed an Oscar.

How to Get Ahead in Advertising (1989) Many jobs call for ethical compromise, and in this devilishly uncomfortable comedy, an adman's anxious doubts about his job manifest as a giant pimple on his shoulder. Soon enough, the zit sprouts eyes and a mouth, and begins persuading him toward new heights of capitalistic venality. As both perpetrator and victim, Richard E. Grant is a whirlwind of neurotic craziness.

Glengarry Glen Ross (1992) A scarring film version of David Mamet's play about the hermetic, dog-eat-dog brotherhood of cold-call real estate salesmen. The movie chronicles an eighteen-hour period in the lives of four small-time, old-fashioned lot hawkers—the sort famous for selling Florida swampland to unwary investors. (We never know whether or not the land the characters sell is legit; the point is, they don't care one way or the other.) James Foley's film catches this crowd at its prettiest: At the outset, company man Alec Baldwin gives them all one week to produce. To help motivate them, he offers an incentive program, in which the top seller gets a Cadillac; "Anybody want to see second prize? Second prize, a set of steak knives. Third prize is you're fired." Too-tan slickster Al Pacino, pathetic whiner Jack Lemmon, hothead Ed Harris, and befuddled family man Alan Arkin face the music in a grim, run-down office, and the way things play out is daunting. Mamet cast a cold eye on the adult workplace as a mercilessly Darwinian playground filled with bullies; it's the ineluctable expression of a free enterprise system devouring itself from the inside out, and anyone facing a new sales job should belly up and take his or her lumps. The minute-to-minute cold reality of the film makes it an indelible skid row chamber piece; who cares who wins the Caddy, if those guys will still be who they are in the end, and still have to work in that office?

Swimming with Sharks (1995) A starter job everyone wants: assistant to a big-deal movie studio executive. Too bad the boss in question is Kevin Spacey at his most half-lidded and megalomaniacal. Frank Whaley is the lackey, and violent vengeance is taken.

Clockwatchers (1998) Lisa Kudrow, Toni Collette, and Parker Posey are corporate temps in this mildly amusing farce about soul-depleting office life. It's rich in intention and wry details, but eventually it turns aimless.

Office Space (1999) A brilliantly unassuming comedy by *Beavis and Butt-head* creator Mike Judge. A stressed-out software drone (Ron Livingston) takes a hypnotic suggestion at its word and ceases to care about his job—doing it or keeping it or even showing up—a disorienting mode of behavior that's mistaken for self-directed confidence by the consultants who've been hired to determine who gets the ax. Although ignored upon its release, this has become the definitive white-collar movie of techno-era America. Gary Cole's smarmy manager, in particular, will leave a heel print on your brain.

Boiler Room (2000) A smart, snappy, and erudite poison-pen portrait of post-Reagan-era greed and entry-level salesmanship, Ben Younger's movie is on the mark about sales culture, masculine prerogative run amok, and capitalism—if only it didn't wimp out with a crime subplot that renders the sales-god ethos secondary. Still, here we have the worst-case scenario of being trained in the art of the merciless sell and of joining an obscure stock-selling rat pit with the ridiculous promise of big bucks hanging over your head. Anyone who's done time at the phones will recognize at least the first half of Younger's film as an authentic working-place hell on Earth. That is, unless you're *one of these guys*, in which case we can't help you.

Human Resources (2000) Laurent Cantet's first film presents a meaty interpersonal crisis for the modernized age of the MBA. A new biz-school grad (Jalil Lespert) returns to his hometown to take a managerial position at the factory where his father (Jean-Claude Vallod) has been working for thirty years. Once the layoffs begin, the bile between the generations begins to flow. Shot ultrarealistically, the movie makes for mesmerizing drama, all of it completely convincing.

Time Out (2001) Cantet's follow-up to *Human Resources* is even more dismaying—a man (Aurelien Recoing) who's been laid off from his consulting job tells his family he has taken a new position, then creeps through the French countryside on a perpetual "business trip" as he attempts to fathom who he really is. The pressure builds up behind the lies, and Cantet's movie ends up saying scary, formidable things about work, family, and a society in which we are defined by our jobs.

Secretary (2002) A troubled girl (Maggie Gyllenhaal), recently released from a mental hospital, lands a secretarial job with a very strange lawyer (James Spader), and gleefully dives in when their relationship slowly evolves into a sadomasochistic liaison. Based on a Mary Gaitskill story, the movie is largely buoyed above its murky perversions by Gyllenhaal, who seethes with conviction.

Workingman's Death (2005) Think you have it bad? Just watch this galling documentary about a handful of the worst livings to be made anywhere on Earth: hauling sulfur in Indonesia; scavenging coal in a condemned Ukrainian mine; selling and buying very fresh meat (some of which still moos) in an open-air Nigerian slaughterhouse; dismantling vast freighters with blow torches and saws on the shores of the Arabian Sea; and more. It's rubbernecking, but it could put things in perspective.

JURY DUTY

"Didja ever hear so much talk about nothing?"
—Jack Warden, *12 Angry Men*

There is rarely much to look forward to in regard to this time-consuming civic duty, but Hollywood has often made a white-knuckle dramatic feast of it; use these films to get your hopes up, or at least to get your antenna twitching for psychodrama and evidentiary disconnects.

***12 Angry Men* (1957)** This famous, play-based stunt was director Sidney Lumet's feature-film debut: a dozen jury members sweat it out in a hot deliberation chamber, deciding on what at first seems an open-and-shut case of urban patricide—until one liberal (Henry Fonda), unwilling to coast on assumptions, slowly turns the room around. It's all "man's man" acting, all the time; the fascinating ensemble cast's most memorable performances belong to Lee J. Cobb, as a rabid bigot, E. G. Marshall, as a conservative intellectual, Robert Webber, as a glib adman, Jack Warden, as a knee-jerk self-server, John Fiedler, as an open-eared nebbish, and Martin Balsam, as a jury captain who's out of his depth.

***Witness for the Prosecution* (1957)** Something of a courtroom-drama paradigm, this Agatha Christie–penned interrogation is an old-fashioned, murder-most-foul mystery; it's very British, and it's carried by Charles Laughton as a wickedly devious prosecutor.

***Anatomy of a Murder* (1959)** Otto Preminger's groundbreaking courtroom psychodrama turns a seamy Southern murder trial into a sweaty, rape-happy psycho circus. James Stewart is the least scrupulous defense attorney in film history, and George C. Scott (in his first-ever film performance) is his army-appointed, junkyard-dog opponent. Lee Remick is unforgettable as a black-eyed slattern whose violated, but incredibly questionable, virtue instigates the whole megillah. This standard-bearing courtroom drama never lets us off easy: here, the issue isn't so much about blood-soaked guilt as it is about the ways in which the system cuts so much slack to bottom-feeders and sociopaths. On this dark planet, justice is a moot point. This was one of the movies that helped shock-start the old Hollywood into what became the brazen American cinema of the 1960s and '70s, and it dates better than last year's Oscar winners.

***To Kill a Mockingbird* (1962)** Based on Harper Lee's novel (the recipient of one of the most famous "first book" Pulitzer prizes ever awarded and still a staple of high school curriculums, the book has never gone out of print), this film takes a hard look at the South in the 1930s. A black man is accused of raping a white woman, and, naturally (given the time and place), his guilt is viewed as a foregone conclusion by everyone—everyone, that is, but one man, played here with Oscar-winning dignity by Gregory Peck. As a courtroom drama, *Mockingbird* is enthralling: Peck's deliberate, calm defense is counterpoint to the seething histrionics of the rest of the characters, both black and white. But it's more than just a trial procedural: it's a tale of childhood disillusionment and enlightenment, and of a father who loves his children so much that he puts himself in jeopardy to demonstrate righteousness in a bigoted world.

...And Justice for All (1979) After the critical success of 1971's *The Hospital* and 1976's *Network*, director Norman Jewison and screenwriters Valerie Curtin and Barry Levinson decided that the modern criminal justice system needed a good satiric drubbing as well. This forgotten farce is sometimes too dark and unpleasant to be very funny—but that's to its credit, and for the most part it's a riot. A vibrantly young Al Pacino is an idealistic Baltimore lawyer who, among his many other cases (all of which are pushed by a rotten system into Absurdistan), is blackmailed into defending a psycho judge (John Forsythe) in a rape trial, and Christine Lahti turns in a smart and uniquely sexy performance that should've made her a star. This film is lacerating in a way that today's movies have forgotten how to be.

Absence of Malice (1981) There's no jury in this movie, and no real courtroom, either— just a scene of a judge and a court stenographer in an empty office. But what a scene it is—in it, Wilford Brimley takes no prisoners and shames veterans Sally Field and Paul Newman in what may well be the best one-off adjudicator performance in the history of cinema. Field is an earnest reporter who picks up a lead about mob son Newman's suspected illegal activities; problem is, he's completely innocent, and the collateral damage inflicted during Field's investigation ruins the lives of other innocent people. It's an examination of truth and morality that questions widely held principles about both, including whether reporters should become intimately involved with the subjects of their research (but who *wouldn't* get involved with Paul Newman?).

The Verdict (1982) Newman returns to the courtroom, this time as a lawyer, in this shadowy, brooding legal drama, in which an over-the-hill Boston alcoholic takes a medical malpractice suit to court in order to redeem himself and his career. A little formulaic, it turns out, in the Grisham style (before there was Grisham), and less gritty than one would've hoped. Even for director Sidney Lumet, the 1970s were over. Robust supporting players include James Mason, Charlotte Rampling, and Milo O'Shea as the judge.

The Juror (1996) Trash, really, but a movie aimed directly at jurors—at least, at jurors who can identify with single mom Demi Moore, who's serving on a mob trial and is, as a result, stalked by Alec Baldwin's sadistic hit man.

The Devil's Advocate (1997) Lawyers *are* evil, literally, in this serious pulp epic, wherein hotshot Keanu Reeves takes a high-profile job under Al Pacino's Mephistophelian master of the universe and slowly becomes aware that he has, in fact, sold his soul to the devil. Full of terrific New York ambience and great supporting performances, the movie is, underneath the wild thriller stuff, a tense and bright debate on the moral relativism at the heart of the justice system.

***Runaway Jury* (2003)** John Grisham's judicial fiction machine grinds on; if you enjoy the easy equations, legal curlicues, and moral simplicities, this double-crossing melo-drama could make your own jury duty routine a little more scintillating. As could ***The Firm* (1993)**, ***The Pelican Brief* (1993)**, ***The Client* (1994)**, ***The Chamber* (1996)**, ***The Rainmaker* (1997)**, and ***The Gingerbread Man* (1998)**.

DIVORCE

"There is no winning, only degrees of losing."
—Danny DeVito, *The War of the Roses*

A touchy category, but nonetheless a major life event for a substantial portion of the population—and how anyone chooses to weather and remember it is a matter for the individual to decide alone. How can movies help? They can make you cry when you otherwise wouldn't, make you laugh when you shouldn't, satisfy feelings of vengeance, contextualize your private hell within historical and social lines—it's your call. Whether you're furious, miserable, delighted to be free, or some confused morph of extremes, you'll find something here to suit your state of mind.

***The Private Life of Henry VIII* (1933)** A crotchety early talkie about history's most notorious serial divorcé, played with plummy brio by an Oscar-winning Charles Laughton. Good luck finding a worse husband (or ex-husband) figure in the entirety of movies. Merle Oberon and Elsa Lanchester flare briefly as two of the six wives.

***Dodsworth* (1936)** Based on Sinclair Lewis's novel, this drama focuses on a retired auto exec (Walter Huston, never showing off) who discovers, despite his goodwill and best efforts, that he has nothing in common with his banal, snobbish wife (Ruth Chatterton). The prospect of Mary Astor waiting in the wings only agitates the situation, which is executed with simple gravity and grown-up good taste.

***Suspicion* (1941)** To trust or not to trust—that is the *real* question. Joan Fontaine, still lost and unsure of herself after *Rebecca*, marries half-lidded hunk Cary Grant, and life becomes a half-hidden nightmare of possible lies, potential crimes, and circumstantial sin. Spoiler alert: in the end, Grant's ice man is revealed to be innocent (innocent, at least, of trying to push Fontaine's demure wife off a cliff), but don't believe it—during the film's production, the studio demanded a Grant-positive climax, so director Alfred Hitchcock reluctantly appeased them. Then again, maybe he didn't. It's a wonder Grant remained a star after playing this role; watch the movie, and you'll never trust him again.

***Double Indemnity* (1944)** Based on the seminal James M. Cain noir novel that spawned a billion "scheming bitch" thrillers, this expert Billy Wilder–directed night of the soul is all about a rich, spoiled California wife (Barbara Stanwyck) who hates her husband so much (but loves his money) that she arranges for Fred MacMurray's cynical insurance guy to kill the sop. Of course, that's not the limit of her depravity; no one is safe, least of all the horny jerk she roped in. As far as prenup advocacy goes, this film is the Book of Genesis.

***Gaslight* (1944)** A remake of a rarely seen 1940 British film of the same title, this Victorian suspense-fest positions naive maiden Ingrid Bergman in a new marriage with secretive cad Charles Boyer, who, it becomes apparent, is out to drive her mad. Boyer was hard to buy as a romantic lead after this film—he's that oily—but it's Bergman who won the Oscar. The term *gaslight*, meaning to compel mental instability in another by denying the obvious and making the victim second-guess everything he or she knows to be true, became a usable verb in the English-speaking world as a result of this film, and remains so today.

***Unfaithfully Yours* (1948)** A ray of hope, but one expressed with fanged smile: Preston Sturges's rapier-like farce is a study in lurking distrust, not infidelity. Rex Harrison is a brazen, wealthy, egomaniacal symphony conductor who is given cause (the hows and whys are what Sturges and his company of quirksome character actors are best at) to suspect his nubile American wife (Linda Darnell) of cheating. Half of the subsequent fallout plays out in the would-be cuckold's mind as he conducts three different pieces in front of a packed house, imagining three different homicidal scenarios. Sturges was the best dialogue writer in town, and the movie sparkles with sharp eloquence, as well as with a spirit of both brute folly and forgiveness.

***Voyage in Italy* (1953)** Ingrid Bergman left her first husband and children for Italian director Roberto Rossellini in 1949, so it was perhaps inevitable that Rossellini (always an interrogatory artist) would cast her in this introverted movie about a couple (Bergman and George Sanders) whose marriage silently implodes during an Italian holiday. Canonized by some; forgotten by most.

***Diabolique* (1954)** This French thriller quickly became, even more so than *Gaslight*, the movie paradigm of the gaslight phenomenon, by which the marriage between an evil lout and a fragile woman comes under fire from secret plots and manufactured intimations of madness. There's a triangle—wife Vera Clouzot, hubby Paul Meurisse, and lover Simone Signoret—but saying more would spoil your enjoyment (if it hasn't already been spoiled by the unnecessary 1996 remake).

Dial M for Murder **(1954)** Another marital murder scenario, played out in grimly plain style by Alfred Hitchcock in (for the most part) a single-room set, and featuring a very uncomfortable pair of scissors. Ray Milland is the slimy plotter, and there's little we can understand about him because he wants to kill Grace Kelly. Who would want to kill Grace Kelly?

The Tingler **(1959)** Like *House on Haunted Hill*, William Castle's other Vincent Price seether, this movie gets its narrative fuel from a marriage gone toxic, leading a hate-filled husband to do unimaginable things. (See "Halloween," p. 16.)

La Notte **(1961)** Italian existentialist Michelangelo Antonioni pares his despairing vision of relationships and love down to its essentials: a successful writer and his wife (Marcello Mastroianni and Jeanne Moreau) spend the whole film going to parties, meeting people, and flirting—neither of them quite realizing until the morning that their marriage is dead. That's it; as in a Raymond Carver story, the cataclysms are what's really happening underneath the trivia of modern life.

Contempt **(1963)** Easily meta-film master Jean-Luc Godard's most orthodox movie, this adaptation of Alberto Moravia's novel *A Ghost at Noon* does, nevertheless, subvert its own commerciality at every step, down to bathing Brigitte Bardot's nude scenes (which were dictated by the producer) in washes of primary color. On the surface it's a razor-sharp lampoon of international film productions just like this one (Jack Palance plays an idiotic Joseph E. Levine–ish producer who has a red Ferrari and a hair-trigger checkbook), but it's actually a doomed marital romance whose astounding key scene is a thirty-minute set piece involving two people alone in an apartment. Even when the characters speak the same language (which is hilariously infrequently) they cannot connect, and the marriage between a playwright (Michel Piccoli) and his too-young wife (Bardot) slowly crumbles like a burning house—but out of view and between the lines of dialogue. The cumulative impact is achingly, exquisitely sad in ways you never expect. The plaintive Georges Delerue score makes it hurt.

The Soft Skin **(1964)** Director François Truffaut turns a simple story of marital infidelity into a precise, grim suspense film—a well-known publisher (Jean Desailly) carries on an obsessive affair with a stewardess (Francoise Dorleac) and struggles against all odds to keep the relationship a secret from his wife and daughter. It's essentially a Cold War espionage thriller, but instead of the Western world being at stake, it's a conventional upper-middle-class home.

Who's Afraid of Virginia Woolf? **(1966)** The archetypal marriage-as-hell modernist play still packs a bruising punch in this unforgotten film version, with Elizabeth Taylor and Richard Burton allowing alcohol to reveal their union's festering sores, and George

Segal and Sandy Dennis as naive husband-and-wife witnesses subjected to brutal, whiskey-driven social pressure. If you envy others' domestic tranquility, step up and take a dose of disenchantment.

Rosemary's Baby (1968) Suspecting your spouse of ulterior motives and secret agendas is one thing, but here's the scale's farthest point—your husband is setting you up to be raped by Satan and to bear the Antichrist. As the hubby, John Cassavetes should set off the alarms right away (but then again, so do many nice women's real partners). He's *too* effective; imagine the visceral jolt we'd have gotten if Robert Redford, whom director Roman Polanski originally wanted for the role, had been cast.

The Honeymoon Killers (1970) A must-avoid scenario that, here, is graced with the authentic quality of a sweaty dream endured by clenching a mouthful of pillowcase. Based on the trial transcripts of the infamous 1950 "Lonely Hearts Club" murder case, Leonard Kastle's film recounts the exploits of porcine ex-nurse Martha Beck (Shirley Stoler) and seedy Spanish conman Raymond Fernandez (Tony LoBianco), who were convicted of murder and executed in Sing Sing after years of robbing lonely women they'd met through a correspondence club: with the pugnaciously jealous Beck posing as his sister, Fernandez would agree to marry each spinster or widow, and then make off with her cash. The tense hothouse psychodramas produced by the scams eventually resulted in the simple, ruthless disposal of the more recalcitrant victims.

An Unmarried Woman (1978) Paul Mazursky's late-coming feminist-movement anthem film, in which complacent wife and mother Erica (Jill Clayburgh) watches husband Martin (Michael Murphy) walk out on her (she vomits, actually), then struggles, in a man's world, to set herself straight without relying on a guy. Bursting with recognizable characters and scenarios—some truthful, some stereotypical.

The Woman Next Door (1981) Gérard Depardieu is a comfortable suburban dad whose world is rocked when a new couple moves in next door and he discovers that the wife (Fanny Ardant) used to be his lover. François Truffaut casts a hypnotic eye on the tension between sexual obsession and middle-class security—and on the suffering that results from it. This is one film that should be seen by every husband and wife *before* divorce proceedings begin.

Shoot the Moon (1982) A thorny character study of a husband (Albert Finney) at sea and torn between an unsatisfying affair and a wife (Diane Keaton) who's beyond bitter. One of the best Hollywood films of the 1980s, it deals with real people and the emotional chaos that real actions produce, and offers no easy answers.

Betrayal (1983) Another dissective play about marriage, this David Jones–directed Harold Pinter number traces the reverb on a tense relationship (between Ben Kingsley and Patricia Hodge) invaded by a friend/lover (Jeremy Irons), and it does so in reverse:

we open with a postmortem of the infidelity and trail backward through the years to its drunken point of origin. Acted within an inch of its life, the film is hypnotizing.

***Paris, Texas* (1984)** Marriage dissolution as existential parable: amnesiac Harry Dean Stanton wanders mutely out of the desert after some cataclysmic rupture—we learn what's happened only at the end of the movie, and it has to do with wife Nastassja Kinski. A great film from Wim Wenders, from an original script by Sam Shepard.

***Heartburn* (1986)** Based on Nora Ephron's roman à clef about her marriage to Carl Bernstein, this Mike Nichols–directed film comes equipped with Jack Nicholson as the philandering journalist-husband and Meryl Streep as the oblivious food-writer wife. Sadder than it is funny, it's also a cautionary tale: if you're going to cheat on your wife, be sure she's not a writer, or you may find your own career achievements overshadowed by a bare-all bestseller oozing with your boorishness.

***The War of the Roses* (1989)** A black comedy that takes a bitter divorce to the limits as the embattled couple arms to the teeth, each determined to hang onto the house they both dearly love. The plenitude of ripping satirical outrages may leave you feeling a little uneasy unless you, yourself, have a hankering to lock your ex in a sauna and turn up the heat, or indulge in any number of other sadistic, destructive revenge scenarios the film offers. Can't we just get along? Michael Douglas and Kathleen Turner pair up again, as if to suggest that this is what became of the happy, bickering twosome last seen frolicking at the end of 1985's *The Jewel of the Nile.*

***Husbands and Wives* (1992)** Woody Allen made this noncomedy as he was breaking up with Mia Farrow (while maintaining an affair with her adopted teenage daughter, remember), and the caustic script, in which Farrow's hapless wife is set adrift during a scattering of broken marriages, leaves a bad taste in the mouth. Take from it what you will, depending on your circumstances.

***La Séparation* (1994)** Christian Vincent's film about marital dissolution is mercilessly frank. At the same time, it picks no heroes or villains, and it draws no convenient conclusions. Based on an acclaimed novel, the movie opens as only a movie could: with an idyllic scene in which love-struck dad Pierre (Daniel Auteuil) videotapes his sleeping two-year-old son, getting close enough to the toddler to see his drool and hear him breathing, while narrating in a whisper. It's obvious right off the bat that Pierre and his unhappy wife Anne (Isabelle Huppert) share little, at this point, beyond their love for their son. Things escalate when Anne announces she's having an affair, and Pierre, thinking either that he can win her back by being understanding or that Anne's extramarital joy will ease the home's tensions, agrees to stay together as a couple. Because we are conditioned to want happy endings, we hope he will win her back, but Pierre is too angry, and even after Anne's protracted affair dissolves, the two continue to drift apart, leaving Pierre, for one, lost. The film is raw and real and electrifying, especially if it's territory you're familiar with or dread in your bones.

Dolores Claiborne (1995) Stephen King always appreciated the narrative idea of an abused woman finally picking up arms against her husband, and here his novel gets a long, too-respectful treatment—filled with good acting and menace, but not nearly nasty enough.

Lost Highway (1997) David Lynch takes on marriage—at least, on one of this movie's many levels. The first half of this prickly, violent, often sickening film is a chilling exploration of marital anxiety, in which suspicious jazz musician (and Lynch doppelganger) Bill Pullman and brunette-bewigged wife Patricia Arquette are "visited" in their L.A. apartment by an unknown force, which videotapes them as they sleep. (The tapes are left on their doorstep.) The druggy action is almost abstract—in one scene, Pullman discovers and wordlessly explores a secret room hiding in the shadows of his bedroom hallway—and is often horrifying. The suspicion that Arquette may be having an affair perverts the film's entire universe, down to the wicked confrontation at a party between Pullman and Robert Blake as a white-faced homunculi who insists he is in Pullman's apartment as they speak. In an incredibly powerful, dreamlike evocation of infidelity, Pullman calls home to verify, and it's true—or is it merely suspicion, or estrangement, or existential hunger? You decide.

Intolerable Cruelty (2003) In this saber-toothed Coen brothers satire, there are no limits to the damage married people will inflict on each other once the wheels of divorce are set in motion. The joke is that both marriage and divorce are both hypercapitalist business maneuvers, waged like a war in which all's fair, the wounded are shot, and spoils go to the happy victor. George Clooney is renowned divorce shark Miles Massey, whose cartoonishly mercenary tendencies find a worthy adversary not in opposing counsel, but in glamorous serial bride Marilyn Rexroth (Catherine Zeta-Jones). That they're soul mates in their take-all cynicism is the subtlest irony in this loud, brassy, wholly unsubtle movie; love and trust are impossible, but they can't help but be drawn to each other. It's a brutal portrait, and it may have cathartic powers, especially for men. (Clooney's character eventually grows genuinely earnest, but Zeta-Jones's whispery vampire remains a duplicitous double-crosser to the end.) Whatever: Clooney is a high-octane marvel; packing in a year's worth of comic tics and double takes into one performance, he makes viewer depression virtually impossible.

COMING OUT

"I really wanna kiss you, man."
—River Phoenix, *My Own Private Idaho*

A pivotal life moment if ever there was one, with no corollary among the experiences of the hetero majority. Resonant gay films are not huge in number, but the tradition is not new and the best of them have a universal relevance.

Michael (1924) This forgotten German Expressionist treasure by Carl Dreyer is as antiquated in its ideas about art and class as it is thoroughly twenty-first century in its subtle depiction of gay love. Cowritten by Mrs. Fritz Lang, Thea von Harbou, the film explores a tragic love triangle among a "master" artist (filmmaker Benjamin Christensen), his young model-boyfriend (an unrecognizable Walter Slezak), and a penniless Russian countess (Nora Gregor).

Mädchen in Uniform (1931) Made on the eve of Hitler's ascension to power, this powerful and sensitive early-talkie melodrama about a monstrously oppressive girls' school was banned in Germany for its overt depictions of lesbian love. Or was it because of how gay desire represented the only salvation in the face of militaristic dehumanization? Cowritten and directed by women (Christa Winsloe and Leontine Sagan, respectively), it's a forgotten breath-stealer.

Un Chant d'Amour (1950) This notorious semipornographic short, directed by budding writer and former crook Jean Genet, is a potent twenty-five minutes about men in prison. But it's euphoric—Genet converts the grim, deprivative lifestyle of the inmates into an achingly romantic tribulation, in which the walls and bars that separate his lonesome, lovelorn muscle men become the fetishized definition of their desire. Another avant-garde unmissable: Kenneth Anger's **Scorpio Rising (1964)**, a half-hour mood piece that essentially defined American gay iconography and nascent queer culture for several generations of horny guys.

Desert Hearts (1985) A modest, pure-hearted period indie in which a buttoned-down 1950s professor (Helen Shaver) goes to Nevada for a quickie divorce and ends up falling for a rancher's saucy daughter (Patricia Charbonneau). The convert-a-straight scenario, ripe as it is with dramatic discovery, has rarely been as convincing or sexy.

Maurice (1987) Edwardian England was not the best environment for letting your same-sex preference hang out, and this E. M. Forster adaptation is the *Brokeback Mountain* of snooty Brit-lit movies. (Unsurprisingly, the novel wasn't published until years after Forster's death.) Here, the mutual attraction between two upper-class students (Hugh Grant and James Wilby) is battered on the anvil of English propriety, leading one to tragically repress his true self in exchange for a "normal" social existence and the other to fall off the aristocratic grid by embracing his bliss.

My Own Private Idaho (1991) See "Road Trip," p. 267, and try not to dwell on the confluence between River Phoenix's tragic death and the lonesome, doomed odyssey of his street hustler in this film, a gay *Rebel Without a Cause* for the late twentieth century.

The Living End (1992) A road movie apotheosis: no one's ever had as much a reason to fuck the system (sometimes literally) and take off for the horizon as guerrilla director Gregg Araki's HIV-positive pair of hard-luck misfits (Craig Gilmore and Mike Dytri). *L'amour fou* is this crude indie's modus operandi—these guys can't keep their hands off each other—and Araki makes up for what his film lacks in technical polish with scads of attitude.

Happy Together (1997) Wong Kar-Wai's wall-climbing melodrama observes in typically Wongian fashion (poetically, lushly, fragmentedly) a hot sexual union between two men from Hong Kong (Leslie Cheung and Tony Leung) in the tropical skids of Buenos Aires. Desperate, sweaty, fatalistic, and ironic—what more could you want?

Brokeback Mountain (2005) Ang Lee adapted an E. Annie Proulx story into this perfectly conceived, hyperromantic tearjerker, a realist gut-punch that pits its closeted cowboy lovers (Heath Ledger and Jake Gyllenhaal) against society in a way that movies usually reserve for interethnic pairings—they're a virtual Tristan and Isolde. Despite being notoriously frank about man sex, the movie pays off with the most genuine and gracefully executed heartbreak of any American film of its decade.

GRIEVING

"We're all citizens of a different town now, a place with its own special rules and its own special laws."
—Sarah Polley, *The Sweet Hereafter*

We're not suggesting that movies should be a major part of anyone's grieving process—and in any case, most of these wrenchingly sad films should be treated carefully, like isotopes, by anyone whose wounds have not begun to heal. But eventually, maybe, a serious film can serve the same purpose as a great novel: to let you see your experiences reflected in a world that has been broken, too—and healed itself.

The Crowd (1928) King Vidor's silent masterpiece chronicles the experience of an ordinary urban man—something of a Hollywood first—from his first New York job to the tragedy of his sudden death. Magisterially done, and without relying on dialogue.

Ikiru (1952) This Akira Kurosawa rite opens with the image of an X-ray; a narrator tells us that semicatatonic government clerk Watanabe (Takashi Shimura) has stomach cancer but doesn't know it yet. When we first see him (in a scene in which the narrator tells us that "it would be boring to talk about him now" because he is "barely alive") Watanabe is huddled within walls of moldering bureaucratic paperwork. Learning of his death sentence, Watanabe sheds the responsibilities of his life, but becomes even more miserable drinking and whoring; it's only when we're informed, halfway through the film, that the poor man has passed on that we begin to glimpse what happened next. Via flashbacks augmenting his coworkers' drunken debate during his wake, we find out that Watanabe spent his last months politically bulldozing through modern Japan's mountainous infrastructure—just to transform a public waste area into a usable playground. Mourning becomes a secondary concern; instead, the focus moves to the question (which both the deceased and his observers ponder) of how Watanabe made his life useful to others around him.

Hiroshima, Mon Amour (1959) Using a Marguerite Duras screenplay, New Wave metaman Alain Resnais had a big international hit with this brooding postwar art film, in which a Japanese man and a French woman have dreamy sex and talk about their mutually tragic pasts. She lost a lover in the Resistance; he lost his whole family at Hiroshima. Comparatively speaking, the film's emotional freight is too heavily invested in her relatively minor psychodrama. Nevertheless, the film is impassioned and glamorous, yet heartfelt and powerful.

Solaris (1972) Andrei Tarkovsky's most grounded film takes place, ironically, largely in space, aboard a semiderelict space station circling the titular planet, which has played some scary games with the minds of the station's crew. Sent to investigate, a psychologist (Donatas Banionis) is soon accompanied by a replica of his wife (Natalya Bondarchuk), who killed herself years before. Given a second chance, their relationship begins to spiral toward the same sad end. The badly missed metaphysical master of the 1960s Soviet "thaw," Tarkovsky was no pulpster, and *Solaris* is a long, soulful, funereal mystery, with fascinating images and a central conundrum derived as much from basic existential questions as from sci-fi writer Stanislaw Lem's more theoretical novel.

Grave of the Fireflies (1988) A Japanese anime for those of us who have no normal use for the genre, Isao Takahata's tribulation of a movie follows two orphaned children trying to survive in wartime Japan after the Americans firebomb their town. That it's a cartoon might suggest to you that the film is, by nature, an unaffecting exercise, but this is an intensely poetic piece of work that can run over you like a tank, and since it's based on a semiautobiographical novel, there's never a doubt that it's earned its ferocity. Produced by Hayao Miyazaki's acclaimed Studio Ghibli, and the care shows.

Men Don't Leave (1989) Fleshing out a grown-up, uplifting vibe in the mourning process that says "it's time to move on," this Paul *"Risky Business"* Brickman drama has Jessica Lange's soft-spoken widow Beth weather attempts, by her children and a quirky neighbor, to help her get back to the business of living. The give-and-take is sweet and genuine; the real gut-wrenching scenes—spoiler alert—are reserved for the youngest son (Charlie Korsmo), who must deal with the loss of his father via an unfinished tree house.

Olivier, Olivier (1992) Polish writer/director Angieszka Holland's mastery peaked, before she came to Hollywood and made *The Secret Garden*, with this emotional mystery about the loss of a child. Such a fate devastates a French family when their nine-year-old son vanishes. Six years later, a gawky but beautiful teenager (Grégoire Colin) enters the picture, claiming to be the long-lost boy. The question of whether he is or isn't remains a nettlesome matter, and meanwhile the highly dysfunctional family members deal with him in their various ways. Challenging, suspenseful, and never less than sincere (Brigitte Roüan is cataclysmic as the mother), it's a movie that careens in your skull for days after watching it.

Blue (1993) The first film in Krzysztof Kieslowski's Three Colors trilogy, with *White* and *Red*; each film utilizes, somehow, the flag-symbolic shades of liberty, equality, and fraternity. *Blue's* notion of liberty is disquieting: we open with a car crash; wife and mother Julie (Juliette Binoche) lives through it, but her husband and daughter perish. "Freed" from her old life, her delicate features frozen with exhaustion and grief, Julie empties her life of belongings, memories, and attachments, changing her name and losing herself in the anonymous crush of Parisian life. The movie doesn't have much in the way of direction, momentum, or dramatic payoff, but a lot of people thought it profound.

Fearless (1993) A great, overlooked film of the American 1990s, this throat-grabber from director Peter Weir begins with a catastrophic airliner crash, then follows the dazed path of a survivor (Jeff Bridges), with a post-traumatic sense of invulnerability. The film's second story thread is where it leaves its bruises: a young mom (Rosie Perez) is ruined by grief after she fails to hold onto her baby son during the crash. The two of them enact a dubious, free-for-all self-cure, and the fallout—particularly when Perez dares to smell someone else's baby in a mall, or faces off against the dubious condolences offered by airline company grief therapy—is brutal and beautiful both. Be careful; it plays for keeps.

The Crossing Guard (1995) Sean Penn's second directorial effort plays like you think a day in the life of this most serotonin-challenged actor might, but the grim seriousness is affecting. Jack Nicholson plays a bitter, lowlife jeweler whose daughter was killed by a drunk driver (David Morse); when the culprit gets out of prison, our hero is waiting or him with an ill-conceived plot for revenge. Slam it for pretension and derivativeness (of the films of John Cassavetes, mostly) all you want, but the intent is pure, the characters are real, and the actors (including Jack's real-life ex-girlfriend Anjelica Huston, as the dead girl's more sensible mom) are muscular.

Ponette (1996) Jacques Doillon's harrowing film may very well be the best, most grueling, and in the end most truthful and transcendent film ever made about children or about the mechanics of grief. Don't watch it on a lark, particularly if you're a parent; after viewing it, you'll feel as if you've been scoured with steel wool inside and out. You see a dead-real emotional reality happen before your eyes, and there's no forgetting it. The situation is purposefully simple: as we open, a pint-sized four-year-old named Ponette (Victoire Thivisol, a best-actress winner at the Venice International Film Festival) is in the hospital with a broken arm after a car wreck that killed her mother. As she is jockeyed around, during the transitional post-funeral period, from her aunt's house to a live-in preschool to finally her father's home, Ponette undergoes her own tribulation: she refuses to accept her mother's death and move on. Nobody around her has much time or patience for the child's inconsolable grief, and so she must go the road alone, attempting to collate what little she understands about God and Heaven into a reasonable scheme by which she can once again see or at least speak to her mother. Just negotiating the simplest aspects of life requires Herculean strength, and a playground confrontation with an it's-your-fault-your-mommy's-dead bully has the reverb of a napalm strike. What *Ponette* does best is quietly but indelibly express the plight of children as they attempt, with such inadequate tools, to survive under the merciless wheels of the adult world. When Ponette finally makes it to her mother's graveside, collapsing and pawing at the soil, it's as if you're staring into the sun. All the more amazing, then, that Doillon finds deliverance for Ponette, in what may be either a simple dream experience or an unsentimental blast of secular magical realism. This isn't merely a movie—it's a mesmerizing ordeal by cinema.

The Sweet Hereafter (1997) Canadian social surgeon Atom Egoyan adapts Russell Banks's novel, perfectly, about a remote northern town and how it is shaken at its footings by a fateful bus crash. The film's adeptly constructed sense of scattered community doesn't mitigate the tortures of bereavement, which are all executed by a brilliant cast with what feels like absolute fidelity. The accident scene itself can make your heart stop, but it's the film's patient study of people cut loose in their own lives that's unassailable.

All About My Mother (1999) Pedro Almodóvar's sunny, melancholy hit begins, more or less, with its narrator-hero's accidental death, after which his aggrieved mother (Cecilia Roth) searches out the father the boy never knew—an AIDS-afflicted transvestite living in Barcelona—and melds in with an ad hoc family of mothers, actresses, pregnant nuns, and semiwomen of various stripes. Never trite but generally affirmative.

Under the Sand (2000) A quiet, oblique, and, finally, hypnotic piece of psychological knife work, François Ozon's movie happens almost completely on Charlotte Rampling's face. An aging European lioness famous (for thirty-five years now) for icy beauty and her own emotional instability, Rampling has seasoned into an intricate and persuasive grande dame, and here she proves her chops, as a woman who, on a drive to her vacation home in France, loses her husband. He never turns up (alive or dead) and so Rampling's quasiwidow must carry on, living in a kind of grieving suspension before cracking up altogether.

The Pledge (2001) Sean Penn's third film is just as miserable as *The Crossing Guard*, but here, the tale of death and survival is adapted from a novel by Swiss moralist Friedrich Durrenmatt, and it has a ghostly, existentialist shape to it. Jack Nicholson, again, plays a detective who vows to catch the killer of children (when one distraught father, trying to see the body of his dead daughter, asks, "Why wouldn't that be a good idea!" Nicholson's detective replies, "Because we hardly dared to look ourselves"). Giving credence to clues no one else cares about, the cop eventually stakes his life on his suspicions, retiring and planting himself in the desert with a new identity, forever on the lookout for what might just be a phantom—or evidence of an obsession that's out of control. Penn has never lost a child, so his constant attention to that dynamic could be seen as opportunistic. But the film plays honestly.

Solaris (2002) With astonishing hubris, Steven Soderbergh remakes the Andrei Tarkovsky Soviet sci-fi opus three decades later—and, stunningly, his film is better, in some ways, than the original. It's emotionally clearer, better acted (George Clooney swaps wounded gravitas for easy charm, and Jeremy Davies out-quirks the competition), and unencumbered by Tarkovsky's exhausting longueurs. It may be too laden with exposition, and it may not have as much cosmic weight to it, but the hero's grief is front and center, and the dilemma of having your suicidal dead wife return for more of the same failed marriage is heavy stuff.

21 Grams (2003) A positively toxic film about grief from Mexican filmmaker Alejandro González Iñárritu. The story is fractured into a disorienting scramble of past and present; only toward the end can you fathom the actual order of events, which center on two dead children and three traumatized, addiction-plagued adults (Sean Penn, Naomi Watts, and Benicio Del Toro). Given the kamikaze commitment of the actors (Watts and Del Toro were both nominated for Oscars), it's a scouring experience.

Birth (2004) A hypnotic, confident tour de force that centers on a beautiful widow (Nicole Kidman), and the little ten-year-old creepazoid (Cameron Bright) who asserts that he is the reincarnation of her dead husband. But the metaphysical suggestions (coscripted by Buñuel's former screenwriter, Jean-Claude Carrière) turn out to be merely a device to scrutinize the woman's gangrenous case of grief, and Jonathan Glazer's film is crafty, subtle (Kidman's manner sometimes suggests the presence of prescription tranquilizers, but not in a way that calls attention to itself), and, in the end, heartrending. There's also this, for what it's worth: several bright critics have noted how the film features scores of visual echoes of Buñuel's 1929 surrealist assault *Un Chien Andalou*, itself a madcap dream parable about lost love. Maybe.

RETIREMENT

"You don't think about getting old when you're young."
—Richard Farnsworth, *The Straight Story*

Retirement is the bonus you get for completing the thankless task of growing old; we, like the movies, are never sure how to feel about what amounts to a big vacation that was withheld from you until you're close to death. We shouldn't look at it that way, of course—retirement is all about the attitude you bring to it, even if the movies tend toward ruefulness.

She Wore a Yellow Ribbon (1949) The second film of John Ford's Cavalry trilogy hands John Wayne a rare character role, as an old, retiring colonel facing one more Indian siege. Typically simple-minded politically, but full of autumnal warmth.

Tokyo Story (1953) Perhaps the greatest and most emotionally incisive film in the corpus of Japanese great Yasujiro Ozu, a filmmaker whose expert visual restraint and sensitivity to his culture's social repressions might just make him the wisest and most eloquent filmmaker the medium has yet to see. Most of his films are generational struggles, however gentle and woeful, and this masterful work pits an aged couple (Chieko Higashi-yama and the great Chishu Ryu) against their uncaring children and the modern postwar age. Few other films so amply repay your attention, and Ozu's infinite resources of generosity could take the edge off of your own nascent sense of bitterness.

Touchez Pas au Grisbi (1954) Neglected director Jacques Becker's noir centers on an aging mobster (Jean Gabin) who is living comfortably after a career-capping heist, but is sucked into the underworld again by both his sense of righteousness and a conniving chorus girl (Jeanne Moreau). Decades before Quentin Tarantino's realization that criminals have kitchens, too, Becker's weary crooks were brushing their teeth and going to bed early.

The Tall T (1957) The westerns made by actor Randolph Scott and director Budd Boetticher, often with screenwriter Burt Kennedy (who penned five out of seven), remain some of the most incisive, unpretentious, and knowledgeable genre movies of the 1950s. Naturalistic, weathered, fatalistic, and never less than adult, this perfect example—in which Scott's hardened cowboy (the actor was almost sixty when he made the film) gets himself kidnapped, along with a family of greenhorns, by Richard Boone's scalawags—helped to reforge the dynamics of the genre and clean out the mythic baloney. In doing so, the film paved the way for Sam Peckinpah, Monte Hellman, and the very idea of an "antiwestern." Suddenly, in American action dramas, the acquired experience of an aged man meant something. The series' other films are just as fine; check out *Seven Men from Now* (1956), *Decision at Sundown* (1957), *Buchanan Rides Alone* (1958), *Westbound* (1959), *Ride Lonesome* (1959), and *Comanche Station* (1960).

Wild Strawberries (1957) Ingmar Bergman's art-house touchstone, in which a septuagenarian professor (Victor Sjöström), after having maintained a life of cold, aloof sternness, confronts the hollowness of his life and the joys he neglected. Filmed in a free-associative, dreamy surrealism, this much-hailed beauty helped make Bergman's international reputation, and it's still affecting.

The Firemen's Ball (1968) Milos Forman's ultrarealistic, observational satire about a small town in Communist Czechoslovakia that throws a party for the retiring octogenarian fire chief. Of course things spiral out of control. Forman's last film before defecting to Hollywood.

Harry & Tonto (1974) One of the very few Hollywood films to sympathetically attend to the social waywardness of being over sixty-five—and, in this, it's almost the American counterpart to Ozu's *Tokyo Story*. Oscar winner Art Carney plays a restless retiree whose New York building is being torn down; as a result, he decides to launch out on a road trip, accompanied only by his cat, to visit his somewhat neglectful children and to see the country. Director Paul Mazursky brings his full measure of Brooklyn-Jewish warmth and post-Catskills humor to bear.

The Sunshine Boys (1975) Neil Simon blasts away at the elderly, as crotchety, semisenile ex-vaudeville partners George Burns and Walter Matthau drive young 'un Richard Benjamin and each other crazy. Shticky, and funny enough if it doesn't chafe.

Going in Style (1979) By this point in Hollywood history, the popular 1970s cute-old-man routine was getting tired; here, Art Carney, Lee Strasberg, and George Burns are three pensioners who decide to rob a bank. Of course, plenty of retirees can sympathize.

Strangers in Good Company (1990) A blast of gorgeous, melancholy fresh air, this modest Canadian movie couldn't be simpler: a busload of old women get stranded in a hunk of pleasant country, and talk. Director Cynthia Scott cast each of the eight characters—a Cockney, a nun, a Mohawk, and so on—with nonprofessional actors who, essentially, play themselves, each recounting the crooked path of her life: her raptures and losses and intersections with history. Punctuating the flow of dialogue are the women's individual streams of snapshots that illustrate their lives from birth to present. Movies that so appreciate the accumulation of life and memories are as rare as ten-ounce pearls.

***Ma Saison Préférée* (1993)** André Téchiné's searching, meaty drama is a rich, sophisticated portrait of a familiar theme: the bruising self-absorption of modern adults in light of their disregarded, aging parents. Two embittered siblings (Catherine Deneuve and Daniel Auteuil) attend to their dying mother (Marthe Villalonga); no punches are pulled, and the neurotic family conflicts are worked by fevered pros.

***Wrestling Ernest Hemingway* (1993)** A septuagenarian mismatched buddy movie, in which one rangy old fart (Richard Harris) befriends another (Robert Duvall) and shows him how to live life like, well, a foolhardy extrovert. It's trite, except for the prodigious talent of Duvall, who so inhabits the role of the shy, gentlemanly Cuban barber you'd swear he grew up in Havana. Harris breaks into a sweat performing, but Duvall owns the film by the virtues of precision and modesty (the actor's *and* the character's).

***The Straight Story* (1999)** There are only two things stranger than the true story of Alvin Straight, a seventy-three-year-old Iowan who drove his riding lawn mower across two states to see his long-estranged, dying brother—that Disney would hire David Lynch to make the movie, and that the film itself would turn out to be such a dignified, country-wise, utterly humane masterpiece. Lynch neglects his impulse toward psychomania, and instead applies the surgeon's skills and well-traveled ear we've been overlooking all these years, and there may not be a better Hollywood film about aging, midwestern landscape, or the friendly social vernacular of flyover America. As Straight, Richard Farnsworth (who would die the year after the film's release) brings more than chops and wit to the table; he's the real deal—a living authenticity, unsentimental and enthralling.

***Fighter* (2000)** Documentary filmmaker Amir Bar-Lev takes two Czech Holocaust survivors—angry "bring it on!" boxer Jan Wiener and life-embracing optimist/novelist Arnost Lustig—back to the places of their memories (among them Terezinstadt, the labor camp where Lustig spent five years and Wiener's mother was murdered). Along the way, the two friends' opposing philosophies clash, mend, and clash again, forming a dialogue not only on grief but also on bitterness, aging, remembrance, and living in the present.

***About Schmidt* (2002)** Jack Nicholson plays a genuine person for once in his latter-day career—a retiree who's fed up with his wife and disconnected from his daughter, whose upcoming marriage compels him into a road trip via a massive mobile home. Director Alexander Payne goes for every big joke at his aging star's expense, but the movie's got a rueful backbeat and a stunningly poignant ending that makes it all feel necessary.

***Ladies in Lavender* (2004)** Two gray-haired sisters (Maggie Smith and Judi Dench) sharing a seaside cottage in Cornwall find a Polish young man washed up on their beach like a tired crab. His beauty, earnestness, and talent stir the dying embers of hearts well past their prime. The real treat here is watching the two Dames performing in tandem.

I II III **IV** V VI

ALTERED STATES

SICK DAY

"Leave the gun. Take the cannolis."
—Richard Castellano, *The Godfather*

What to watch when you're laid up on the coach, feeling like crap? Something that's not too challenging but also not dull, familiar but not done to death, serious but not ponderous, and, most of all, engagingly narrative. Long movies, we think, are terrific when you're under the weather—you've got an entire day to kill, after all—but a certain buoyancy and epic confidence are important, too.

IV

***The Hunchback of Notre Dame* (1939)** A whimsical choice; we can't pinpoint exactly why this splendid adaptation of Victor Hugo's classic novel makes for such good sick-day viewing, but it does. Charles Laughton is Quasimodo, Maureen O'Hara is the gypsy girl, the Parisian locales are faked beautifully, and director William Dieterle hits plenty of arresting notes—particularly in the nearly silent moment when the bell ringer swoops down to save the persecuted maiden.

***Laura* (1944)** The chattiest, dreamiest, and wittiest of noir mysteries, Otto Preminger's film begins with a murder and a romance—cool cop Dana Andrews falls for the dead woman, personified by Gene Tierney's wall portrait. Then Tierney's heroine walks in from a weekend away, and no one's sure who the body belongs to. All in all, the film is virtually owned by Clifton Webb, the feyest and most acidic character actor of the 1940s.

***Notorious* (1946)** Ingrid Bergman's troubled souse is convinced, by Cary Grant's implacable OSS agent, to leave behind her wanton Miami lifestyle for some undercover work in Rio, which certainly compromises their budding affair. This is arguably Alfred Hitchcock's most perfect movie, perhaps because the drama is completely composed of wary looks, dawning realizations, unspoken questions, and lurking suspicions. Grant is so understated he barely opens his mouth when he speaks, and Bergman is a sad and wounded beauty. Amid the pregnant meanings and the most superfluous MacGuffin in Hitchcock's catalog, Ben Hecht's script plumbs the psychology of patriotism, social mores, and passion all at once. All this and a screen kiss that might make you lift your head off the pillow in anticipation.

***The Third Man* (1949)** Director Carol Reed fashions one of *those* movies—one that despite its standard cast and familiar plot, is positively intoxicating, and can become almost an addiction. Perhaps credit extends also to sardonic screenwriter Graham Greene and the trademark zither score, but this beloved saga of postwar Vienna, in which American schmo Joseph Cotten comes to town to look for his old buddy Orson Welles, is told that his pal just recently died, then staggers around as things really percolate, is essential Movieness, and an effortless watch.

The Bridge on the River Kwai (1957) One of maybe a dozen Best Picture Oscar winners that has a real-world brain in its head, this wide-canvas David Lean World War II fave is long, rich in clarified drama (thanks to the struggle between Alec Guinness's proud, Geneva Conventions–obeying officer and Sessue Hayakawa's equally proud Japanese camp commandant), and adroitly engineered to snowball to an astonishing, but absolutely believable, action climax.

The Great Escape (1963) This perennially popular World War II POW-camp adventure is the least traumatic war film you can imagine—a precursor to TV's *Hogan's Heroes*, it's peopled with glib movie stars doing "outwit the Nazis" shtick and exhibiting the Allies' "we can take it" wherewithal. As you might guess, it's not an emotionally demanding film: Steve McQueen suffers time in solitary with a mitt and baseball, James Garner manages to scrounge everything but the kitchen sink in the middle of nowhere, Charles Bronson's "Tunnel King" digs toward the fences despite his claustrophobia, and so on.

I Am Cuba (1964) A vertiginous Cuban-Soviet coproduction that dizzyingly propagandizes on the Cuban revolution's causes and experiences, as revealed through director Mikhail Kalatozov's superhuman, gravity-resistant camera. This movie is all visuals and little character or plot, so dozing is permitted.

IV

The Flight of the Phoenix (1965) Old-school, "man's man" adventure stuff, in which a planeload of craggy "actor's actors" (James Stewart, Dan Duryea, Ernest Borgnine, Richard Attenborough, et al.) crash-land in the Sahara and struggle to rebuild the aircraft. They're convincingly more uncomfortable than you are, and you'll be reminded to keep up on fluids.

2001: A Space Odyssey (1968) Stanley Kubrick's languorous sci-fi behemoth is mesmerizing, nap-inducing, provocative, long, and enigmatic enough to make the day pass without giving yourself a chance to indulge in feeling miserable. At the same time, it's transporting in a way that few other movies are—you feel like you've *been* somewhere, even if you never get off the couch.

Little Big Man (1970) Director Arthur Penn (of 1967's *Bonnie and Clyde* fame) was never a subtle craftsman, and this shticky yet intelligent rendition of Thomas Berger's big, absurdist farce fit him like a glove. Dustin Hoffman plays a 121-year-old man who claims to have been everywhere and witnessed everything, from the death of Wild Bill Hickock to Custer's Last Stand.

The Godfather (1972) What could be better? It's even easier than usual to overlook the dark themes at the heart of Francis Ford Coppola's seductive, well-loved masterpiece when you're under the weather. What's left: mighty Greek-style tragedy, played out in soft, shadowy umber, period tweed, and melodramatic Sicilian-ese, by arguably the best cast ever assembled for a major Hollywood film. And it's nearly three hours long.

The Godfather Part II **(1974)** Same goes here—like *The Godfather*, this three-plus-hours film is meaty and epochal, yet effortless. Double feature, anyone? We advise against cutting corners by watching *The Godfather Saga* (1977), which splices the two features together into a linear time line that only emphasizes the freestanding thinness of *Part II*'s separate strands—and who said the individual films were hard to follow in the first place? Also, forget *The Godfather Part III* (1990), a relatively graceless and tired retread.

1900 **(1976)** Bertolucci's sumptuous, mammoth folly (see "Summer," p. 79) is Italian history as megafresco, stuffed with stars, alive with old-world affirmations, and long enough to last all day—don't settle for an edited version that runs less than five hours.

The Kingdom **(1994)** A smorgasbord for the couch detained: Lars von Trier's almost five-hour-long Danish miniseries is a comedy about a haunted hospital, the hallways of which are clogged with hilarious social satire, clairvoyants, a runaway pregnancy, illicit liaisons, and truly scary ghosts. Often outrageous but never dull; the same goes for ***The Kingdom II*** **(1997)**, which is just as long and even crazier.

Being John Malkovich **(1999)** Perhaps the closest a Hollywood movie has ever gotten—and probably will ever get—to the free-associative shotgun spray of Salvador Dali's and Luis Buñuel's *Un Chien Andalou*, this first film by the team of director Spike Jonze and screenwriter Charlie Kaufman is an ingenious, incredibly entertaining Rorschach blot of a metacomedy that says a truckload about celebrity, movies, sexual identity, control, and much, much more. The primary metaphoric vehicle is a mysterious, slimy tunnel that leads directly from a small door in an obsolete office building into the consciousness of actor John Malkovich. After fifteen minutes spent in Malkovich's head, however, tunnel travelers are interdimensionally chucked out onto the shoulder of the New Jersey Turnpike, but the orgasmic thrill of living inside Malkovich's skull (and what we see of that experience is, not incidentally, less than thrilling) spurs the characters (including office clerk and formerly unemployed puppeteer John Cusack, his frumpy—yes, frumpy—wife Cameron Diaz, and sultry business chick Catherine Keener) to repeat the experience and steer Malkovich's actions into fulfilling their sexual fantasies. Plenty of sequences suggest a consciousness on a chemical ride: a pet chimpanzee flashes back to his own orphanhood in the jungle; Charlie Sheen shows up (as himself), blabbering on about "hot lesbian witches!"; and then there's the climactic homicidal chase through Malkovich's tortured subconscious.

The Da Vinci Code **(2006)** Crowd-pleasing, eternally topical conspiracy-theory fun and games, in which Tom Hanks, Audrey Tautou, and Ian McKellen essentially recite plummy thickets of ancient history (and heavy strands of complete blarney), all of it pleasantly amounting to little beyond well-read nonsense. Accompaniment: tea with brandy.

INSOMNIA

"Let me sleep. . . ."
—Stellan Skarsgård, *Insomnia* (1997)

Often enough, movies are your best remedy for a bad bout of sleeplessness—but only certain movies, movies that regard the idea of narrative pacing with a land tortoise's prehistoric disinterest. A key factor is language—nearly all of the suggested features below are foreign-made and come shouldering vast thickets of subtitles, and virtually nothing on God's green Earth will lapse you into helpless slumber like an honest attempt to read subtitles off a television screen at three in the morning. But the movie itself must also have a forceful narcotic effect, while not being merely dismal and dull. You don't want to be tempted to turn it off and watch soft-core porn instead.

IV

***Napoléon*(1927)** Abel Gance's pioneering, vividly visualized epic chronicles only the first half of the mad conqueror's life, but if you're lucky, you won't make it past the school years. There's not a boring frame in this fabulous mastodon, which is part of the strategy; it may not be possible for the average person to focus on an ordinary silent movie when they'd rather be sleeping; that would just allow for too much temptation to switch to more contemporary, unhelpfully distractive programming. But Gance's film is wild, unpredictable stuff, and you'll feel compelled to stick with it until your eyes fall shut.

***Last Year at Marienbad* (1961)** The jury is still out on this piece of meditative, French-art-film flimflam. Outrageously popular in its day as some kind of postmodern, existentialist dream drama, today it's difficult to watch without succumbing to a narcoleptic seizure. Alain Resnais directed Alain Robbe-Grillet's conscientiously abstruse screenplay as if he'd been in a coma along with the actors (including the effervescent Delphine Seyrig), who wander around a huge manor estate lazily attempting to figure out if now is now or then or soon to be, and whether or not they'd met last year in Marienbad, or ever. Hypnotic after a fashion, but indisputably lulling.

The Sorrow and the Pity (1970) Marcel Ophüls's famous epic documentary about the Free French Resistance fighters is over four hours long, and in most prints the endless subtitles are also faded and difficult to read—perfect. Like many World War II documentaries (the very long ones that feature lots of subtitled interviews and little footage of concentration camps), this epochal essay is an effective sleep-inducer that you feel obligated to watch for as long as you can stay awake. You shouldn't experience shame over not finishing it—it's quite possible that, on home video or DVD at least, no one ever has. Actually, all of Ophüls's movies—because they are very long, and therefore have no inclination to move quickly—have the same barbiturate-like impact.

The Traveling Players (1975) Greek master Theo Angelopoulos makes movies in the Antonioni-Bergman-Tarkovsky tradition, full of long traveling shots that sometimes cover several city blocks, encompass multiple threads of simultaneous action, and roll on methodically for fifteen or twenty minutes at a time. It can be a revelatory way to watch cinema—his *Landscape in the Mist* (1988) is one of the great, underappreciated epiphanies in the art form. *The Traveling Players* is a similarly mind-boggling masterpiece; if only you could stay awake in its presence. Unlike the comparatively melodramatic and compact *Landscape*, this earlier, nearly-four-hour film is almost entirely metaphorical, following a nomadic theater troupe through the gray Greek townships during decades of dictatorship, civil war, and social upheaval. Despite the calamities, there's nothing here to jar you awake: no close-ups, no involvement with a single character, no clear story. Just brooding movement, milling crowds, and rueful talk—it's like history sitting on your chest. Good luck.

Kings of the Road (1976) German New Waver Wim Wenders cemented his international reputation with this signature work—a three-hour black-and-white movie about a pair of modern wanderers—a movie projector repairman and a haunted hitchhiker—driving around Germany. They rarely say anything of importance, and nothing terribly dramatic happens to them. As a statement about the postwar culture Wenders grew up in, it's a stunningly eloquent film. As entertainment, it's trance-inducing.

Shoah (1985) This landmark film, the Everest of Holocaust documentaries, clocks in at nearly nine-and-a-half hours—which doesn't mean very much in and of itself if you intend on sleeping as soon as possible. But knowing that the film is essentially endless can have a seriously soporific effect. Claude Lanzmann's movie isn't merely a movie; it's a monument to the murdered millions, and as such, it should be regarded with reverence. But it's also a talking-heads documentary, free of archival footage, and it can therefore be useful as a late-night sleep aid. (In truth, though, we'd opt for one of Ophüls's films, as unfocused and ramshackle as they are, over *Shoah*, which can be enthralling and heartbreaking in ways that may not promote sleep.)

The Decalogue (1988) Krzysztof Kieslowski's greatest work, and something of an ideal choice for the insomniac who wants it all—to catch up on both a world masterwork *and* sleep. This made-for-Polish-TV monster is approximately ten hours long, and broken into ten segments. Each segment is a freestanding minimovie, each ironically examines one of the Ten Commandments, and all of them take place simultaneously in and around the same Warsaw housing project. You can watch this behemoth in small or medium hunks; that fits the work's structure just fine. In fact, watching this bruising, fascinating epic late at night, with red corneas and in haphazard spurts, might be the *best* way to experience Kieslowski's quizzical spiritualism and modern malaise.

Hotel Terminus: The Life and Times of Klaus Barbie **(1988)** Ophüls's magnum opus of unconsciousness. We have a friend, no insomniac, who tried for over a year to watch Ophüls's interrogatory account of the Barbie trial, but who couldn't stay awake for more than twenty minutes of it, no matter what time of day he tried to watch it. An important historical portrait, and a vital exploration of fascism and cultural responsibility, but also the cinematic equivalent of a shovel brought swiftly to the head.

Insomnia **(1997)** This Norwegian film is not long, slow, or particularly snooze worthy, but if you feel lonesome in your sleeplessness, it might best be taken as an expression of empathy. Join Stellan Skarsgård's sullen Swedish detective as he finds himself sent to arctic Norway in the summertime—when there is simply no night—to investigate a murder, and finds it impossible to get any sleep. As his investigation quickly becomes self-incriminating, his battle with insomnia (and with the inexorable sunlight that stretches into his hotel room twenty-four hours a day) takes its vicious toll; the film's cool visual evocation of dissolving consciousness could give those who are actually sleep deprived the shivers. It won't necessarily send you off to dreamland (that goes triple for the lame 2002 American remake starring a sandbag-eyed Al Pacino), but it knows what you're going through.

IV

Waking Life **(2001)** Richard Linklater's free-associative animation wanderingly glances upon a vast cast of chatterers, ranters, and speculators, all of them digitally cartooned so that everything, including the background settings, levitates, morphs, and seethes. As much as it's an intellectual exercise, it's also a semiconscious boat ride down a river of dreaminess. (See "Spiritual/Philosophical Crisis," p. 215.)

The Piano Tuner of Earthquakes **(2006)** This supremely dreamy feature film by superhuman animator twins Timothy and Stephen Quay takes place inside of a warped, Tuscan-sunlit fantasyscape, in which a robotics mechanic/piano tuner falls in love with a kidnapped opera diva on a maniacal toy engineer's island. Really, the story is so lugubrious and vague that it seems to deprive the frontal lobe of oxygen, thereby igniting subconscious associations and daydreamed conclusions. The movie itself is one looming automaton, down to the stunning dream sequence in which the ineffectual hero ventures forth into a blue birch forest, where his pillow waits for him under a tree and the mad doctor's servants run in silent backward fits. It may not be inappropriate to incorporate the movie into your own dreams as you nod off.

The Science of Sleep **(2006)** Michel Gondry's trippy, semiconscious comedy is so narratively challenged that you may feel compelled to doze even as the film is sympathetically fueling your dreams with craziness. Rarely confident in the knowledge of being either awake or dreaming, Gael García Bernal's impish hero is the anchor to a free-associative burble of non sequiturs and thrift-store surrealisms.

POST-OP RECOVERY

"Let there be dancing in the streets, drinking in the saloons, and necking in the parlor!"
—Groucho Marx, *A Night at the Opera*

IV

Like "Sick Day" times a gazillion. So you've had surgery or some other severe form of medical procedure; maybe your movements are restricted; perhaps you're in a hospital bed, with sutures or casts or IVs or whatever. There really is no day in your life that is more in need of movies—movies that burn with humor and joy, that reacquaint you with the life force. This is cinema viewing as remedy: under any circumstances, these films are holy balms for the soul because they offer a vision of life defiant of pain and drudgery. Under *these* circumstances, they could make your otherwise downtrodden year.

Animal Crackers **(1930)** The second of the Marx Brothers' films (after 1929's *The Cocoanuts*), this dusty, sarcastically musical vaudeville farce involves a sham "explorer" (Groucho), a society party thrown in his honor, a stolen painting, a pair of suspicious musicians (Chico and Harpo), and so on. The bros' vim could not be contained even by the primitive early-talkie technology.

Love Me Tonight **(1932)** Rouben Mamoulian's early talkie musical begins with tailor Maurice Chevalier more or less assembling a morning song out of his Paris neighborhood's natural noises, and from there it just gets sunnier, sillier, sharper, and bouncier. It's impossible to be unhappy watching this film.

Duck Soup **(1933)** Any day is ripe for this life-giving fruitcake. (See "Summer," p. 76; "Optimism," p. 225.)

Twentieth Century **(1934)** Howard Hawks offers up screwball comedy at its fastest and sharpest, with Carole Lombard's outraged star and John Barrymore's ham-hock of a Broadway director riding the titular train as he tries to lure her back to the stage from Hollywood.

Top Hat **(1935)** There may have never been a film subgenre so lovable and yet so utterly meaningless as the Fred Astaire–Ginger Rogers musical—the plots are little more than misunderstandings distended by dance numbers, and it's all frivolous and joyful and happy to be alive. The stars themselves are enchanting because of their essential unlikeliness—ridiculously graceful while hoofin', but otherwise awkward, silly, and hilariously unsuited to each other. *Top Hat* may be the best of the run (and with Irving Berlin songs to boot), but ***Swing Time*** **(1936)** and ***Shall We Dance*** **(1937)**, with songs by Jerome Kern and the Gershwins, respectively, are also good choices.

The Miracle of Morgan's Creek **(1944)** Wartime pregnancy via Preston Sturges's directorial efforts, Sturges's screenplay (a comet of wordplay and effervescence), and Sturges's faithful company of character clowns (including Eddie Bracken, William Demarest, Porter Hall, Torben Meyer, and Chester Conklin). (See "Pregnancy," p. 138.)

Rear Window **(1954)** Like you, James Stewart is laid up—with an absurdly phallic leg cast—and so, bored, he spies on the movie-like dramas unrolling in his neighbors' apartment windows, until one of them seems to become a murder mystery (viewed, as they usually are, from a safe, dark distance). One of Alfred Hitchcock's most valuable essays on discomfiture and audience implication. It's not a celebration of healing per se, but being helpless has never been so riveting.

The Producers **(1968)** Mel Brooks's first film and conceptually his funniest; amoral theatrical producer Zero Mostel and neurotic accountant Gene Wilder contrive to make a killing on a flop show, which naturally hits it big. Zesty, booming with Mostel's comic life force, and infinitely quotable.

The Hospital **(1971)** Before *Network*, screenwriter Paddy Chayefsky took a cudgel to the state of modern American medical care with this chaotic, blackly comical satire about an urban hospital that does more damage to its patients than good. You'll be glad to have been discharged.

Raiders of the Lost Ark **(1981)** One of the handful of times that Steven Spielberg's patented overmanipulations and blue-tinted "sense of wonder" doesn't curdle in our bellies, this George Lucas–inspired yarn is blessedly free of UFOs and dinosaurs, and is set, rather rowdily, in a 1930s pulp-serial world in which the instantly iconic adventurer/archaeologist Indiana Jones (Harrison Ford) fights Nazis for the sake of Biblical artifacts. Good-natured and distracting without being patronizing.

There's Something About Mary **(1998)** The sweetest comedy ever to be choked with semen, scrotum, boob, cripple, and dead animal gags, Bobby and Peter Farrelly's breakout farce gets away with anything by virtue of naked nerve, visual gravity, and the unwillingness to allow a comic situation to pass before it's squeezed completely dry. Ben Stiller plays a shy high school misfit who, because he's kind to her retarded brother, gets asked to the prom by blonde goddess Cameron Diaz; after prom night is scotched (we won't spoil it by saying how), fifteen years go by, and Stiller's desperate nebbish finds his lost ideal woman with the help of a slimy detective (Matt Dillon) who has aims of his own. But the constant presence of cabaret folk artist Jonathan Richman sitting in trees and singing the ballad of Diaz's loveliness should be clue enough that this reckless beast isn't about plot. The Farrellys are masters at shotgun-style comedy, and the killers here are many, from Matt Dillon's struggle to revive Mary's doped-up pooch, to the mysterious misplacement, and then galling discovery, of a stray dollop of semen. Make no mistake: the Farrellys respect no limits to indecency, and if you have zero tolerance for, say, mockery of the handicapped, think twice about watching this. Think twice, too, if you're recovering with stitches—you'll pop 'em.

The Death of Mr. Lazarescu (2005) Whatever stage you're at after your medical trial, you'll be happy to be in better shape than the hero of this daunting, chilly, grimly chucklesome Romanian film, in which a deplorably ill-kept old man is shuttled from one ill-run hospital after another as his precarious health quickly deteriorates. Two and a half hours of unremitting realism—there but for the grace.

HEARTBREAK

"The old dreams were good dreams—they didn't work out, but I'm glad I had them."
—Clint Eastwood, *The Bridges of Madison County*

Movies have attended to the wounds of the heartsick since the medium's very beginnings, and they've tended to wallow in the experience rather than seek a rescue from it. Wallowing can be good.

Wuthering Heights (1939) A film that is unjustly maligned today (and more fully hailed in "Valentine's Day," p. 25), it holds a unique place of honor in our home, where just one bar from Alfred Newman's score can bring all-business adults weeping to their knees. The ultimate broken-heart story, tinged with metaphysical urgency and executed beautifully—no other version has come close to capturing its indescribable sense of loss.

Waterloo Bridge (1940) Right after the long haul of *Gone with the Wind*, Vivien Leigh stayed in Hollywood long enough to make this lowdown brute of a tragic melodrama (based on a Robert E. Sherwood play), in which the romance between an aristocrat and a dance-hall girl is scotched by World War I, economic necessity (read: prostitution!), and shame. The film uses "Auld Lang Syne" like a cudgel, and Leigh is lovely.

How Green Was My Valley (1941) The well-read Richard Llewellyn novel by way of director John Ford, this portrait of Welsh coal-mining country gets you right *here*. Packed with Ford's Celtic stock company of actors, plus Walter Pidgeon as a schoolteacher, Oscar winner Donald Crisp as Dad, and Roddy McDowall as the family's youngest son.

Brief Encounter (1945) Scored to Rachmaninoff, this world-famous Noël Coward–David Lean tragedy-in-a-teapot recounts, simply, the doomed romance between a conventional British housewife (Celia Johnson) and a conventional British doctor (Trevor Howard), each of whom is married to someone else. Nothing dramatic happens between them, and that's the picture's deliberate strategy—it summons the pathos of what *doesn't* occur, as opposed to what disastrously might've been.

Lilith (1964) A sublime and forgotten beauty, this brooding Robert Rossen–directed movie features a young Warren Beatty as a New England sanitarium worker who falls under the spell of a psychotic patient (Jean Seberg). Shot on location beneath overcast skies, it's a time capsule of its era, and it ends up packing a vicious wallop.

Modern Romance (1981) Albert Brooks, as the film's writer, director, and star, trumps all comers in this definitive portrait of a narcissistic schlemiel in the throes of post-breakup agony. Laser-like in its social surgery and brutally funny (all at Brooks's own expense, of course—he embodies every man at his most pathetic and oblivious).

Chungking Express (1994) Wong Kar-Wai is world famous for his fractured, lovelorn fairy tales, which buzz around Hong Kong and trail after young, lonely obsessives who are strung out on unsuccessful coping strategies and searching for love in every wrong corner. This popular minimasterpiece is actually divided into two equally significant stories, in which two city cops struggle with heartbreak and magical thinking. Similar, and also recommended, are Wong's **Fallen Angels** (1995), a more complex interwoven narrative, also full of post-noir fatalism and urban melancholy, and **Happy Together** (1997), a doomed gay romance playing itself out in the hothouse of a Buenos Aires flop-joint. His *2046* (2004) is something else altogether—see below.

The Bridges of Madison County (1995) Author Robert James Waller's schmaltzy bestseller was adapted into a humane, astringently acted film about middle-age romance. Sort of a middle-American *Brief Encounter*, it features Meryl Streep as the unfulfilled farmer's wife, and Clint Eastwood as the good-hearted nomadic photographer. Of course, the relationship can't last.

IV

Jude **(1996)** Far from being another cutesy, waistcoat-and-bustle Merchant-Ivory weekend getaway, Michael Winterbottom's adaptation of Thomas Hardy's *Jude the Obscure* is stark, gnarly, and breathtaking. Its rigorous, assaultive visual form and naked intensity never shrink from the clean truth of catastrophe, ill fortune, and poverty. Neither does Jude himself; he's played by Christopher Eccleston as a help-less individualist—smart but out of synch, impulsive, luckless, and condemned to struggle. His story is a gauntlet of crushed dreams (wanting to be a teacher, he ends up a stonemason), battles with propriety, and heartbreak. Kate Winslet, as Jude's unpredictable cousin and soul mate Sue, is effortlessly cherishable and clever, and the bond between the two is so palpable and genuine that their fated romance has the torque of a cosmic action. Even if you know the novel going in, nothing prepares you for the film's darkness.

Chasing Amy **(1997)** Kevin Smith's comedy could be bravely characterized as the *Wuthering Heights* of 1990s slacker comedies. It's another smart-assed Smith movie, but it's also the painful, lonesome answer to the empty sex banter of his earlier films (*Clerks*, *Mallrats*), abetted by the greatest clinch in modern indie film history. Smith's alter ego here is Holden (Ben Affleck), a cult comic artist. As far as Holden is concerned, everything's hunky-dory between him and his irascible partner Banky (Jason Lee)—until Holden meets Alyssa (Joey Lauren Adams), a sexy comic artist who happens to be a devout lesbian. Undeterred, Holden starts arranging his life around the time he spends with Alyssa, until one rainy night, he desperately lets loose with a filibuster on true love that breaks Alyssa's sex-pref resolve. Their ensuing relationship is far from peaceful, and Smith runs various sexual politics through the ringer in the most graphic manner ever attempted in American scriptwriting; the reverb of it all throbs with real feelings and frustrated inadequacy.

The End of the Affair **(1999)** Adapted from the Graham Greene novel and filmed by Neil Jordan with all the intelligence that work requires, this is all about wartime love (between married woman Julianne Moore and family friend Ralph Fiennes) as a defi-ance of—and, finally, a bloody deal made with—a hard-bargaining God. One of the best British films of the 1990s, and predictably underappreciated.

In the Mood for Love **(2000)** So lavishly heralded since its first appearances at festivals that you wonder if any movie could sustain such noise, Wong Kar-Wai's bewitching, elusive, time-haunted tone poem is a Hong Kong art film in which we're shown only part of the never-resolved story, and in which a romance that never quite happens is the worst tragedy of all. Sumptuously conceived visually and edited into a series of potent glimpses, the movie constantly catches you up short—particularly if you've got your heart set on knowing more than the characters themselves do. In Hong Kong in 1962 (a place and time that Wong remembers and evokes very clearly) apartment owners would often rent out single rooms to young couples, and so on the same day

IV

Mr. Chow (Tony Leung) and Mrs. Chan (Maggie Cheung) each move in to neighboring flats, their spouses elsewhere for the moment. For all intents and purposes, their spouses never show up: they frequently travel for their jobs, and even when they are home, Wong deliberately keeps them off frame—their faces and personalities are another unknown for us. Before long, the two pick up some hints that their spouses are having an affair, and their own relationship blooms into one of mutual melancholy, although they are hardly allowed even a sexy embrace, much less a full-on consummation. The movie needs to be seen twice, so that our highly developed expectations as filmgoers can be washed away into irrelevance; only then can we see what Wong has done: made a film that watches, sweats, and agonizes like a consciousness caught in a passionate whorl.

Eternal Sunshine of the Spotless Mind **(2004)** This Chinese-box mystery is actually a romantic comedy—albeit one that's been Rubik's Cubed and set adrift in an unmoored consciousness by Charlie Kaufman's beautiful screenplay. Jim Carrey stars as a shy nebbish in love with Kate Winslet's bipolar tramp; once dumped, he seeks out a small firm that will literally wipe his memories of her right out of his brain. Of course, it's not that easy, and neither is the film, since much of it takes place in a beleaguered subconscious that's being technologically erased as we watch. In the end, though, the lovelorn mood trumps the gimmickry.

2046 **(2004)** This multiheaded monster of a movie—which was years in the making, remaking, postponing, and editing—is director Wong Kar-Wai's magnum opus. It conflates several narratives—some set in and around a rented room in historically based 1960s Hong Kong, some imaginary and futuristic—and several women, none of whom quite fills the hole in the heart of Tony Leung's laconic journalist, who was first made miserable in *In the Mood for Love*. Form, mood, and affect drubs narrative content, and the steamroller of sadness rolls right over you.

IV

MS. LONELYHEARTS

"I've had three lovers in the past four years, and they all ran a distant second to a good book and a warm bath."
—Renee Zellweger, *Jerry Maguire*

Simply put, these are films that ache in sympathy for the unlucky, lonely women in our midst—or that dramatically spell out what those women may think they already know: that men are untrustworthy, amoral beast-things who treat the female of the species like steak bones. Whichever way works for you.

Dr. Jekyll and Mr. Hyde **(1931)** No mystery to what this old chestnut says about the bestial nature of man, but in this version, Fredric March is made up like some kind of baboon-man in a top hat, and his realization of a violent male id set loose is scary and queasy, even if the scene in which Miriam Hopkins gets whipped happens off camera.

I'm No Angel **(1933)** What better company, if you're without a man and frustrated, than Mae West, a woman's woman who's built like a battleship, is in complete control of her sexual identity, and is ready to use up men like tissues, with no more than a smirk and tossed bon mot? West remains an invigorating, optimistic object lesson in how to be comfortable in your own skin, how to love sex for sex's sake, and why you need never rely on a man.

El **(1952)** In the years he spent making movies in Mexico, Luis Buñuel trained his satiric muscles at the expense of old-world masculinity, with all of its demonic urges, childish tempers, and sexual frustrations. In this barbed semidrama, a rich man nets a young wife, then succumbs to jealousy psychopathy. (In Buñuel's ***The Criminal Life of Archibaldo de la Cruz*** **(1955)**, the pathologies seep into murder, necrophilia, and fetishism.)

Rachel, Rachel **(1968)** Perhaps the most sensitive portrait of feminine loneliness in the post-Eisenhower period, this Paul Newman–directed drama gets under the epidermis of a wilting-lily, thirtysomething schoolteacher (Joanne Woodward) who hopelessly embarks on an aimless affair as she otherwise faces her grim middle years alone. The profound sympathy brought to the heroine's plight by all concerned keeps this film very far from being depressing.

Husbands **(1970)** Generally regarded as the lesser of iconclast-realist John Cassavetes's films, this wallow in masculine ugliness follows three drunken middle-aged fools (Cassavetes, Peter Falk, and Ben Gazzara) on a midlife tear in response to burying a fourth friend. The grim acting-out behavior is, of course, the point, but even when they're sober, these guys are obnoxious louts.

Alice Doesn't Live Here Anymore **(1974)** Ellen Burstyn snagged an Oscar for this unpredictable, somewhat odd tale, in which the heroine—a single mother who works as a diner waitress and dreams of becoming a club singer—tries to keep the future looking bright in the Arizona flatlands for her smart-mouthed son (Alfred Lutter), even as patient hunk Kris Kristofferson waits out the brawls. Martin Scorsese directed, clearly without having ever met a midwesterner.

The Stepford Wives **(1975)** Try to find a more savage indictment of middle-class marriage than that hidden in this hooey, written by Ira Levin (who, evidently, had a mother-whore fixation of his own; see *Rosemary's Baby*). Idealistic young wife Katharine Ross and her bland, rich husband move into an exclusive suburban enclave, and she slowly discovers that the women are being replaced, one by one, by mindless, obedient androids. Literally. The 2005 remake turned the premise into a campy joke.

Thelma & Louise **(1991)** Single, alone, and discouraged? Rather than resume the soul-crushing hunt for a suitable, or even bearable, mate, consider entertaining the notion that's at the wide-eyed core of this seminal, postfeminist war chant: the solution to your problem is to *run*. There aren't many males of the breed worth one of your air-borne toenails, and, since males run the world, your best bet is to stick it to the man, grab a gun, climb into a big, brightly painted vintage automobile, and make a break for the frontier. This remarkable movie actually makes this dead-end gambit seem worth the price: Susan Sarandon and Geena Davis, both smashing in faded denim and desert-wind-swept hair, revel in all things masculine (cool cars, firearms, the West, teaching lowdown varmints a thing or two about how to talk to a lady), then simply take their own spectacular exit rather than submit to the laws of patriarchal privilege. As a rebel yell, it couldn't be more extreme—or more fun. Anyway, you can't be blamed for thinking you'd rather drive off a cliff than endure another round of speed dating.

IV

Next Stop Wonderland **(1998)** Perhaps the definitive turn-of-the-millennium, single-urban-chick ode, with Hope Davis soldiering on through the dating scene. The plot gets tiresomely quirky, but Davis is dynamite.

The Personals **(1999)** A superb, wise, and witty Taiwanese film about being single and what to do about it, Chen Kuo-fu's movie starts off as a kind of universalized "unmarried gal in the big city, hunting for a mate" movie (something like an Asian *Next Stop Wonderland*). Slowly, it is revealed that the lovely ophthalmologist heroine, Jiazhen (Rene Liu), is a three-dimensional character, with secrets and hidden temperaments, and eventually Chen's film turns the corner into searing drama. Structured as more or less a series of teahouse meetings between Jiazhen and the men who answer her personal ad, the movie is like a succession of dozens of minimovies, each shot by Chen in a distinct style, and each involving Jiazhen's gentle interrogation and/or tolerance of the lonely men as they ritualistically vomit out their lives, desires, woes, proposals, and even fetishes.

Erin Brockovich (2000) A film designed to win its star an Oscar if there ever was one, Steven Soderbergh's movie sets up Julia Roberts as a working-class single-mom heroine for the oppressed, legally battling corporate giant Pacific Gas and Electric on behalf of the scores of poor locals who have endured decades of tumors and other illnesses thanks to the illegal use and dumping of poisonous chemicals. Filthy with character details and robust righteousness, the film is also notable for its dismissal of love and even parenthood in favor of doing justice, fighting the good fight, and working your ass off at something you believe in.

You Can Count On Me (2000) A literate, mature indie about a single mom (Laura Linney) who's stuck in her childhood home after the early death of her parents, saddled with an obnoxious boss and an evasive boyfriend, and raising a son who needs a man around the house. Trouble rolls into town in the form of her screwed-up brother (Mark Ruffalo). Sounds slight, but it adds up—to a portrait not just of a woman's love life, but of her *entire* life, and all the emotional complexities it entails. Both stars are remarkable; Ruffalo found himself a career after this film, and Linney was nominated for an Oscar.

IV

Dog Days (2001) An Austrian film by Ulrich Seidl that paints a dire, horrifying view of lifeless, brainless suburban existence in what's normally considered a quaintly cultured and upscale nation. The treatment of women here could put you off men for two lifetimes.

Mulholland Dr. (2001) Hollywood's foremost idiosyncratic director, poet of the irrational, and one-man narrative anarchist, David Lynch is an all-American original, and this award-winning doozy is pure Lynch: frustrating, maniacal, loopy, and utterly, charmingly nonsensical, it treats genre conventions like toilet paper and the usually reliable concrete aspects of event and character like ethereal daydreams. Its characters—primarily dewy heroine Naomi Watts—start out as amusing archetypes, morph into things that have no names, and end up figures in a hallucinogenic tragedy. Notoriously, Lynch's film began as a CBS pilot that got dumped; with the help of French investors, Lynch took what had been an open-ended, meandering beginning to a tapestry TV series (in the *Twin Peaks* vein), added more than forty minutes of additional footage, and turned it on its head. The main "story" involves Betty (Watts), a sugar-spun Canadian girl come to L.A. for fame and fortune. She's not in town for even one day before a sultry brunette (Laura Elena Harring) shows up in her shower, calling herself "Rita" after a Rita Hayworth movie poster in the bathroom because she doesn't remember who she is. The two rather delicately set out to uncover the mystery, which includes movie-producer gangsters, a car wreck on the eponymous road, and a young director (Justin Theroux) who's having a rather Lynchian experience while casting his new film. In one of the movie's stunning left turns (which is where Lynch continued the narrative after his initial TV pilot was dumped), the two women, having found out a good deal but solved nothing, climb into bed together and initiate a lesbian affair that the rest of the movie proceeds to look at through a nightmarish prism. Once Lynch's camera plunges into a mysterious black box with a triangular keyhole, *Mulholland Dr.* runs off the traditional-movie rails, becoming increasingly heartbroken and wrenching.

***The Piano Teacher* (2001)** A lonely-spinster saga like no other, in which Isabelle Huppert, in all of her regal, early-autumn power, plays a piano instructor who becomes involved with a young man (Benoît Magimel), even as she nears the edge of masochistic madness. Brutal, stunning, and uncompromising in its anger.

***Auto Focus* (2002)** Paul Schrader's terrific biopic of TV actor and *Hogan's Heroes* star Bob Crane (Greg Kinnear), who apparently enjoyed quite a life as a remarkably guileless satyr before his body turned up in an Arizona motel room in 1978. While the case is still officially unsolved, this film points the finger at Crane's longtime partner in hedonism, John Carpenter (Willem Dafoe); together, the two make for a galvanizing portrait of the male of the species in hypnotic thrall to its own restless penis.

***Enough* (2002)** Jennifer Lopez runs from battering hubby Bill Campbell—and realizes she's going to have to train for a bone-breaking confrontation.

***Roger Dodger* (2002)** Campbell Scott, playing a paragraph-spouting pickup artist who's up to his ears in manipulative techniques and "wisdom," takes his naive nephew out for a night on the town. This is what you want to keep a wary eye out for, ladies.

***Friends with Money* (2006)** Writer-director Nicole Holofcener's film analyzes a very particular dynamic—that of being a luckless and careerless lonely girl (Jennifer Aniston) in an L.A. circle of friends (Catherine Keener, Frances McDormand, and Joan Cusack) who are all married and rich. Seems preposterous, given the casting, but nobody in this country uses as sympathetic a microscope as Holofcener when examining the conundrums of modern women, and Aniston is convincing and sad.

IV

MR. LONELYHEARTS

> "Thousands, literally thousands, of songs about heartbreak, rejection, pain, misery, and loss."
> —John Cusack, *High Fidelity*

Men pine lonesomely, too—and their beleaguered, schlubby hearts can also divide time spent between needing empathy and venting rage about modern woman's vacuous, soulless, often materialistic behavior. Since most movies are made by men, there's no shortage of candidates.

The Blue Angel (1930) Stuffy prof Emil Jannings throws away his life for Marlene Dietrich—wouldn't you?—and is reduced to a humiliated cuckold and vaudeville clown. The credible beauty of this film-school classic is Dietrich, who plays not a caricatured vampiress, but a common, even warm-hearted hussy.

The Devil Is a Woman (1935) From *The Blue Angel* to this nutty chintz—star Marlene Dietrich and director Josef von Sternberg moved from gritty German morality play to cartoon misogyny. Here, Dietrich is a man-eating Spanish dancer who's faithful to no man. The military chumps (Cesar Romero and Lionel Atwill) are merely hapless pawns, despite their bluster. Great if you're feeling bitter, yet jonesy for 1930s chiaroscuro.

Double Indemnity (1944) The concept of the "femme fatale" was old hat when James M. Cain wrote his vicious thriller *Double Indemnity*, but (with some help from this film adaptation, which was coscripted by Raymond Chandler and director Billy Wilder) he made the man-eating antiheroine into *the* dramatis persona of the postwar era.

Leave Her to Heaven (1945) For sheer feminine acidity, no other actress of Hollywood's Golden Era could touch Gene Tierney, whose ridiculously opalescent beauty and silky overbite could be turned on a dime into misanthropy. This weird melodrama features her most discomfiting portrait of homicidal jealousy, for the likes of which new hubby Cornel Wilde is far from prepared.

Susana (1951) Luis Buñuel's early Mexican phase (1947 to about 1960) was dominated by feverish, satiric melodramas in which men revealed themselves to be fetishistic beasts without control over their instincts or neuroses. This film presents the same type of story, but about the opposite sex: a psychotic young woman (Rosita Quintana) escapes from a sanitarium, embeds herself in a normal, peaceful Mexican family, and slowly tears it to pieces.

The Shrike (1955) With a title like that, who would cast June Allyson in the starring role? That's what director and costar Jose Ferrer did, in this theatrical domestic noir about a successful stage director driven mad by his spiteful, calculating, deranged wife. Allyson's toothy sweetness makes her a galling, untrustworthy creature here, and the scenario powerfully evokes an angry man's scream for help.

David Holzman's Diary (1967) A mockery of the then-new personal documentary movement, and a film seemingly made by one man—L. M. Kit Carson as a New York nobody who decides to make a "vérité" documentary about his life, his West Side apartment, his street, and, most of all, his relationship with a sensible girl (Eileen Dietz), who grows increasingly fed up not only with being filmed, but with Holzman's introspection as well. In reality, the film was written and directed by Jim McBride.

Le Samouraï (1967) Alain Delon is the epitome of lonely cool in this celebrated Jean-Pierre Melville neogangster fable, as a disciplined, trench-coated assassin whose emotional armor is penetrated by a nightclub chanteuse, making him prey for the cops and the underworld.

The Swimmer (1968) The loneliest lonely-man movie ever made, based on what you'd think would be an unfilmable John Cheever short story: Burt Lancaster is a Connecticut family man who, apropos of nothing, appears in a neighbor's yard and dives into the pool. He proceeds to "swim" a long circuit of his rich neighbors' pools, "going home," as he says. It's a journey that reveals along the way what the pool owners already know: that this buoyant, athletic guy has nowhere to go.

Play Misty for Me (1971) The primordial predecessor to 1987's *Fatal Attraction* (see below), Clint Eastwood's film has the laconic star playing a L.A. disc jockey who's stalked by a maniacal, needy fan (Jessica Walters). Creepy crawly in the extreme.

Betty Blue (1986) An even more alarming scenario: sharing sexual obsession with an out-and-out bipolar harridan (Beatrice Dalle). Jean-Jacques Beineix's exhaustive film is drenched with sex and full of masculine fear.

Fatal Attraction (1987) The movie that put an entire generation of American men off one night stands, this glossy, calculated, trashy film still raises the "I'm better off alone" hairs on your neck, particularly during the suicide-attempt scene, in which privileged family man Michael Douglas truly visits the Land of Holy Shit.

What Happened Was... (1994) This chillingly mundane portrait of a first date that never should've occurred is an adaptation of a play (both the play and the adaptation were written by Tom Noonan, who also directed and stars in the film). Even so, it's less theatrical than brutally personal, and the observations about modern mating, lonesomeness, and communication breakdown are white hot. Noonan plays an antisocial white-collar dweeb who's invited into the home of a desperately lonely, not-too-bright coworker, played with nerve-racking honesty by Karen Sillas. She's lovely, but out of her element in the Manhattan power zone; he's a solitary misfit who seems superior and ambitious (he lies about being a writer), but is actually an unmitigated zero. What ensues between them is a naked sketch of urban despair, and once Sillas begins reading her deranged, vanity-published children's stories aloud, things get very, quietly crazy. A winner at the Sundance Film Festival—and a shining example of what can be done with a small budget, one room, and two people—Noonan's movie is menacing, creepy, and, finally, scary. Unattached, lonely singles should be forewarned: it pays to be picky.

Fallen Angels (1995) Hong Kong filmmaker Wong Kar-Wai is a culty, art-house phenomenon with a pop-eyed visual style (comprising equal parts MTV camera crank, Hong Kong claustrophobia, New Wavey *l'amour fou*, and abbreviated rock 'n' roll attention span), and a permanently forlorn heart. Like Wong's *Chungking Express*, this rambunctious ode lovingly yet crazily zooms around the tight corners of contemporary Hong Kong. The movie involves, on one hand, an embittered hit man (Leon Lai), whose life migrates anonymously from job to job as dictated by the Agent (Michelle Reis), an efficient gal Friday who sets up his temporary pads, does the paperwork, pays him—and is secretly in love with him. On the other hand, the film is also the story of a mute (and slightly deranged) ex-con (Takeshi Kaneshiro) whose ersatz living is made by breaking into shops after closing time and maniacally compelling reluctant customers to buy from him. These two engaging and often hilarious tales crisscross at several points; in Wong's Hong Kong, everybody—however supercool they may be—is abandoned and searching for elusive connections.

Heavy (1995) Superreal, uncompromised, and blazingly homely, *Heavy* is a movie that's covered with honest work blisters—nothing interests first-time writer-director James Mangold quite as much as simply watching ordinary people do their jobs. The central figure is a grade-A palooka: Victor (Pruitt Taylor Vince) is an inarticulate, obese pizza cook who's stuck in a lonely rut as wide as the Hudson Valley. Doting on his mom (Shelley Winters), who owns the joint, and otherwise keeping to himself (so much so, in fact that Vince has maybe twenty-five lines in the whole film), Victor silently melts down once Callie (Liv Tyler) hires on to wait tables. We would, too. The film seethes with revealing moments, and none of its characters—not even Deborah Harry's overseasoned bar slut—remains an easily pigeonholed type for very long.

Fight Club (1999) Taking the emasculating numbness of modern civilization to task, David Fincher's runaway train of a movie roasts the post-tech world's masculine frustration on a spit, forming a hilarious, vivid, almost apocalyptic vision of lost modern men. Edward Norton's unnamed protagonist is a white-collar nobody whose empty life creates both an inability to sleep and an addiction to catalog consumerism; into this void stumbles Tyler Durden (Brad Pitt), a closet anarchist and lowlife who lives off the grid in an abandoned house; together, the two men act out their frustrations by simply beating each other into pulps in a bar parking lot every Saturday night. Others join in, and the ritual eventually becomes an underground tribal cult, a secret club in which the joys of hitting and being hit are their own means and ends. Unfortunately, the scenario escalates into a silly kind of fascistic anarchism, but there isn't a more volatile and cathartic film about frustrated maleness in the Hollywood canon.

High Fidelity (2000) In this adaptation of Nick Hornby's farcically self-pitying novel, John Cusack plays a going-nowhere record store owner and pop-music obsessive who, after his latest relationship collapses, takes the viewer on a tour of his past romances.

The Brown Bunny **(2003)** If, and only if, you can somehow push aside the rampaging narcissism on display in Vincent Gallo's dizzy, sad film, you might be able to feel his pain as a cross-country bike racer who travels from east to west, meeting women but haunted by a lost love. A late-in-the-game pornographic plot twist is actually the film's most rueful moment.

MIDLIFE CRISIS

"All of the sudden, it's closer to the end than it is to the beginning."
—William Holden, *Network*

If you're having a full-on middle-age breakdown, complete with sports cars, face lifts, jewelry debt, or trophy concubines, no movie can help you. But if you've yet to succumb, the right film might serve as an effective replacement for such shenanigans. Movies, quite sensibly, tend to dissect the midlife crisis, and they often make nasty sport of it even when they're sympathetic, so if immerse yourself, you can feel as if you passed through the gauntlet without any of the psychological damage that comes with it.

IV

The Roman Spring of Mrs. Stone **(1961)** Vivien Leigh, looking her age with a vengeance, revisits Tennessee Williams country as a retired actress who spends her days drifting through Italy and falling in with gigolo Warren Beatty. Pitiful if you buy into it; silly and potentially comforting if you don't.

8½ **(1963)** Federico Fellini's great, revered movie about the inner tumult of a worshipped Italian filmmaker who doesn't know what to do next. Because it is dreamy and impressionistic, and aims its harpoons straight at Fellini's own sense of self, it's the only film in which the man's absurdist style seems eloquent and meaningful. The movie receives a gratuitous homage from Woody Allen's ***Stardust Memories*** **(1980)**.

The Arrangement **(1969)** At some point in his fifties, Elia Kazan had a nervous breakdown, then wrote a novel about it, and then adapted the book for the cinema; the result is arguably the first Hollywood movie ever to deal explicitly with the concept of midlife crisis. Kirk Douglas is the fracturing American Man, Deborah Kerr is his patronizing wife, and Faye Dunaway is the young hottie who turns him upside down.

The Rain People **(1969)** Shirley Knight, pregnant and pissed, is a Long Island housewife who one day decides she's had enough—and simply begins driving, eventually taking in hitchhiker James Caan, who turns out to be a young, brain-injured ex-football player on his way to a job to which he may not be welcome. Francis Ford Coppola directed; it's his first film from an all-original screenplay.

The Wild Bunch (1969) Sam Peckinpah invented the "antiwestern," and one way in which this bloody, existentialist subgenre differs from the westerns that came before is in its focus on how the western culture was dying out right along with its vestigial witnesses. The outlaw cowboys here (William Holden, Ernest Borgnine, Warren Oates, and Ben Johnson) are old, paunchy, bitter as hell, and ready to throw their lives away for one last fight, deep in Mexico, because the world they once knew has no more frontier and no more tolerance for lawless independence. Other, earlier cowboy stars (John Wayne, Randolph Scott, et al.) were able to age within the genre, but only in the days of Wild Sam did the fate of aged prairie men signify the evaporation of an entire way of life.

The Hospital (1971) Paddy Chayefsky's gritty but lunatic comedy about a chaotic and often terminally dangerous urban hospital is centered on one of the 1970s' great portraits of middle-age angst: George C. Scott, as a doctor tortured by professional doubt and personal terror.

Last Tango in Paris (1972) Director Bernardo Bertolucci brings Marlon Brando to Paris, where, grieving for his dead wife, he begins a purposefully meaningless and empty sexual liaison with a pert Eurobabe, played by Maria Schneider. Massively titillating in its day, but now more appreciated as a powerful probing of the aimless, mateless male animal in middle life, regardless of the city or sexual position.

The Passenger (1975) Jack Nicholson was only thirty-seven when he made this mysterious Michelangelo Antonioni masterwork, but the scenario is tempting to every aging human: confronted with a white man's body while working in an African country, a disgruntled reporter looking to escape his life swaps identities. Of course, it doesn't turn out well—the corpse belonged to an arms runner, and his history is in hot pursuit.

Network (1976) Featuring quite possibly the most thoughtfully written script in Hollywood history, Paddy Chayefsky's torrential satire on the television industry wasn't so far-fetched at the time, and it's turned out to be so prophetic that today's jaded high schooler might think it tame. It's a movie to be savored for many reasons, among them the autumnal crisis endured by aging network exec Max Schumacher (William Holden), who faces the business end of his career just as Faye Dunaway's irresistibly amoral company hotshot lures him into an affair. He knows it's all a soap opera cliche, and she hardly knows soap from real life, but in the meantime there's real heartache here, with Holden and his wife (Oscar winner Beatrice Straight) bravely facing—in painful, human terms— the desperate confusions of fading love and angry devotion. It's a notably sympathetic portrait because it's so viciously honest, and anyone in his or her fifties can find understanding company in Holden's melancholy, hound-dog visage.

Serial (1980) As the Ramones said, it's the end of the seventies, it's the end of the century—and Martin Mull's middle-class family man, lost in his own suburban L.A. existence, is watching his family and world implode in new age cultisms, media idiocy, sexual-revolution legacies, and California trendiness. The script, by Michael Elias and Rich Eustis, is snarky as hell.

The Border (1982) Jack Nicholson finally embraces his middle-aged spread, as a border patrolman who cleans up his corrupt ways and complacent middle-class lifestyle when confronted with the genuine suffering of the Mexican poor. Sounds programmatic, but it's a nascent 1970s film, full of thorny character.

Tempest (1982) Paul Mazursky's idea of a midlife crisis puts a carefree John Cassavetes, overpowered by a renewed zest for life, on a Greek island with new girlfriend Susan Sarandon, tempestuous daughter Molly Ringwald, and horny native Caliban figure Raul Julia. Ebullient and crazy—and no slouch on Shakespearian business, either.

Shirley Valentine (1989) At long last, a midlife crisis movie about a woman who's actually in the middle of her life. Manchester working-class housewife Shirley (Pauline Collins) addresses the camera as if she's revenging all the ridiculed English women in *Alfie* (that 1966 Michael Caine–as–womanizer affront), venting her frustration and disappointment at who she's become and how she lost herself along the way. She hitches a free trip to Greece to discover, thankfully, that being over forty doesn't have to mean an end to skinny-dipping in the Aegean Sea and drinking retsina by sunset. Unembarrassed by the film's staginess, Collins looks like a real middle-aged woman whose hips have borne children and whose chin hasn't been lifted above her eyebrows.

Where Angels Fear to Tread (1991) The most barbed of E. M. Forster's novels makes for the least-seen film of the 1980s–90s Edwardian literature adaptation fad. Helen Mirren plays a proper English widow who, while on holiday, falls for and marries an Italian lower-class charmer, thus prompting criticism and social strife from her friends.

Affliction (1997) Writer-director Paul Schrader's film, based on Russell Banks's acclaimed novel, is a difficult movie to warm up to, but it's true to itself and the thorny discomfort of aging out of your own usefulness. Exploring the simple descent of a self-destructive, middle-class, northeastern man with big family problems, the movie is so frosty and clinical it can make your eyes water. Nick Nolte is Wade Whitehouse, a nowhere man scrambling to hold onto his dissolving life in a small, weather-beaten, one-horse New Hampshire town. Wade's a glorified traffic cop and odd-jobber who gets no respect, and his life is, in many ways, already over: his marriage is shattered, and his sparse relationship with his daughter (Brigid Tierney) is uncommunicative and spiteful. Plagued

IV

by a toothache, haunted by a childhood of abuse, beleaguered by the unfailingly kind intentions of his waitress girlfriend (Sissy Spacek), and struggling to rearrange custody for a daughter to whom he has no idea how to relate, Wade suddenly loses his job as well, pushing him right over the edge. It's essentially a character study, and one that could make your own fifties seem a whole lot sunnier.

After Sex (Post Coitum Animal Triste) (1997) Brigitte Roüan's superb psychodrama-comedy might be the best of a popular French subgenre: the "older woman, younger stud" tragedy, usually starring Isabelle Huppert. Here, Roüan herself (at age fifty or so) plays a wife, mother, and successful publisher who falls to pieces over a rather despicable Latin hunk.

Sunday (1997) An introverted middle-aged man (David Suchet) living in a Queens homeless shelter is confronted on the street by an aging English woman (Lisa Harrow), who says she recognizes him as a famous film director—no one is telling *us* anytime soon what's "true" and what isn't. The spooky mating dance between these two emotionally battered pilgrims eventually becomes profoundly deranged, compounding fantasy, lies, movie plots, and the chilly truth. Director Jonathan Nossiter keeps the mystery alive in the filmmaking as well, shooting the autumnal badlands of Queens as if it were Nagasaki.

American Beauty (1999) Absurdly overrated and over-Oscared, this popular film about a suburban man's self-immolating midlife ya-yas is witty and professional, but it lays on the "middle-class family as embodiment of all things evil" spiel way too thickly. Kevin Spacey got an Oscar for, essentially, knowing where the laughs were.

Bread & Tulips (2000) Silvio Soldini's adroit and, finally, soft-headed comedy focuses on slow-smiling, relentlessly kind Licia Maglietta as an Italian mom left behind on a family tour-bus vacation in northern Italy (her husband and teenage sons are self-involved lugs, but the film only skirts the satiric potential of a family so dopily masculine that the mother could actually be forgotten at a road stop). She deflects her irritated husband's telephoned efforts to get her home, jumps a bus to Venice, and essentially searches for a new life—which she finds without much ado, in a community of semieccentric florists, cross-dressers, waiters, and losers. The film makes no bones about being a wholesome, feel-good vacation of a movie, and the viewer is encouraged to enjoy Venice much as the heroine does.

Sexy Beast (2000) Jonathan Glazer's film—the meanest, leanest, and most mysterious of recent British crime movies—is also something like an anxious elegy for middle-aged peace and quiet. As in, that is exactly what Gal (Ray Winstone), a relaxed, overtanned, porcine ex-crook living with his gorgeous ex–porn queen wife DeeDee (Amanda Redman) in a Spanish villa, cannot find. Into his lazy hedonism comes Ben Kingsley's Don Logan—a wiry, jug-eared sociopath so hard-core you can hear murder in his most innocuous utterances—on a mission to recruit Gal for a job back in London. Most of Glazer's film takes place in and around Gal's house as Logan hectors, insults, threatens, menaces, pummels, and coerces Gal, often fearsomely, into reentering the crime life. We don't need to be told what Logan is capable of, or what everyone else has already experienced with him, because we see it in their eyes. Confident, mature, deeply conceived, and convincingly inhabited, it's a surprisingly humane film—despite the close-range shotgun spray—and Gal's plight is impossible to *not* empathize with.

Wonder Boys (2000) Middle-aged literature professor Grady Tripp (Michael Douglas) is having a bad day: his wife has just left him, he's having an affair with his boss's wife (she also happens to be the chancellor of the university), and his editor is coming to town expecting a finished manuscript—of which he's written very little, although he's already used up a full ream of paper in the attempt. His own "wonder boy" years as star author far behind him, he embarks on a snowy Pittsburgh weekend odyssey that ends up involving a stoned literary prodigy (Tobey Maguire), a transvestite, a dead dog hidden in a trunk, a manuscript more promising than his own, and the stolen jacket of Marilyn Monroe. Michael Chabon's novel of midlife crisis is wisely centered in the academic milieu: is there any more constant reminder that you're past your prime than being surrounded by the flush of youth 24/7? We could feel our own age lines expand as we watched, but that doesn't mean the movie isn't smart, quick, witty, and lovable—it is.

Yi Yi (2000) How difficult is it to make a truthful movie about family? Think of some. Can't? That's how difficult it is. Bearing the emotional complexity and depth of a great novel, Edward Yang's film (the title translates as "one one" in Chinese, or "one by one") resonates on so many levels that it may take several viewings to sop them all up. *Yi Yi* trains its wise gaze upon a family's often unexamined middle years—when children seem to be nothing but trouble, aging parents begin to die, jobs become outmoded, and lost opportunities begin to seriously haunt. The family in question is the Jians, which consists of middle-aged software executive N.J. (Wu Nienjen), his troubled wife Min-Min (Elaine Jin), their teenage daughter Ting-Ting (Kelly Lee) and seven-year-old son Yang-Yang (Jonathan Chang). As the family attempts to nurse a comatose grandmother by talking at her bedside, each in his or her own way, N.J.'s life becomes a litany of dissolving or restructuring chaos: his business is failing, his wife suffers a midlife crisis and retreats to a mountain temple, and he stumbles into Sherry (Ke Suyun), an old sweetheart who has since married an American insurance broker but who pines, as N.J. does, for their perished first love. No synopsis could do justice to Yang's naturalistic textures, breath-catching moments, and affecting rhythms; at nearly three hours long, it's a five-course meal of a movie, with drinks. This one's for mature moviegoers for whom most movies have come to resemble brainless carnival rides, not works of art.

Calendar Girls (2003) In youth-obsessed America, where it's entirely possible to start feeling over the hill at age twenty-five, this film is a refreshing, good-natured slap in the face: a comedy, based on a true story, in which a group of Yorkshire women nervily bare all for a yearly fund-raising calendar, which becomes, as we see, a sensation. These women aren't making fitness videos on the side, either—these are real bodies, belonging to undoctored women (including Helen Mirren, Julie Walters, and Linda Bassett) who are willing to be judged by a shortsighted world. The script isn't overly sweet, although the saucily affirmative tone and the wheezy tai chi coda are trying.

49 Up (2005) Michael Apted's *Up* films began as a BBC news program exploring an old Jesuit maxim: "Give me the child until he is seven, and I will show you the man." This is the seventh film in forty-two years, and the average Britishers who were chosen arbitrarily in 1964, when they were merely second-graders, have grown up, grown out, lost hair, and suffered traumas, and now they face the down slope of their lives. (Their passage from cherubs to weathered middle-aged adults is complicated, of course, by fact that the film series itself has intruded on their lives—a point made by several participants.) In each of the *Up* films after the first, Apted has made liberal use of footage from the previous films, and while each installment becomes a chastening portrait of time, modern life, aging, and regret, this latest entry is even more so. Undoubtedly, *56 Up* will be leveling.

PARANOIA

"Is it safe?"
—Laurence Olivier, *Marathon Man*

When paranoia sets in, there's nothing like a few compatriotic movies that agree with your darkest moments: they *are* out to get you, the system *is* engineered to squeeze you like an orange, and things *are* only going from bad to worse. It's no accident that several of these films are based on true stories, and several more *could* be happening, *right now.*

Invasion of the Body Snatchers (1956) Don Siegel's unbeatable Cold War parable, set in a small California town, about alien pods falling to Earth and systematically swapping out real, emotional humans with conformist robotic replicas. More than just a pulp exercise in paranoia, it's a searing indictment of Eisenhower America, and it's almost unbearably suspenseful.

The Wrong Man (1956) Alfred Hitchcock's only film that's based on a true story, in which Henry Fonda's unassuming musician is mistaken for a wanted criminal and sucked into a grim maelstrom of bureaucratic terror. Chilly and, as far as Hitchcock movies go, underrated.

Peeping Tom (1960) Michael Powell's chilling film rivals Alfred Hitchcock's *Psycho* as the 1960 movie that upset the universal-audience applecart. (Afterward, children just *had* to be kept away from some movies.) It might be the most perverse British film ever made, and it's something of an understatement to say that England wasn't ready for Powell's creepy vision—the film killed Powell's previously distinguished career. The story revolves around Mark (Karl Boehm), a soft-spoken German fellow in modish London, working on movie sets, living in an apartment house and, we learn (not too slowly), murdering women with a spiked tripod leg (his third leg!) as he films them with a 16mm camera. We see the film he shoots often, including one early scene wherein Mark has a kind of symbolic orgasm during a victim's death screams. Powell lays out the character's warped world quietly and effectively, tracing the unforking path of trauma and perversion immediately back to Mark's father, who experimentally terrorized the boy and filmed his reactions to the abuse.

IV

The Trial (1963) Orson Welles's baroque adaptation of Kafka's novel focuses on an average guy (Anthony Perkins) in a mysterious totalitarian state who's accused of who knows what by who knows whom, and yanked into a nightmarish metaphoric version of modern bureaucracy, in which the ultimate goal is maintaining power, not pursuing truth. Welles's frantic postproduction dubbing (he provided many of the actors' voices himself) only adds to the sense of dislocation.

A Report on the Party and the Guests (1966) Jan Nemec's Czech New Wave howl of discontent, this furious parable on Soviet Bloc–era oppression had been supposedly "banned forever" in Czechoslovakia, presumably for sharing the blame for totalitarianism between the government and its subjects. Picnickers are accosted by mysterious police figures; as if in a dream, all of them are then invited to an outdoor banquet, during which the innocent conform to the suspicions of their victimizers and start betraying each other. When a rebel (played by director Evald Schorm) emerges, everyone agrees he should be run down and apprehended, even though they never learn why they're there.

Seconds (1966) One of the greatest and creepiest of paranoia movies from the Vietnam era, John Frankenheimer's unforgettable film has the authentic, gritty chill of a bad dream endured while breathing through a pillow. It's the kind of crazy, scary, thoroughly morbid film that Hollywood not only doesn't make anymore, but also was probably surprised, like we were in 1966, that it *ever* made. Pudgy, dyspeptic John Randolph stars first as a phobic, unhappy businessman who is approached by a huge, seemingly all-powerful Company that will, for a price, provide individuals with a completely new identity and life. Reluctantly, Randolph becomes "reborn," his death faked with some-one else's body, his life restructured, and his face remodeled into Rock Hudson's. Not any more sure of himself, Hudson becomes a Malibu artist and tries to blend in as a happy bachelor. But it isn't so easy: his sense of unease and lostness remain, he knows he's living a lie, and the Company constantly surrounds him with agents and employees, forever fearful of having their cover blown by an inexperienced cli-ent. Hardly free to do as he chooses, the poor guy makes a mess of this life, too, and when he returns to the anonymous halls of the Company and demands to be recycled once again, he finds he's caught in a harrowing bureaucratic nightmare that's as Kafkaesque as it is ruthlessly capitalistic. This was a major studio film with a big star, yet it's shot in a fish-eyed, claustrophobic style reminiscent of avant-garde films and berserk independents. You can always feel the ceiling lowering on you, and the characters breathing down your neck.

THX 1138 **(1971)** A purist's dystopia by first-timer George Lucas, this film offers a despairing, antiseptic vision that often encloses its numbered, hairless drone-humans in complete whiteness. Robert Duvall is the restless prole who decides that a lab rat's life isn't enough.

The Conversation **(1974)** Between the *Godfather*s, Francis Ford Coppola crafted this nerve-racking essay on privacy and surveillance; Gene Hackman is a bugging expert who's so good at his job that he's emptied his life rather than be bugged himself. Murder might result from one assignment, sending him on a guilty, destabilized tear—which in turn makes him the subject of the surveillance he's always dreaded. Indelible.

The Parallax View **(1974)** In the paranoid post-JFK/RFK/MLK world, Warren Beatty's rogue reporter sniffs out a conspiracy behind a politician's murder and ends up inside an assassin training program. Director Alan J. Pakula was the dark prince of Nixon-era paranoia, and this neglected chiller is crazy with institutional menace. For more Pakula fun, check out *Klute* **(1971)**.

Three Days of the Condor **(1975)** Back in the 1970s, the CIA had cred only as a cabal of evil, black-op mercenaries. That's how they're portrayed in this wintry suspenser, in which Robert Redford's agency schmo survives an office massacre and goes on the run. In this film, even the mailmen are suspect.

Marathon Man **(1976)** Paranoia of a different stripe—William Goldman's bestselling yarn puts Dustin Hoffman's postgrad in the path of backstabbing Cold War combatants and elderly Nazis, as they argue over a booty of war diamonds. Laurence Olivier's dentist Mengele is the stuff of lifelong memories.

Invasion of the Body Snatchers **(1978)** Philip Kaufman's inspired remake of the 1956 Cold War nail-biter transfers its anxieties to post-hippie San Francisco, an entire society already undergoing neurotic stress. The textures of the film—from the linty mange of the pods to the soundtrack's insistent background screams—can drive you right up the wall. In a good way.

The Entity (**1982**) Paranoia to the nth degree: Barbara Hershey plays a woman who is inexplicably plagued—and repeatedly raped—by some kind of horny, invisible ghost. Supposedly based on a true story. The music alone can shake your trust in the world.

1984 (**1984**) George Orwell's cautionary tale about a futuristic fascist England is done right by director Michael Radford, down to the film's deliberately antiquated visual style—it's an incarnation of the future as seen from 1948. John Hurt is Winston Smith (looking exactly like existential litterateur Samuel Beckett—coincidence?), Richard Burton is the government's voice of persuasion, and the rats play themselves.

Brazil (**1985**) Who would've thought that the man behind those air-brushed cutout animations of *Monty Python's Flying Circus* would eventually arrive at this, an anachronistic, technophobic vision of a preposterously British bureaucratic future that pushes Orwell's *1984* through the Play-Doh Fun Factory and ends up somewhere far north of the Ministry of Silly Walks? Terry Gilliam uncorked every bottle in his cellar for this hellzapoppin experience, which chronicles a lone Everyman (Jonathan Pryce) trying to find joy and righteousness in a neofascist dystopia in which misprinted paperwork can get an innocent man "erased" and ductwork is so maniacal that repairmen have become covert vigilantes (Robert De Niro gives a nice turn in a SWAT uniform). By taking out newspaper ads and holding a clandestine screening for the Los Angeles Film Critics Association, Gilliam shamed Universal into releasing this visually berserk film unmutilated—right down to the catatonic climax.

JFK (**1991**) Maybe this Oliver Stone blitz should be listed under "Election Day" (although that may depend on your political predilections), but it's also our modern era's most convincing paranoiac screed. Much of the movie—which revolves primarily around actors like Kevin Costner acting out one of several semipossible conspiracy scenarios regarding the events that occurred in Dealey Plaza on November 22, 1963—is questionable, but just as much is not. At least credit Stone for having the *cajones* to have Costner's Jim Garrison, unraveling a plot that reaches straight to Lyndon Johnson, spit the word "facism" during his in-court summation.

Kafka (**1991**) One of us still likes this movie, which makes for a grand total of two fans worldwide, if you're counting screenwriter Lem Dobbs's mother. Steven Soderbergh cashed in his *sex, lies, and videotape* cachet on this comic, Gothic faux biopic, in which Franz (Jeremy Irons) becomes an ersatz detective investigating a rash of seamy murders in old Prague. Shot in antiquated black and white until the story passes through a portal, at which point it blooms in color. Unjustly maligned—or so the minority thinks.

Shadows and Fog (1992) Woody Allen does Kafka—and rips the processes of fascist anti-Semitism *and* the informant methods of Stalinist Communism. But really it's just Allen, dithering about during a foggy night as a serial killer lurks and too many guest stars loiter at the fringes in the tiny sections of Manhattan that still look, vaguely, like turn-of-the-century Prague.

Body Snatchers (1993) "Where are you gonna go?" rasps pod-Mom Meg Tilly to her panicky husband in this third version of the deathless Jack Finney sci-fi novel—and, because we've seen the previous two films (Don Siegel's 1956 original and Philip Kaufman's 1978 remake), we know there is, indeed, nowhere to run. Goosey and creepy, Ferrara's rendition, in which the takeover of the Earth by emotionless aliens begins not in a small town or in San Francisco but on a southern army base, de-emphasizes the story's just-add-water paranoia by locating the invasion in the place where America's "fear of the Other" throbs strongest—the military—and by focusing on an already broken family, complete with a disassociated teenager who *already* thinks her stepmom is a pod person.

IV

Cube (1997) A high-concept, polished Canadian sci-fi indie, Vincenzo Natali's movie is an ingenious but stagy attempt at beginning where Sartre's play *No Exit* left off: five individuals suddenly find themselves, for no apparent reason and with no idea how they got there, trapped inside a fourteen-by-fourteen-foot square room made of steel and Plexiglas. That room has six doors—one on each wall, one in the floor, and one in the ceiling—that lead to other identical rooms with doors, and so on. Oh, and some of those rooms are booby-trapped with high-tech weaponry. A lean study on feeling lost inside a bureaucratic modern world.

Gattaca (1997) Andrew Niccol's frosty, philosophical dystopian vision involves a future corporate world wherein genetic engineering is standard practice—when a couple decides to have a child, the future parents select its attributes and have the kid created in a lab from their respective genetic strands. In such a world, the only kind of disadvantaged background you can have is to have been conceived the natural way (and indeed, those who are conceived naturally are labeled "invalid"). Workplaces require certain genetic requirements, a test for which can be quickly made from a stray hair, a flake of shed skin, or a drop of urine or blood. Ethan Hawke plays Vincent, a "faith-birth" who is determined to beat the system, rise up through the ranks, and eventually be shipped out to a planet colony. His plan begins with striking an illegal deal with a crippled athlete (Jude Law) to assume his identity and use *his* hair, skin, and blood. Needless to say, fate dogs Vincent's heels—every time he sheds a hair, he's at risk of being outed. Niccol hits home runs with his details: the urine sample that *is* a job interview; the relentless hunt for stray hairs and skin; the walk-in genetic analysis shop that costar Uma Thurman uses as if it's an ATM. Superficially a parable on racism and classism, the film is, on a deeper level, a harrowing look at life in the ultimate police state—one structured around biology.

***The Matrix* (1999)** Enough has been written, blogged, theorized, treatised, and rhapsodized about this box office behemoth that it hardly requires our boost, except perhaps to say that it does posit an extreme form of dystopia—one that isn't even there. The sequels were significantly less interesting.

***Caché* (2005)** Michael Haneke's quasi-metaphysical domestic thriller, in which a bobo French couple (Daniel Auteuil and Juliette Binoche) become victims, shall we say, of history's own surveillance. A masterpiece that grows in your head long after you see it—but pay attention.

SPIRITUAL/PHILOSOPHICAL CRISIS   **IV**

"God is a luxury I cannot afford."
—Martin Landau, *Crimes and Misdemeanors*

In an age when spacious thinking is frowned upon, movies—unlike most pop music—can pose the large questions, address basic metaphysical issues, express cosmic doubts and urges, and flesh out the big moral doozies that any of us could face at any time. If you're doubting your faith, plagued by existential angst—or just wonderin' about you, us, and the universe—movies, and particularly these movies, are uniquely equipped to provide the narratives and psychodramatics necessary for contemplative thought.

***The Passion of Joan of Arc* (1928)** Danish heavyweight Carl Dreyer shot this French film using bare, expressionistic sets, the immolated saint's actual trial transcripts, and a stage actress named Maria Falconetti, who delivered what many have considered to be the most beautiful and affecting film performance of all time. Of course the issue at hand is spiritual integrity—do you surrender your beliefs, or *say* you do, in exchange for clemency from an evil empire? Who does God's work, anyway? One of the faithful, Dreyer was intent on communicating the tormenting experience of spirit-body conflict, and this well-worn art-house cornerstone still astonishes.

***Diary of a Country Priest* (1950)** Robert Bresson's act of cinematic penitence details the largely internalized tribulations of a sick, weak priest in an unhappy French village; his efforts at salvation and rescue are often seen as betrayals and uselessness. The film's formal approach is austere, undemonstrative, and so pure it hurts.

***The Flowers of St. Francis* (1950)** Early in his neorealist career, Roberto Rossellini crafted this rather joyous chronicle of the saint and his band of comical monk followers, who strive toward ascetic divinity but end up wrestling with folly, pride, and the nature of happiness. The only film ever to view early Catholicism's semi-Buddhist attitudes as strategies toward joy.

***Ordet* (1955)** Another ascetic, in his fifth decade of filmmaking when this movie was made, great Dane Carl Dreyer crafted this theatrical, definitive version of Kaj Munk's miracle play about a soul-sick family finally rescued by a single act of impossibly powerful faith. Intended as a cleansing experience, both spiritually and cinematically.

***The Incredible Shrinking Man* (1957)** Some guy (Grant Williams) inhales some toxic fumes and begins to shrink—suddenly, his furniture and clothes don't fit, his wife doesn't know what to do with him, and a common house cat becomes a serious threat to life and limb. Written by Richard Matheson, this 1950s piece of pulp organically poses some deep philosophical questions about man and the cosmos, and it doesn't pretend to answer them.

***Meetings with Remarkable Men* (1979)** A film version of the book by Armenian mystic/teacher G. I. Gurdjieff, this movie traces Gurdjieff's early days of roaming through Asia, searching for spiritual answers and experiencing life and death. More of an introduction to Gurdjieff's writings than a spiritual experience itself.

***Crimes and Misdemeanors* (1989)** One of Woody Allen's richest films, and one that dares to take on the weightiest of moral dilemmas, as Martin Landau's tortured Manhattan ophthalmologist is confronted with saving himself, his wife, and his lifestyle from the destructive forces of Anjelica Huston's unstable girlfriend. What can we live with? What price can we, and others, pay for peace and happiness?

***Mindwalk* (1990)** A three-way debate about life and meaning, set in Mont Saint-Michel at low tide, among a scientist (Liv Ullmann), a politician (Sam Waterston), and a poet (John Heard). The discussion rarely actually rises to a boil, but it's interesting nonetheless, particularly when Ullmann's reclusive egghead explains quantum physics in basic terms, and the men find the concept reflected in ideas about their own work.

***The Double Life of Veronique* (1991)** It's difficult to articulate exactly why Krzysztof Kieslowski's film is such an epochal experience, but it has everything to do with his worshipful attention to dewy star Irène Jacob, to the opalescent, "world through a teardrop" cinematography of Slawomir Idziak, and to the fundamentally enigmatic tale cowritten by Krzysztof Piesiewicz: two women (both played by Jacob), one a choir soprano in Poland, the other a music teacher in France, exist simultaneously but are unaware of each other. Crisscrossings, unbalanced awarenesses, sudden deaths, secret connections: how do you film inner disassociativeness, or spiritual awakening? Don't ask, just watch. There's no possible way to beg for more concrete conclusions from this magnificent movie's scenario than Kieslowski wants to give you; you either enter into this languid world of sensual reverence, global ghostliness, and never-ending questions or you leave the room. Are the two women in fact the same, an otherworldly bifurcation discovered by chance—implying a secret government of spiritual tissue beneath the surface of life? Or is it coincidence, which itself becomes a metaphor for the story of a life, for time, and for the role that luck plays in the supposed significance of our lives?

The Rapture (1991) Novelist Michael Tolkin takes on American evangelical culture—making up most of the cultural particulars—by way of a wayward nympho (Mimi Rogers) who tastes salvation, devotes her life to God, and carries the belief in self-sacrifice and anticipation of the end times to its horrifying climax. In the end, Tolkin affirms the Book of Revelations—but dares to suggest that belief is not enough.

Dream of Light (1992) Only Spanish master Victor Erice's third feature in three decades, this patient, observational essay began its public life at Cannes in 1992 under its original title, *The Quince-Tree Sun,* which is understood, in the film, as the name for a morning glow in early autumnal Spain, when the light hits the ripe quinces in a certain way. The film pursues that light in an almost radical way, patiently tracking the creation of a single painting by hailed Madrid artist Antonio Lopez Garcia, a still life of a quince tree in the artist's small courtyard. Garcia is an old-school brand of craftsman, and the process takes many weeks; a lengthy and wordless opening sequence follows the artist as he prepares his canvas, positions his easel, mixes his paints (at first, for a preliminary color study), fashions a plumb line (to determine the exact center of his composition), and even drives nails into the dirt so he'll stand in exactly the same place every day. Erice intercuts Garcia's attentive work with scenes of visitors, his wife's daily ministrations, and a team of laborers fixing the walls in Garcia's old house, and the effect is a genuine experience of life and art that movies rarely produce. Not a true documentary any more than it is a "narrative" film in the traditional sense, Erice's work is a meditation on creation and on the life that must surround it.

Naked (1993) A brilliant, unsettling, breathtakingly ballsy spew of discontent, Mike Leigh's most bilious film centers on Johnny, a twentysomething Manchester street rat whose vicious wit and endlessly inventive monologues about "the End" constitute his interface with the world. Played by David Thewlis (a Best Actor winner at the Cannes Film Festival), Johnny is a nonstop volcano of bitter diatribe and verbal laceration, talking in a blistering rant so he won't have to hear the inevitable silence. Wading into battle with women, old girlfriends, strangers, hookers—anyone and everyone, really—Johnny is at the tail end of a narcissistic spiritual search, whether he knows it or not, and just because he faces the abyss doesn't mean that he will stop asking questions and demanding meaning.

Being Human (1994) Elliptical, strange, and quietly mysterious, *Being Human* is Scottish director Bill Forsyth's tremendously risky and bizarre conception of a Hollywood movie: a five-part, noncomedic (but hardly unfunny) omnibus film (starring Robin Williams) that ranges from neolithic times to the 1990s and that concerns the perpetual failure of men to meet the responsibilities allotted them by society. Each Williams persona, from fated caveman to Roman slave to post-yuppie weekend dad, is faced with a web of painful circumstances that precludes convenient answers. Magnificently photographed (you'd think the stone-age sequences would be absurd, but they're breathtaking), Forsyth's film favors the director's odd, charming rhythms and dangling non sequiturs. Most arrestingly, the movie's central subject is paternal angst, regardless of the sometimes fantastic plotlines (one story involves a 1500s Spanish shipwreck off Africa). Williams's Cro-Magnon family man loses his entire family to Vandal pillagers; his 1990s counterpart suffers no less as he spends a weekend with children he barely knows and cannot connect with. *Being Human* (an unfortunate title) is an offbeat, searching film that dares to never give us what we want from mainstream movies—easy solutions, affirmations, and closure.

Seven (1995) A famous, too frequently copied Hollywood serial-killer thrill machine, this film is built for maximum gross-out—except that it also has Morgan Freeman's fierce moral gravity, and a dead-serious take on its "seven deadly sins" formula that raises all sorts of questions about moral relativism and religion's capacity for persecution in the name of sanctity.

Taste of Cherry (1997) An unequivocal masterpiece, Abbas Kiarostami's Cannes Film Festival winner has the electric charge of an elemental experience. Though its plot is spare and short-story simple, the filmmaking is so rigorous, so intensely focused, and so unsentimental that it can shock you awake from today's universal movie-consuming torpor. If you can, watch the film before you read the rest of this entry; not knowing precisely where the film is going is an important part of its mystery and power. For a good half hour you don't know what the film's about—the viewer watches from the passenger seat as a weathered, middle-class man (Homayoun Ershadi) rides in a Range Rover through the Tehran outlands (a landscape that gives you the impression that Iran is one huge, desolate construction site), searching for a man to help him. There are many laborers, but the man is picky. Eventually he selects a few (a Kurdish soldier, an Afghan seminarian, a Turkish taxidermist) and tersely explains his offer: for a sizable payment, he requires only that someone come to a predetermined spot on a hill where a grave has been dug and perform one of two tasks: if the man has succeeded in swallowing sleeping pills, then he must be buried; if he's alive, he is to be helped out by his hand. Since suicide is a strict Muslim taboo, the man has difficulty enlisting aid, having at times to glumly cajole his applicants like an exhausted real estate broker. The textures of Kiarostami's film—down to the immaculate camerawork, long suspenseful traveling shots, and bare-bones editing—are neorealism redefined and exploded. But the questions at its center are everyone's.

After Life (1998) A peaceful, soothing Japanese launch of lyricism that imagines the next world to be prefaced by a week of gentle counseling, during which the recently dead must choose a single fulfilling memory to take with them into eternity. Director Hirokazu Kore-eda locates a hundred poetic pearls in a scenario that suggests a Taoist remake of Albert Brooks's *Defending Your Life*.

What Dreams May Come (1998) Ersatz New Zealand visionary Vincent Ward had his last Hollywood shot with this poundingly romantic dream tribulation, in which a dead Robin Williams, enjoying a digitally splashed-out heaven, must travel down to the depths of the underworld to save the soul of his dead (by suicide) wife (Annabella Sciorra). No painterly, impressionistic (or expressionistic) idea has been left out, and the oddly affecting thing about the film is that everybody involved seems to mean it.

Waking Life (2001) This whacked movie-movie is a radical departure even for semi-indie director Richard Linklater: returning to the loquacious non sequitur setup of 1991's *Slacker* (in which the camera is treated more or less like a wandering contagion), Linklater has at the same time fashioned a series of rants and spouted theories about consciousness, life, and meaning, voiced by over fifty characters, all of whom were shot on digital video. We don't see them, though; using digital animation software, Linklater rotoscoped the entire film, allowing some thirty animation artists to re-create the movie's action and thematic thrust using expressionistic, painterly images that range from the uncannily accurate to the loopily caricatured. As the subjects bounce from quantum physics to neoevolution to André Bazin to alternate realities to social outrage and political disillusionment, Linklater's visuals bounce, too. Everything floats in this movie—eyeballs, hands, sidewalks, backgrounds, even the visualized thoughts of the speakers. It's a mood piece, a rhetorical exercise, and a metaphysical board game, all wrapped into one.

Northfork (2003) Twin filmmakers Mark and Michael Polish are responsible for this supremely odd meditation on midwestern loneliness, in which suited company men descend on a small Montana community in the 1950s to persuade them to move before a dam is built. Beautiful and slow, the film features multiple angels—as well as Nick Nolte, as a priest nursing a sick boy who may or may not be half-occupying the next world. In the distinctly imperative DVD supplements, what may've seemed vague in the film crystallizes as Nolte talks about watching his own mother die, convinced that she was, in fact, occupying two planes at once.

Spring, Summer, Fall, Winter . . . and Spring (2003) Lovely to look at and filled with improvised Buddhist exercises, this Korean film takes place entirely on a gorgeous man-made lake, in the center of which floats a monk's shack. Five seasons (spanning decades) transpire, tracing the hardly simple spiritual education of a young boy. The tug-of-war between the body's need for satisfaction and the mind's need for purity is vividly played out.

DESCENDING INTO A GOOD FUNK

"Why did God give me life? What is it but hunger and pain?"
—Laurence Olivier, *Wuthering Heights*

Everybody does it sometimes—we enter a state of morbid melancholia, and we don't want to come out of it. But we would like company, if only that of a movie that understands dark woe and the sting of self-pitying tears. The only way out is through to the other end—and these, some of the most depressing films ever made, can provide a good shove.

Freaks (1932) A moral fable/exploitation thriller wherein gothic director Tod Browning uses real circus freaks to essentially play themselves as they're duped and mocked by "normals," then exact a ferociously unpleasant revenge. Yikes.

Wuthering Heights (1939) This Brontë adaptation, discussed lavishly elsewhere in this book (see "Valentine's Day," p. 25), is a premier weepy purgative—once you're through, you'll be soaked and exhausted. This is a movie-movie universe in which dead lovers' ghosts are pined for and chased by their abandoned paramours, and a young Laurence Olivier means every word he says. It's under our family's skin, this movie, and we may even tend to over-recommend it. But we wouldn't trade it for a hundred more artful or modern movies.

Random Harvest (1942) No other film will test your tolerance for melodramatic, tear-jerking foolishness as intensely as this Greer Garson–Ronald Colman weeper, in which a dance hall chanteuse falls for an amnesiac millionaire who regains his memory and forgets about her, therein initiating a years-long saga of brink-teetering hope and time-tested love. Garson, because she is one of her era's sexiest and warmest personages, makes this mothball soar, and she'll yank the bawls out of you come hell or high water.

Long Day's Journey into Night **(1962)** Eugene O'Neill's autobiographical plunge into the nightmarish dissolution of a Southern dynasty hobbled by addiction, mental illness, bitterness, and drink gets a definitive, post-Method realization by young TV vet Sidney Lumet. Four loquacious but scarred souls—father Ralph Richardson, mom Katharine Hepburn, and sons Jason Robards and Dean Stockwell—batter themselves against each other and the darkness of the approaching night. Although the energetic acting delivers a measure of élan, O'Neill's dramatic thrust is a harsh downer.

Repulsion **(1965)** Roman Polanski comes to England, where he locks repressed, shy, blonde Catherine Deneuve in her vacationing sister's apartment for a weekend, then delivers one psychotic, hallucinogenic episode after another. A wicked thriller with a gravely unhappy center, even if you don't really know *how* unhappy until the final, revelatory shot.

Mouchette **(1966)** Rigorous, undemonstrative, and mysterious, French master Robert Bresson has never been a crowd pleaser, if only because of the amount of entertaining movie stuff he leaves *out* of his films. But his projects can scour you, and this merciless passion play (from a novel by the happy-go-lucky Georges Bernanos) tracks the downward progress of a country teenager (Nadine Nortier) who's systematically neglected, used, and abused by everyone around her, until, silently, a point of no return is reached. As much a social critique as a penitence, the movie will not let you alone.

Titicut Follies **(1967)** What could possibly be more depressing: in the 1960s, novice documentarian Frederick Wiseman somehow got permission to film inside the Bridgewater, Massachusetts, State Prison for the Criminally Insane, where patients were routinely stripped naked, force-fed through their noses, and humiliated by guards. There's plenty of room to question the presumptions behind Wiseman's hands-off technique and whether the patients were being treated fairly by the filmmaker, if not anyone else. But the film is a sledge to the gut, and it should be seen. The Massachusetts state government effectively banned the film for years, but even so, it has been credited with helping to initiate a nationwide cleanup of state institutions.

Salesman **(1969)** A cataclysmically eloquent portrait of postwar America as wasteland, the Maysles brothers' documentary follows four very real door-to-door Bible salesmen as they essentially sell their souls for the chance to grift uneducated working-classers in the name of Christ. Shot in serotonin-depleting black and white, it's a horror movie of Beckettian purity, so real you can smell the Camel-blighted car interiors.

Wanda **(1970)** The American New Wave rarely got bleaker than this film, in which a clueless, directionless, spiritless, deadbeat mother (Barbara Loden, who also wrote and directed) falls in with an incompetent bank robber (Michael Higgins) and watches her already bottomed-out life take yet another step down the social ladder. A scalding, hard-core tribulation.

Salo, or the 120 Days of Sodom **(1975)** In this, the last film he made before he was murdered, Pier Paolo Pasolini aptly took Sade's monstrous, dryly titillating epic subversion about evil aristocrats, holed up in a mansion with a small army of young boys and girls to defile, rape, and kill at their whim, and transposed it to 1945 fascist Italy. Generally speaking, the film is not as sickening as it's been touted to be, which can only be a good thing; it's just a colorless, stultifying, zombie-like itinerary of revolting debaucheries. This film not only hates women, men, vaginal sex, anal sex, and *people*, but it seems most of all to hate itself.

Sophie's Choice **(1982)** Meryl Streep reaped an Oscar playing a Polish shiksa and Auschwitz survivor with devastating secrets, and though the film is filled with life and melodrama, it's a blues catalyst from beginning to end. Streep will haunt your dreams, the camp sequences are as hopeless as any in an American film, and Marvin Hamlisch's score wraps it up into a lovely, downbeat package. Parents in particular should be careful when selecting this film—be sure you're looking for a good sob, because you will find it.

The Second Circle **(1990)** Famous today for the one-shot megastunt *Russian Ark*, Alexander Sokurov made his best, if most depressing, film twelve years earlier. In a Russian outland still laboring under Soviet bureaucracy (or the lack thereof) after the empire's fall, a young man tries to bury his dead father—a virtually Herculean task given the red tape and lack of infrastructure. It'd be funny if it weren't crushingly grim.

Mother and Son **(1997)** On one level a pioneering act of visualization, Alexander Sokurov's fame-making art film has a story so simple it could barely sustain a poem: somewhere in a remote cabin, a grown son cares for his dying mother, much as a mother would nurse a sick child. The film's "action" is comprised simply of his acts of kindness, the demonstrations of deep affection the two exchange, and the passing of a single day, from morning light to twilight. At one point, the mother asks to get out of the house, and so the son carries her, through a deserted village nearby, as well as through the landscape, which, as Sokurov photographs it, is the film's third protagonist. It's as if Sokurov reinvented the Earth—the hills, fields, mountains, forests, and stormy skies we see possess a vivid, eye-popping strangeness. Amid the warped, vivid style is a mother-son love unmuddied by dramatics, and a pragmatic vision of death as a natural process.

I Stand Alone **(1998)** Beware this fearsome beast—Gaspar Noé's first feature is a repellant portrait of an aging nobody who happens to be teetering on the edge of homicidal psychosis. Then he falls over. Looking away is at times necessary; feeling filthy and miserable at the end is inevitable.

Rosetta **(1999)** Almost a remake of Bresson's *Mouchette* (see above), this dire odyssey, from Belgian filmmakers Jean-Pierre and Luc Dardenne, follows the dead-end daily existence of a desperate, bitter teenage girl (Émilie Dequenne) who has an rummy mother, few—pathetic—employment opportunities, and no end of exhausting trouble with the neighboring lowlifes.

Requiem for a Dream **(2000)** In bringing Hubert Selby Jr.'s heroin-junkie novel to the screen, indie star Darren Aronofsky tried to render the experience of being fueled by an overdose of bad dope for the audience. Three beautiful users (Jared Leto, Jennifer Connelly, and Marlon Wayans), plus Ellen Burstyn (as Leto's Brooklyn mom, descending into her own circle of hell by way of television delusions and diet pills), head down, down, down into that burnin' ring of fire, and the attention-deficit energy of the filmmaking keeps your head above water until the final, climactic quartet of grisly climaxes, which are so harrowing you may feel as if Aronofsky lured you in with fun and paid off with hellacious misery. Which he did.

IV

BAD DAY AT WORK

"Can anybody tell me what's wrong with this picture?"
—Michael Douglas, *Falling Down*

Impulse renting at its most immediate: on the way home after a rotten day at work—rotten enough to haunt your stomach afterward and prompt scenarios in your head in which the boss, the building, the company—whatever—simply falls into a lava pit. Or perhaps the problem is you: the job doesn't fit; your life needs a paradigm shift; you're dying of boredom. Generally speaking, the movies here present job situations that are astronomically worse than yours could ever be.

The Crowd **(1928)** Reputedly, MGM producer Irving Thalberg asked director King Vidor how he'd like to follow up the success of his World War I epic *The Big Parade*, and on the spot Vidor suggested this film about the average American wage slave. James Murray stars as a nearly anonymous family man who works at a desk in a massive, almost Kafka-esque bureaucracy—hardly the American dream he'd imagined. Tragic, expressive, and beautiful.

Salesman **(1969)** A brutally depressing documentary about four door-to-door Bible hawkers; however bad your job is, it's better than this hollow-souled ordeal, where earning the paycheck you need to keep the home you never see—by selling expensive malarkey to poor families—is virtually impossible.

Harlan County USA **(1976)** Likewise, this acclaimed, Oscar-reaping documentary about a 1973 Kentucky coal miners' strike opens a window on a work life that has to make your problems seem puny—mining is one sort of nightmare all by itself, but consider how much worse it would be if you risked being murdered for asking the boss to implement basic safety measures and pay you a living wage. (See "Labor Day," p. 52.)

9 to 5 **(1980)** Three female coworkers (skittish Jane Fonda, all-biz Lily Tomlin, and sassy secretary Dolly Parton) are grossly mistreated at the hands of their chauvinistic boss and, after sharing a round of booze and grass, fantasize about exacting their revenge. In this day and age of corporate downsizing, reduced pensions, increased health costs, and presidential speeches about "haves and have mores," who wouldn't want to entertain this proletariat fantasy? Tolerate the dated talk about "women's lib" and enjoy the retributive buzz.

Henry: Portrait of a Serial Killer **(1986)** The grimmest and most believable of homicidal fantasies, this squalid indie may be useful as a vehicle for venting: impassive maniac Henry (Michael Rooker) kills and butchers virtually anyone who causes him discomfiture, including "my mama." Based loosely on the case file of Henry Lee Lucas.

Meet the Feebles **(1989)** A vicious, saber-toothed parody of *The Muppet Show*, Peter Jackson's early, low-down Kiwi comedy features no humans—just a vast cast of Jim Henson–type creatures lost in a nightmare of vomit, viscera, disease, hate, and violence while struggling to produce a variety show. It's a one-joke scenario that peeks below the waist of the puppets only to discover one vice-ridden horror after another: there's a satyric rabbit dying slowly of a sex disease; a knife-throwing junkie frog given to 'Nam flashbacks; an elephant slapped with a paternity suit by a chicken (he insists the child isn't his, but the kid *is* half-chicken, half-elephant . . .); a rat who shoots S&M porn loops in the sewers with an udder-ringed cow and a cockroach; and so on. You'll forget your workday entirely.

Joe Versus the Volcano **(1990)** John Patrick Shanley does for dreary, wage-slave daydreams what he did for Italianate romance in *Moonstruck*, following nowhere man Tom Hanks out of a Kafka-esque work life and into a supremely silly adventure involving a fake terminal illness and a tropical volcano.

Falling Down **(1993)** Politically it's a shambles, but this Hollywood venture into the frustrations and alienations of low-rung American white-collar workers is loaded with cathartic set pieces, beginning with one in which a buzz-cut conservative (Michael Douglas), who's just been laid off from his job as a defense worker, abandons his car in a freeway traffic jam. He goes on to enact unmoored, increasingly violent confrontations with road construction pointlessness, Korean storekeepers, fast-food-restaurant rule keepers, gangbangers, bigoted militiamen, golfers (!), and so on. The only thing missing from this film, in fact, is the hero's seemingly obligatory attack on his workplace and boss.

A Single Girl **(1995)** An electric, mesmerizing French import that makes much from very little, Benoît Jacquot's breakthrough drama stars Virginie Ledoyen as Valerie, a young, exceedingly modern girl with an overactive bullshit detector and little patience for fools. After an argument with her boyfriend, during which she reveals she's pregnant, Valerie begins her first day on her new job as a Paris hotel's room-service waitress. The movie simply observes as she delivers breakfasts, whether it's to an empty room or to a copulating couple; Jacquot fills the film with long shots of Ledoyen walking restlessly down hotel corridors, sometimes doing her job, sometimes stealing time alone to smoke or make phone calls. Shot and cut with a jeweler's blade, the movie makes the narrative significance of work potently realized.

Office Killer **(1997)** Photographer and art diva Cindy Sherman crafted this cheesy, somewhat sophomoric Gothic gotcha, with Molly Ringwald, Jeanne Tripplehorn, and Carol Kane as coworkers in the antiquated office of a failing magazine, where Kane's pent-up drudge accidentally kills one snotty yuppie, then decides to go for the whole office.

A Merry War **(1998)** Based on George Orwell's early novel *Keep the Aspidistra Flying*, Robert Bierman's quirky comedy follows the erratic path of a restless, high-strung London ad writer (Richard E. Grant) who, disgusted with his own success in an essentially amoral career, quits his job to devote himself wholly to writing verse. He hungrily—too hungrily—embraces poverty, discomfort, loneliness, and suffering along his way, driving his already exasperated fiancée (the ever-lovely Helena Bonham Carter) nuts. The self-destructive path is backlit by entrancing dialogue; screenwriter Alan Plater ladled whole unedited gobs of Orwell's sparkling screwball verbiage into the film, and Bierman, whose only notable previous credit was the wildly dissimilar *Vampire's Kiss*, did all he could to help by staying out of the way. Grant, as dynamic and nerve-racking here as ever, is practically a one-man show, berating his potted aspidistra (the story's beleaguered symbol for bourgeois complacency) and looking misfortune down with both bloodshot eyes. Bonham Carter is just as dishy, though, and the two of them together—possibly because they seem to oppose each other like night and day—are a hoot.

Monday Morning **(2002)** A scathing and obliquely hilarious comedy of wage slavery and its discontents, this French film, directed by the masterful Georgian emigré Otar Iosseliani, follows the trajectory of a disgruntled factory man as he cuts loose with a weekend of smoking and drinking in Italy—and then goes home. Iosseliani never dictates how you should react to his hero's deadpan travails, but instead lets you find your own sense of life in the long, distantly observed scenes of human folly. So, if you pay attention, it's hilarious *and* strangely moving.

CATHARSIS

"This ain't something else. This is this!"
—Robert De Niro, *The Deer Hunter*

It's one of the movies' primary achievements since the 1960s: the narrative bolero that steamrolls toward a climax of cathartic violence (physical, emotional, or otherwise), which can function on you like a master session of shiatsu massage. Psychoanalyze your desire for such release if you must—but meanwhile, if you feel the need for a veins-in-your-teeth explosion, these are the films that best do the job.

Straw Dogs (1971) Sam Peckinpah's nasty, jungle-law fable plays out in the English countryside, where a nebbishy Yank mathematician (Dustin Hoffman), inaptly married to a saucy Brit slut (Susan George), is slowly beset upon by the yowling vigilante locals. The climax, in which Hoffman's inner Hun emerges in the defense of his home and wife, is jolting, unsettlingly realistic, and unsensationalized.

The Deer Hunter (1978) This large-scale blitz of unhappy Americana finds its cathartic crest long before the movie's end—and no sequence in any war film will wring your nerves dry of fluid like this film's central Russian roulette set piece.

Come and See (1985) Possibly the greatest and most appalling war film ever made, this Belarusian beast, filmed by Russian director Elem Klimov (who then retired, saying there was nothing left to say), follows the progress of a peasant youth (Aleksei Kravchenko, in a performance that brands itself on your cerebellum) as the countryside around him is torn asunder by the Nazis. In a slaughterhouse this extreme, there's no heroism—just carrion and guilt-ridden survival.

Bad Lieutenant (1992) A belly-crawl through the urban gutter, Abel Ferrara's willfully abhorrent movie depicts a miserable day in the life of a monstrous, self-detonating wretch whose depraved behavior is a simple but gut-roiling reflection of his environment. Ferrara was reportedly determined to earn an NC-17 from the MPAA even if it meant shooting more scenes; he needn't have worried. The lengths to which he and his star, the inestimable Harvey Keitel, go to rub our noses in lowlife are brave and crazy. A fallen prince of the city whose drug ingestion rate could power Washington Square for a full late-night hour, Keitel's very bad cop indulges in abusive sexual combat, compulsively self-jeopardizing gambling, hapless violence, and the aforementioned consumption of every chemical he can find, most commonly crack. This *Inferno* without Virgil begins in earnest when Keitel is given a pivotal case: a devout nun is brutally raped, and though she knows her attackers, she refuses to identify them. By the time the lieutenant starts shooting smack (shown in close-up scenes) and visions of Christ begin to appear, we're set up for a full-scale *katharsis*, and we're as committed as Ferrara and Keitel to finding some kind of salvation.

***Fearless* (1993)** This post-traumatic-stress masterpiece about the survivors of a plane crash pounds you in many ways before you get to the film's end—which is when director Peter Weir finally lets you experience the crash itself; endured by people we've gotten to know (and the loved ones they've lost), the entire event is shot inside the plane, and it's scored in a plaintive crescendo with Gorecki's Symphony No. 3, which was written as a requiem about the Holocaust. Puts you through the mill.

***Will It Snow for Christmas?*(1996)** Sandrine Veysset's austere, humane, uncompromised debut, which won France's Best Picture César Award, is a naturalistic tragedy about the day-to-day life of a farm family: the beleaguered mother (Dominique Reymond) and her seven adoring children, all of them illegitimate, are virtual slaves to the father, a domineering cretin whose legit, in-town family enjoys every luxury while the farm family scrapes for wood, food, and electricity. Veysset's film is far from melodramatic, but the movie's thrust—etched in every scene's authentic details—is the desperate love between mother and children, and the lengths each will go to save the other from hardship. In the unforgettable end, we're left wondering whether we've witnessed a disaster narrowly deterred or a horrible dream from which we've all awoken. Either way, it's euphoric.

IV

***Pola X* (1999)** A psycho fantasist with an Erich von Stroheim–like thirst for trouble, French filmmaking whirligig Leos Carax likes to typify himself as a tortured artist who's misunderstood by society, and, judging by *Pola X*, he's not far from wrong. Adapting Herman Melville's heavily ironic *Pierre, or the Ambiguities*, the movie is charged with visual urgency—you never know what's coming at you (or how you'll see it), be it a breathtaking landscape, sudden handheld motorcycle smack up, or a holy-cow graphic sex scene. It's a trial by fire: Pierre (Guillaume Depardieu) is a successful young novelist who's living in an enormous Normandy chateau with his gorgeous mom (Catherine Deneuve) when his comfortable life and upcoming marriage to an aristocratic girl are turned upside down by the appearance of Isabelle (Katerina Golubeva), a feral, dark, emotionally crippled waif who claims to be Pierre's half sister. As a movie, it's not a tidy experience, but it'll hit you in the throat.

***Dancer in the Dark* (2000)** Notorious, admired and loathed in equal measure, and largely misunderstood, Lars von Trier's movie is an excoriating experience—a trying, tormented, and thrilling movie ordeal that questions the righteousness of God by way of musical numbers and intense melodrama. Elfin Icelandic diva-ette Björk (who won a Cannes Film Festival Best Actress award for her work here) stars as a thickly bespectacled Czech immigrant who's slowly losing her sight. A single mother who works in a pressing plant, she is determined to save enough cash to pay for an operation that might save her son's similarly beleaguered sight. Once her savings are robbed, her path becomes a nightmare of maternal defense and gallows martyrdom. Von Trier's real subject is melodrama itself—its profusion of coincidence, misery, and cruel redemption, and the bullshit salvation that show tunes, musicals, and other such forms of pop culture blithely promise.

OPTIMISM

"Always look on the bright side of life!"
—Eric Idle, *Life of Brian*

This category is self-explanatory, really; whether you are newly embracing the positive, having your upward gaze reaffirmed, or are badly in need of a change in perspective, these are the films (cherry-picked from a plenitude of optimistic films) that can best restore bounce to your step.

Various Buster Keaton shorts (1917–1928) Because, unlike Chaplin, he doesn't beg for your approval, because his triumphs are always self-effacing and genuinely heroic, and because his screen persona could be defined as laconically optimistic, Buster Keaton remains an avatar of upbeat cinema, and a guiding light through a world in which nothing—not even falling buildings or speeding locomotives—is cause to get upset. You needn't be selective with Keaton's features, but don't overlook his shorts particularly the extraordinary two-reelers he made with Roscoe "Fatty" Arbuckle and Al St. John between 1917 and 1920, as well as *The Goat* **(1921)**, *Cops* **(1922)**, and *The Love Nest* **(1922)**.

Horse Feathers **(1932)** The Marx Brothers, American university life, speakeasies, varsity football espionage, the "college widow," harp interludes, Thelma Todd without underwear, Groucho singing "Whatever It Is, I'm Against It" and answering the ass-kissing set-up line "Oh, professor, you're full of whimsy," with "Can you notice it from there? I'm always that way after I eat radishes."

Duck Soup **(1933)** In *Hannah and Her Sisters*, Woody Allen's morbidly obsessed character, on the brink of suicide, accidentally catches the last act of *Duck Soup*—which restores his love of life. That scene has the integrity of an obvious truth. ("What if the worst *is* true?" Allen's persona concludes. "What if there is no God, and you only go around once and that's it? Well, don't you want to be part of the experience?") If there was ever a film that could rescue a psyche from the bowels of darkness, this is it. Groucho is a newly appointed head of state, Harpo and Chico are double agents, and Zeppo is, well, Zeppo. But who cares; other comedies, what with their plots and all, must have "arc" and some kind of conflict, but no such contrivance dampens the Marxes' irreverent, childlike universe. This film is nothing less than a font of undiluted, obstinate joy. Hail, Freedonia!

Captain Blood **(1935)** And so the world met Errol Flynn, one of the most hypnotizing and seductive human beings ever caught on film, a preposterously graceful and buoyant force that in vital ways epitomized the holy gravity of movies. Maybe he wasn't a trained showboater, but a gallery of Flynn lines, movements, close-ups, smiles, and gestures comes close to defining the pleasure of the medium. His oeuvre of pirate movies, period swashbucklers, miscast westerns, and kid-lit adventures never helped his stock value, but still, there was no swatch of hoary dialogue Flynn couldn't make sound deft, and no scenario that could bury his élan. This adaptation of Rafael Sabatini's novel was Flynn's first starring vehicle; it's a robust pleasure, and youthful brio still spills from its frames.

My Man Godfrey **(1936)** This sunny, adorably eccentric Carole Lombard farce bubbles and grins like a kid at Disney World. (See "Anniversary," p. 148.)

Bringing Up Baby **(1938)** The combination of director Howard Hawks and star Cary Grant gives off royal fireworks in this screwball trifle about a paleontologist, a socialite (Katharine Hepburn), a leopard, and an errant dinosaur bone. Frantic, high-tension comedy has rarely come as fast, thick, and razor-sharp, although ***His Girl Friday*** **(1940)**, Hawks's and Grant's redo of *The Front Page*, is right up there, too. Once upon a time, Hollywood was all about a zest for living.

A Woman Is a Woman **(1961)** Only Jean-Luc Godard's second feature film, this is a brilliantly uplifting rip through the musical comedy genre—the entire film, in which bubbleheaded Angela (Anna Karina) tries to get boyfriend Emile (Jean-Claude Brialy) and buddy Alfred (Jean-Paul Belmondo) to impregnate her, and teeters on the verge of bursting into a full-on musical number, but never really does. Irresistible joie de vivre.

Band of Outsiders **(1964)** Jean-Luc Godard's 1960s films, even the politically radical and socially outraged ones, are brimming with joyful love of movies—which, by Godard's definition, includes crazed passion for women, pulp fiction, Paris, American movies,

IV

pop music, and Anna Karina, his wife and muse. This perfect quasi-noir gem—from which Quentin Tarantino cribbed his production company's name, A Band Apart—is about a heist, but it's really about hanging out and goofing off and being in love with Karina. As if to prove it, Godard revolves the film around a long central sequence in which the three protagonists loiter in a café, flirting, drinking, waiting, and eventually performing together an infectious, syncopated variation on the dance the Madison. After that, what could be important?

What's Up, Tiger Lily? **(1966)** An irresistible, merry concoction from first-time director Woody Allen, who took a crummy Japanese spy comedy (1965's *International Secret Police: Key of Keys*), and redubbed it into a global battle for an egg salad recipe. The memories of moments and lines from this simple ace in the hole never die.

The Discreet Charm of the Bourgeoisie **(1972)** As if in answer to his own masterpiece *The Exterminating Angel*, in which dinner party guests inexplicably find they cannot leave the dining room, Luis Buñuel made this late-career world-beater in which six friends (including Fernando Rey, Bulle Ogier, Stéphane Audran, and Delphine Seyrig) continually attempt to have dinner but are always interrupted—by terrorists, by sex, by error, by the disclosure of a theater audience watching them on a stage, and so on. Invigoratingly irreverent and life affirming as only Buñuel could be.

Monty Python and the Holy Grail **(1975)** That this farcical masterpiece is richer, minute by minute, in comic invention than virtually any other film made anywhere may be an arguable point for some, but not for us. You have to see it ten times to rope in all of the jokes, but what makes the Python boys particularly valuable here is their palpable joy in *telling* those jokes: the six members (Michael Palin, Terry Jones, Eric Idle, John Cleese, Graham Chapman, and Terry Gilliam) play forty or more roles among them, and all are seized throughout with the high spirits of inventive kids playing in the woods. This movie's an essentially bottomless life-giving institution. (The same goes for their next film, the superbly sustained *Life of Brian* **[1979]**, in which the New Testament and its blind followers get a right flogging.)

Airplane! **(1980)** The shotgun farce that made Mel Brooks look sophisticated—and yet, there's something inspired and joyous about its steamrolling assault of crude sight gags, surreal equations, and puns, puns, puns. There's no reality being made fun of here—instead, the film takes aim at the rapturous ether of old movies (*The High and the Mighty* and the *Airport* films, predominantly) with childlike play of language and outrageous nonsense.

The Gods Must Be Crazy **(1981)** Rumor has it that during the years that this gentle, bizarre South African comedy (released as a product of Botswana, because of the wide embargo during the Apartheid era) loitered in theaters, psychoanalysts were recommending it to their chronically depressed patients. It begins as a "documentary" about tribal life in the bush, and—almost imperceptibly—becomes a fable about a bushman (N!xau) who tries to rid his people of a troublesome Coke bottle after it's dropped from a high-flying plane. The lead actor's hilarious expressions of bewilderment were genuine—up to that point, he had avoided all contact with modern civilization. The movie has a quirky merriment to it that's strangely infectious.

Monty Python's The Meaning of Life (1983) The Python crew's final film—cobbled together from their piles of material and glued into place with the sheerest of thematic ideas— is a sloppy, inspired explosion of derisive invention. As is usually the case with Monty Python offerings, you could quote from it all year long (as do, perhaps, the jury members of the 1983 Cannes Film Festival, who awarded it the Special Jury Grand Prix), but the moments we like to remember when we're searching for a bit of cheer include the bawling fetus dropping from behind Terry Jones's legs before the "Every Sperm Is Sacred" musical number ("Oh, get that, would ya, Deirdre?"), the fake expressions of concentration on the students' faces during Oxford don John Cleese's live sex lesson, the Grim Reaper relishing the moment when he gets to point out *"the salmon mousse!"* . . . and so, infinitely, on.

Kiki's Delivery Service (1989) A young apprentice witch in a coastal New England village, her struggles, longings, and eventual triumph—anime master Hayao Miyazaki brings a grinning humanity to conventional kid stuff, and the results here (and in his other films, particularly **Spirited Away [2001]** and **Howl's Moving Castle [2004]**) are warm, unpredictable, and thrilling.

Pleasantville (1998) The wackiest scenario in 1990s Hollywood: two contemporary teens (Tobey Maguire and Reese Witherspoon, playing brother and sister) are magically dropped into the black-and-white world of a stereotypical 1950s TV sitcom, where everything is trouble free and nothing ever changes. Except, of course, that now things *do* begin to change—and a crazily conservative universe learns about the glories of color, sex, modernism, passion, art, and, at the end, change itself.

South Park: Bigger, Longer & Uncut (1999) Never underestimate the shine a fierce dose of obscenity can put on your disposition. This exceptionally profane film features the popular TV show's trademark imagery (which resembles a puppet show put on by idiot fifth graders), dumbly visualized 2-D protagonists, edge-of-hysteria voice characterizations (mostly done by creators Matt Stone and Trey Parker), and enthusiasm for school-age scatology, in which few gross-out gratuities are left unexpressed. However scattershot, Parker and Stone's satire is pump-action, and the effect is bracing. It was even Oscar-nominated, for the song "Blame Canada."

Amélie (2001) Jean-Pierre Jeunet's massively popular digitized romance, in which serendipitous French gamine Audrey Tautou pursues love with a primitive's faith in coincidence, signs, fate, and magical thinking—which the film expresses in every frame, using every trick in the newly written book.

8 Women (2002) More Gallic whimsicality, but impossible to resist: there's a dead body in a manor house, and eight French actresses (Catherine Deneuve, Isabelle Huppert, Ludivine Sagnier, Fanny Ardant, Emmanuelle Béart, and others) vamp around, sing, and butt heads trying to solve the case. Light as chiffon and adorable.

Team America: World Police (2004) Hands down, the most bruisingly, heart-attack-funny film of the new millennium. Trey Parker and Matt Stone make a Jerry Bruckheimer–style action flick (about an elite band of patriotic spy cops), but with marionettes, a la the old Gerry and Sylvia Anderson TV series *Thunderbirds*. In this case, though, the marionettes are puking, gun-toting puppets who have graphic sex and get maimed by gunfire. The politics of the film are slippery—Hollywood liberals get trounced, but military thinking and political power are ripped to shreds. However you read it, your ribs will ache.

APOCALYPTIC DREAD

"Listen to me as if I were Cerberus barking with all his heads at the gates of Hell."
—Albert Dekker, *Kiss Me Deadly*

Just when we thought we were done with the Cold War . . . the dogs of war are yelping again. Clearly, there's no expiration date on mankind's (or, more aptly, governments') ability to place the planet in serious jeopardy, and rarely since World War II have movies slouched in imagining the upshot.

Kiss Me Deadly (1955) This first apocalypse film made post-Hiroshima is classically gritty, pulpy, and tin-pot. Ralph Meeker (as Mickey Spillane's Mike Hammer, even though director Robert Aldrich threw most of Spillane's book out the door in creating this adaptation) tries to find out what happened to a hitchhiker he picked up and ends up confronting black-box secrecy and black-market atomic shenanigans. True, the unearthed menace only takes out a beach house—or so it seems—but you have to start somewhere.

On the Beach (1959) The grim flip side of *Kiss Me Deadly*, this morose nightmare (based on Nevil Shute's bestseller) focuses on a group of Americans in Australia (Gregory

Peck, Ava Gardner, Fred Astaire, Anthony Perkins, et al.) as they wait for the radiation cloud to reach them. Mature and decidedly unhysterical, Stanley Kramer's film still packs a punch.

Panic in Year Zero **(1962)** This raw American International Pictures cheapie is so expressive that it presages scores of actual crises that have occurred since the film was made (comparisons to post-Katrina New Orleans accompanied its unceremonious 2006 DVD release). This is the Cold War on the ground: a camping family of four (led by Ray Milland, who also directed the movie) instantly begins to modify its behavior after hearing about nuclear attacks on nearby cities. How quickly and thoroughly do we abandon law and order in order to stay alive? Milland's icily pragmatic dad begins to loot, terrorize, and indulge in vengeance killing; it's clear evidence that the darkness awaiting our descent from civilized comfort is cold indeed.

The Birds **(1963)** Look again at this thing—this strangest and most consciously surrealist Hitchcock film may be the most deeply irrational movie ever made by a Hollywood studio. The nature-gone-berserk scenario has no reasonable foundation, so the extraordinarily evocative set pieces—the bird-covered jungle gym; the attack on the phone booth; the torrent of birds pouring in through the fireplace; the final world-of-perched-birds apocalypse—touch at some primordial dread that a world we've taken for granted might begin to behave in threatening ways we don't understand.

IV

Dr. Strangelove or: How I Learned to Stop Worrying and Love the Bomb **(1964)** This Stanley Kubrick outrage limns a militarist arms-race world in which a maniacal general (Sterling Hayden) deliberately begins World War III, a pentagon officer (George C. Scott) pitches for nuclear Armageddon as if it were a baseball team, the fact of modern weaponry is reduced to one phallic gag after another, and, everywhere you look, Peter Sellers holds the fate of the world in his shaky hands.

Fail-Safe **(1964)** Unjustly overshadowed by *Dr. Strangelove*, which was released the same year and was based on the same premise, this white-knuckle drama of warhead face-off pits President Henry Fonda—and the inept arms-race establishment around him—against the Soviets when bombs are sent to Moscow due to a malfunction. Shot in grim black and white and staged like the most suspenseful early-TV drama ever made, Sidney Lumet's movie is little more than talking heads, but it holds you in a vise.

The Last Man on Earth **(1964)** The Italian-made (and wretchedly dubbed) first adaptation of Richard Matheson's *I Am Legend* has a weary Vincent Price proceeding with the sorry, post-plague tasks of killing zombie-like vampires by day and drinking himself into depression by night. Remade, rather hippie-ishly, as ***The Omega Man*** **(1971)**, and recently as the Will Smith–led *I Am Legend* (2007), but the definitive film version of Matheson's novel awaits.

The War Game (1965) Peter Watkins's first film, a BBC-commissioned documentary about the probable effects, according to the British government's own reports, of an atomic attack on England. The movie was fearsome and disconcerting enough to get officially banned in England—and, consequently, to get what would be the filmmaker's lifelong career as a cultural exile started off with a bang.

Colossus: The Forbin Project (1970) High-concept Cold War sci-fi—a giant supercomputer is built, at the U.S. government's behest, to monitor and control all of its nuclear arms (thus negating the possibility of human error and violence). Unfortunately, the computer links up with the Soviet's identical machine and essentially, with a few electrical pulses, takes over the world. Coldhearted and scary.

No Blade of Grass (1970) Pulp moviemaking wild man Cornel Wilde offers up an apocalyptic view of a future in which pollution triggers a worldwide famine and a global descent into savagery.

The Crazies (1973) George Romero's sloppily assembled cheapie has the military quarantine a virus-infected town, only to have the contagion-maddened populace fight viciously back. The governmental cure out-terrorizes the disease, revolutionary paranoia becomes a nerve-racking reality, and the gritty visions of neighborhood-invading army trucks and hazmat-suited infantry are the stuff of childhood nightmares.

The Last Wave (1977) As something of a riposte to the glut of Christian horrors like *The Exorcist* and *The Omen*, director Peter Weir's gloomy countdown to doomsday follows a stuffy Aussie corporate lawyer (Richard Chamberlain) through the various stages of the end times as envisioned by the ancient Aborigines.

Akira (1988) An almost inexplicable sci-fi nerve shredder, this hallowed Katsuhiro Otomo anime follows a testy band of cycling youths in Neo-Tokyo as one of them crosses paths with a long-secret government project that transforms him into a burgeoning telekinetic monster. The detailed images of wholesale urban destruction are awesome and harrowing. *Akira* has had many imitators that share an anarchist's eye for cataclysm, including **Ghost in the Shell (1995)**, **X (1996)**, **Metropolis (2001)**, and **Ghost in the Shell 2: Innocence (2004)**.

Miracle Mile (1989) Ignored by audiences and critics when it hit theaters in 1989, Steve De Jarnatt's runaway train of delirious paranoia, postnuclear dread, and madcap domino-theory madness poses an inevitable Cold War–age question—if you found out the world was going to end in an hour, what would you do? We meet our painfully average, trombone-playing hero (Anthony Edwards) amid the prehistoric panoramas in the L.A. museum adjacent to the famous La Brea Tar Pits that mark one end of the eponymous stretch of Wilshire Boulevard. In a diabolical, Rube Goldberg–esque series of circumstances that involves a missed date, a burning bird's nest, and an all-night diner, Edwards's schlub answers a ringing pay phone—*never* do that—and hears a panicked voice tell him, "This is the big one—we're locked in! I'm talking about nuclear fucking war!" From there, it's Chicken Little time, and the entire city gets whipped up into a predawn seizure over what might be, in the end, just a crank call. Los Angeles has always been the sweatiest, most incendiary, most apocalyptic of American cities, and this movie exploits like no other its unique midsummer's-night feeling of expectant crisis.

The Day of the Beast (1995) Nobody knows blasphemy quite like the Spanish, but no Spaniard besides the late, great Luis Buñuel may have ever gotten quite as much fun out of skewering Catholic norms than snot-nosed young filmmaker Álex de la Iglesia, and this Revelations farce is as tasteless as it is inventive. The filmmaker's got a great, simple premise that allows for almost any sort of profane action you can imagine: a theological scholar cracks the cabbalist code of the Book of Revelations and discovers the impending arrival date of the end times. He immediately buses to Madrid alone, determined to commit evil (the crimes are, at first, ridiculously minor) and sell his soul to the Devil so that he can get close enough to the Antichrist to kill him, sacrificing his own life and soul in the process. De la Iglesia runs his ludicrous scenario down the boulevards of Madrid like a crazed bull, eventually arriving at a meeting with Satan himself.

Safe (1995) Director Todd Haynes nailed the perfect mood and scenario for a 1990s quasi-version of Sartre's *Nausea* with a story that can come off sounding like either a disease-of-the-week TV movie parody, a comedy about affluent alienation, or a sci-fi essay on paranoia. It's all three: Julianne Moore is Carol, a perfect, ambition-less, spoiled, hermetically sealed California housewife, blandly taking her wealth for granted and filling her days with shopping and beauty parlor appointments, who eventually begins to suspect (as the viewer has from the beginning, thanks to Haynes's unworldly camera movements) that there's something dreadful happening under the skin of her life, waiting to surface. When some kind of unknowable "environmental illness" creeps up on her, it's a visceral metaphor for her inner crisis of comfort and emptiness. Very often we just watch Carol as she listens to the mad machinery of her body; because Haynes has built an atmosphere drenched in anxiety, when her nose bleeds, it's apocalyptic. The movie is textually flawless and viscerally invasive.

The Trigger Effect (1996) A pungent little B movie from screenwriter and first-time film director David Koepp: upper-middle-class suburban existence for new parents Elisabeth Shue and Kyle MacLachlan, already a tense affair, becomes a fractured social contract when a blackout strikes and everyone quickly begins thinking "live or let die."

Deep Impact (1998) Prior to September 11, moviegoers may not have looked to disaster movies like *Deep Impact* for an emotional workout, but that's what we got; this is one of the most upsetting and painful pulp movies a major studio has ever released.

The plot is simple: a comet is speeding to Earth, and we must do everything we can to stop it or get the hell out of the way. We send a crew (Robert Duvall, Mary McCormack, Ron Eldard, Jon Favreau, and Blair Underwood) into space to try to implant atomic bombs on the comet's surface; we try to shoot it out of the air with Triton missiles—a plan so doomed to failure we don't even see it enacted; we're just told about it by the sorrowful president (Morgan Freeman). We build underground caves in which a few select million will hide for the two years it takes for the planet to reacclimate. We worry, a lot. The film is filled with good-byes—of panicked parents handing their infants over fences so that they might survive in the caves, more panicked parents imploring their teenage kids to save themselves, and so on. At the heart of every scene is the insistence that the end of the world means, for us as a whole, the end of our children.

***Last Night* (1998)** Canadian actor/writer/director Don McKellar's first feature is an abstracted comedy in which there is no nighttime, everybody knows exactly when the world will end (how, exactly, it will end is never articulated), and the only issue anyone has left to face is the question of what to do with the last day, the last evening, the last hour. Sandra Oh's efforts at last-minute shopping for her and her husband's final dinner together are squelched when her car is overturned by a mob, then stolen; Callum Keith Rennie decides to satisfy his every sexual fantasy before midnight, including having sex with his high school French teacher (played by an aged Geneviève Bujold). David Cronenberg's buttoned-down gas company exec commits himself to calling every customer to assure them of continued service, while McKellar's single loner is plagued by needy people, particularly his mother (Roberta Maxwell), who cooks a Christmas dinner even though it's not Christmas, and who rewraps all of her grown children's old toys as gifts. Aptly, this delicate, ironic indie gets more passionate as it nears the end time.

***Songs from the Second Floor* (2000)** Swedish art-film director Roy Andersson's radical film, shot in distanced, vanishing-point compositions and often without cuts within each scene, chronicles the absurdist, haunted last days of a city of losers and nowhere men, flogging their own weaknesses and failures as supernatural phenomena proliferate and the population—often seen blocks away, whipping themselves—seems on the verge of an apocalypse.

***Donnie Darko* (2001)** Richard Kelly's freshman psychological epic is one of the best and most affecting portraits of teenage disconnection, one of the best "Halloween in suburbia" films ever made, and a scary glimpse of an all-American end of days. It didn't help (although, depending on your take, perhaps it does now) that the movie, which features a jet engine falling through the hero's roof as a catalytic event, was first released just weeks after September 11. That this seemingly prophetic piece of work takes salvation so seriously makes it especially potent. At any rate, *Donnie*

Darko can apparently become a life-realigning event for the right viewer; just ask the millions of teens who've discovered this hand grenade on DVD and video.

28 Days Later (2002) Shooting on digital video, Brit hotshot Danny Boyle revamps the George Romero zombie scenario by blaming a virus for the problem and expanding the red-eyed flesh eaters' actions to include more than a stumbling walk. Because it's cheaply made without stars, Boyle's movie has an intense edginess—you're never sure that you won't be faced with something not sanctioned by test screenings and Burbank marketing teams. A desiccated London, brought to its empty-streeted knees by what the story says is only four weeks of rampant infection, is powerfully realized.

Time of the Wolf (2003) Michael Haneke, director of 2001's *The Piano Teacher* and 2005's *Caché* sets up a kind of ultimate domestic nightmare: a family vacation is interrupted by murderous outlaws, sending the mom (Isabelle Huppert) and her two kids into the country landscape, which slowly shows signs of having been ravaged by an unmentioned catastrophe. We're never told why, but society dissolves; survival is all there is, between stacks of burning livestock and impromptu social units made up of hungry strangers, holed up in abandoned train stations. A gripping masterpiece, the film was largely misunderstood in theaters, and, alas, due to Haneke's faithful depiction of pitch-black night, it's not perfectly suited to video or DVD.

IV

Dawn of the Dead (2004) The team of pros who assembled this big-budget remake of George Romero's take on Armageddon in the mall learned from Danny Boyle's *28 Days Later* that human-munching zombies are more frightening if they run, so we return to the mall, this time with crowds of drooling, rotting-flesh Olympic sprinters close on our heels. This film begins with an electrifying ten-minute collapse of society, but then Romero's not-so-clever template takes hold.

War of the Worlds (2005) Steven Spielberg's take on H. G. Wells devolved quickly into formulaic nonsense, and it was far too tainted with Scientological baloney. But the initial crash-boom-bang of the Martians' emergence, set in Bayonne, New Jersey, and done with superhuman care for weird light, odd winds, architectural collapse, and offscreen horror, is close to neorealistic. If *something* came to town and dealt out the end of New Jersey as we know it, this is what it'd feel like.

An Inconvenient Truth (2006) Davis Guggenheim and Al Gore's sobering essay on climate change is the only documentary in this category, but if it's global fear you crave, this film will speak to you. (See "Earth Day," p. 57.)

LIKE A BIG CUPPA BLACK COFFEE

"We're on an express elevator to Hell—going down!"
—Bill Paxton, *Aliens*

Action movies didn't really know how to rocket and throb until Sam Peckinpah fetishized the shoot-out in the late 1960s. Since then, moviemakers have become increasingly committed to making films move quickly, at the expense of intelligence, narrative, character, theme, and even visual clarity. Still, there are a handful of movies for which the electrically edited, masterfully shot action sequence *is* the narrative and theme. Here are some that can make your blood pressure spike—which you may, on occasion, like it to do.

Sorcerer (1977) William Friedkin's majestic and martyred remake of Henri-Georges Clouzot's relatively tame *The Wages of Fear* doesn't move that quickly, because it doesn't have to; the saga of four crooks in exile who attempt to drive old trucks loaded with nitroglycerin through the Amazonian jungle in order to put out an oil-rig fire, this film has a massive built-in electrical charge. What's more, Friedkin fulfilled the premise's potential by placing his actors and trucks in real-life jungle environments you just cannot imagine; the images of the desperate characters trying to drive their juggernauts across rope bridges in the middle of monsoons are absolutely believable (no special effects here), and are, therefore, hair-raising.

The Road Warrior (1981) The action film as absurdist thrill machine—this postapocalyptic farce is tough to swallow this many years later (even in 1981, the idea of irradiated nuclear-wasteland outlaws wearing fuchsia Mohawks was a bit much), though its all-for-the-gasoline plot, when nobody seems to really go anywhere, seems to mark this film as a clearly intended bit of satire. Anyway, the crazy road action is impossible to resist, and George Miller directed and cut the film with his finger on our pulses.

The Terminator (1984) James Cameron came out of nowhere with this high-strung, low-budget rocket, which propels itself by a rather ingenious time-travel storyline and introduces the world to a new Arnold Schwarzenegger, the implacable destruct-a-thon android from the future. (The old Arnold was just a bodybuilder.) This was one indie filmmaker who earned his place at the table—with just a few cars, a few sawed-off shotguns, and a parking garage, Cameron managed to forge an adrenalinized experience that felt new.

To Live and Die in L.A. (1985) The master of the "omigod" urban car chase, director William Friedkin, who directed 1971's *The French Connection*, returned in the New Wavey 1980s to give us this cold-blooded exercise in hell-or-high-water law enforcement, in which cop nobodies William J. Petersen and John Pankow, strung out on the rush of danger, hunt down Willem Dafoe's counterfeiter in Los Angeles County's nastier outskirts. At least one of the best rush-hour auto derbies of all time.

Aliens (1986) James Cameron cemented his foothold on moviegoers' adrenal glands with this rowdy, hair-raising sequel to the brooding 1979 sci-fi horror flick, turning the stalking game between aliens and humans into a Sergeant Rock–style armed-combat mayhem. Shot with perpetual strobe, piled high with cataclysm upon cataclysm, and crafty enough to extrapolate the space carnivore's peculiar biology into a queen-bee dynamic, it's a stunnah. This movie also marks a defining cinematic moment (really, the most profoundly emotional and metaphorically resonant experience in the history of science fiction film), in which what had been a perfectly executed haunted-house thrill ride became something much larger: the saga of Ellen Ripley (Sigourney Weaver)—it is hers, not the aliens'—as a postfeminist odyssey through the cosmic horrors and endless pressure of biological imperative. The four Alien films so far (2004's *Alien vs. Predator*, being an idiot detour, doesn't count) may have had the last word on the price of maternal survival and the evolutionary martyrdom of host biology. It's not often that a Hollywood film, much less an action movie franchise, attains epic sublimity.

A Better Tomorrow (1986) The first John Woo gangster film, made in Hong Kong, starring Chow Yun-fat, and featuring, for the first time anyone saw, urban gunfights in which characters shoot with two automatics at once, and even fire away while diving through the air. It's a solid, mournful melodrama to boot, but Woo rewrote the action-film rules here, and filmmakers are still ripping him off.

Iron Man (Tetsuo) (1989) Handle this radioactive Japanese feature with asbestos mitts, or you'll be sorry. An all-out, sixty-nine-minute assault on propriety, narrative, good taste, and subconscious logic, Shinya Tsukamoto's film is both living nightmare and ferocious social commentary; there's virtually no way to describe it except perhaps as a bad dream about biophysically invasive technology, in which metal of all sorts and origins attacks a salaryman protagonist (pop star "Tomorrow" Taguchi) and morphs him into something other than merely human. Maybe.

The Killer (1989) For many in the United States, this film served as the official introduction to John Woo's frantic gangster universe, a madcap rain of bullets in which Chow Yun-fat's retiring, guilt-ridden assassin faces off against both the cops and his own syndicate, which has put out a contract on him. At the time it was released, this movie amped up everything we thought we knew about action films. Woo tripled the dose, applied a balletic sensibility to the combat, instilled the weepy drama with a Douglas Sirkian intensity, and the result is dazzling.

Bullet in the Head (1990) John Woo takes his operatic-seizure style to Vietnam in 1967, where a handful of buddies run from a gangland shooting and end up running black-

IV

market arms and getting captured by the Vietcong. Stealing shamelessly from *The Deer Hunter*, the movie is nonetheless grandiloquent, yowlingly sentimental (friends scream their mutual love as they shoot at each other), and ferociously exciting.

Hard-Boiled **(1992)** Woo's last film before he emigrated to Hollywood and began struggling with giant budgets, American unions, and duller actors. Chow Yun-fat stars, as usual, as a mercenary cop going after the mob; the climax, in and around a hospital, entails Chow blasting away while holding a swaddled newborn.

Killing Zoe **(1994)** Executive-produced by Quentin Tarantino, this queasy, hilarious heist nightmare follows the adventures of Eric Stoltz's laconic young safecracker to Paris, where he plans to meet up with sleazoid pal Jean-Hugues Anglade for a doomed bank robbery, which is complicated by an overenthusiasm for heroin and an angelic hooker, played by Julie Delpy. The manic energy and humor of the film is formidable; Stoltz has never been better (except, perhaps, in 1994's *Pulp Fiction*), and Anglade is a revelation of Gallic nihilism and high-strung evil.

Speed **(1994)** Big hit, Keanu Reeves, speeding bus, L.A. Such a cable-TV staple that most of us are sick of it by now, but you may not be.

Starship Troopers **(1997)** Whatever else it is, which is plenty, Paul Verhoeven's movie had to be the most misunderstood F/X sci-fi blockbuster of all time. Based on a pulpy Robert A. Heinlein novel from the 1950s, and featuring enough gadzooks digital imagery to fill a mainframe, *Troopers* is not an action film that doesn't work (as many unfairly claim) but a vicious, balls-to-the-wall piece of social satire, and easily the funniest Hollywood film of 1997. In this film's hilarious idea of the future, the world has one fascist government, and its elite "citizens" battle "bugs," an alien race of house-sized arachnids who hurl their spore into space and thereby direct meteors toward Earth. In this neo-Nazi, space-age version of *Archie*, there's even a Jughead (Jake Busey) and a competing Betty (Dina Meyer) and Veronica (Denise Richards). Casper Van Dien, as the Archie-like hero, is so absurdly handsome his every close-up dares us to laugh, but Richards's voluptuous face is beyond belief—is she a special effect, too? At the same time, the action is outrageously, mind-blowing fast, silly, and fearsome; the "bugs" wreak violence so hairy and gory that it, too, becomes a running gag.

Ronin **(1998)** After years of bum assignments, director John Frankenheimer came back with this Robert De Niro spy thriller, a white-knuckle film that moves fast, dallies little, and has at least two of the most upsetting car chases ever filmed.

Memento **(2000)** A movie whose very narrative structure knocks the wind out of you every few minutes: Guy Pearce, suffering from short-term memory loss, scrambles to retain his fix on who killed his wife and who, exactly, the other characters in the film are, even as they conspire to frame or kill him. The film, too, rewrites itself constantly, taking two steps back for every step forward, and it's such a radically different way to watch a movie that it's riveting.

***Time and Tide* (2000)** Tireless Hong Kong director-producer Tsui Hark's espionage thingy has a plot; we just can't tell you quite what it is, although it has something to do with a young punk taking a job as a bodyguard and dealing with rampaging South American gangs. But the vertiginous pyrotechnics are breathtaking, the stunts are ridiculous, and the action editing is tight and cause for cardiac arrest.

***Wonderful Days* (2003)** A Korean anime set in a *Blade Runner*–ish dystopian future, this film was retitled *Sky Blue* in the U.S. market (for reasons unknown). Not heavy on plot work, it is nevertheless hypnotic visually—fusing CGI, traditional animation, detailed background art, and real-life photography, often in a single scene—and the battles are ripping.

***The Departed* (2006)** Martin Scorsese's stormy, gory, hectic, hilarious Americanization of the 2002 Hong Kong hit *Infernal Affairs*, in which mob boy Matt Damon becomes a mole within the police, cranky cop Leonardo DiCaprio goes undercover in the Boston mob (ruled by Jack Nicholson, here at his Jackest), and each man is instructed to ferret himself out. Kudos to Scorsese and screenwriter William Monahan for forcing the adrenaline to rise as the film plunges on, instead of getting its web of narrative crisscrosses tangled and talked out.

IV

TIPPLING, ETC.

"My advice to you is start drinking heavily."
—John Belushi, *National Lampoon's Animal House*

A natural companion to movies, strong drink has been duly celebrated in many movies, and since drinking makes you blissfully stupid above all things, and drunkards love company, these are exactly the films we recommend be viewed with a icebox o' beer or a full complement of 'tails. Since this category must suffice as a discussion of weed and other organic or synthetic recreational substances, we also consider the films that can be criminally, cripplingly hilarious—or philosophically fascinating (while perhaps not intending to be)—when enjoyed under the influence. *Skol!*

***It's a Gift* (1934)** Every W. C. Fields film is a saga of the pickled man looking for peace in which to tipple, and though this sourest of comic masters doesn't imbibe much in this paper-thin comedy, every trial is a hungover ordeal—in particular, the nap Fields's irate family man attempts to take on his porch, and which the world conspires to disrupt.

Maniac (1934) During the Depression, a second, not-quite-legit film industry operated on the fringes of Hollywood, beyond even the so-called Poverty Row studios. This was the exploitation racket led by a loose-knit coterie of opportunists nicknamed the Forty Thieves, who would cobble together taboo-busting movies (sometimes no more than glorified stag reels), dress them up as "educational," and barnstorm them around the country, showing their films in hired theaters and getting out of Dodge before any protest or legal action could be taken. The most prominent figure in this low-life stratum was one Dwain Esper, "King of the Celluloid Gypsies," whose list of credits masks a busy uncredited career of stealing footage, rereleasing old films in the guise of new, editing two films together to make a third, and so on. *Maniac*, a dramatic treatise on psychosis, is his premier achievement, insofar as he made it himself (and thus proved himself to be the worst judge of performance in the medium's history), and insofar as it is a howling, ridiculous train wreck.

IV

The Thin Man (1934) This film's recommendation in "Anniversary" (p. 147) assumes a bit that your marital bliss also enjoys plenty of midday cocktails, since Nick and Nora Charles, as devoted as they are to each other, are rarely without a snort. Prohibition saw its fair share of drinking, but this banter-filled joy constitutes a celebration of its repeal, which came just a few months before production.

Reefer Madness (1936) This musty anti-dope polemic was made to scare audiences in the 1930s, but, helplessly, it only succeeded in cracking up much hipper, and higher, viewers during some of the country's first "midnight movies" in the 1970s. Watching it now, it's difficult to believe it wasn't conceived and executed by master satirists. Dwain Esper claimed (once the forgotten, public-domain film had gained notoriety and earning power, thanks to the new drug culture) to have produced this film himself, but he couldn't prove it (credit for directing goes to down-and-out French vet Louis Gasnier), and its actual provenance—who funded it, and why—remains a mystery.

The Sin of Harold Diddlebock (1947) Writer-director genius Preston Sturges and reemerging silent star Harold Lloyd had their last gasps with this frantic screwball, about a buttoned-down nebbish gone haywire after his first drink. It's the scene with the drink that makes the film a must-see: Edgar Kennedy, master of the grumpy slow burn, is the secret-artiste bartender rising to the occasion, and the pas de trois between him, Lloyd, and crony Jimmy Conlin is priceless.

The Quiet Man (1952) Being Irish helps when taking in this ethnic daydream, but being soused may be imperative. (See "Saint Patrick's Day," p. 29.)

Glen or Glenda? (1953) Edward D. Wood Jr. may not have been the *worst* filmmaker who ever lived—define your terms, please—but he certainly was the most guilelessly inept, the most sunnily idiotic, and the most stunningly oblivious. But he was many other things as well: carnival geek, pure-hearted transvestite (he boasted of storming the beaches at Normandy wearing silk panties under his marine issue), world-class rummy, suicidal leech, homeless pornographer, and the axis of a loony cabal of mid-century Hollywood outskirters that included the psychic Criswell, budding transsexual Bunny Breckinridge, Swedish wrestler Tor Johnson, and aging horror star/dope addict Bela Lugosi, all of whom appeared in his films. Penniless, broken, and pie-eyed, Wood eventually died hammering out deranged porn novels between whiskey runs, and he was duly forgotten until his cheap-to-lease films began appearing on late-night TV stations around the country. The films themselves worked their peculiar magic on several generations of Americans, and the Wood legacy became part of our common culture (culminating with Tim Burton's biopic valentine, *Ed Wood*). Watching the films, of which *Glen or Glenda* is the first, is in a very real sense like entering the dead-end dreams of an authentic American nut. Given this movie's erratic semidocumentary structure, earnest narration, surreal stock footage of elephants, and pioneering advocacy of fetishism, you won't believe it's dead serious, but it is—Wood's films are so committed and personal they smack of dementia.

IV

Plan 9 from Outer Space **(1959)** Ed Wood's masterpiece, if only for its nutlog excess of ambition (relatively speaking), non sequitur dialogue, misreadings, outrageously inept performances, mismatched cuts, and head-shaking discombobulations. There's no plumbing the full depths of the disjunctures in evidence here, from Wood's apparent belief that we'll think the zombie stalking through the film is the dead Bela Lugosi, even though the guy is a foot taller than Lugosi and covers his face with a cape (it was, in fact, a chiropractor friend), to Wood's peerlessly crazy writing. (Everyone can pick their favorite boners—there are so many; we like, "Modern women. They've been like that all down through the ages. Especially in a spot like this.") As Criswell the alcoholic psychic intones in his ludicrous prologue, "You are interested in the unknown. The mysterious. The unexplainable. That is why you are here." Amen.

Donovan's Reef **(1963)** "Not the whiskey, you dope!" John Wayne hollers from off-camera at a bottle-grabbing Lee Marvin as they engage in one of many buddy-enemy brawls; Marvin sensibly puts the liquor back on the bar and throws a beer bottle instead. This story of sodden sailors in the tropics is just as indulgent of boozy logic, in the typical way of director John Ford's lazier movies. But if you're slamming 'em, Marvin and Wayne are solid company.

The Saragossa Manuscript **(1964)** Overlooked Polish director Wojciech Has's medieval magic act, based on a once-famous, now forgotten 1805 metanovel, is a boisterous, Borgesian genre epic that has its wicked genre—a collision of Chaucerian fable, Tarot imagery, and corpse-strewn anamorphic landscapes—all to itself. The tale begins when two opposing soldiers sit down in the middle of a war-torn Spanish house to read a mysterious manuscript, which tells the tale of another officer's journey cross-country to Madrid. His odyssey is perpetually frustrated by agents of evil and temptation (including Inquisition terrorists), who tell other stories, from which still more stories creep. Casting nearly the entirety of 1960s Film Polski (including fated star Zbigniew Cybulski), Has even reaps from Méliès and Griffith to evoke the movie's yesteryear sense of superstitious angst. Larky, seductive, and owed debts by both Lars von Trier and Terry Gilliam, the film will keep your brainpan muddled for hours.

***Orgy of the Dead* (1965)** An Ed Wood film that makes the black-and-white work of his earlier phase seem like *Citizen Kane,* this skid-row hilarity was written by Wood but actually directed by gutter hack Stephen Apostolof, for all that it matters *who* was behind the camera. It stars a booze-swollen Criswell—the dead-eyed psychic pal Wood employed in *Plan 9 from Outer Space*—as some King of the Graveyard, or something, who commands "the spirits" (actually, a parade of second-rate L.A. strippers) to dance before him. Overdubbed comic commentary is provided by a bystanding werewolf and mummy. That's it, but you've got to admit—it's not quite like anything you've ever seen or heard.

***The Last Movie* (1971)** Dennis Hopper's follow-up to *Easy Rider* lands uneasily in a remote Peruvian mountain village that's hosting a Hollywood shoot (featuring director Sam Fuller); shit happens, movies get remade and re-envisioned, drugs get taken, narrative laws are dropped off a cliff. Fiendishly inconclusive.

***The Rocky Horror Picture Show* (1975)** Where were you in the late 1970s, when this accidental phenom took root in American culture and invented the idea of "counterpoint dialogue"? (The systematized audience participation culture that sprung up around this unlikely film began spontaneously in a Greenwich Village theater in the fall of 1976.) *Rocky Horror* literally had 'em dancing in the aisles—as well as shooting water guns, throwing toilet paper, and shouting predetermined responses at the screen. Adapted from a play by Brit Richard O'Brien (who plays Riff Raff), it set the bar for "cult" cinema and cultists' commitment (who dresses in costume to see a favorite film anymore?). More than thirty years after the age of video should have killed it off completely, it still draws crowds that dutifully reenact a previous generation's self-created camp routine. Needless to say, few of us—then or now—go straight. Throw a party with this one if you dare—you'll be cleaning up the debris for days afterward—or see if the movie is as much wacky fun now that you can finally hear it.

***Eraserhead* (1977)** David Lynch's feature debut, and one of the creepiest, most original American films ever made. Everything here is freestanding subconscious metaphor, from the run-down industrial decor and the hero's frumpy couture to his haunted radiator, the pungent worms he pulls out of his uncooperative wife at night, and his baby—a slimy, rodentine puppet creature that represents the ultimate unprepared-parent bad dream. It's also funny as hell—though where you'll laugh, and why, we couldn't say.

***National Lampoon's Animal House* (1978)** The case for this drunken nostalgic rip being a more eloquent cultural portrait than its lowbrow reputation suggests is made in the "Autumn" section (p. 87), but its most obvious utilization today is as a beer-blast anthem that's as carefree and irreverent as a senior-year bender. Here is a world in which beer bottles fly from offscreen into the characters' appreciative hands (watch early on when just such a projectile accidentally wings freshman Tom Hulce's blonde date in the head; befitting the spirit of the movie, she's hardly fazed).

***The Kids Are Alright* (1979)** All rock groups worthy of the genre drink, but few ever seemed to have as much blotto fun as the Who, on stage and off, and this archival documentary is an adrenaline shot of rowdy fun. All by himself, dead or not, Keith Moon is a larger-than-life ad for living irresponsibly and half in the hat.

***Altered States* (1980)** Whatever you're on, this hell-bent sci-fi melodrama (derived very loosely, by novelist/screenwriter Paddy Chayefsky, from the experiments of Dr. John Lilly, author of *The Center of the Cyclone*) is a raging hoot, complementing some of the densest and most quickly read scientific dialogue the movies have ever known with absolutely crazy mutative imagery. This is the film in which the world discovered William Hurt, who rants psychophysiological inanities whenever he's not lodged in foam rubber prosthetics that are meant to represent humankind's prefetal essence, or something. Ken Russell directed.

***Arthur* (1981)** A rather embarrassing 1980s artifact, this winsome recruiting poster for giggling inebriation still kicks up a few laughs, thanks largely to Dudley Moore's puckish enthusiasm and John Gielgud's laconic delivery, but also to the seductive charm of being completely, nonsensically three sheets to the wind and—crucially—being so rich that it doesn't matter a whit.

***Cutter's Way* (1981)** Itself a kind of distorted Hemingway daydream, this superb, character-based Santa Barbara mystery, directed by Czech emigré Ivan Passer, is all about slacking, drinking, and living off society's grid and in the heat. John Heard's growling, irreverent 'Nam vet cripple, Jeff Bridges's noncommittal beach boy gone to seed, and Lisa Eichhorn's wounded post-hippie all drink far too much and spend their days sleeping it off, with only a murder to upset their dozy routine.

***Heavy Metal* (1981)** A Canadian-made fantasy cartoon based on tales from the American comic *Heavy Metal* (not, it should be noted, from its French source mag and counterpart *Métal Hurlant*), held together by way of a perfectly idiotic story thread, and voiced by *SCTV* vets. Still, it's groovy and psychedelic, baby, and some of it is irrationally funny.

IV

S.O.B. **(1981)** Blake Edwards's Hollywood satire has aspects to it that dated badly in 1981, and worse now, but underneath the comic plot (which is funny enough, despite the showbiz creakiness), there's the "all drinking, all the time" lifestyle of the entourage around the insane hero (Richard Mulligan, mugging monstrously, as a suicidal director), led by Robert Preston (as a fabulous Dr. Feelgood—"*Tomato juice!*"), Robert Webber, and William Holden, playing his own drinking self, after a fashion; he died after shooting this movie by falling drunkenly and cutting his head on a night table. Thus was born the legend of the William Holden Drinking Helmet, must-have paraphernalia among the dipsos we knew in the 1980s.

My Favorite Year **(1982)** Another portrait of drunken high spirits, loosely based upon Mel Brooks's experience as a young underling working on Sid Caesar's *Your Show of Shows*, where for a week he was assigned to keep watch on toasted guest star Errol Flynn. Peter O'Toole, at his florid, chandelier-swinging best, plays the Flynn character with inebriated glee.

Barfly **(1987)** You don't want to emulate the behavior depicted in this film (based on Charles Bukowski's short stories)—in fact, the movie is realistic enough about catastrophic alcoholism to maybe scare you straight. But it's also a comedy, and Mickey Rourke's boozy comic instincts are funniest when you yourself are also slowed down a little by drink.

Naked Lunch **(1991)** David Cronenberg beats all comers at making explosively inspired movies out of what were thought to be absolutely unfilmable novels—he made J. G. Ballard's *Crash* into an almost tasteful existentialist tale of devotion, and he made William S. Burroughs's *Naked Lunch*, a free-associative junkie nightmare famous for its surrealist prose, into a droll comedy. The less you know, the better; we'll just say that the comic points are crispy dry, and the drug-addled, hypersexualized imagery is a total freak-out.

Tribulation 99: Alien Anomalies Under America **(1991)** Though it clocks in at under an hour long, this berserk found-footage collage film may be the greatest doped-up conspiracy-theory epic ever made. San Francisco anarchist/artist Craig Baldwin assembled a new, secret history of the twentieth century out of cold news, UFO rumors, sci-fi movie tidbits, industrial footage, Bible-school instruction shorts, and his extraordinary imagination, which sardonically links the CIA, Castro, atomic testing, the 1976 Chilean coup, a plot to alter the Earth's axis, and an alien/inner-Earth invasion by the "Quetzals," all of it coming at you in ninety-nine fast chapters, narrated in a hostile growl.

Ed Wood **(1994)** See *Glen or Glenda* and *Plan 9 from Outer Space* first, and it will become clear as to who Ed Wood was and why Tim Burton made this bizarre, sad, wickedly funny biopic about him. Once you're a member of the club, *Ed Wood* comes off as a ravishing, lovelorn portrait of a very real all-American loser dizzy with his own

dead-end daydreams. The film is propelled by Wood's poignant relationship with the
morphine-racked Bela Lugosi as the latter faced the grave, and the sense of lives lived
within the lurid, intoxicating shadow of Movies is palpable and evocative. Part of the
triumph here may be casting: Johnny Depp is superb in his stylized take on Wood,
Martin Landau won an Oscar for his letter-perfect Lugosi, and Bill Murray, Patricia
Arquette, Jeffrey Jones, and ex-wrestler George "the Animal" Steele populate the
fringes. Hilarious and graceful, Burton's film knows enough to leave Wood himself
as an enigma.

Texas Chainsaw Massacre: The Next Generation (1994) Starring native Texans Renee Zellweger and Matthew McConaughey before they became magazine covers, this fourth-
generation sequel to Tobe Hooper's 1974 indie sensation is a psycho piece of work, an
absurdly nonsensical genre spoof that, while making very little sense, may showcase
the performance of McConaughey's career. He's the miscreant family patriarch—a
yowling, nose-biting, script-chewing bull goose loony with a homemade hydraulic leg
that makes Rutger Hauer look like Steven Wright. Holy moly.

Congo (1995) Let's get this straight: a language-equipped ape, a CIA agent, a hippo
attack, an African revolution, King Solomon's mines, spontaneous skydiving (talking
ape included!), Tim Curry with an Eastern European accent thick as a wool rug, and
an onslaught of albino gorillas fended off with a laser gun that needs a giant diamond
in it to run? Outrageous, campy nonsense, mistaken by many people for a failed
action film.

IV

The Fifth Element (1997) Despite being in English and starring Bruce Willis, this is a
French sci-fi epic, in which there's little science to speak of, and plenty of high-as-a-
kite fantasy and futuristic surrealism. If Gary Oldman, as a villain named Zorg who's
going berserk, doesn't clue you in, you'll know you're lost when you get to the performance of a blue-skinned octopoid opera diva belting out an aria from *Lucia di Lam-
mermoor*. Written by director Luc Besson when he was a teenager.

Fear and Loathing in Las Vegas (1998) Terry Gilliam's blasted film of Hunter S. Thompson's
infamous book is, for what it's worth, a sharp evocation of the warped experience of
LSD, and it could spark a flashback. On one level, it's about two drooling, drug-addled
cretins, Raoul Duke (Johnny Depp) and Dr. Gonzo (Benicio Del Toro), misbehaving on
a scale that would shame an African despot. On another, it's about an apocalyptic lost
weekend that is an escape from, response to, and conceptual-art commentary on the
middle-class bad dream that is midcentury American life. Del Toro, as the monstrous,
puke-prone, knife-wielding sociopath of the two, is an unforgettable presence, but it's
Depp's movie. His Duke is just as fearlessly stylized as his Ed Wood, possessed of a
mannered diction that sounds like Mel Blanc doing Alexander Haig, and a loopy body
language that aims to mime the conflicting influences of amyl nitrate and blotter acid.

Half-Baked (1998) Proudly sophomoric, this comedy is scrupulously aimed *only* at pot heads, in that it focuses euphorically on the wonders, rituals, and fetishism of marijuana to the virtual exclusion of anything else. If you're not on that wavelength, and don't have fond memories of being on that wavelength in your youth, you'll be left out in the cold. Dave Chappelle, Guillermo Diaz, Jim Breuer, and Harland Williams are crispy roommates who decide to answer their money problems by dealing; nonsense ensues. Breuer is a howl as the most thoroughly toasted of the quartet.

Pi (1998) Darren Aronofsky's ferociously inventive debut movie (an award winner at the Sundance Film Festival) doesn't tell a story so much as jack it into your nervous system. In many ways, it's the ultimate paranoid conspiracy movie, as well as the ultimate cinematic expression of chaos theory, numerological obsession, and the very human hunger for order in a mad world. And it was made for sixty thousand dollars. Cheap, rough, messy, and primitive, but full of ideas, the movie follows the (largely interior) progress of a reclusive mathematician (Sean Gullette), whose entire apartment is a hard-wired, do-it-yourself computer devoted to discovering the secret code beneath what he sees as the ultimate system of ordered chaos—the stock market. After his homemade computer happens upon a potentially significant string of digits and crashes, the nervous brainiac is stalked by both mercenary Wall Street personnel and a Kabbalah sect intent on discovering the secret code hidden within their ancient texts—a number that may be the very name of God.

The Adventures of Elmo in Grouchland (1999) Deceptively infantile, this *Sesame Street* opus could be more simply titled *Elmo Goes to Hell*, in that it follows the beloved red furball into Oscar's trash can and through a dimensional portal to an filthy, underground anti–*Sesame Street* that's as metaphoric as any Antonioni junkyard and that is occupied by Dada-spouting grouches who howl in agony at "The Alphabet Song." Once embarked upon his own *Inferno* without a Virgil, the angelic Elmo struggles to retrieve his sacred blankie from Huxley (Mandy Patinkin), a juggernaut of preening greed who labels everything "MINE," acting out the universal dialectic between capitalistic hunger and socialistic reason. (Indeed, every toddler learns Marx the hard way in those inevitable "sharing" skirmishes.) Along the way, a cleavage-heaving Vanessa Williams shows up as the Queen of Trash, injecting a subtext of seductive sex magick into the brew; St. Elmo, though amused, is not tempted. Instead, Elmo's authentic trial comes in the harrowing moment when he recognizes in himself Huxley's doppelganger. As surely as *Teletubbies* is a tot *Videodrome*, Elmo's passion is Milton for millennial kindergartners.

Bad Santa (2003) Possibly the nastiest and most hilarious movie about overdrinking ever made. Billy Bob Thornton is a raging, misanthropic drunk so far gone he's practically incontinent, but it's impossible to pity him since he's such a cretin. The squalor and bad taste that fuels Terry Zwigoff's film is so complete it'd be depressing if it weren't so appallingly funny.

The Saddest Music in the World **(2003)** Canadian quasi-avant-gardist Guy Maddin makes films that resemble no one else's—conscientiously antiquated, deliberately unprofessional, and soaked in a brine mixture of ironic campiness, melodramatic fervor, and outlandishly absurd comedy. Often his films resemble actual film-history discards, deteriorating remnants of ancient industries working in obscure genres. Here, he invokes both Soviet-silent Supremacist design and amateur super-8 productions in an Oedipally angsty five-way romance saga that centers around a brewery-sponsored "saddest music in the world" contest and the mopey culture of Winnipeg beer guzzling that surrounds it. The various rounds' winners get, as their prizes, a chance to actually slide into a giant vat of foamy beer.

A Scanner Darkly **(2006)** Philip K. Dick was surely one of the most dope-addled authors of William S. Burroughs's America, and Richard Linklater's version of his druggiest book captures the disorientation and humid paranoia of addiction almost *too* well—it's digitally rotoscoped, so the action, the actors (which include Keanu Reeves, Winona Ryder, Robert Downey Jr., Woody Harrelson—a cast custom built for epochal dopiness), and even the scenery float in painterly swatches. It could be a blast, but the jittery, lost, grim narrative—Reeves plays a narc so wasted he's not quite aware that he's surveilling himself—could also put you off tripping forever.

IV

GIRLS' NIGHT OUT

"You really wear that suit."
—Jennifer Lopez, *Out of Sight*

Good either for prepping for a voyage into partyland or as the first act (or the entirety) of a ladies' evening out, with strong drinks, gossipy banter, and no familiar men sniffing about.

The Way We Were **(1973)** We have to confess that the popularity of this Barbra Streisand vehicle remains a bit of a mystery to us—you're either a Barbra-ite, or you're not. Streisand's character here is a righteous political activist, and how Robert Redford, who's about as sexy in this film as he ever was, could tolerate her for the span of even a lunch date is beyond us. There are a few genuinely touching moments, especially in the famous last scene, but chances are you already know if you and your girlfriends are suckers for this one.

An Officer and a Gentleman **(1982)** A favorite among the women we talked to, whom we dare say represent something of a core sample of "pubescent in the early 1980s" American femininity. Maybe it still rings bells because of its intimate grittiness, which makes it more swallowable and identifiable a Cinderella story than 1990's *Pretty Woman*; after all, Debra Winger's factory worker isn't quite a streetwalker (then again, neither was Julia Roberts's supposed lady of the evening), and Richard Gere's navy bad boy doesn't lift his lady up to the castle his *Pretty Woman* tycoon clearly could afford. Both movies depend entirely on their actresses' open faces and joie de vivre, and Winger—a forgotten wonder today who provided sorely needed fire in the movies of the Reagan era—is completely winning.

Dirty Dancing **(1987)** Popular demand alone warrants this revered hit's inclusion; hordes of women flocked to theaters to see it, and even now, years later, all of them still sigh when it's mentioned. There may be a certain amount of early summer rosiness involved, but enjoyment of this flick requires that you have acquired the taste for Patrick Swayze's muscly dance instructor or that you identify somehow with Jennifer Grey's budding post-teen.

Tequila Sunrise **(1988)** It's a sultry L.A. summer, and successful restaurateur Michelle Pfeiffer faces a daunting decision: cop Kurt Russell or crook Mel Gibson? If they were ice cream, you'd want a scoop of each, and that's exactly what Pfeiffer opts for—but since Gibson has never been more beautiful before or since, she does eventually settle on him, *in a hot tub*. The plot won't override chitchat, noshing, or awed gasps of appreciation. Important: commit first to forgetting everything you've learned about Gibson since 2004.

Women on the Verge of a Nervous Breakdown (1988) Pedro Almodóvar's estrogen-fueled neo-slapstick farce involves betrayed women, goldbricking men, girlfriends with more man troubles, homicidal impulses, a dangerous pitcher of gazpacho, and a deep lust for romantic folly. Redefines the word "romp" for the post-feminist era.

sex, lies, and videotape **(1989)** Four characters: a shallow and amoral lawyer (Peter Gallagher), his prudish wife (Andie MacDowell), her trampy barmaid sister (Laura San Giacomo), and a mysterious stranger in town—James Spader, as an old college friend with an impotence problem, a closetful of other issues, and a predilection for videotaping women as they talk about sex. Justly renowned, funny, and sneakily sexy.

Thelma & Louise **(1991)** The ultimate female-bonding anthem movie—see "Ms. Lonelyhearts," p. 195.

The Truth About Cats & Dogs **(1996)** A *Cyrano de Bergerac* retread for the phone sex age, this gentle and unambitious romantic comedy stars British hunk Ben Chaplin in the Roxane role, Uma Thurman as a hot ditz with legs as long as her bad-luck roster of rotten boyfriends, and a sharp, lovely Janeane Garofalo as the film's Cyrano, a talk-radio veterinarian/animal psychologist whose alluring voice and carbolic wit thoroughly melt Chaplin's butter. A mammoth masturbatory phone date sets a Hollywood standard, while Garofalo's on-air gig is entertaining enough to make you wish it were a real show.

Walking and Talking **(1996)** Nicole Holofcener's chick flick depends absolutely and generously on the verve and candor of Catherine Keener and Anne Heche, as lifelong buddies negotiating their own mutating friendship as one faces marriage and the other faces loneliness. The film has the easy rhythm of a three-hour girl talk phone call, and all the actors run like linebackers with their unpredictable and witty (but not too witty) characters. Keener is particularly radiant and raw in a way that justifies the whole movie—a dozen emotions can register on her face all at once. Watching her come up with something to say in an embarrassing situation is like watching a Japanese table-tennis pro play himself.

Out of Sight **(1998)** A girls' club natural, this film is better watched once the chatter fades, because there's not an iota of novelist Elmore Leonard's snappy banter you can afford to miss. A great, comical neo-noir on one hand, this Steven Soderbergh gift also proves the theory that sex starts in the brain. The pas de deux here, amid a cast of supporting eccentrics, is between Jennifer Lopez's federal marshal and inveterate bank robber George Clooney; Clooney's fast-thinking, humane crook knows what he wants from the get-go, but Lopez's savvy fed—the pop-culture star's best role by far—struggles mightily between her cop instincts to catch him and haul him back to prison and her desire to ride him like a pony (a yearning every woman in the room will be sharing). Absolutely the best sotto voce flirt talk heard in a movie since, well, maybe ever, and that's what counts for grown-ups.

There's Something About Mary **(1998)** See "Post-Op Recovery" (p. 189) for a full-on appreciation, but don't overlook the all-girl possibilities here—you can scream over the low-down, man-beast humor without feeling self-conscious.

Holy Smoke **(1999)** Jane Campion's larky, absurdist satire/melodrama/I'm not sure what it is takes as its subject cult membership versus deprogramming. The film is after bigger fish, of course, and seems framed to be a rather demented parable about gender combat. Campion is generally addicted to feminist anthems, and here common sense and character sometimes have to wait it out as the film goes bonkers with estrogen. On a trip to India, Aussie free spirit Ruth (Kate Winslet) becomes besotted with a local guru and commits herself, harmlessly, to his cult. Her white-trash family back home spends the family bank account on "exit counselor" P.J. (Harvey Keitel), a no-nonsense, American-outlaw type in cowboy boots and hair dye. Once Ruth is cornered for her deprogramming, all hell breaks loose: in more or less complete control of her mind, her emotions, her body, and her sexual allure, Ruth mocks, insults, and sleeps with P.J. until he is in fact deprogrammed himself. Campion has a lot to say here, and not so much narrative room to say it; expect a coherent, cohesive movie at your peril.

Kissing Jessica Stein (2001) Fed up with looking for love but feeling pressure from her mother to land a husband, the sassy, ditzy heroine of the title (Jennifer Westfeldt) finds instead the bisexual Helen (Heather Juergensen), who's already convinced that girls can scratch the itch that men can't seem to reach. Trouble is, how does a nice, straight Jewish girl bring home a woman—especially one who's not a doctor? Written by the two actresses, the script is fierce, smart, and funny as hell.

Ocean's Eleven (2001) Women born in the 1960s seem to fall into two categories when polled: those who have the hots for "man's man" George Clooney and those who prefer the boyish perfection of Brad Pitt. In this flick, you get both of 'em, plus Matt Damon, Julia Roberts, a thick cast of charming comic pros, director Steven Soderbergh (keeping the neo–Rat Pack thing light as a feather), and a heist in which no blood is spilled.

The Devil Wears Prada (2006) A vitriolic dig at the fashion-magazine industry—what could be better?—with Meryl Streep making an Oscar-nominated meal out of the megalomaniac queen bee modeled on Anna Wintour. You'll all get the fashion-label in-jokes and trendy digs without worrying about a nearby man scoffing or raising an eyebrow.

BOYS' NIGHT OUT

"Are you gonna bark all day, little doggy, or are you gonna bite?"
—Michael Madsen, *Reservoir Dogs*

Few men will actually want to stay home to watch a movie together (even if that movie is *Reservoir Dogs*) when they could be hitting the local fleshpot or ranging about in public half-cocked. But if you and your buddies want something to prime the tank before you head out, decide to lie low for a night, or are past the age when the alternatives sound like fun, check these out.

***The Lives of a Bengal Lancer* (1935)** One of the premier buddy adventure movies, in which sardonic British Army pals (Gary Cooper and Franchot Tone, plus petulant newbie Richard Cromwell) face Afridi invaders on the Indian frontier. Politically incorrect, but rousing.

***Gunga Din* (1939)** Even better—three colonial officers and comrades (Cary Grant, Victor McLaglen, and Douglas Fairbanks Jr.) battle an onslaught by Thuggee rebels while attempting to get Fairbanks's aw-shucks soldier boy out of his marriage commitment (to pale Joan Fontaine). Fun-loving star power and a rather childish sense of irreverence carry the day, and those qualities have made this a boy's Saturday-afternoon-on-the-rug favorite.

***The Killers* (1964)** Genre hard guy and *Dirty Harry* auteur Don Siegel directed this remake of the 1946 noir (itself an nervy extrapolation of the very short Ernest Hemingway story), placing the task of deciphering the backstory not in the hands of an investigator, but in those of the assassins themselves (Lee Marvin and Clu Gulager)—after they've shot their target (John Cassavetes) and begin to wonder why they were paid to do the job. Made for TV, but deemed inappropriate for that medium due to violence and sex, so it was released to theaters instead.

IV

***Faster, Pussycat! Kill! Kill!* (1965)** Exploitationeer Russ Meyer was famous for his nudie films starring huge-breasted women, but this notorious quasi–biker thriller features virtually no skin—just big-bosomed strippers (led by the unforgettable Tura Satana), rebelling against the Man and hitting the high road in search of excitement and vengeance. Which they find, at the expense of innocent lives and the dignity of some weak-kneed men. A deeply hilarious cult favorite.

***The Good, the Bad and the Ugly* (1966)** The boys inside of men love big, cool, dramatic confrontations, schematically broken down by label, where either an actor says next to nothing (like Clint Eastwood) or eats the scenery (like Eli Wallach). Sergio Leone's mega–cartoon western of three men, the Civil War, and a cache of hidden loot is long, patient (go ahead, get a beer; no need to hit pause), and full of machismo run awry.

***Point Blank* (1967)** Perhaps the most perfectly Marvinesque of Lee Marvin movies, in which he plays a returned hood determined to extract the money he's owed from an amorphous criminal syndicate that's not so different from multinational corporations. Of course, he kicks ass. Was Marvin—with his torpedo-shaped head, alligator eyes, snoring-dinosaur voice, and lightning-strike body English—the most mesmerizing, original presence American movies have ever known? It might be a guy thing.

***Bullitt* (1968)** Would that we could all follow "the Tao of Steve," as the 2000 indie comedy suggested. In this San Francisco cop drama, Steve McQueen is the epitome of experience-hardened coolness that Humphrey Bogart used to embody—and that everyone's been trying to copy since. Includes the first of the great urban car-chase sequences.

***The Getaway* (1972)** More McQueen, this time in a much nastier on-the-run crime scenario, courtesy of director Sam Peckinpah. Ali MacGraw, the future Mrs. McQueen, is along placidly for the ride, and Al Lettieri (*The Godfather*'s catalytic antagonist) makes a great growling villain. But watch Steve, who's all bitter grace under pressure.

***Going Places* (1974)** A wildly misogynistic (or is it?; Pauline Kael didn't think so) comedy about two itinerant rogues (Gérard Depardieu and Patrick Dewaere) who roam the countryside hunting for fun, free sex, and a chance to offend middle-class sympathies. They get shot, hunted, hounded out of town, humiliated, and sexually abused; in the meantime, they double-team vapid girl-toy Miou-Miou, schoolgirl Isabelle Huppert, and paroled convict Jeanne Moreau. Director Bertrand Blier began his successful auteurist run here, and just four years later his film *Get Out Your Handkerchiefs* won an Oscar.

***The Man Who Would Be King* (1975)** *Gunga Din*'s male-bonding principle, upscaled for the 1970s. John Huston fashioned a leveling macho tearjerker out of an old Rudyard Kipling story, in which two renegade British officers (Michael Caine and Sean Connery, in their prime) decide to traipse into unexplored Kafiristan (now part of Afghanistan), in order to become kings. Executed with love and conviction; you'll never hear "The Minstrel Boy" again without welling up.

***Mad Max* (1979)** Postapocalyptic Australia, where survival in the semisavage outlands is all a matter of driving. Mel Gibson wasn't a star yet; after director George Miller's lawless, punked-out follow-up, ***The Road Warrior* (1981)**, he was.

***Southern Comfort* (1981)** A boisterous, riveting, unpretentious voyage into men-in-the-wilderness territory (see "Camping and Hiking," p. 271, for the others), wherein a squad of idiot redneck National Guard members offend the Cajun trappers deep in the Louisiana swamps, and get picked off one by one as they try to find the interstate. Powers Boothe and Keith Carradine have the only IQs; Fred Ward, T. K. Carter, Alan Autry, Peter Coyote, Lewis Smith, and others are gator fodder.

***Predator* (1987)** Arnold Schwarzenegger leads a cadre of muscled mercenaries into a Central American jungle on some covert mission, but battles instead a tentacle-faced alien creature. Director John McTiernan delivered the filmmaking chops needed to make this hooey watchable.

***Frankenhooker* (1990)** A giggly trailer-trash cousin to David Cronenberg by way of EC Comics and sideshow taboo, director Frank Henenlotter had a great exploitation run in the 1980s—this comedy might be the *least* transgressive movie he made, though it has its fair share of absurd gore and sexual heebie-jeebies. A wannabe mad scientist

(James Lorinz, peerlessly nerve-racked) reconstructs his fiancée using hookers' body parts; tasteless hijinks ensue.

Reservoir Dogs (1992) The best movie Don Siegel never made, Quentin Tarantino's debut is a justly famous, lean, sweaty anxiety attack of a film. A carefully constructed genre study, it's something of a bull in a genre shop—literal aspects of *The Killing, The Wild Bunch, The Taking of Pelham 123, Point Blank,* and John Woo's Hong Kong shotgun weddings are co-opted and exploited. A heist movie in which we never see the crime, just the preparations and the blood-soaked aftermath, Tarantino's film is a field day of macho confrontations, raucous Mametian dialogue, and corrective realism—blood never spurts into the air; it just leaks out into a black lake. We know we have membership in this neo-noir, film-head cabal when we immediately understand what quiet psychopath Michael Madsen means when he smiles at Harvey Keitel's bleeding-heart after a toe-to-toe and quips, "I bet you're a big Lee Marvin fan."

IV

PARTY SOFTWARE

"I just can't cope with the freaky stuff."
—Leslie Carlson, *Videodrome*

Parties, particularly those thrown and attended by anyone under forty, should be webs of intersecting and conflicting input. But what to put on the TV, with music blasting from elsewhere? Here are our eye-popping recommendations for adding visual snap to your next event.

Les Vampires (1915) Using single shots of condensed action and space, French pulp-meister Louis Feuillade outpaced D. W. Griffith in his own time in terms of inventiveness, mise-en-scène, and visual sophistication. Watching this nearly seven-hour crime serial, in which the titular gang of thieves lurk inside walls and scale buildings, is like glimpsing a century-old dream that's been somehow preserved, and it's no surprise the original surrealists worshiped it. Musidora plays Vampire ringleader Irma Vep, Paris plays an empty, Chinese-box version of itself, and narrative logic is taffy-twisted into a sense of moviegoing euphoria. It's more than a movie—it's an epic subconscious event, and it's hard to not watch.

Aelita (1924) Based on a novel by Leo Tolstoy's distant cousin, this Soviet silent is the world's first space-travel melodrama—and an anti-royalism screed that's remembered most fondly today as an orgasm of futurist set and costume design.

Metropolis (1927) Fritz Lang's bad and beautiful ultra-opus depicts a futuristic society of elites and slaves that is brought crashing down by the socialist activism of a young woman (Brigitte Helm) and the scheming of a lovelorn, robot-manufacturing mad scientist (Rudolph Klein-Rogge). The politics are hogwash, but visually the movie's a candy store.

The Man with the Movie Camera (1929) Dziga Vertov, one of the Soviet Empire's premier montage-happy propagandists, presents a portrait of 1920s Russian life, a portrait of the moviemaker as portraitist, and a portrait of cinema itself as a liaison between life and artifice. Meanwhile, Vertov's images, edited together in a expressive fashion, remain wild and startling.

A Midsummer Night's Dream (1935) Shakespeare, by way of Warner Brothers and German Expressionist theater impresario/codirector Max Reinhardt, whose only film this is. The charming but odd incongruity of James Cagney as Bottom notwithstanding, this is a fairyland feast for the eyes, a tidal wave of ethereal mist, toy-shop forests, dancing goblins, flying goddesses, and stardust.

Pandora and the Flying Dutchman (1951) Ghosts, love, and transmigrated souls, on a beach inhabited by Ava Gardner, in unearthly color photography by Jack Cardiff, with designs and compositions by Man Ray. In other words, a surrealist Hollywood film André Breton would've swooned for.

Invaders from Mars (1953) William Cameron Menzies transformed a subpar kid's pulp version of a Martian invasion tale into one of the most chilling, weird, and unforgettable sci-fi films of the 1950s. It's as clammy and uncomfortable as a bad dream; the rarely used Cinecolor process is employed here, and the film looks to have been compromised by rot from the very beginning.

The Night of the Hunter (1955) Portly actor Charles Laughton directed only one film, but no one's been able to get over it—a noir mixture of Beatrix Potter and EC Comics, in which fake preacher Robert Mitchum chases after two orphaned kids and their doll full of money. From Shelley Winters's corpse sinking under a lake to the forest animals observing the children's raft flight down the night river, it's a unique experience.

Touch of Evil (1958) As much a seething, death-haunted scuttle through the darkest landscape Hollywood ever invented as it is a spectacularly moody triumph of pure filmmaking hubris, Orson Welles's anti-masterpiece is far from a prototypical film noir—it rants, raves, explodes, shrieks, shocks your eyeballs, and bends the world around its bruise-swollen finger. Whether you choose the original version (which was sloppily edited by the producers) or the recent restoration (reedited in accordance with a fifty-eight-page memo left by Welles), this dirty, low-budget B flick is racked with looming expressionism, motifs from Delvaux and Tanguy, a visualized partial prophecy of *Psycho* (which would come out two years later), and more compositional imagination than any ten other movies. In the grand scheme of things, *Touch of Evil* stands second only to *Citizen Kane* in the Welles oeuvre, second to none in the legacy of true, lowdown noir, and, finally, uniquely alone in its own shadowy universe.

THX 1138 (1971) George Lucas's first film offers up a dire, glum dystopian vision of a dehumanized future in which the hairless, white-suited humans are often simply stranded in endless whiteness. Quite a different sensibility than we came to know through thirteen-plus hours of Skywalker-ness, but by far the more interesting—and visually, it has a disarming starkness that grabs your eyeballs.

Tommy (1975) Ken Russell's wack-a-doo filmization of the Who's rock opera is more of a costumer's camp orgy than the kitsch parable on rock stardom that Pete Townshend intended. Leave the sound on and you get Jack Nicholson tonelessly moaning "Go to the Mirror"; leave it off, and you'll still be stunned by the image of Ann-Margret swimming in a pool of baked beans.

Zu: Warriors of the Magic Mountain (1983) Perhaps the paradigmatic Hong Kong fantasy film from the industry's feverish heyday, this Tsui Hark opus is a torrent of flying wizards, insane magic, and martial arts swordplay. This is the kind of raw, maniacal energy that *Crouching Tiger, Hidden Dragon* glossed up and made safe for middle-class audiences.

Bram Stoker's Dracula (1992) Francis Ford Coppola saw an opportunity, in this retread of the most-often-filmed novel of all time, to break his piggy bank of lurid, neo-Gothic visual ideas: independent shadows, blood that drips up, stop-motion vampiresses, nickelodeon nostalgia, double-exposures, ad infinitum—even if you've seen it, you probably haven't seen, or noticed, *all* of it.

Riki-Oh: The Story of Ricky (1992) A rather astonishing, starkly stylized Hong Kong blood flood set inside a privatized prison, where the enraged hero punches his enemies' eyes out, their bellies open, and their heads in half until someone attempts to strangle him with intestines and the warden turns into a snot-drooling ogre. You've been warned.

Conspirators of Pleasure (1996) The unapologetically demented, dank movie universe of Czech animator Jan Švankmajer is an acquired taste, but one that offers up astonishing rewards once you've made the leap. Švankmajer loudly proclaims himself a "militant surrealist," although this masterful film has little of his trademarked animation—the disjunctions and dreamy weirdness are mostly live, and all are conspicuously mundane. Like Buñuel before him, Švankmajer doesn't need to make pretty pictures to invoke the irrational—all he needs is a room, a few household objects, and the will to subvert. All of the film's six Prague-based characters compulsively pursue the same thing—sensual satisfaction. A magazine vendor devises a machine to massage and masturbate him in synchronization with the TV appearances of a beautiful news anchor; the anchor herself eases the pain of a lonely marriage by fondling live carp; her husband hammers together a battery of self-stimulators out of nails and fur; and so on. Švankmajer employs no dialogue (except for a few glimpses of news broadcasts), but this uproarious *and* discomfiting experience is nevertheless wildly satiric, roasting every sweaty act of self-absorption.

***Decasia* (2002)** A film *about* the decay of nitrate-stock film. Bill Morrison's found-footage movie uses film material of any variety and from any source—he hunted the world's lesser archives for ill-preserved film that had begun to dissipate. Here we have travelogues, old Asian serials, home movies, test shots, circus footage—you name it. The images are all compromised, in varying ways and to varying degrees, by decay; in one clip, a fin de siècle boxer seems to throw jabs at a metamorphic column of liquidy rot.

IV

WORLD TRAVELER

FAMILY TRIP

"Roll 'em up!"
—Chevy Chase, *National Lampoon's Vacation*

Movies are like miniature trips, and when gearing up for a family vacation, you could do worse than to skip triple-checking your packing list and instead soak up the vibe of being on the move and teach your kids a little something about the world in transit. Too bad there aren't many watchable films that offer those opportunities. Most of the films recommended here, suggested half-tongue-in-cheek, are outrageous "what's the worst that could happen?" scenarios, which may help you maintain perspective on the road. These movies are not, in any case, intended as viewing entertainment *during* the trip itself—shut off the DVD player in the minivan and look out the window, fer Chrissake.

Blondie Takes a Vacation (1939) The third film of this protracted, deathless series (twenty-seven films and a TV series inside of twenty years) has the Bumsteads of *Blondie* comic-strip fame head to the mountains and decide to help run a hotel. Some vacation.

Gidget Goes Hawaiian (1961) Deborah Walley takes over as the popular 1950s–'60s teen, going grumpily to Hawaii with her parents and getting involved in new romantic misunderstandings. For period obsessives only.

National Lampoon's Vacation (1983) This is actually two movies: seen when sober, it's an only occasionally winning Chevy Chase comedy about the worst family vacation ever; seen while under the influence of a certain organic substance we keep hearing about in the news (and from friends who certainly knew more about it in their 1980s youths than they do now), it's a gaspingly hilarious Chevy Chase comedy, filled with dry moments *between* the jokes that are, for some, priceless.

Lost in America (1985) Or maybe *this* is the worst vacation on film—don't throw down an extreme-scenario gauntlet if you don't want Albert Brooks to step up and take the gold. Here, he's a fired ad exec who leaves L.A. with wife Julie Hagerty and a head full of road movie cliches and *Easy Rider* memories. He doesn't get far, and the comedy of discomfort that ensues is peerless.

The Mosquito Coast (1986) Well, this'll take the cake: if your dad is Harrison Ford, and he strands you and your family on a Central American jungle coastline so you can create paradise away from the evils of society, then you've won the Worst Vacation Ever sweepstakes handily. Ford is fascinatingly out of character as a deluded utopian, and director Peter Weir knows how to turn the screws.

Little Miss Sunshine **(2006)** Jonathan Dayton and Valerie Faris's indie hit (pulling in nearly a 1,000 percent return on investment in a year in which *Mission: Impossible III* couldn't even break even) has a familiar outline: a contentious, eccentric extended family hits the road in a puttering VW bus—in this case, to participate in that most revolting of American rituals, the preadolescent beauty pageant—but it's executed with consummate wit and Swiss timing. The charm of this film might boil down to the cast: give pros like Alan Arkin, Steve Carell, Toni Collette, and Greg Kinnear some open road, and they will race like the devil.

RV **(2006)** A fairly rotten, rote family comedy with Robin Williams, but it actually entails a trip in a contemporary recreational vehicle, so for some who have no high-comedy expectations, it might serve as a nice pre-trip appetizer.

EXOTIC TRAVEL

"This must be the place where they empty all the old hourglasses."
—Bob Hope, *Road to Morocco*

The art of pumping up for a trip to tropical locales requires you to turn a blind eye to political and socioeconomic realities, and instead immerse yourself in the colonialist daydreams of yesteryear, when "exotic" wasn't a taboo word, Third World natives were important only insofar as they happily brought you drinks, and equatorial landscapes were pristine and luxurious. "Tropical" is a fantasy state of mind, after all; cultivate it now, before you leave.

Tabu **(1931)** Fed up with the Hollywood studio system, German emigré director F. W. Murnau went to Tahiti with pioneering documentarian Robert Flaherty—a more ill-fitting match one cannot imagine—to make a film; they fought, and Flaherty left, and the movie that resulted from the excursion is an odd infliction of tropical nature on Murnau's filmography. It's also one of the last genuine silent films, yet it has no title cards. A simple, tragic, native romance, filmed with locals and without a smidge of Western condescension toward Asian "others," it's a marvel of sun-blazed intimacy, and the sexiest film made anywhere in the 1930s.

Qué Viva México! **(1932)** Soviet master Sergei Eisenstein went to Mexico at the dawn of the sound era and cavorted about with a camera, shooting the local populace being essentially Mexican—or so he'd have us think. It's all very studied, and basically unfinished, but gorgeous and unabashedly tropical.

Red Dust **(1932)** Clark Gable and Jean Harlow, sweating and bickering on an Indochinese rubber plantation. Actually, the film was shot in Hollywood, but so what—it's Gable and Harlow!

Flying Down to Rio **(1933)** We can still wistfully recall the days when, in the movies at least, Third World vacation spots were playgrounds for rich people who dressed in tuxedos and gowns, danced, ballroom style, under the palm trees, and nuzzled in the equatorial moonlight. This lovable old movie introduced the pairing of Fred Astaire and Ginger Rogers (but as the second leads, after Dolores Del Rio and Gene Raymond), and it features splendid tunes (by Vincent Youmans and lyricists Gus Kahn and Edward Eliscu) and a good amount of pre–Production Code bralessness—all under a fake Brazilian sky.

Lost Horizon **(1937)** Going to Tibet? It's fair to speculate that more westerners have gone to the Himalayas on holiday because of this woozy Frank Capra fantasy than because of any other cultural ignition. It's pure Hollywood, with Ronald Colman finding and refinding his Shangri-La, but the dream lives on.

V

One Night in the Tropics **(1940)** Like *Flying Down to Rio*, but with Abbott and Costello instead of Astaire and Rogers.

Black Orpheus **(1959)** One of the great midcentury import hits, this vivid Brazilian film is an infectious retelling of the Orpheus-Eurydice myth, set during Carnavale and feverish with hip-swiveling hustle, exploding local color, and sleeve-worn heart. Never underestimate the raw energy of South American partying.

Hell in the Pacific **(1968)** A simple, boys-at-play war game: Lee Marvin and Toshiro Mifune are soldiers stranded on a Pacific atoll during World War II, driving each other nuts (with very little dialogue) and acting out the war in miniature. John Boorman directed.

The Color of Pomegranates **(1969)** Georgian artist Sergei Paradjanov, after the eye-opening primitiveness of his 1964 film *Shadows of Forgotten Ancestors*, grew more abstract in his storytelling and more hellzapoppin with his folk-art imagery. This demanding and astonishingly beautiful film depicts the life of Armenian poet Sayat Nova (which Paradjanov mixes with the myth-tales of Nova's own writing), and it's a fabulous visitation of ancient Russian-Arab-Turkish-style fusion, as seen in the most surreal icon art. Similarly, Paradjanov's *The Legend of Suram Fortress* **(1985)** revivifies a Georgian folk legend and explodes with *that* region's specific cultural flavor, recalled from lost centuries.

La Vallée **(1972)** New Guinea is visited by western hippies searching for paradise—or, more accurately, by a film crew documenting the paradise lost of the 1960s. (See "Being in the 1960s," p. 295.)

Club Paradise **(1986)** Exotic holiday comedies used to involve tuxedos and evening gowns, idealized equatorial moonlight, suave nightclubs, and Hollywood-style canoodling, but come the late century, they turned instead to Club Med craziness. Such is the case with this rather pallid but not completely unrewarding Harold Ramis comedy. A handful of *SCTV* alumns provide some zing.

Blissfully Yours **(2002)** A quietly rapturous Thai film, from festival favorite Apichatpong Weerasethakul, which entails little more than three unmoored souls retreating into the jungle for a picnic. That's it: there's nothing but sex, eating, hiking, and naps in the sun. Blissful is the word most viewers use.

The Big Bounce **(2004)** How can you go wrong with this one? Based on an Elmore Leonard novel, the movie is set in Hawaii, directed with snapping fingers by underutilized genre pro George Armitage (*Miami Blues, Grosse Point Blank*), and graced with likable star Owen Wilson, as a small-time criminal who's angling for a big score despite his better judgment and the advice of sympathetic local judge Morgan Freeman.

The Wild Blue Yonder **(2005)** Far out, man: Werner Herzog weaves a sci-fi parable around two sources of found footage that just can't get any more exotic. Film shot inside a NASA shuttle that was sent into orbit in 1989 becomes footage of humans lost in space, performing antigravity rituals; film shot under the sea ice in the Antarctic Ocean becomes images of a poisoned alien planet with a sky of ice. Vital to each of these visual orchestrations is the achingly mournful soundtrack mass, a fugue (arranged by Herzog) by Dutch jazz cellist Ernst Reijseger, Senegalese vocalist Mola Sylla, and a five-man Sardinian shepherd choir.

DOING EUROPE

"Is Phaeton misbehaving with his Persephone?"
—Simon Callow, *A Room with a View*

A vacation in Europe isn't just a matter of place; it's also a matter of mind-set: no one wants to visit the public housing projects of London or the industrial parks of Vienna. What you want is the *old* Europe—the gargoyle-encrusted architecture, the Tudor villages, the misty side streets of Paris, the vineyards and churches and castles that have been there, gathering mold and legends, forever. Luckily, movies want the same thing more often than not.

Under the Roofs of Paris (1930) René Clair was one the filmmakers for whom the technological burdens of early sound were not a crippling impediment but an inspiration. This love triangle confection is a fascinating litany of ingenious narrative gimmicks and formal flourishes, as well as a swoony, romantic evocation of the city in the period between the world wars. Same goes for Clair's _Paris Qui Dort_ (or _The Crazy Ray_) (1925), _Le Million_ (1931), and _À Nous la Liberté_ (1931).

Marius (1931), _Fanny_ (1932), and _César_ (1936) Based on his stage plays, producer-screenwriter Marcel Pagnol's landmark trilogy (he directed _César_, and he may as well have directed the other two) is a gabby, boisterous, no-bullshit paean to provincial Frenchness, love, Marseilles, and working-class dreams. Stagy, but shot on location, and the source of many old French-culture saws, especially among the French.

Boudu Saved from Drowning (1932) A Parisian bum (Michel Simon) is rescued from a Seine suicide and brought into the unhappy home of a petite bourgeoisie, where chaos reigns. Stereotypes die in the sun of director Jean Renoir's humanism; the class conflict is never as rote as Hollywood's 1986 remake, _Down and Out in Beverly Hills_, would lead you to believe. In any case, you can see Renoir discover what it means to visually evoke the unpredictable flow of life, and the character of a city, with composition, movement, and depth.

L'Atalante (1934) Jean Vigo's only full-length feature film, made before he died of complications from tuberculosis at age twenty-nine, this classic quasi-romance involves a Parisian barge, a marriage, the exquisite Dita Parlo, too many cats, and a pair of pickled hands. And Michel Simon, as a kind of Caliban. A dream snared on celluloid, this movie could convert an open-minded viewer into a cinephile forevermore.

Desire (1936) Whether actually shot in France or merely in Los Angeles County (seemingly unverifiable claims assert each), this Frank Borzage–directed confection pits Gary Cooper and Marlene Dietrich, at their least solemn, against each other. Photographed by Charles Lang, it certainly has a "sunny morning in the _jardin_" feel to it.

A Canterbury Tale (1944) Michael Powell and Emeric Pressburger's crazy wartime ode to the Kent countryside modernizes Chaucer and invokes a sweet, melancholy sense of life proceeding in wartime that few films could summon. The plot involves a strange serial harasser who dumps glue into the hair of local girls to, we find out later, ethnocentrically dissuade them from dating the boys stationed at the local army base. But the mood and landscape are dreamy.

The Third Man (1949) The ultimate Vienna postcard-movie. (See "Sick Day," p. 182.)

An American in Paris (1951) This big, fat Oscar-winning musical features Gene Kelly and Leslie Caron warbling and dancing all over Paris (actually, it's mostly sets on the MGM lot). If this film's airy, lovey-dovey vibe doesn't appeal to you, why go to Paris at all?

The Quiet Man (1952) As if you need to be told to sit down to this totemic Irish American saga before actually going to Ireland. Shot in Counties Mayo and Galway, and, in spots, on Hollywood sets. (See "Saint Patrick's Day," p. 29.)

Roman Holiday (1953) Audrey Hepburn won an Oscar her first time out with this expert postwar romance (she's a bored princess; Gregory Peck's a cynical American reporter), shot entirely in Rome and utilizing virtually every recognizable tourist spot in the city, from the Spanish Steps to the Colosseum.

Funny Face (1957) The Hollywood musical goes to Paris for real, finally, with Audrey Hepburn as a philosophical model and Fred Astaire as a photog smoothie. Gershwin music, Givenchy fashions, Richard Avedon images, simple and lilting dance numbers, Hepburn actually singing her songs, and famously unseasonable (for Paris) rainy weather.

The Umbrellas of Cherbourg (1964) Both flamboyantly faux and scrupulously anti-ironic, Jacques Demy's fame-making masterpiece of bitter sugar is an addictive, hypnotizing pleasure. Were movies really ever this buoyant, this gracious, this brave? Demy held silly love songs and Candyland visuals to be principles of faith, and this is his masterpiece, a simple wartime tragedy in which every utterance—even "pass the bread"—is sung in a Michel Legrand–composed lilt. It's something like being buried alive in lollipops. Stranger still, it has the air of being completely artificial—aren't all movies, really?—yet the whole thing was shot on location in the lovely seaside town of the title, an area of France in which Demy grew up and that he never left.

Claire's Knee (1970) Eric Rohmer's films are *all* vacations in the sun (well, OK, not *Perceval*, what with its fake armor and cardboard trees). This much-loved masterpiece from Rohmer's Six Moral Tales, characteristically, involves the masculine ego's use of women (here, a certain teenager's certain body part becomes the hero's obscure object of desire), but it's honey sweet and set in France's lovely Haute-Savoie.

The Conformist (1970) One of the great European films, made when director Bernardo Bertolucci was only twenty-nine, this startlingly beautiful character study and essay on fascist collaborationism and political cowardice is by no means just an evocative Euro-travel primer; it's essential viewing for anyone who cares about movies. Even so, the film's passage from World War II–era Rome to Paris to the snowy Alpine forestland between the two cities is as powerful as a dream.

Ryan's Daughter (1970) This heavy-footed David Lean melodrama may be useful primarily as a rather grandiloquent, travelogue-like portrait of County Kerry. God knows what the natives think of it, but to a traveler's eyes, the scenery is dazzling. (See "Saint Patrick's Day," p. 30.)

Death in Venice (1971) Your Venice getaway is bound to be better than Dirk Bogarde's in this Luchino Visconti wail of despair, adapted from Thomas Mann's novel and referencing Gustav Mahler at every opportunity. But as photographed by Visconti compadre Pasqualino De Santis, the city is gravely gorgeous and dripping with atmosphere.

The Spirit of the Beehive **(1973)** Thanks to Generalissimo Francisco Franco, Spain never had the cinematic New Wave it deserved, but it does have this sweeping, poetic, elliptical work from Victor Erice, about two peasant girls, the vast and sun-reflective Castilian plains, a village showing of 1931's *Frankenstein*, and a dark-eyed drifter. Essential viewing.

A Little Romance **(1979)** *L'amour* between two precocious young teens—an American girl (a fresh-faced Diane Lane) and a French boy (one-shot-wonder Thelonious Bernard)—on the streets of Paris, and their flirtation takes us on quite the tour: Parisian markets, the Champs Elysées, the Tuilleries, and more. In an effort to pledge their eternal love, they run away to Venice to kiss under the Bridge of Sighs in a gondola at sunset, and they treat us to Italy in the bargain. Laurence Olivier accompanies them, trotting out a French accent that sounds as unassailable as his German accent in *Marathon Man*.

V

Local Hero **(1983)** Possessed with an unpredictable sense of gentle, organic humor, Scottish director Bill Forsyth's one-of-a-kind comedy brims with quirkiness, hilarious non sequiturs and Celtic warmth. There's hardly a moment that can be predicted with any assurance, and there are few outright jokes. Instead, the movie's remarkable wit and wisdom seeps out of its many characters, who seem to have such a distinct life outside of the movie that the town in which it was filmed (and especially its lone, pivotal phone booth) has long since become a real-life mecca for film-crazy tourists. The story trails MacIntyre (Peter Riegert), an American oil company executive sent to Ferness, a remote Scottish shore town, with a mission: to buy the place out from under its inhabitants. His boss, an eccentric oil magnate (Burt Lancaster), also instructs him to keep a keen eye out for comets—or anything unusual—in the Scottish skies; even so, between the visiting Soviet submarines and the appearances of a research scientist-cum-mermaid (Jenny Seagrove), celestial wonders turn out to be among the more ordinary things about this obscure northern corner of the world. That MacIntyre isn't really of Scottish descent ("My folks changed their name when they got off the boat from Hungary," he explains. "They thought MacIntyre was American.") becomes one of the film's typically subtle drolleries: in Ferness the native Scots all call *him* Mac. Forsyth's unique movie is all savorable texture and relaxed hilarity, and it becomes more enjoyable with each viewing, long after the "what happens next?" reflex has faded. With lovable, upbeat rhythms all its own, Forsyth's slice of life has become a cult movie in the best sense of the word: it's a film people live in rather than see once and forget, a movie designed for those who savor every sip of champagne and never worry about getting a headache.

A Room with a View **(1986)** Halloween is possibly the only day we cannot see being a perfect occasion for this Merchant-Ivory benediction; among other things, it's a travel-brochure sell job the likes of which Florence and Surrey have never gotten before or since. (See "Summer," p. 79.)

Jacquot **(1991)** French New Wave director Jacques Demy was the movement's crazy daydreamer, a rhapsodic gentlemen who so loved the northwestern coastal towns in which he grew up, he returned to them in his films again and again. Well, after he died, his widow, Agnes Varda (who made her first feature before any of her famous compatriots had), went back to Nantes to film the memoir he never made, in which a starry-eyed French boy in the 1930s falls in love with movies. Demy's films are folded into the mix, and the result is simply the loveliest elegy one filmmaker has ever made in memory of another.

Les Amants du Pont-Neuf **(1991)** Also known in the United States as *The Lovers on the Bridge*, this big, fat, eccentric, world-class blast of filmmaking energy details the romance of a pair of emotionally crippled homeless waifs (Denis Lavant and Juliette Binoche) living on the eponymous Seine bridge. The characters' symbiotic passion is communicated not through the actors, who are largely tense with survival, but through the kaleidoscopic visuals—director Leos Carax achieves moments of spectacle and absurd poetry that seem unbelievable even as they're being viewed: the water-skiing-under-fireworks epiphany; the subway corridor of flames; Binoche's candlelit after-hours trip to a museum to inspect a Renaissance masterpiece before her eyesight fails altogether (a scene that would be stolen in 1996's *The English Patient*). Carax had a vision, certainly, and he routinely risked everything to get it on film, even recreating Paris on scale sets in the south of France. It is, in any event, a Paris you've never seen before.

Enchanted April **(1992)** Soft-centered and crowd-pleasing, this Merchant-Ivory-wannabe romance (based on an early-twentieth-century novel) chases after stressed-out Londoners (including Miranda Richardson, Polly Walker, Joan Plowright, Alfred Molina, and Jim Broadbent) on a lusty vacation in Genoa.

Before Sunrise **(1995)** Ethan Hawke and Julie Delpy's just-met soul mates get to know Vienna as most of us would: by walking. We experience their journey in real time, so the mundane alleyways, shops, and parks they pass along the way are just as significant as the famous tourist sites. (See "Dating," p. 129.)

When the Cat's Away... **(1996)** Enthralling, affectionate, tough, and vigorously realistic, Cedric Klapisch's loose-limbed movie is concerned entirely with capturing the natural rhythms, textures, and fascinating minutiae of ordinary life. Fittingly, the story is deliberately mundane: a lonely Parisian girl (Garance Clavel) decides to blow town for a weekend and leaves her cat in the care of an elderly neighbor; upon returning, she's informed that the cat escaped, and she combs the Bastille section of Paris in her sad search for the runaway pet. This is how you depict a city in a narrative movie—not with plot, but with texture and people and patience. The search for the cat is, in fact, a MacGuffin, a loose structure through which Klapisch closely examines the closely knit neighborhood just as it is about to vanish. It's a vitamin shot of pure cinema—simple, real, and sublime.

Russian Ark **(2002)** You don't need to go to The Hermitage, in St. Petersburg, if you see this remarkable film by Russian filmmaker Alexander Sokurov, which takes a tour of the world's largest museum (and, in the czar's day, the world's largest private residence) in one roving, restless digital-video shot. Never mind that the film intersects with a century of Russian history along the way; the instruction here is in the location. Once you've experienced this gargantuan remnant of the imperial age, you'll know why the Russian Revolution happened.

Before Sunset **(2004)** If, via *Before Sunrise*, you've already been to Vienna with Ethan Hawke and Julie Delpy, you can hardly resist strolling through Paris with these motor-mouths, nine years later and with a lot of baggage. (See "Valentine's Day," p. 28.)

Everything Is Illuminated **(2005)** Jonathan Safran Foer's postmod novel couldn't have made for a coherent movie—and it didn't—but this is the only film you're likely to find about a naive American (Elijah Wood) journeying into the heart of modern, comically semiprimitive Ukraine in search of his roots.

The Illusionist **(2006)** Quite a pleasant ham hock of a fable, about a magician (Edward Norton) and his entanglements with the aristocracy, set in turn-of-the-century Vienna but actually shot—fabulously, by Dick Pope—in the old neighborhoods of Prague. The result does both cities justice.

SNOWY VACATIONS

"Nothing like fresh powder."
—Vin Diesel, *XXX*

Some vacationers bask; others blast away—and winter sports aficionados head to the snow for the adrenaline, not the atmosphere. But at the same time, the heady buzz attained by experiencing the lofty meeting of mountainous snow and cold blue sky shouldn't be taken for granted. Movies, as always, can get you there first.

Downhill Racer **(1969)** Robert Redford, at his brooding, youthful peak, is a hunky but narcissistic jerk of a hotshot on the U.S. Olympic Ski Team who clashes with coach Gene Hackman. Much of the slope action is real, and was shot during actual international competition in Austria.

On Her Majesty's Secret Service **(1969)** Each James Bond movie has its handful of distinctive elements; besides being the one episode in the series starring George Lazenby, and the only one in which Bond experiences serious, tragic romance (with Diana Rigg; can't blame him), this is the Bond film that features Alpine snow, villain headquarters that boast a certain "mountain lodge" coziness, and lots of ski chases.

The Great Ecstasy of the Woodcarver Steiner **(1974)** Werner Herzog loves to find surrealities in the ordinary world, and so this documentary featurette chronicles the experience of a champion German ski-jumper who, in Herzog's vision, never seems to land, but is always sailing, in midflight, against a blue sky.

Never Cry Wolf **(1983)** Conservationist Farley Mowat was once stationed by the government in the Canadian Arctic to research the danger wolves pose to caribou herds. He proved that there was barely any, and then he wrote a book about it, and *Black Stallion* director Carroll Ballard made it into a film, with a careful respect for the realities of living in subzero temperatures and for the beauty of the land.

Aspen Extreme **(1993)** Cliched, hokey flick about the strained friendship and moral dilemmas of two ski instructors in Aspen. Don't bother unless you're a ski junkie.

Cool Runnings **(1993)** A feel-good bobsledding drama based on a true story and set in Calgary during the 1988 Winter Olympics; nothing accentuates frosty Canadian snowscapes like a team of fish-out-of-water Jamaicans. (See "Olympiad," p. 111.)

Himalaya **(1999)** The first Nepalese film to be widely seen outside of its native land (albeit one shot with a French crew), this movie is cast largely with nonprofessionals. The story is mythically fundamental: a struggle between a sensible, ambitious young warrior and a superstitious but wise village chief over the village's pivotal caravan run—a journey that entails leading yaks down the mountains to trade salt for grain before the winter arrives. It's a simple movie, but the visual and largely visceral odyssey over that treacherous landscape is, in the end, strangely haunting.

XXX **(2002)** Subpar James Bond–wannabe hooey with Vin Diesel, he of more muscle than enunciation capability, as an extreme-sports spy, or something. Entails trying to out-ski an all-digital avalanche.

ROAD TRIP

"I'm a connoisseur of roads. Been tasting roads my whole life. This road will never end. It probably goes all around the world."
—River Phoenix, *My Own Private Idaho*

We define road trips as car trips sans family; most of the movies that fall in this coolest of subgenres are existentialist parables that find life significance in the relationship among driver, car, and road, and often end in fatalistic tragedy. Which only makes them cooler.

Sullivan's Travels (1941) Road trips in golden-age Hollywood mostly meant actors in rocking cars in front of back projection, but if you let that turn you off, you might gloss over this stupendously witty film-industry farce by Preston Sturges, about a pretentious writer/director (Joel McCrea, playing what may be meant, in a winking way, to be Sturges himself) who longs to abandon the comedies that have made him famous and make a film about "suffering"—so he launches out into the world, with a sharp-tongued waif (Veronica Lake) in tow.

Detour (1946) Road movie ideogram, skid row bad dream, and the answer to the decidedly unmusical question *how could things get any worse?* Edgar G. Ulmer's famous, dirt-cheap film noir follows real-life Tinseltown lout Tom Neal as Al Roberts, a hitchhiker on a desperate ride to nowhere. He's accompanied by Ann Savage as sex-starved, consumptive Vera Whatever Her Name Was, who soon enough engages the self-pitying hero in a spare, motel-room *No Exit* nightmare from which he never quite escapes.

Out of the Past (1947) A much more polished, but no less enthralling noir act of cinematic "despair on the road," Jacques Tourneur's hard-bitten thriller has small-town mystery man Robert Mitchum revisit his secret past by getting involved with gangster Kirk Douglas and his female problems. Moody, tense, and cynical, as the best noirs are.

Weekend (1967) Jean-Luc Godard's view of capitalist Armageddon, plunging into the sewer trough of bourgeoisie materialism. A matter-of-factly homicidal middle-class couple embark on a car trip to visit her sickly father, for money's sake; immediately they enter a provincial landscape of bloodthirsty drivers, ceaseless car wrecks, imaginary personas, cannibalistic revolutionaries, and feral consumerism ("My Hermès handbag!" Mireille Darc's antiheroine screams after a burning crash). The layers of social critique here are so many that even Marxists—spouting rhetoric, toting rifles, and eating tourists in the woods—are roasted in the film's furnace.

Easy Rider (1969) The first self-consciously "road movie–ish" road movie? Traveling across the South with Peter Fonda, Jack Nicholson, cinematographer Laszlo Kovacs, and a skeleton crew, director-star Dennis Hopper understood that the very fact of ceaseless travel, across byways and social landscapes American movies had always ignored, was in itself a revolutionary statement. The 'Nam-era idea of semioutlaw road-rangin' became crystallized, and "Born to Be Wild" became the road anthem for generations of drivers.

***Two-Lane Blacktop* (1971)** In many ways the ultimate American road movie, Monte Hellman's long-martyred piece of backroads existentialism is mythic yet as real as highway weeds. Nearly catatonic, James Taylor and Dennis Wilson are, respectively, the Driver and the Mechanic; their life is a series of impromptu drag races against local drivers, and with their custom dragster in a primer-gray '55 Chevy shell, they almost always win. Warren Oates (whose credit reads "G.T.O.") is a slumming dude with a hot car he knows nothing about; the cross-country race between the two vehicles that passes for the film's plot is arrived at so casually you could miss it. Along the way, the wager is neglected and forgotten; just drive, man. Laconic, grittily shot, and totally devoid of visual showboating and campy, *Easy Rider*–esque counterculture hipness, Hellman's masterpiece thrusts viewers into the dusty, dirt-poor midday of American road culture (most of it "found"), surrounded by overgrown flatlands, vanishing points, and the angry chortle of car engines. (The cars are listed as cast members.) The druggy rhythms, the elliptical dialogue, the meaningless forward motion—the movie itself is like a long drive to nowhere.

V

***Kings of the Road* (1976)** A signature Wim Wenders movie, in which a depressed young husband takes up with an introverted movie-projector repairman and travel, significantly, the border between East and West Germany. Nothing much happens, except the road.

***The Road Warrior* (1981)** In this famous, massively successful Aussie atomic-wasteland thriller, the road travel is perpetual, circular, and farcically pointless. But the driving scenes will spike anyone's EKG.

***Drugstore Cowboy* (1989)** Gus Van Sant's second film (but first full-fledged masterwork) follows the expressionistic journey of four dope heads (Matt Dillon, Kelly Lynch, James Le Gros, and Heather Graham) as they live on the road, rob drugstores, and eventually come apart at the seams.

***Powwow Highway* (1989)** Two Cheyenne tribesmen drive south to New Mexico in a Buick, in one of the 1980s' best and most culturally resourceful road movies. As polar opposites, the mountainous and philosophical Gary Farmer and the wiry and politically outraged A Martinez are superb.

***My Own Private Idaho* (1991)** The ostensible subject at hand is Seattle street hustlers, but Gus Van Sant's unique masterpiece is a magical mystery tour of deadpan energy, Shakespearean mockery, and rebel-yell lust for dropping off of society's radar. As a comically exhausted narcoleptic punk who's constantly awakening in strange places,

River Phoenix was a martyr idol for his generation. A crazy, beautiful creation, as eloquent about lost highways as any film.

A Perfect World **(1993)** "You ever been in a time machine?" calm psycho-killer Kevin Costner asks his young, kidnapped passenger in this Clint Eastwood chase movie. "That there's the past," he says in pure road movie patois, pointing to the ass end of the highway they're on, "and up there, well, there's the future. This here is the present—enjoy it while you can." Nothing else need be said, except this: fast-forward through the Laura Dern scenes.

Western **(1997)** A long, loose, meandering French buddy road movie that happily disconnects from popular notions of narrative propulsion and necessity, Manuel Poirier's film is a naturalistic charmer that paints a fond portrait of small-town France as seen through the eyes of two foreigners, a shoe salesman from Spain (Sergi Lopez) and a diminutive Russian vagabond (Sacha Bourdo). Chance meetings, hitchhiking, car theft, weddings, drinking, romance—the journey is truly aimless, and often doubles back on itself. It's a movie you have to live with, relax into. The title is something of an antigenre statement—see, Poirier's saying, this is a *French* western—no guns, horses, and simple morality here. Like so many French films (going all the way back to Renoir's masterpieces from the 1930s), *Western* is really about the fine texture of human relationships—the minute kindnesses, recriminations, hopes, empathies, and camaraderie.

ON A CRUISE

"The motion of the cool green sea will soothe my tortured soul; thank you, and bon voyage to us all!"
—Alfred Molina, *The Imposters*

A mode of luxury travel that ain't what it used to be—the picture we have of Fitzgeraldian heroes wearing tuxes on deck, finding love by ocean moonlight, and chasing wacky stowaways has long ago given way to the modern cruise-ship reality of a retired middle-class crowd whose agenda generally does *not* include adventure, romance, comedy, and crazy drinking. Which is why, if you're taking the dive, you need a cinematic appetizer to edge you back toward the old dream.

His Wooden Wedding (**1925**); ***Isn't Life Terrible*** (**1925**) Two two-reelers by forgotten comic Charley Chase that actually, wonderfully, take place largely aboard a luxury cruise ship. Chase is hilarious, and the modern myth of high-end sea travel is portrayed in its infancy. Both films are available on the Kino-produced DVD ***The Charley Chase Collection Vol. 2.***

Monkey Business (**1931**) The first and greatest comedy feature about stowaways on a cruise ship, this Marx Brothers farce is unbridled, high-octane silliness, but everyone is dressed to the Gatsby nines (except the gangsters, a newly popular archetype in 1931), and the childlike experience of simply running amok amid luxury-consuming adults is infectious. You might have fun on your own voyage, but not this much.

China Seas (**1935**) A voyage to Singapore during a typhoon might not usually sound appealing, but if Clark Gable is the ship's captain, women will be stampeding the gangplank. He's already spoken for by Jean Harlow, as a loosey goosey with a cast-iron mouth and a marshmallow heart. Her brash talk soon has the typhoon brewing on board as well, and he gives her the deep freeze and betroths himself to a British aristocrat. Shipboard shenanigans include an attack by Malay pirates, redeeming heroics, boozy sing-alongs with the officers, and a drinking game called Admiral Puff Puff Puff, which is probably fun even if you're not playing with Jean Harlow in a clingy dress. The high China seas, by way of the MGM studio water tanks, knock the ship about and put the tough-talking fun in a pressure cooker.

A Night at the Opera (**1935**) The Marx Brothers' debut at MGM, and an overrated disappointment, largely due to the imposed romantic plot and musical numbers. Its single scene on a luxury liner, for which the film is primarily remembered, is also the most famous ship scene in Hollywood history: Groucho's small stateroom is invaded, in a drip that turns into a flood, by every kind of innocent interloper, from delivery boys and manicurists to the engineer's assistant ("I had a premonition you were going to show up!") and a girl looking in all the wrong places for her Aunt Minnie. "If she isn't in here," Groucho tells her, "you can probably find somebody just as good."

History Is Made at Night (**1937**) A fairy-tale romantic melodrama from women's-film fantasist and director Frank Borzage, about a socialite (Jean Arthur), her violently jealous ex-husband (Colin Clive), and the bystanding headwaiter rogue (Charles Boyer) who saves her. The hopscotch plot ends up on a cruise ship that's scheduled for a fated rendezvous with an iceberg.

The Lady Eve (**1941**) Even if you're the type who gets seasick in a wading pool, there's something undeniably alluring about a 1940s cruise-ship liaison, and you're not going to find a cuter and funnier dynamic than Barbara Stanwyck in a midriff-baring dress purring "Why, Hopsy!" at befuddled millionaire Henry Fonda. She's part of a card-sharp trio out to fleece rich suckers, and he's the chump. Preston Sturges wrote the devil out of this fluff in his customary fashion, and it might feature the hugest studio-built luxury boat ever dreamed up, with mansion-like ballrooms, sumptuous banquets, and endless moonlit decks.

Ship of Fools **(1965)** Katherine Anne Porter's thick bestseller, by way of director Stanley Kramer, in which a vast array of tortured characters play out their dramas on a Mexican ship sailing to pre-Nazi Germany. Vivien Leigh, in her fading light, stars, alongside Lee Marvin, Simone Signoret, Oskar Werner, Jose Ferrer, George Segal, et al.

Voyage of the Damned **(1976)** An ambitious but forgotten historical drama, it's not a fun vacation film, but it is based on actual events: in 1939, hundreds of German Jews are loaded onto a cruise ship by the Nazis, who promise them sanctuary in Cuba; once the ship begins its journey, however, it can find no port that is willing to take her. A big cast (Faye Dunaway, Oskar Werner, Lee Grant, Wendy Hiller, Julie Harris, Orson Welles, James Mason, Ben Gazzara, and many, many more) pull out all the histrionic stops.

The Imposters **(1998)** After the 1930s, the luxury-ship-stowaway comedy fell, more or less, into remission until Stanley Tucci (who wrote, directed, and stars here) con-cocted this happy vaudeville about two lousy thespians (Tucci and Oliver Platt) who find themselves, quite by accident, on a cruise ship among European anarchists, spies, grieving ex-royalty, a pompous theater star (Alfred Molina), a suicidal nightclub singer named Happy Franks (Steve Buscemi), and sundry other broadly played types (including a Nazi-esque ship officer, triumphantly personified by Campbell Scott). It's so unpretentious and dizzy, the entire cast conga-lines right off the set at the end, to boppin' tango music.

Master and Commander: The Far Side of the World **(2003)** Patrick O'Brian's literate, seafar-ing Aubrey-and-Maturin novels finally hit the screen, by way of director Peter Weir. Napoleonic warfare, survival at sea, and meticulous period flavor are all subsumed, as they should be, by the two protagonists (played by Russell Crowe and Paul Bettany) and their ironclad, platonic bond to each other. Supposedly, 90 percent of the film was shot on the water.

Pirates of the Caribbean: Dead Man's Chest **(2006)** Ripe blockbuster cheese, but one that packs in a cannibal tribe, a voodoo queen, a ship-consuming monster cephalopod, the Flying Dutchman, Davy Jones's locker, Davy Jones himself (Bill Nighy, with a captivating squid puss), a seaport tavern brawl, the infamous East India Company (as the ultimate corporate villain), and a cannon-blasting sea battle. Plus Johnny Depp, pounding so hard on his Keith Richards imitation that it seemed inevitable Richards would be cast as his father in the next sequel.

CAMPING AND HIKING

"Who has the ability to survive. . . ."
—Burt Reynolds, *Deliverance*

With or without a family in tow, this particular type of vacation is, like the cruise-ship journey, not quite what it used to be. Is there wilderness left against which to pit our survival skills? Or are we now faced with just campsites and RVs? Chances are, wherever you're headed could stand to be a bit wilder and more dangerous; happily, movies can put you in just that frame of mind, as most "wilderness" movies are fierce Jack London–esque dramas of life and death. At worst, they might encourage you to be perfectly content with the campground's general store and built-in pool.

***Northwest Passage* (1940)** The Hollywood adaptation of the Kenneth Roberts bestseller (written as one of a pair; the second never got finished) about the Revolutionary-era westward push of Rogers' Rangers, complete with on-location shooting in Idaho's Salmon River Mountains, Spencer Tracy, no technology whatsoever, and frontier life so rough that someone resorts to cannibalism.

***Man in the Wilderness* (1971)** Perhaps the inaugural film of what became the unsung mini-genre of men-in-the-wilderness movies, and based on a true story. An 1800s trapper (Richard Harris) is left behind in the northern woods after a bear attack, yet he survives and perseveres with vengeance on his mind (said vengeance to be exacted upon his compatriots, not the bear). The veracity of the mountain locations and the physical commitment of the actors make it a very tactile film.

***Deliverance* (1972)** What kind of wilderness trip you're thinking of taking with this film recently under your belt we couldn't rightly say, but the "men against the forest, the river, *and* the locals" dynamic has never been executed with as much terrifying grace. Shot in the woods of Georgia and South Carolina, and using loads of "found" people and places, John Boorman's masculine morality play has a believable grit to it that makes the action seem not only convincing but inevitable. Consider yourself lucky if you find a place this wild now (which is part of the movie's message), but going there in a canoe after watching the movie will seem as attractive as ocean swimming after your first viewing of *Jaws*.

***Jeremiah Johnson* (1972)** The Jack London–est of the men-in-the-wilderness sagas, this authentic-feeling mountain man story marks the moment in Robert Redford's career when he went from being a congenial romantic idol to an inexpressive, self-regarding Movie Star. But the film itself, true to its tradition, is fascinated by trapping, hunting, survival tricks, and Crow lore. Shot entirely in the peaks of Utah, including Redford's own Sundance ski resort.

***Dersu Uzala* (1975)** Akira Kurosawa coproduced this survival saga using the Soviet Union's filmmaking apparatus, and the Siberian result is muscular and icy. An army officer gets stranded in the highlands, and a Tuvan hunter befriends him; their only adversaries are the elements, which are horrendously formidable. After watching this, you'll definitely feel as though you've been there.

***Shoot* (1976)** More wilderness and more men. This time, the guys are competing ex-military who are hunting wild game in the Canadian woods; after an accidental killing, they're hunting each other. Cliff Robertson, Ernest Borgnine, and Henry Silva lead a cast of aging actors as they emote in the forest.

***Rituals* (1978)** The *Deliverance* template again, involving doctors being stalked by a maniacal killer during a hunting trip. Hal Holbrook is the only face worth recognizing. Shot in Canada, of course.

***Southern Comfort* (1981)** A Reagan-era men-in-the-wilderness potboiler from director Walter Hill, with disgruntled national guardsmen Powers Boothe and Keith Carradine facing off in the bayou against vengeance-minded Cajuns. It's an anxious, hairy-chested blast, but in terms of pre-vacation fodder, the film only makes a good case for the Louisiana swamps being as mysterious and dreadful as any Gothic forest.

***A River Runs Through It* (1992)** Robert Redford adapts Norman MacLean's memoir of two brothers, their minister dad, and the trouble the reckless son runs into in 1920s Montana. What's more important is that for these fellas, fly fishing in unspoiled wilderness is a presiding vocation, a form of dance art, and a symbol for life lived in communion with nature, not in ignorance of it.

***Surviving the Game* (1994)** Richard Connell's short story "The Most Dangerous Game," updated with social commentary. Ice-T is the ghetto waste case selected as prey and brought to the woods by wealthy white guys Rutger Hauer, F. Murray Abraham, John C. McGinley, and Gary Busey.

***The Edge* (1997)** David Mamet writes a "combat with nature" melodrama, the trick of which is that a famous writer and brainiac (Anthony Hopkins), lost in the mountains, must use his vast store of book knowledge to survive, even as he discovers that co-strandee Alec Baldwin is actually plotting to bump him off. Plenty of breathless suspense in the Canadian forest.

***The Blair Witch Project* (1999)** We're joking. Other men-in-the-wilderness movies at least capture the countryside, but you shouldn't really watch this ill-shot, skeletal bad trip before launching into unfamiliar woodland—that is, not unless you are completely resistant to movie-borne impressions. If you are, what's the point?

Old Joy **(2006)** American movies don't come much smaller, subtler, or swoonier with tactile experience than Kelly Reichardt's festival hit. In Portland, Oregon, one old college friend calls another: let's get lost, just for a few days, in the Cascades. Mark (Daniel London) is a watchful, even-tempered father-to-be with a high-pressure job; Kurt (Will Oldham) is an unmarried searcher, still living the West Coast dorm ideal, with odd jobs, a head full of weed, and stories of spiritual awakenings. They head for a hot-springs retreat in the forest, can't find it, camp elsewhere, then arrive at it and kick back. That's it, but we see much more: this might be the only film ever specifically made about that universal moment when the bonds of youth begin to rust, fade, and become irrelevant under the pressures of age and responsibility. The moist Northwestern wilderness around the protagonists is unforgettably sensual, but it's the men's unspoken conflict—with the onslaught of time as much as with each other—that haunts your thoughts.

V

URBAN U.S. OF A.

"This is really a great city; I don't care what anybody says."
—Woody Allen, *Manhattan*

The great American city—there are scores of movies that evoke the flavor—historical or present, idealized or not—of the country's great metropolises.

San Francisco **(1936)** The authenticity factor is almost nil in this Hollywood romantic drama set in 1906 San Fran (Clark Gable is a swingin' saloon owner, Jeanette MacDonald is his latest chanteuse, and Spencer Tracy is his priest buddy), but since most of the city was leveled by the earthquake and fire that climaxes the film, this may as well be how we remember the place in its original heyday.

In Old Chicago **(1937)** A virtual remake of *San Francisco*, this film pitches an elder son (a Gable-like Tyrone Power) against his moral-minded bro (Don Ameche) and his ma Mrs. O'Leary (Alice Brady), whose cow supposedly started the fire of 1871 and burned *this* city to the ground. Cities are all about their own invented nostalgia, aren't they?

City for Conquest **(1940)** Just a by-the-book Warner Brothers boxing saga, with James Cagney rising from the street to an unhappy fame as a champ. But rarely in the old Hollywood has a film taken such time to elegize New York's lower neighborhoods and immigrant classes, here done in ripe prose that'd make a pretentious novelist blush.

Saboteur **(1942)** A bristling little Hitchcock ditty, in which Robert Cummings is mistakenly pursued for military sabotage. The famous climax occurs atop the Statue of Liberty—you'll never get closer to it without going there yourself.

Sweet Smell of Success **(1957)** Auteur and movie maven Paul Schrader recently listed this dark, bitter pill of a noir as one of the top fifty films belonging to an all-time cinema "canon." We wouldn't go that far, but we will say that it's a rascally, grueling drama, about a PR hack (Tony Curtis) who's willing to do nearly anything to get a leg up from powerful columnist Burt Lancaster. Set and shot in Manhattan, no other mid-twentieth-century film did the city so well.

Vertigo **(1958)** San Francisco's house movie, so famously entangled in the city's landmarks that for years now, tourists have easily found guided tours of the places featured in the film, in the order in which they're seen. Of course, the substance of the film is something else—James Stewart, two Kim Novaks, a ghost, a fear of heights, and a psychosexual obsession so subtly but clearly delineated by director Alfred Hitchcock that this film remains one of the most perverse in Hollywood history.

V

Bullitt **(1968)** Steve McQueen, a black turtleneck, a Mustang, and the hills of San Francisco. (See "Boys' Night Out," p. 249.)

California Split **(1974)** Robert Altman, smack in the middle of his premier era as the gimlet-eyed prince of all-American satire, does Las Vegas—Elliott Gould and George Segal descend into a maelstrom of obsessive gambling that climaxes, for better or worse, with a bone-chilling Big Score. Less a comedy than an existential ordeal, perhaps, but the town is frozen for future study.

Chinatown **(1974)** Being the hub of Movieland, Los Angeles has produced many odes to itself, but none as acidic, sunburned, and wide awake as Roman Polanski's neo-noir, hailed amply elsewhere (see "Summer," p. 78).

Manhattan **(1979)** Woody Allen's love letter to the island of Manhattan—in pearly black and white, scored to Gershwin, and dense in irony and lifestyle tips for the New York–deprived. No cheap Jewish jokes, either.

Atlantic City **(1980)** A great American city—decaying tourist trap, haven for lowlife, repository of dreams, schizophrenic, gentrified-neglected mess—is the backdrop to Louis Malle's film, which largely involves a romance of sorts between dapper has-been septuagenarian Burt Lancaster and casino trainee Susan Sarandon.

Broadway Danny Rose **(1984)** Was New York at its New Yorkest in the 1950s? Woody Allen's painfully lovely small-time showbiz ballad features Allen's low-rung talent agent, Mia Farrow's floozy, and Nick Apollo Forte's comeback-kid lounge singer, all mixing it up in a 1950s-ish world of nightclubs, back offices, liaison flats, and very real spots like the Carnegie Deli. So flavorsome it makes most of Allen's other New York movies seem generic.

The Big Easy **(1987)** The most New Orleans–ified film ever made is tipsy on everything that made the pre-Katrina hub famous: sunlit bayous, dancing at Tipitina's, voodoo in Storyville, Mardi Gras floats, institutional corruption, and an overall Cajun flavor so palpable you can taste the pepper in the gumbo. In addition to providing an authentic N'Awlins feel and foot-tapping creole-Cajun-zydeco soundtrack, this flavorful Jim McBride movie also offers Dennis Quaid's irresistible grin (in its way as life-loving as the city's reputation), and a foreplay scene (with Ellen Barkin) that just doesn't quit, no matter how many repeated viewings (ahem) some of us may sneak.

Bugsy **(1991)** Not every American city has an origin myth like Las Vegas does, and if you love Sin City, you'll dig this too-serious Barry Levinson–Warren Beatty tribute to Vegas-planning, psychopath gangster Bugsy Siegel. If you don't agree that Vegas was worth all of the angst, the money, and the bodies in the desert, you're not going there, anyway.

Heat **(1995)** Michael Mann's epic tale of cops and robbers weaves multiple stories into its Robert De Niro–Al Pacino "last of the hard men" struggle, but it is also very much an L.A. story; the city is captured in all its smoggy sprawl, glamour, economic disparity, freeway craziness, and industry. Likewise, Mann's ***Collateral*** **(2004)** hits the same note (while driving around with Tom Cruise's contract killer and Jamie Foxx's cabbie), but with a difference: because it's shot on digital video, you see the lit city at night, partially illuminated by smog-reflected neon, like never before.

Ocean's Eleven **(2001)** More Vegas, only newer, courtesy of Steven Soderbergh, an all-star cast on a drinker's vacation, and the understandable inspiration to remake the awful Rat Pack original and co-opt its reputation for cool.

BUSINESS TRIP

"We have to first get out of this bar, then the hotel, then the city, and then the country. Are you in or you out?"
—Bill Murray, *Lost in Translation*

No type of travel needs a cinematic booster shot as much as the business trip, which, by definition, is not a journey you *want* to take. These movies cover all the bases, because just about every work trip would benefit from any jolt of drama, action, crisis, or comedy.

Bad Day at Black Rock **(1955)** A one-armed man (Spencer Tracy) in a black suit gets off the train at a semiabandoned desert town haunted by its wartime sins, and quietly, methodically demands justice. Stranger in a strange land, indeed.

Duel **(1971)** Steven Spielberg's first film (or, at least, his first television movie to net theatrical distribution in Europe), this lean, mean tribulation features Dennis Weaver as a traveling salesman who is being stalked on the wide open highways by a malevolent gas trailer truck (whose driver we never see). A Kafka-esque parable for those who must drive for a living.

Local Hero **(1983)** See "Doing Europe" (p. 262) for a rhapsodic dissertation on this fish-out-of-water treasure about a quixotic working vacation.

The Accidental Tourist **(1988)** A pallid but award-winning version of Anne Tyler's terrific novel, notable not so much in this context for its business trip drama, but for the tale's rather poetic view of work-compulsory travel and the quiet struggle between appreciating change and wanting things to stay the same.

Barton Fink **(1991)** Auteurs Joel and Ethan Coen won at Cannes with this rich casserole, in which a self-righteous, Clifford Odets–like 1930s playwright (John Turturro) goes to Hollywood to cash in on scriptwriting and enters a deranged dream factory of uneasy stereotypes: a Faulknerian lush (John Mahoney), a splenetic producer (Tony Shalhoub), a megalomaniacal studio head (Michael Lerner), and, best of all, a traveling sales agent (John Goodman) who's all aw-shucks working-class congeniality and sweaty psychomania. The hotel itself is a character business travelers won't forget.

Irma Vep **(1996)** Olivier Assayas's lovable film is an improvised behind-the-scenes satire detailing the doomed contemporary Parisian production of a remake of *Les Vampires*, Louis Feuillade's 1915 kinky crime serial. Hong Kong star Maggie Cheung stars as her bewildered self, out of her element and cast (by the movie-in-a-movie's director, played by Truffaut vet Jean Pierre Léaud) as the leather-clad arch villainess Vep, a French movie icon with no counterpart in this or any other country. Speaking no French, Cheung wanders through a labyrinth of crew squabbles, logistical impossibilities, lesbian crushes (the costume designer has a meltdown over her), and directorial nervous breakdowns, eventually realizing, as do we, that the film she's there to make is doomed. Everything about *Irma Vep* suggests spontaneous combustion, down to the remarkable scene in which Cheung tries to answer foolish questions put to her by a snotty, pro-Hollywood French journalist—questions that Assayas had actually been asked in real life; Cheung counters them with unscripted honesty.

Fear and Loathing in Las Vegas (1998) A sputtering monster of a movie, Terry Gilliam's adaptation of Hunter S. Thompson's book is faithful with a vengeance—this hard-charging freakazoid isn't nearly as funny as its source material because it takes that source's nightmarish misanthropy at its word. It'll seem as strange as Martian rocks to anyone for whom Thompson's book is not a crucial adolescent reading memory. At its heart, it's a psychedelic buddy road movie subjected to a chemical peel, leaving only raw wounds behind. Thompson's book began as an assignment for *Sports Illustrated* to cover an annual desert motorcycle race. Loading up a used convertible with every variety of abusable substance known to the 1960s, Thompson headed to Las Vegas with his obese attorney, Oscar Zeta Acosta, and proceeded to forget the race in favor of exploring the limits of acceptable behavior in a town where limits are meaningless. If you don't want to be in whatever town you're stuck in, this is one way to address the situation.

The Wind Will Carry Us (1999) Iranian filmmaker Abbas Kiarostami spins one of his most pungent mysteries: a media crew travels to a remote mountain village to, perhaps, film the expiration of a legendary matriarch. Except the crew stays out of sight, the old woman is mostly rumored about, and the head of the expedition, a well-meaning urbanite with an unreliable cell phone, can never get a straight answer as to what's going on or what he should do. The experience—of the time, the uncertainty, the village, and its disinterested inhabitants—is the thing.

Lost in Translation (2003) A much-acclaimed film about a business trip meeting of hearts: Bill Murray plays an aging movie star who's in Tokyo to do a TV ad; Scarlett Johansson is a photographer's wife who's been left to her own devices. Loneliness does the rest. A little too dizzy with touristy views of Japan, but mature and heartful.

The Matador (2005) Say you're Greg Kinnear, as a semidesperate contractor who's begging for jobs. You're out of town; you're alone; you have a drink in a bar—and in comes Pierce Brosnan, as a whiskey-sodden, socially barbaric hit man, looking at his last days and in need of a helping hand. Things don't go well.

Syriana (2005) The business voyage as variegated nightmare: Stephen Gaghan's tri-fold drama about the contemporary nexus between Middle East oil, the American government, and multinational corporate interests bottoms out to bad trips for CIA op George Clooney, lawyer Jeffrey Wright, and corrupted economist Matt Damon. Come to think of it, the Pakistanis left jobless in the desert have a lousy time of it, too.

SPRING BREAK

"Experience—that's what separates the girls from the Girl Scouts."
—George Hamilton, *Where the Boys Are*

You'd think the "Exotic Travel" section would suffice for those high schoolers and college kids who are blessed enough to light out for a sex-crazed, booze-soaked beach somewhere for the spring vacation (they've worked *so* hard!). But here are a few thematically pertinent candy corns as well, for the pop-history-minded young student.

V

Spring Madness (1938) Lew Ayres and Burgess Meredith are two Harvard undergrads looking to hightail it to Russia for a term of study, except coed Maureen O'Sullivan intends to keep them on campus for the seasonal dance. Absurd fluff, based on the wisecracking play *Spring Dance* by Philip Barry, who rewrote an original Smith College production for Broadway.

Where the Boys Are (1960) Four college chicks (Yvette Mimieux, Paula Prentiss, Connie Francis, and Dolores Hart) go to Fort Lauderdale to meet boys (think future husbands, not one-night stands).

Palm Springs Weekend (1963) Another relatively sexless teen comedy, it is instead all bumbling romance, California style. Stars Connie Stevens, Troy Donahue, Stefanie Powers, and Robert Conrad.

Girl Happy (1965) Elvis goes to Fort Lauderdale! He's a rocker who's hired by gangster Harold J. Stone to watch over virginal daughter Shelley Fabares as she cavorts on the beach. It has songs: "Spring Fever," "Do the Clam," and "Fort Lauderdale Chamber of Commerce" are among them.

Where the Boys Are '84 (1984) Hopeless remake of the 1960 stinker; the sex that was left out of the original is put back in here, but barely.

FLASHBACK

The movies we've seen during our lifetimes function as our own personal reels of sense memories, but because cinema often endeavors to faithfully crystallize or re-create a specific era, films also serve as a kind of *cultural* memory well, into which we can escape and get lost, and find ourselves at liberty in, say, 1890s Europe or 1940s New York or the intoxicating meadows of the 1960s. There's hardly a more effective or encompassing way to wallow in nostalgia. Although the authors of this book are tail-end baby boomers, we are particularly prone, on an unpredictable basis, toward a craving for the prewar decades, while friends of ours would revisit the 1960s every day if they could. Thanks to film, the past is a coalition of countries we can visit at any time.

RETURNING TO THE NINETEENTH CENTURY AND THE FIN DE SIÈCLE

"A kind of hieroglyphic world. . . ."
—Joanne Woodward, *The Age of Innocence*

All right, so we're not *remembering* the 1800s here, but idealizing them like crazy, in a escapist reverie of aristocratic decor, manners, couture, and geography. But not always—many of the films listed below recall the rough edge of late nineteenth-century frontier life, which, of course, today can have its own charm.

VI

***Electric Edwardians* (1900–1913)** This feature-length, newly titled collection of early "actualities" was shot by traveling Brit cine-ethnographers Sagar Mitchell and James Kenyon, who simply toured England and photographed public life—parades, fairs, school processions, factory workers going home, ad infinitum. It's doubtlessly invaluable as archaeology—no other visual record of the era in Great Britain is nearly as rich—and as viewing, it's primeval cinema, a fragile window on an extinct universe. The DVD extras include a raft of additional Mitchell and Kenyon shorts, including footage of the announcement, in Blackburn, of Queen Victoria's death.

***Les Vampires* (1915)** This decisively weird, hypnotic early-century French thriller serial, which details the unearthly, convoluted tale of a Parisian underworld called the Vampires and their devoted adversaries, was one of the first major film projects to be filmed on location in a real city, and so the forgotten World War I–era spaces of Paris are frozen in time.

***The General* (1926)** Buster Keaton's most famous and beloved comedy, this American classic involves an average Joe, a girl, a war (the Civil War), and a train, all of it perfectly in period. Based on a true story of wartime espionage and heroism. Unable to use the actual *General* locomotive engine, Keaton revamped a similar engine to match it.

***Alexander's Ragtime Band* (1938)** A bouncy, cheesy musical about ragtime, set in 1915 San Francisco and featuring period-style songs by Irving Berlin, most of them sung by the inimitably throaty Alice Faye. Tyrone Power, Don Ameche, and Jack Haley do the more-or-less irrelevant plot stuff.

***The Strawberry Blonde* (1941)** The Gay Nineties are mustered up in stilted Warner Brothers fashion in this melodrama, which has dentist James Cagney pining for Rita Hayworth and not appreciating Olivia de Havilland, and someone eventually plays "And the Band Played On." Pure studio sausage, and fun, as always, for the stars.

Heaven's Gate (1980) Michael Cimino's infamous, nearly four-hour-long western—a ballooned account of the 1892 Johnson County War—supposedly sunk United Artists. But all of its budget, and all of its director's care, are there on the screen: the period accuracy is awesome, and the scale tremendous. Vilmos Zsigmond's mistily gorgeous cinematography is virtually an act of frontier mourning in and of itself.

Impromptu (1991) France of the 1830s, done with a vampy high-culture smirk and inspired stunt casting, as George Sand (Judy Davis) pursues Frederic Chopin (Hugh Grant), while Franz Liszt (Julian Sands), Alfred de Musset (Mandy Patinkin), Eugene Delacroix (Ralph Brown), and Marie d'Agoult (Bernadette Peters) buzz around them.

The Age of Innocence (1993) Martin Scorsese's version of Edith Wharton's novel is, like the book, a triumph of obsessive detail that temporarily obscures the machinations of a heartbreaking story of love, manipulation, and late nineteenth-century social restriction (Daniel Day-Lewis is engaged to Winona Ryder but pines for Russian countess Michelle Pfeiffer). Pfeiffer hardly provides the mesmerizing fire that's needed here, but the cast is otherwise fine, amid New York's most beautiful surviving turn-of-the-century architecture.

Little Women (1994) Louisa May Alcott's famous novel has been filmed several times, but no other adaptation captures the feel of the Civil War era that this lovely rendition delivers. The March sisters' lives are made up of small, intimate moments among characters who didn't branch out much beyond their family and immediate neighbors, yet their story feels larger than if it had centered on the war itself. The period details are completely authentic: the songs the sisters sing, the books they read, the way they speak and what they wear. A beautiful movie with faultless performances (there's never been a more perfect Laurie than Christian Bale) and a score that will sweep you back in time.

Topsy-Turvy (1999) A consistently delightful, superbly timed, and impeccably staged wedge of Brit pop history, *Topsy-Turvy* is a Mike Leigh–directed saga of the mid-career fall and rise of operetta maestros Gilbert and Sullivan (Jim Broadbent and Allan Corduner). Expansive, wise, ingenious, and performed to within an inch of its life; few movies are as faithful to the spirit of historical time and place. Leigh's other films are justly famous for their intense contemporary realism, and the same degree of passionate fidelity adheres here. Primary among the film's many pleasures is Broadbent, whose belchy, plummy way with stinging dialogue is unparalleled. But the entire cast is entrancing—few period films feel as genuinely inhabited as this one.

Gangs of New York (2002) Martin Scorsese's long-awaited 1800s epic turned out dreary, bloated, simplistic, and often idiotic, but there's a bargeload of effort devoted to period detail, from clothes and food to tavern interiors, alleyways, and the Five Points themselves. Daniel Day-Lewis stands above the fray, wielding a nutsy Brit-Brooklyn accent.

***Peter Pan* (2003)** The flat-out best version ever of J. M. Barrie's story of the Lost Boys and the Darling family, because it actually pays attention to the surfaces of the late 1800s, it respects the well-source of Victorian fearie lore and childhood paraphernalia from which Barrie's tale sprang, and it has pubertal subtext—unavoidable, c'mon—oozing out of its skin. Kudos to director P. J. Hogan.

LIVING THE HIGH LIFE OF THE ROARING TWENTIES

"One guy isn't enough—she's gotta have a convention."
—Groucho Marx, *The Cocoanuts*

VI

From where we sit today, the 1920s was an almost primitive cultural era: entertainment technology was still in its infancy, the old century's ways of life still held sway, and everybody was dizzy with wealth, post–World War I élan, wild crime, unstoppered drink, and the new idea of universally experienced glamour. The 1930s had the Depression to sober it, and the '40s had World War II, but the '20s had no brakes.

***Foolish Wives* (1922)** Erich von Stroheim's film is typical of him: a pulp melodrama of infidelity, set in Monte Carlo, amid the international rich and its predatory underclass. The director's fame for overwhelming detail make his films, including ***Blind Husbands* (1919)**, ***Merry-Go-Round* (1923)**, and ***Queen Kelly* (1929)**, peerless time capsules of their era's more garish cultural elements.

***The Last Flight* (1931)** A rarely seen sad dream that best echoes the tone of F. Scott Fitzgerald's fiction; a disillusioned band of World War I flyers go on an aimless, suicidal drinking spree through Paris and Lisbon, roping in a careless ditz along the way to Endsville. Arguably the only film to legitimately sing the ballad of Gertrude Stein's "lost generation."

***Death Takes a Holiday* (1934)** Concerning the idle rich, for whom every season is summer, this semiforgotten fantasy (remade decades later, at twice the length, as *Meet Joe Black*) is vintage "lost generation, in tuxes and satin gowns, loiters with martinis on a marble veranda at midnight." Until, of course, Death (a stunningly stiff Fredric March) decides to visit and see what being mortal is like.

The Roaring Twenties (1939) Not that different from the many other 1930s Warner Brothers gangster films, which is more than enough reason for us to enjoy it, plus this one has James Cagney and Humphrey Bogart, seething.

The Fortune (1975) One of the best and wittiest of the comedies made during the 1970s "look back in fondness" craze, Mike Nichols's film—about a pair of nitwits (Warren Beatty and Jack Nicholson) who attempt to murder ditzy heiress Stockard Channing—is so summer-before-the-Crash hazy that the cinematography itself seems light-headed with humidity. The 1920s atmosphere is all sun, white linen, old convertibles, improperly paved country roads, palm trees, and screwball, like a Gatsby scenario with its pants down.

The Great Waldo Pepper (1975) Way back when, escapist "nostalgia" was not a dirty word, but was, in fact, a tempting cultural fad. This George Roy Hill doodle explores the barnstorming culture of Middle America between the wars, following Robert Redford's big-cheeked biplane aviator who, having missed World War I, longs for sky-high glory, even if it's over cornfields and in the movies.

Once Upon a Time in America (1984) The gangster epic as fractured opium daydream, tripping back and forth in the skull of a Jewish hood (Robert De Niro) until the past, present, and future more or less mush into a mournful opera of betrayal and guilt. Along for the pageant: James Woods as a weasely cohort, Elizabeth McGovern as the trollop that got away, Tuesday Weld as a decaying slattern, and Joe Pesci as an unlucky rival. Directed by Sergio Leone, the man that made Clint Eastwood famous in *A Fistful of Dollars*, this reckless monstrosity spends its plot, characters, and themes like a drunken sailor: settle for nothing less than the nearly-four-hour version, but even then, the film can barely contain so much *stuff*. 1890s New York childhoods, teenage hookers, Prohibition, hits, rapes, backstabbings, lost love—Leone left nothing out, making this the buddy elegy flip side to *The Godfather*'s familial moan. With, ironically enough, one of Ennio Morricone's most heartfelt scores.

The Cat's Meow (2001) A true Hollywood scandal fictionalized rather adroitly: in 1924, pioneering producer Thomas Ince died, perhaps after being shot—maybe accidentally, maybe not—aboard the yacht of William Randolph Hearst (Edward Herrmann), in a scenario that also involved Charlie Chaplin (Eddie Izzard), actress (and Hearst's mistress) Marion Davies (Kirsten Dunst), and Louella Parsons (Jennifer Tilly), who would soon become a lifelong columnist for Hearst Newspapers. A return to fluency by director Peter Bogdanovich.

VI

EVOKING THE 1930s

"Well, bless my blonde heart."
—Elaine Shepard, *Topper*

Grace under pressure: the 1930s represent the first great social drama that's still remembered by many Americans. Of course, you don't have to belong to that club to enjoy these films, whether your goal is to share the decade's escapist tendencies (movies made then routinely limned a Roaring Twenties, tux-and-gown lifestyle) or to love the sun-drenched fad of seminaturalistic movies about the Depression made after *Bonnie and Clyde*.

Gold Diggers of 1933 (1933) The essence of the 1930s cannot be found properly in the Astaire-Rogers musicals, which exist in a trouble-free world of cavernous hotel suites and sequined gowns. It's located in the earlier Warner Brothers musicals of the decade, the ones that feature the shaky singing of Dick Powell, Ruby Keeler, and Rogers, too, as well as stories that evoke concerns about mass poverty—only to explode, onstage, into Busby Berkeley kaleidoscopes. While **42nd Street (1933)** is seen as the form's peak moment, we prefer this, the first Gold Diggers film: it's looser, crazier, and more surreal, in a penny-arcade kind of way. But if you see all of the best of them, including **Dames (1934)** and **Gold Diggers of 1935 (1935)**, you'll get their wacky pieces mixed up in your head in any case, to the point that they become one mosaic of desperate chorines, cigar-chomping financiers, and a mythical New York no less cruel than the real one.

Mauvaise Graine (1933) Billy Wilder made one film in France on his way from Berlin to Hollywood, and this is it: a droll piece of melodrama about a spoiled rich boy who falls in with dopey Parisian car thieves. Spiced with café life, "Apache" styles, and European insouciance. With Danielle Darrieux, at the kick start of her sterling career.

Topper (1937) If you've been wondering why in this day and age, when Hollywood seems to be doing nothing but recycling old movies, no one has thought to remake *Topper,* consider this: it's essentially a story in which driving drunk at breakneck speed around dangerous curves with your feet on the steering wheel of a convertible is seen as not just funny, but also as a paradigm for living the good life. Party animals George and Marion Kerby (Cary Grant and Constance Bennett, bouncing screwball dialogue like Ping-Pong champs) become ghosts because of such antics, and they soon learn they've got a pretty short resume for applying for residence in Heaven. They set out to do a good deed: loosening up repressed bank president Cosmo Topper (Roland Young), who is henpecked by his propriety-conscious wife and who leads as dull a life as you can imagine. A kind of morality-tale act of retribution on Roaring Twenties hedonism, *Topper* is also completely 1930s in its battery of platinum blondes in slinky sequined evening dresses, men in tuxes and top hats driving roadsters, bankers in fedoras, and dancing in nightclubs.

The Grapes of Wrath (1940) As from the photographs of Walker Evans, the Depression's grueling impact flows out of this film's images (shot by Gregg Toland the year before he did *Citizen Kane*), and director John Ford, in his most somber period, keeps the cast—all of them caught in the glare of poverty, like real people of the 1930s—battered and sad.

They Shoot Horses, Don't They? (1969) This movie, based on Horace McCoy's novel, makes Steinbeck look like an optimist—here is a 1930s dance marathon viewed as an existential metaphor for life: jobless and hopeless, you dance in circles until you virtually die. It's been noted recently that this film's potent central conceit is not far at all from the gladiatorial competition inherent in most reality shows; the human race remains a spectator blood sport. The desperate victims on view include Jane Fonda, Michael Sarrazin, Bruce Dern, Susannah York, and Red Buttons.

Emperor of the North Pole (1973) The only Hollywood movie made about Depression-era hobos, this film beautifully evokes the overgrown Southern landscape and the decade's tone of hungry squalor. At the same time, it's a weird, hairy-chested, "man's man" movie about a psychotic train conductor (Ernest Borgnine) who faces off against a mythologized superbum (Lee Marvin). A lovable oddity, down to the chain fight. The title is a bit of hobo lingo meaning "king of the heap," but the reissue (and video) title tried to be literal and dropped the "Pole."

VI

Paper Moon (1973) Peter Bogdanovich's grim comedy about the Depression, in which Tatum O'Neal's raw-mouthed orphan latches onto Ryan O'Neal's fumbling, Bible-hawking con man (more out of hope for love, home, and a sense of belonging than for loot), has a formidable period thrust. The glowering black-and-white cinematography, the desolate midwestern towns, the exhausted faces of the poor, the empty Kansas skyline—every frame of this film makes you feel like you landed in 1936 without a nickel in your pocket. It's largely forgotten now, but it justly received acclaim back in 1973; the sorely missed Madeline Kahn practically steals the movie in a mere twenty minutes, but she lost the Best Supporting Actress Oscar to Tatum, who remains the youngest winner ever of an Academy Award.

The Sting (1973) Nostalgia mondo: this Oscar-filthy con-game comedy was super hip in 1973; it seems merely diverting today, but since it deals with a back-alley gambling scam (run by grifters Robert Redford and Paul Newman), it does a tasty job of painting a portrait of the 1930s as it was experienced by the lower classes, in fringe corners of every city. Of course, the anachronistic Scott Joplin retro score sells it to the cheap seats.

Hard Times **(1975)** Screenwriter Walter Hill comes into his macho own as a director with this laconic, "man's man" Depression drama, which details yet another long-forgotten American subculture activity: bare-knuckled street fighting. Charles Bronson is the new hitter in town with a private past; James Coburn is his gabby manager.

Bound for Glory **(1976)** An eccentric and largely undramatic biopic of progressive folk demigod Woody Guthrie (played sweetly, if mildly, by David Carradine), this Hal Ashby movie is better viewed as a lyrical tone poem about Depression-era America—a vast world of grand natural vistas, railway hoboes, migrant labor, and moldering urban landscapes, all of it rapturously photographed by fellow radical Haskell Wexler.

Pennies from Heaven **(1981)** This peculiar movie musical, derived from a Dennis Potter BBC series, brings the 1930s back in a unique way: with the original popular recordings of the day, straight off the old, scratchy records, lip-synched by Steve Martin, Bernadette Peters, and others as they live out a pathetic tale of economic destitution in a mythical studio-set city that, during the song sequences, frequently turns into a glitzy fantasy realm. And then back again: the undulation of sky-high oldies and dour "reality" is disarming and fascinating.

Ironweed **(1987)** A roundly drubbed bomb, this Hector Babenco adaptation of William Kennedy's Pulitzer winner does get a good deal painfully wrong (those ghosts!)—but the Depression-era homeless of Albany, New York, isn't an easy subject. Jack Nicholson and Meryl Streep are excellent, the realization of the past is convincing, and the whole damn thing is, despite the missteps, wildly sad.

O Brother, Where Art Thou? **(2000)** Joel and Ethan Coen revisit the subgenre of Depression-era films—kinda—with this hillbilly comedy, using the framework of *The Odyssey* and lustily yanking on every broad gag they could find. Our Ulysses (George Clooney) escapes at the outset from a Mississippi chain gang shackled to John Turturro and Tim Blake Nelson. His odyssey winds through its preordained (by Homer) route as he runs from the law, meets the sirens, and confronts the Cyclops (in the form of John Goodman's one-eyed Bible salesman); he goes on to thwart the dancing KKK before falling into the strident Mississippi gubernatorial race between two Huey Long–ish candidates. Taking its title and milieu from Preston Sturges's unbeatable *Sullivan's Travels*, the film is a rambling picaresque, chockablock with 1930s details (a bipolar Baby Face Nelson, a Robert Johnson–esque guitarist who's sold his soul to the devil, and so on), blessed with a heavenly bluegrass soundtrack, and soaked in lovely Southern light.

Road to Perdition **(2002)** An overproduced Oscar bid for both director Sam Mendes and star Tom Hanks, this gangster saga (based on a Max Allen Collins graphic novel) about a mobster and his son taking revenge on his own clan is rather stale, but again, the money spent on recreating a rainy, sepia 1930s pays off.

Sky Captain and the World of Tomorrow **(2004)** An inspired triumph of design-maven atmosphere—a retro sci-fi actioneer, executed almost completely with digitals (only the actors are real), conceived and shaped to resemble not 1930s sci-fi movies, but their posters, along with comic-book illustrations, art deco advertising, and pulp paperback covers. The story involves vigilante superhero pilot Jude Law's battle against waves of behemoth robot attacks, but it's the look of the film that says it all: it's the dream of every between-the-wars fantasist fulfilled, presented in ways no actual 1930s film could have achieved. It's the ultimate in nostalgia for a past that never existed—not even in cinema.

RELIVING THE 1940s

"Who are you, really, and what were you before? What did you do and what did you think, huh?"
—Humphrey Bogart, *Casablanca*

Pop culture finally grows up—welcome to gloss, bop, polished banter, nationalistic fervor, lost innocence, the communal feeling of wartime, Chuck Jones's Bugs Bunny, Glen Miller, female independence, postwar disillusionment, and the bitter taste of noir.

. . . One of Our Aircraft Is Missing **(1941)** The often eccentric British team of director Michael Powell and scripter Emeric Pressburger together made the first great English film about World War II during the war itself—their effort is crisp, dry, and matter-of-fact. A downed bomber crew in Nazi-occupied Holland seeks out help from the native population; the happily brave and efficient cooperation between the two contingents, under the German noses, says scads about the British temperament during the conflict.

Casablanca **(1942)** Possibly the greatest, and certainly the most perennially popular, movie of its decade, this movie is almost a bible of twentieth-century impulses, character types, bits of catchy dialogue, and pulp-melodrama pangs of emotion. But it reflects its decade masterfully, down to its neutral political stance, its swipes at Vichy, its knowledge of European histography, its use of World War I and the Spanish Civil War as backstory, and its genuine sense of global tension.

The Palm Beach Story **(1942)** Preston Sturges, in the middle of his home-run streak, directed this ditzy comedy about a poor inventor (Joel McCrea), his desperate wife

(Claudette Colbert), an amorous millionaire (Rudy Vallee), and a raft of screwball misunderstandings; the stars are backed by Sturges's inimitable stable of supporting comics (most of them playing members of the notorious Ale & Quail Club, drunk as skunks, with hunting rifles a-blazin'). Nothing at stake here except supersonic dialogue and merry nonsense, the likes of which only Sturges, in the 1940s, could accomplish. Sturges's *Hail the Conquering Hero* (1944) is also an eloquent take on the decade, with an explicit skewering of wartime fervor.

Action in the North Atlantic (1943) An overlooked World War II flag waver, in which Humphrey Bogart captains a merchant marine ship from Halifax to Murmansk. Action is what you'd call it—in a day of old-fashioned special effects, this movie accomplishes amazing sea-battle detail. Less patriotic per se than it is matter-of-fact about Allied efforts as a perilous job that needed doing.

The Bells of St. Mary's (1945) The war may have been winding down, but America needed this Leo McCarey movie like a black eye needs ice—in it, Bing Crosby's Father O'Malley (returning to the character for which he won an Oscar in 1944's *Going My Way*), lands in

a new urban parish and butts heads so gently with the head nun (Ingrid Bergman) that you'd swear they were in love. But it's not a romance; it's just people being kind to each other in a world soaked with suffering. Who can blame 1945 America for loving it?

The Best Years of Our Lives (1946) William Wyler's heartbreaking postwar ballad does an extraordinary thing for its day—it focuses entirely on the workaday lives of ordinary midwestern Americans as they pick up the threads of their lives. Sure, there's a little melodrama (Teresa Wright falls for unhappily married vet Dana Andrews), but for the most part the "story" adheres instead to the ordinary trials of the day: the moment when reunions grow awkward; the struggle of going back to work; family squabbles; getting your parents (and your girlfriend) used to the fact that you have hooks instead of hands. Oscars all over the place, and it's easy to see why: for a moment, Wyler sucked the Hollywood out of American movies—and replaced it with real people.

Julia (1977) Lillian Hellman's bestselling memoir *Pentimento* turned out to be mostly fiction, but it had at least one good yarn in it: Hellman's own lifelong friendship with a woman—as well as the established playwright's fame and safety—are put to a wartime test when she's asked to smuggle Resistance funds into Nazi Germany. The 1940s movies made during the 1940s are almost all Hollywood, but here, the period is trapped in all of its details, and the acting—by Jane Fonda (as Hellman), Vanessa Redgrave (as Julia), and Jason Robards (as Dashiell Hammett)—is a pleasure.

The Postman Always Rings Twice (1981) A decidedly unglitzy view of the decade in which James M. Cain wrote this vicious, horny noir, wherein a drifter (Jack Nicholson) links up with a greasy-spoon maenad (Jessica Lange) in a plot to kill her immigrant husband (John Colicos). Screenplay by David Mamet.

Radio Days (1987) The free-form nature of this overlooked sweetheart allowed writer-director Woody Allen to affectionately fold in virtually everything he remembered about the age of his early Brooklyn adolescence, as well as tons of other details he just made up out of love of the era. (See "New Year's," p. 13.)

Enemies, a Love Story (1989) This thoughtful, embraceable saga, based on a novel by Isaac Bashevis Singer, is set in the New York Jewish community in the late 1940s, a time when traumatized refugees and camp survivors flooded into the city and the Catskills were a new haven for *yiddishe* immigrants. Singer's story is a doozy: one well-intentioned Polish Jew (Ron Silver), living in Coney Island and married to the goy maid (Margaret Sophie Stein) who'd hidden him from the Nazis, maintains a passionate affair with a unstable fellow escapee (Lena Olin). She becomes pregnant, so he marries her, too, albeit off the books—and that's about when his *other*, first wife (Anjelica Huston), whom he thought had perished in the camps, shows up, leaving him with three wives and no sensible plan of action. Paul Mazursky directed, and it's the finest, most deeply felt movie the 1970s-cinema vet ever made.

VI

Safe Conduct (2002) Bertrand Tavernier's vast, witty, smooth-sailing portrait of the French film industry under the Occupation, as seen through the experience of real-life screenwriter Jean Aurenche (who wrote 1948's *The Walls of Malapaga,* 1949's *Occupe-Toi d'Amelie*, and 1952's *Forbidden Games*, and who died in 1992 at age eighty-eight), and director Jean Devaivre (who assisted filmmakers Maurice Tourneur, André Cayatte, and Richard Pottier during the war). Here the details aren't just physical but ethical as well; even if it weren't the most heartfelt valentine the French films of the 1940s ever produced, Tavernier's juggling act involves so many points of view and episodes that the movie might be the wily Gallic veteran's best film ever.

The Good German (2006) Steven Soderbergh's reincarnation of the postwar global noir—epitomized by classics like **Notorious** (1946), **The Lady from Shanghai** (1948), and **The Third Man** (1949)—is a classy affectation, with plenty of arch compositions, semimannered acting, and retro ominousness, as U.S. reporter George Clooney and ex-Nazi wife Cate Blanchett get embroiled in Marshall Plan intrigue. But because it's realistic about language, violence, sex, and suffering, it's useful as a corrective to thousands of hours of 1940s whitewash.

LOVING THE 1950s

"The cat's in the bag and the bag's in the river."
—Tony Curtis, *Sweet Smell of Success*

The 1950s weren't all "Eisenhower conformity versus greaser-rock 'n' roll," but let's face it, those were the interesting parts. Well, those and the movies the decade produced—which, thanks to the need to compete with television, were getting bigger, wider, odder, and more intense.

VI

The Wild One **(1953)** Marlon Brando, in a leather jacket and on a motorcycle, scaring the bejeezus out of honest small-town folk with his lawless, devil-may-care youthfulness. The movie in which Brando, when asked what he's rebelling against, merely answers "What've you got?"

On the Waterfront **(1954)** Give this politically troubled classic credit for its hard-bitten depiction of the 1950s working class in an era when everything else was showbiz as usual. (See "The Oscars," p. 117.)

Rebel Without a Cause **(1955)** A key film, sprouting from the middle of the decade and masterfully drawing the battle lines for what would later become known as "the generation gap," but more than that: Nicholas Ray's temple-pounding James Dean saga doesn't glamorize the 1950s; its milieu is lower-middle-class, and its social web is stretched to the tearing point. There may not be a clearer emotional portrait of midcentury America.

The Killing **(1956)** The 1950s as a butcher's block: this hellish Stanley Kubrick noir—cowritten by master noiriste Jim Thompson—involves a racetrack heist, but its gray sense of conscienceless doom is sobering, even for its genre. Sterling Hayden, Marie Windsor, and the inimitable Timothy Carey head the cast of soulless predators.

Will Success Spoil Rock Hunter? **(1957)** To many who were there, Frank Tashlin's widescreen, gumdrop-colored comedies exemplify the 1950s—particularly the decade's peculiar ideas of glamour, sex appeal, "modern" decor and style, and new postwar raciness (Jayne Mansfield is a walking sex joke). This isn't the actual 1950s, of course, but the 1950s as imagined by TV-embattled Hollywood and idealized by thrill-hungry audiences. Just as broad and evocative: Tashlin's *The Girl Can't Help It* **(1956)** and the Martin-Lewis vehicle *Hollywood or Bust* **(1956)**.

Thunder Road **(1958)** One of the first threadbare indies produced and cowritten by a popular star—in this case, Robert Mitchum—this is a gritty, modest B movie about Southern moonshiners, starring Mitchum and his son James as brothers (!). Shot on location, a novelty at the time. Bruce Springsteen has claimed he's never seen the film, only the poster.

A Summer Place (1959) A smash hit as the decade wound down, this unadventurous teen romance is now remembered mostly for its theme song, written by film score vet Max Steiner and sung by Percy Faith. But for those that remember, the movie's a time machine.

American Graffiti (1973) The year 1962 was still the 1950s in George Lucas's small California burg, where, for some, Buddy Holly's death marked the end of something grand, and the looming threat of the draft and Vietnam meant that something else entirely was on its way. How could the antiseptic overlord of the Star Wars industry have thunk up something so charming, spontaneous, idiosyncratic, and humane? A 1970s masterpiece, this film marks the beginning of an entire cultural phenomenon: retro cool.

The Lords of Flatbush (1974) Perhaps the best of *American Graffiti*'s residual imitators, this clunky little Brooklyn indie, about a tiny street gang of ne'er-do-wells, goes crazy for the leather jackets, D.A. haircuts, cycle-gang pseudotoughness, and outer-urban ethnic culture. Is this how it was back then? Here is where Sylvester Stallone, Henry Winkler, and Perry King got their breaks.

The Buddy Holly Story (1978) A surprisingly shoddy biopic of the doomed pop star, who despite being famously skinny and small, is played here by a bull-sized, Oscar-nominated Gary Busey. Still, the tragic tale itself was enough to make it a hit, and the music is a gift to the faithful. Holly's plane also carried Ritchie Valens, subject of the equally poignant, half-baked, and popular *La Bamba* **(1987)**; when will the Big Bopper biopic get made?

Grease (1978) The culmination of the 1950s retro fad—and never has a recent era been stylized and repackaged into such garish hootenanny. But you've seen it already.

The Wanderers (1979) Philip Kaufman's retroactively acclaimed adaptation of the Richard Price novel, filmed almost entirely in the Bronx, goofily chronicles the lives of Italian street gangs circa 1963, before Vietnam and the November news from Dealey Plaza. Overdone, but authentic and affectionate.

Diner (1982) Barry Levinson's debut film is a small masterpiece of social anthropology. Here he re-creates the 1959 stuck-in-a-groove lifestyle of six Baltimore guys in their twenties, swapping yucks at the all-night eatery over gravied french fries, like they have since they were kids, and not being much more savvy than their childhood selves about adulthood or women. The semi-improvised banter is fascinating, and the clothes, norms, styles, lingo, and music are all on the money. Steve Guttenberg and Mickey Rourke shine as they did only here, Kevin Bacon and Daniel Stern have rarely had better roles, and Paul Reiser expertly energizes the ensemble with wise-cracks. (The sixth guy, Tim Daly, is a relative dull straight man with dull girl problems.) Guttenberg's slightly dull-witted Colts fanatic is getting married, and the guys collect in the midwinter, in their wool overcoats, to see if it'll actually happen. If it sounds like a hundred other small movies from the 1980s on, you're right—but this is the first of its kind, and it's the best. (Incidentally, this movie also served as a significant "how to" lesson in chatty screenwriting for a young fanboy named Quentin Tarantino.)

***The Long Day Closes* (1992)** The final chapter in British auteur Terence Davies's languor-ous autobiographical film cycle, this rapturously made movie follows *Distant Voices, Still Lives* (1988), which focuses on his older siblings and the tyrannical psychobeast father who wrecked their lives, then succumbed to stomach cancer when Davies was seven, in the late 1940s. *Long Day* is a relaxing return to the childhood years of freedom and peace that followed, until Davies's torturous entry into secondary school at age eleven. Drunk on remembered details, the film often stops dead in its hovering course to simply observe the central family's mum (Marjorie Yates) fuss with laundry and sing "If You Were the Only Girl in the World," but it also ascends, as in the breakout money sequence, which is scored to Debbie Reynolds crooning "Tammy": a sum-it-all-up overhead pan of the young lad playing by his house, dissolving into overhead social portraits of the respective congregations of church, school, and the movies. It's heartfelt, but it's also archaeological.

***Matinee* (1993)** As in *American Graffiti*, the year 1962 belongs, in Joe Dante's per-fect little film, to the 1950s, when film producers like William Castle would cram movie theaters with thrill-seeking postwar kids by tempting them with gimmicks and in-house theatrics. John Goodman plays the Castle persona, who brings his new production, *Mant* ("Half man, half ant!"), to a small Florida town—just as the Cuban Missile Crisis heats up and makes things *really* scary.

***Far from Heaven* (2002)** Frank and Cathy (Dennis Quaid and Julianne Moore) are the perfect 1950s couple: he's a successful businessman; she's a beautiful, impeccable hostess with a flawless home, two well-behaved children, and a loyal housekeeper. The facade cracks when Cathy catches Frank kissing another man—and then finds solace in the sympathetic companionship of her gardener, a courteous, intelligent man who happens to be black. This movie is an homage to the Douglas Sirk dramas of the 1950s, right down to the typeface over the opening credits and the swelling Elmer Bernstein score, and it's a dead-serious "women's film" melodrama. Gloved hands, cocktails before dinner, crinoline skirts, and the ubiquity of casual prejudice—director Todd Haynes's film is almost a deliberate attempt to make the nervy movie about the failure of middle-class surfaces that audiences *should've* had the chance to see in 1956, but that the studios were too timid to make.

Down with Love **(2003)** Sort of the *Sky Captain and the World of Tomorrow* version of the old Doris Day comedies from the postwar era, full of exaggerated "mod" set design, crazy plotting, oldie pop songs, and goofy acting.

Hollywoodland **(2006)** A surprisingly spry biopic of actor George Reeves, whose unmeteoric career led to him playing Superman on TV (1952–58), and eventually to a suicide that might've been a murder. Ben Affleck, as Reeves, and Diane Lane, as Toni Mannix, a Hollywood producer's wife and aging tramp, rise to the occasion, and the film is a bath in postwar semi-affluence. Ignore the Adrien Brody framing story if you can.

BEING IN THE 1960s

"How's your joint, George?"
—Peter Fonda, *Easy Rider*

VI

Like all cultural mythologies, the idea of the 1960s that we have in our heads isn't entirely true—for many Americans, the 1960s weren't very different than the 1950s. But the difference is what matters, and the decade eventually acquired so much historical blood and radical behavior that it was destined to be reexamined through rose-colored glasses very soon indeed. In at least some ways, the 1960s were like the 1920s—but with nudity, real rock music, dope, and a pacifist ideology. All told, the decade would become the most radical of modern American epochs. What's not to love?

Breathless **(1960)** Did the 1960s begin with this earthquaking Jean-Luc Godard debut? Though sniffed at by critic Pauline Kael as "a frightening little chase comedy," this one film changed the rules for filmmakers all over the globe by creating cinematic postmodernism at last, and by refocusing movies away from what they're "about" and toward what they *are*: time, images, light, plastic, and people—watching and being watched. This atom bomb is modest in its outline—a blase scoundrel (Jean-Paul Belmondo) kills a cop and goes on the lam—but Godard used this formula material to rewrite the laws of continuity, narrative priority, and meaning. After this, movies were no longer imitations of life, as it were, but life itself.

Loves of a Blonde **(1965)** Perhaps the keystone film of the Czech New Wave, Milos Forman's feature debut is so ultrarealistic—messy, sensitive to ambivalence, naturally lit, and never "performed"—it could be considered a form of fossilization, capturing the "Prague Spring" Communist thaw like a fly in amber. Forman's heroine (Hana

Brejchova) is a guileless factory girl who, on a night out at the beer hall, withstands the advances of foolish military guys on leave and instead sleeps with a member of the band. Left high and dry, she thoughtlessly arrives on his parents' doorstep in Prague. A warm, wise blast from the past.

The Graduate (1967) The first film to snag onto the Vietnam generation's sense of dissatisfaction with the established priorities of the American empire, this bristling Mike Nichols movie is also a brutal poison-pen portrait of American neo-aristocracy—swimming pools, cheap mansions, sports cars, midday cocktails, and all. As the bachelors-degree rich boy with no forward momentum, Dustin Hoffman became the unlikeliest but, given the film, most inevitable of stars.

Greetings (1968) Brian De Palma, semiacclaimed mechanic of pulp expressionism, was once very funny—this topical farce blasts away at everything in the air back then, from hippiedom to JFK conspiracy obsessives to the sexual revolution. Scatterbrained but full of reckless zest, this was Robert De Niro's first movie, and film school grad De Palma's second. The sequel, *Hi, Mom!* (1970), goes even farther off the cliff, into a mockery of the civil rights struggle.

Psych-Out (1968) A Dick Clark–produced quickie about hippies, hallucinogens, Haight-Ashbury, and a deaf girl (Susan Strasberg) who comes to town to look for her dope-lost brother. Surprisingly smart, due largely to Jack Nicholson's participation as cowriter (for which he received no credit) and costar, playing the one rock 'n' roll druggie who sees the dark end of the tunnel.

Symbiopsychotaxiplasm: Take One (1968) A long-unreleased phantom from the summer of 1968, William Greaves's loopy experiment has Greaves playing Greaves playing a vague indie filmmaker who's shooting a film about marital rupture in Central Park. With three mutually interrogating cameras going at all times, the set and surrounding passersby (including cops) get folded into the Godard-vérité mix, which is often prismed out for us as a split-screen triptych. Eventually, the discontented and cerebral crew begin filming themselves complaining about Greaves (and his script) when he's not there. "Stop acting!" someone hollers early on—it's laid-back grooviness, but nothing if not sophisticated.

Easy Rider (1969) Not a very good movie, when all is said and done, but few other American films shook things up so violently. On a nothing budget and on the road, director-star Dennis Hopper made a true indie about America while emitting gassy ideas about "America"; in the process, he taught the world how to smoke a joint. At the time, this was the movie that expressed a generation's yearnings, and, inevitably, its suspicions that there might be nowhere to finally run to. Jack Nicholson, as a boozy lawyer catching a whiff of freedom, got his first Oscar nomination for his performance here.

Fruit of Paradise **(1969)** Czech cinema anarchist Véra Chytilová's film begins with a ten-minute Garden of Eden overture of tripled images, rotting textures, and crazed editing that would've made avant-gardist Stan Brakhage stomp his foot and yowl; after that, it's an entrancing hippie-dippie oratorio on gender combat that doesn't retell Genesis so much as slip it a microdot. Her previous and more famous work, ***Daisies*** **(1966)**, is a more linear attack, yet even more absurd.

Valerie and Her Week of Wonders **(1970)** A loopy, sexy, druggy Czech fairy tale about a young girl's coming of age, which involves being beset by vampire father figures, surreal dream sequences, doppelgangers, misty idylls, and what have you. Only in the 1960s.

Woodstock **(1970)** Just as the decade was ending, this monster concert movie introduced the few dozen Americans who don't claim to have actually been there to the century's most socially influential musical moment. Of course, in real terms the 1969 concert itself—which featured Jimi Hendrix, the Who, Janis Joplin, Joan Baez, Country Joe & the Fish, Santana, Crosby, Stills & Nash, among others—made only a medium dent in the popular consciousness; it was this flashy, rough-hewn movie, seen by millions, that established the "mud, nudity, and acid" image of the event for all time, and that made the film's title a catchword for the entire bygone era. Whatever: today, it's a flashback all its own, silly and intoxicating in equal measure. *Of course* an entire generation would claim to have been a part of the humongous, life-loving crowd—who wouldn't want to have that as a firsthand memory?

La Vallée **(1972)** Barbet Schroeder's seductive adventure looks squarely at the 1960s ideas of unbridled freedom, sexual liberty, and the idealization of "natural" lifestyles—and watches them smack into the real Third World, as a self-infatuated group of Eurotrash (led by merchandise-minded rich girl Bulle Ogier) journey into central New Guinea looking for a fabled valley that's never been visited by white men and never been mapped (because it is "obscured by clouds," according to the movie's theatrical subtitle). Will they find it? Will Ogier's heroine find happiness shedding civilization's constraints? Or is it all a big lie? Soundtrack by Pink Floyd.

Coming Home **(1978)** Director Hal Ashby made this potentially treacly romance, between a paraplegic vet and a buttoned-up officer's wife, resonate like a hot day; Jon Voight might be the coolest and most beautiful wheelchair-bound dude in movie history, but the textures of the film are convincing and earnest (although the milieu is relatively fresh—set at a military community and hospital in and around Manhattan Beach, California, the film really was shot in Manhattan Beach). Jane Fonda is her usually vivid, pre-sellout self, and both of them earned and won Oscars. With a wall-to-wall soundtrack haze comprised of the Rolling Stones, Richie Havens, Jefferson Airplane, and more.

Who'll Stop the Rain **(1978)** This was the year in which movies began to seriously address the fallout legacy of our decade-plus involvement in Southeast Asia, and the conclusions were woeful, bitter, and pathetic in tone. This film, from the Robert Stone novel *Dog Soldiers*, involves returned vet Nick Nolte, errant wife Tuesday Weld, a big bundle of smuggled Asian smack, and a greedy gang of pursuing goons (including Richard Masur and Ray Sharkey). Since it's still the 1970s, it's shot so convincingly you can walk right into it.

Hair **(1979)** The 1960s were probably never like anything like this, but Milos Forman's musical adaptation of the stage hit—itself a idealization of the era as it was happening—is a leaping, exuberant hymn to the very vague but infectious notions of free love, peace, present-moment élan, antiauthoritarian defiance, and raw hedonism. Very much an act of nostalgia all its own, the film was released eight months before Ronald Reagan was elected president. Choreography by Twyla Tharp.

Heaven Help Us **(1985)** Life for bursting pubescent boys in a strict Brooklyn Catholic boarding school, circa 1965. A fair but uneasy mix of sensitively observed experience (probably rendered faithfully from Charles Purpura's script) and rude teen comedy (probably dumbed down by the *Porky's*-minded producers). As budding sweethearts, Andrew McCarthy and Mary Stuart Masterson kick-started their 1980s careers.

That Thing You Do! **(1996)** A sweet, giddy, unpretentious love song to one-hit wonders in an age when show business was still an impromptu, hands-on party that practically anyone could join. Tom Hanks's movie pulses with gentle respect for its characters and a genuine ardor for pop music and the middle-class lives it touches. Every time you think there'll be a love triangle, a clash of personality, or a contrived tragedy, the film skips over it gracefully and simply attends instead to the music, the times, and the beguiling characters' delirious fun living out the American dream. "You're way better than anything," says one of start-up pop group the One-Ders' first fans, and damn if she's not close to right: the Erie, Pennsylvania, quartet's first and only hit single (written by Adam Schlesinger) is so adroit and propulsive, you don't mind having listened to it eighteen times by the film's end. The film mostly follows the footsteps of Tom Everett Scott's insouciant drummer, who joins the band (which includes Johnathan Schaech as the self-absorbed songwriter and front man and Steve Zahn as a wisecracking guitarist) with dreams of jazz greatness. It's a small film that aims modestly low and hits every bull's-eye, and the performances are engaging; Zahn, as the group's inspired wisenheimer, and Liv Tyler, as Schaech's selfless girlfriend, are particularly appealing. At the same time, it cuts a slice of the 1960s no one seems to remember anymore—the still-clean-cut, soda-pop Middle America that is just beginning to be raised on rock radio.

Austin Powers: International Man of Mystery **(1997)** By now a franchise and a near-universal cultural gag, Mike Myers's deft retro creation is not at all a parody, as know-nothing critics stated, of the James Bond series, but of the secondary Bondian culture, much of which is self-satirizing, as exemplified by James Coburn's Derek Flint, Dean Martin's Matt Helm, *The Avengers*, *The Man from U.N.C.L.E.*, and the Dick Clement–Ian La Frenais series of spy spoofs. In other words, Myers was aiming at the cheesiest aspects of 1960s culture, not the most popular, and his vapid, hedonistic, terminally trendy 1960s British secret agent—"the ultimate gentleman spy"—is a masterwork of time-capsule comedy. Given to wearing velvet suits, possessed of extraordinarily bad teeth, and behaving generally as if he stepped out of a Richard Lester movie gone rancid (complete with psychedelic musical numbers), Powers, even after he unthaws in the 1990s to chase Dr. Evil, is a rotating-bed, Burt Bacharach–scored wonder, peerlessly evocative of his era as we experienced it in matinees and on TV.

A Walk on the Moon (1999) A midlife dalliance for resurgent star Diane Lane, as a neglected wife and mother who gets turned around by a hunky, hippie clothes merchant (Viggo Mortensen), as Neil Armstrong walks on the moon and Woodstock looms. Thin, but it hit a chord with American women.

VI

LOST IN THE 1970s

"I'm getting away from things that get bad if I stay."
—Jack Nicholson, *Five Easy Pieces*

After the party, the hangover: Nixon, Watergate, Kent State, Cambodia, drug deaths, commune failures. And the movies, perhaps more than ever: learning a lesson from the postwar New Waves in France, Czechoslovakia, Poland, Hungary, Brazil, and elsewhere, American moviemakers opened a window for themselves, in which they made films that respected reality, attended to working-class struggle, and got intimate with adult concerns. That window began closing in earnest in 1977 with the explosion of *Star Wars*, but it was eye-opening while it lasted.

Five Easy Pieces (1970) The quintessential 1970s film—which is to say, it embodies the cynical death of 1960s idealism while establishing another high bar for the new American New Wave's focus on working-class life in all of its dead-ended frustration. Jack Nicholson made himself a star as the rebel son of a family of concert pianists who tries working on an oil rig, but can't settle anywhere. The film's most famous scene, set in a diner and concerning a chicken salad sandwich, sums up an entire generation's dashed hopes and rising rage at a complacent America.

Klute **(1971)** Shot in New York, this mysterious, overwhelmingly atmospheric film masquerades as a thriller (it rather obliquely concerns a serial killer who may or may not be stalking a tempestuous, angry call girl), but it's actually a character study. This is the movie in which Jane Fonda, in a career performance that virtually defined the new, defiant adult woman of the Nixon era, became (and remained, for a few years) the most fearless woman in cinema. We still miss *that* Jane.

The Long Goodbye **(1973)** Robert Altman, in his inimitable style, updates this Raymond Chandler mystery yarn, and Chandler's Philip Marlowe, to 1970s L.A., a sour maze of aging hippies, blithe crime, loneliness, and a certain lack of moral rectitude—something Elliott Gould's singularly schlubby private eye decides to correct on his own by story's end. The case itself involves a friend (baseball star Jim Bouton) who's accused of killing his wife, but various SoCal lunatics are roped in as well, and the film becomes a tapestry of genre jokes, cultural satire, and Altmanesque texture.

A Woman Under the Influence **(1974)** John Cassavetes paved the way for the gritty, truthful Hollywood movies of the 1960s and '70s, and here he pushes the envelope a little wider, in a seemingly improvised, uncomfortably intimate study of a family implosion, which unstable, possibly manic-depressive mom Gena Rowlands causes and devoted but clueless construction worker dad Peter Falk inadequately attends to. As toughminded, cruelly observational, and brave as any American film, it seems to have been shot in the real world, without prearrangement or rehearsal.

Jaws **(1975)** No back-glancing survey of the Nixon-Ford-Carter decade can stand without this famous beaut, the signature monster-movie blockbuster that unified the country in a single movie mind-set for an entire, absolutely unforgettable summer. No money-minting Hollywood hit since has captured its decade as realistically, or given *everyone*—child, teen, and adult—the same fabulous matinee buzz.

Smile **(1975)** Middle America was cool in the 1970s—or at least cool enough to be satirized up and down for its cheesy, oblivious silliness in films like this Michael Ritchie interrogation, which tears apart a second-rate California beauty pageant, from recruitment to training to the final face-off. Everyone—contestants, parents, organizers, judges, choreographers, peeping toms, ad infinitum—gets a vicious lashing, but Ritchie never strains or caricatures. This is how it was, and probably in many ways still is, and it's hilarious and dismaying because you believe every frame.

Network **(1976)** This Paddy Chayefsky–written barn burner is such a brilliantly incisive dismantling of the way network television worked in the 1970s that it has become something like a prophecy in the years since—what was true then is five times as true today. Television goes from being a semi-whorehouse to an out-and-out freak circus in the quest for higher ratings; Sidney Lumet's fastidiously realistic direction and the hair-raising performances of Faye Dunaway, William Holden, Robert Duvall, Peter Finch, et al. make it all tangible and undeniable. Were Hollywood films ever really this sophisticated, this caustic, this ethical?

Annie Hall (1977) The movie that made Woody Allen "Woody Allen," it's a semiautobiographical comedy about the filmmaker's relationship with semiditzy, WASPy Diane Keaton (whose last name used to be Hall), kinda playing herself. A big Oscar winner, and so seminal it quickly became part of our common culture, it's also an unadorned love letter to 1970s New York—this is the way it looked and the way it was, not just for millionaire celebrities, but for everyone.

Real Life (1979) In 1973, PBS ran a documentary series called *An American Family*, about a real upper-middle-class nuclear unit, shot in the family's home. But how could that have been "reality," asks comic Albert Brooks in his first film, which duplicates the scenario to wicked, double-edged-sword effect. As usual, Brooks is the ogre-ish primary target, but the era's relationship to TV and fame are also bludgeoned into pulp.

Dazed and Confused (1993) See "High School Graduation" (p. 124), but if you're a generation older, revel in this Richard Linklater memorial tapestry for its late-1970s specifics: lingo, music (Foghat!), stoner norms—even the way protagonist Mitch (Wiley Wiggins) fiddles with his too-long hair when trying to act cool.

Crooklyn (1994) Another return to childhood, Spike Lee's memoir film (cowritten with two of his siblings) about the filmmaker's youth growing up in 1970s Brooklyn amid five kids, a proud jazz musician father (Delroy Lindo), a no-bullshit mom (Alfre Woodard), and an atmosphere thick with infectious pop songs, Norman Lear sitcoms, urban street games, and a sense of a day and age in which many urban neighborhoods were communities instead of war zones.

The Ice Storm (1997) On the face of it, Ang Lee's thoroughly grown-up movie is a melancholy but bemused Mona Lisa portrait of a very particular time and place: wealthy Connecticut bedroom communities in the early 1970s, when polyester suits were in, Nixon haunted the airwaves, cocktails flowed like monsoon rainwater, and the sexual revolution began to sour the lives of restless suburbanites.

Almost Famous (2000) Has the 1970s fostered more after-the-fact memoir movies than any other decade? Here Cameron Crowe semi-fictionalizes the time he got to go on the road with major rock bands as a teen journalist for *Rolling Stone*. As usual, the story meanders like a haphazard life, but everything—particularly the hot band in question, led by Jason Lee's lanky front man and Billy Crudup's guitar idol—takes you back.

Starsky and Hutch (2004) What do we have here? A semifarcical remake of the old TV show, but one that stars self-satirists Ben Stiller and Owen Wilson, who act as if they're in a crummy 1970s series but around whom a 2004 plot and milieu revolve? But wait, is that Snoop Dogg as Huggy Bear? Is this supposed to be the 1970s, and is it supposed to be a comedy? Or both?

GRADE SCHOOL NOSTALGIA

"A long time ago, but only if you measure in terms of years. . . ."
—Richard Dreyfuss, *Stand by Me*

Doubtless our own childhoods happened differently than the way we all remember them, but who cares: it's the emotion-driven memories that count, and only a handful of movies have faithfully and intelligently spoken to that truth. Any of them could, with a gesture or moment, bring back the prepubertal fire.

I Was Born, But . . . (1932) Like a *Little Rascals* episode writ large and filmed by a meticulous genius, this silent Japanese film by Yasujiro Ozu views the world of two prepubescent brothers from three feet off the ground, as they struggle with the playground hierarchy in their neighborhood and discover, in horror, that their office-worker father is subjugated by the same conflicts. Because Ozu was always concerned with perspective and observation above all things, this film focuses on the real give-and-take of being a boy, and being eight years old.

Zéro de Conduite (1933) This Jean Vigo mini-masterpiece is a vivid snapshot of grade school rebelliousness—you may've forgotten what it was like to spitball a teacher in fifth grade, or what it felt like to *want* to, but this visionary little gem jacks you into that universal spirit in no time flat, and at the same time it acts out your craziest preadolescent wishes of ridiculous chaos. (See "Parenting Tweens and Teens," p. 143.)

The Curse of the Cat People (1944) One of the quiet miracles of 1940s B moviemaking, this is a dreamlike journey into an eight-year-old girl's fantasy world, as the daughter of Kent Smith, the hero from 1942's *Cat People*, now remarried, is visited by the ghost of his first wife (Simone Simon). Shadowy, gentle, and captivating.

The 400 Blows (1959) Like many films found in "Parenting Tweens and Teens" (p. 144), this semiautobiographical French New Wave landmark by François Truffaut is as potent a vehicle for an adult's autobiographical ruminations as it is a guide to the new adolescent's storming terrain. Watch Jean-Pierre Léaud as he watches grown-ups, steals happiness in their absence, and warily regards the world that grates against him at every turn.

Stand by Me (1986) Isn't summer the blazing *belle epoque* of every kid's year, and the forge of most childhood memories? This Rob Reiner–Stephen King film is distinctive, too, for its stinging and hilariously accurate portrayal of how twelve- and thirteen-year-old boys talk to each other, in the late 1950s and now. (See "Summer," p. 80.)

Welcome to the Dollhouse (1995) If you don't remember the killing fields of the seventh grade, this movie's a reminder. It opens in the Theater of Cruelty of the junior high school cafeteria, where finding somewhere to sit, and people who will *let* you sit with them, has all the shivery dread of being lost in a police state without ID. The camera slowly circles around eleven-year-old Dawn Weiner (Heather Matarazzo), standing there holding her tray and surveying the combat zone, her bespectacled face a knot of huddled horror. You've been there.

REMEMBERING HIGH SCHOOL

"The only place different social types can genuinely get along with each other is in Heaven."
—Christian Slater, *Heathers*

The longest three or four years of everyone's life; as in "Grade School Nostalgia," the emphasis here is on movies that evoke the emotional reality, which is far from an easy task. In opposition to the "High School Graduation" section, here is where we put the movies that have a retrospective glower to them—it is only well after we've graduated that it becomes apparent how preposterously stultifying, regimented, and barbaric the dynamic of high school really is.

High School (1968) Frederick Wiseman has made a career of documentaries that stare unblinkingly at the dead soul of American institutions, and his portrait of a Philadelphia high school, where teachers and administrators behave like comatose church elders and students lurk like flogged animals, can make your blood run cold.

Real Genius (1985) A supremely silly 1980s teen comedy about a private high school for scientific geniuses, featuring a fantastically zingy Val Kilmer as the senior class's reigning brain, who has already decided that being smart will not prevent him from being a complete clown. As the new kid in town, Gabe Jarret is *too* convincingly awkward.

River's Edge **(1986)** A key American film of the Reagan-Bush years, and if it was shocking at the time, that's because the era's movies didn't normally rip from the headlines with such cold-eyed matter-of-factness. It's happened more than once in real life: on the edge of some impoverished, delinquent-parent Pacific Coast Endsville, a disaffected teen strangles his girlfriend, then, over the course of several days, shows the body to his friends, who do nothing. Chilly and grim, it's the American high school years as a stoner Samuel Beckett play, abetted by an alert cast—Keanu Reeves began his peerless pot-head routine here, and Dennis Hopper, as a local nutcase, is outstanding (although Crispin Glover, as a maniacally overwrought drama queen in a black wool cap, feels as if he's dropped in from a high school rendition of *Grease*).

Heathers **(1989)** A massively clever, thick-as-a-brick screenplay by Daniel Waters gave this insurrectionary teen satire plenty of ground to tear up—it mockingly endorses, among other things, in-school murder, terrorism, and teen suicide, while dishing homosexuality, teachers, parents, football, and bulimia—all in fun, of course. Winona Ryder's wary clique-follower hangs with the cool, big-haired girls of 1980s Westerberg High (named after Paul, famed lead singer of the Replacements), and has her homicidal fantasies realized by new kid Christian Slater (doing a killer Jack Nicholson). Conceptually it's outlandish, right up to the climactic bomb, but it's also endlessly inventive, line for slangy line, and the feeling of teen social crisis is there.

Dazed and Confused **(1993)** So much baggage for one film to carry; see "High School Graduation" (p. 124) and "Lost in the 1970s" (p. 299).

Outside Providence **(1999)** From Peter and Bobby Farrelly, a relatively straight-faced comedy—semiautobio?—about a working-class Rhode Island pot head (Shawn Hatosy) who is sent, after too many run-ins with the law, to a prep school by his frustrated idiot of a father (Alec Baldwin). Directed by Michael Corrente, the movie surprises everyone who sees it with its observational chops and realism.

Battle Royale **(2000)** Many of us remember high school as a war zone, and in this ludicrous, disturbing, fascinating Japanese film, from crime-epic master Kinji Fukasaku, the feeling is made literal: in some near future on the verge of youth-gang social collapse, Japan's fascist government randomly selects a class of teens and strands them on an isolated island with one imperative: that they kill each other until one student is left standing. It's a very emotional film (try to find a Japanese or Korean film about high school that isn't), and the kids' catalog of slights, betrayals, ostracisms, jealousies, and clique-creation becomes, suddenly, a matter of homicidal payback and adolescent prairie justice. You think *you* had it bad.

Ginger Snaps **(2000)** A small-budget horror film in which a Goth teenage girl (Katherine Isabelle) gets bitten—by something—catches lycanthropy, and essentially undergoes modern movies' hairiest case of puberty. We all know how she feels.

COLLEGE DAYS

"Six years of college down the drain!"
—John Belushi, *National Lampoon's Animal House*

Finally, a genuine cause for nostalgia—your college days are, generally speaking, your taste of irresponsible Nirvana before being launched out into the adult world and forced to work until you die. Thus, many of these films are almost infinitely repeatable, especially in mid-September.

VI

The Freshman **(1925)** Silent comic Harold Lloyd does his higher-education, football-schnook best with this harmless confection, one of his biggest hits. Were college students ever this naive, and was college life ever this innocent?

College **(1927)** Buster Keaton does Lloyd one better, if not very much funnier, as a nerd who tries to become a varsity jock to please a girl. Not as witty or inventive as several other Keaton films, but still visualized and paced with a jeweler's care.

Horse Feathers **(1932)** One of the Marx Brothers' three genuine masterpieces, set on the campus of Huxley College, where Groucho's surreal shyster is again inappropriately given a position of eminence (university president), while Zeppo does time as his son (!) and the film's romantic lead, and Harpo and Chico conspire to peddle football plays to the rival college Darwin. Timeless, hilarious, and full of joy, the film also manages to muster a college's community feel, down to the off-campus speakeasy and the climactic football game itself, which is priceless.

La Chinoise **(1967)** These are college days to moon about—the buildup of 'Nam-era radicalism on French campuses (which culminated the next year, with director Jean-Luc Godard's help, in the May 1968 strikes and popular uprising). Godard here dares to both endorse his Maoist students as they harangue his camera and allow them to establish a kind of auto-critique—politically, the filmmaker seems dubious of the Communist approach, but promotes it because it is the only alternative to capitalist imperialism. See? Ideology and argument like this doesn't happen on campuses anymore, and disjunctive, challenging films like this, though once college favorites, are never screened.

***The Paper Chase* (1973)** A certain varietal of university experience: the crazed, serious graduate life at Harvard Law School, where study groups are a matter of intense political maneuvers and a single professor (Oscar winner John Houseman) instills quaking fear into the tweed-wearing student body. Deft, funny, and realistic, but if you didn't go to an Ivy League school, it might inspire less nostalgia than class envy.

***National Lampoon's Animal House* (1978)** As we've tooted in the "Autumn" section (p. 87), this earthquake of an American comedy isn't just a freshmanic goof-off, but a concerted effort at replicating the dress, norms, spirit, and style of nondescript university life circa 1962. Screenwriters Harold Ramis, Chris Miller, and Douglas Kenney (the last two veteran editors for *National Lampoon*), as well as director John Landis, poured their generational memories into the film.

***The Sure Thing* (1985)** Rob Reiner's second film, and a fairly typical 1980s teen comedy in outline: John Cusack travels across country to meet a rumored-about hot blonde who'll bed him. If little else, Reiner is a sharpshooter with character comedy, and the movie is still simpatico with everyguy college life.

***School Daze* (1988)** For his sophomore feature (after 1986's breakout hit *She's Gotta Have It*), self-made wunderkind Spike Lee fashioned this big-budget, ambitious musical about African American college life in the 1980s (modeled after his own collegiate experiences at all-black Morehouse College in Atlanta). Lee's scorched-earth racial politics are given free run of the place, and they can be bruising, but mostly the movie seems to be a love letter to the personal and cultural moment, at least as much as his later memoir-film, *Crooklyn*.

***SubUrbia* (1997)** An essentially faithful adaptation of Eric Bogosian's play about post–high school slackers killing time in a convenience store parking lot in Any Small Town Shithole, U.S.A., Richard Linklater's film retains the play's formulaic structure, but—like *Slacker, Dazed and Confused*, and *Before Sunrise*—it bursts with precisely observed reality. Effortlessly funny, Linklater's film is also devastating and spooky in its dead-on rendering of twentysomething Middle America nothingness—this is the reality of "there's only the community college." The characters are paradigmatic: Jeff (Giovanni Ribisi), the semicultured cynic still living with his parents; Buff (Steve Zahn), the relentless buzz hound; Tim (Nicky Katt), the quiet sociopath; Sooze (Amie Carey), the talentless but ambitious punkette, and so on. It's all in the rhythms, which are letter perfect, and in the acting—Ribisi is disturbingly believable as the movie's central lost boy, and Zahn's empty party beast is particularly terrifying and real. *SubUrbia* is nearly anthropological in its charting of a near-universal American post-teen experience. If you haven't lived it, the movie might bounce off you. If you have, it's mesmerizing.

Wonder Boys (2000) Though largely told from the point of view of Michael Douglas's menopausal, writer's-blocked lit prof, this Curtis Hanson–directed comedy remains a meticulous evocation of American campus life, which here is somewhat like the lovable hero—stuck in time, floating away from responsibilities as the years pass in a haze of emotional sensation and the pursuit of experience. Because the staff stays put, college life doesn't change much from decade to decade; when you're a student, it feels like the key years in your history, despite the fact that you're there and gone in four years, and the incoming freshmen look just like you. But there's a warmth here, a childlike joy in the free-for-all social norms of the collegiate years, that's hard to find in any other film.

VI

FIRST LOVE

"Do not leave me in this dark alone where I cannot find you."
—Laurence Olivier, *Wuthering Heights*

We've all had one, whether we got to act on it or not. Of our collective emotional tortures, first love may be our most fiery, and our most unforgettable. Movies love this hot spot the way mosquitoes love veins close to the surface, and it's a time-honored pleasure to have the old wound massaged now and then.

Peter Ibbetson (1935) They don't come any more swoony. This Romantic ultraromance, rarely seen before its 2006 DVD-ization, begins in preadolescence, graduates to a cosmically aligned adulthood, and then ascends into the realm of the subconscious. True love survives for the story's separated lovers (Gary Cooper and the somewhat icy Ann Harding) in their shared dreams, which exist in a kind of idealized parallel universe where lovers never age. Makes most other first-love scenarios seem half-hearted; here, neither reality nor death impedes the course of *l'amour*.

Splendor in the Grass (1961) The emotional turbulence of high schoolers found eloquent, melodramatic form in this William Inge story that features Warren Beatty, Natalie Wood, 1920s Kansas, parental pressure, class prejudice, and misunderstood hormonal fireworks. You just wanna weep for those kids. Possibly the best American film of the early 1960s not directed by Alfred Hitchcock, though it's rarely been considered as such.

Love with the Proper Stranger **(1963)** Natalie Wood again, in a movingly realistic drama wherein a Macy's clerk, an innocent Catholic girl, finds herself pregnant from a barely remembered fling with a moody musician (Steve McQueen), who agrees to help her raise the money for an abortion. Out of this, if you can believe it, comes a romance.

Lovefilm **(1970)** A sweet, wise, post-Godardian tour of midcentury Hungarian upheaval, by way of a childhood love grown into wayward adulthood. Directed by István Szabó, who later made splashes with historical tragedies like 1981's *Mephisto* and 1985's *Colonel Redl*.

Two English Girls **(1971)** It's not New Wave hero François Truffaut's most famous or popular film, but it's clearly his best—a sober, exhaustive, bruising inquisition into romance and folly (based upon a novel by *Jules and Jim* author Jean-Pierre Roche) whose cool narrative formalities barely disguise an epic ardor for the tragedies of ephemeral love and youth. The ménage is inverted from *Jules*'s "two buddies and a gal"—Jean-Pierre Léaud's self-analyzing Frenchman indulgently, indecisively, courts two British sisters (Stacey Tendeter and Kika Markham), unable to decide whom he loves more until it is too late. What's sadder, having lost love or having squandered its opportunity?

First Love **(1977)** If Susan Dey, late of *The Partridge Family*, weren't so dewily gorgeous and fascinating in 1977, and if William Katt, equally beautiful, weren't as sympathetic a hero, this earnest, honest essay on postteen romance and its hazards would've sunk from memory. It still hasn't been given its due.

Waking the Dead **(2000)** Director Keith Gordon's film doesn't really work, but it's filthy with tantalizing ingredients: Billy Crudup in the lead, supporting work from Janet McTeer, Molly Parker, and Sandra Oh, a story that head butts 1960s radicalism with the reality of political compromise, and, best of all, the soul-scouring presence of Jennifer Connelly as the idealized Ghost of Heartbreak Past. Just that falling tear during sex, and the way she says "Oh, dear . . . I love that you said that," can do it for you. Ravishing and fascinating both, Connelly is absolutely believable as someone who, once you lost her, would haunt you forever.

Oasis **(2002)** A very odd, but ecstatic and convincing, Korean film in which a criminal misfit (Sol Kyung-gu), after doing questionable time for a hit-and-run, falls in love with the accident victim's sister (Moon So-ri), who has cerebral palsy. Gritty handheld realism meets visionary expressionism in subtle ways, and the performances are transporting.

Punch-Drunk Love **(2002)** So eccentric it can be distinctly off-putting, Paul Thomas Anderson's nebbishy love story will not allow its characters to be pigeonholed—especially Adam Sandler's hero, a self-made businessman with explosive social graces, a chaotic sense of masculine pride, a violent and impulsive anger, a troubled relationship with his many harpy-like sisters, and a yen for Emily Watson's ordinary working girl. But the unpredictability is bracing, and the love story is hard-won.

My Summer of Love **(2004)** A very odd quasi-lesbian teen-love idyll, in which a poor British scamp and a sultry, neglected aristocratic daughter bond, share, smoke, defy convention, have sex, and eventually confront their unavoidable class differences. Directed by Polish emigré Pawel Pawlikowski, and featuring star-to-be Emily Blunt.

A Very Long Engagement **(2004)** French serendipity-fantasist Jean-Pierre Jeunet caught hell from his homeland for this digitized epic about World War I, fated love, and post-battlefield fallout; the powers that be even denied it a possible foreign-language Oscar nomination because Jeunet used American money to make it (as if international coproductions haven't been common coin since the salad days of David Lean). Sébastien Japrisot's novel is an intricate detective story infused with magical thinking, and the film remains faithful both to its headlong lovelorn-ness and to the authentic horrors of early-century warfare. Audrey Tautou plays a crippled girl who will not accept the news of her fiancé's death at the Somme, and the film revisits, again and again, from different and endlessly complicated perspectives, what happened on that blood-soaked patch of no man's land in 1916.

VI

RESOURCES

What movies are available to consumers, and in what format, are questions with ever-changing answers. Here are some alternative resources we love, to be perhaps resorted to when Netflix or your local Blockbuster lets you down. Of course, ardent pursuers of particular films are urged to first check eBay and Amazon for "used" copies, usually available at substantial discounts. In addition, never forget to explore your public libraries, which often have VHS collections packed with out-of-print titles, and never ignore the schedules of Turner Classic Movies, IFC, Eurocinema, the Sundance Channel, and other up-and-coming cinephiliac cable stations.

ONLINE RENTALS AND DOWNLOADS

Facets Multimedia (www.facets.org): By far the largest plumbable collection in the nation.

Film Fury (www.filmfury.com): A fascinating start-up that offers direct downloads of feature films, but whose scant inventory is restricted entirely to cloudy TV prints of semiforgotten public domain titles.

Gameznflix (www.gameznflix.com)

GreenCine (www.greencine.com): Like Film Fury, this is a video-on-demand renter of public domain films; it's also a sweet film-culture blog.

Intelliflix (www. intelliflix.com)

Liberation Video (www.liberationvideo.com): A picky and politically progressive collection.

Lovefilm (www.lovefilm.com)

Peerflix (www.peerflix.com)

Video Advantage (www.videoadvantage.net)

Video Library (www.vlibrary.com)

RETAILERS AND DISTRIBUTORS

The Criterion Collection (www.criterionco.com)

Docurama (www.docurama.com)

DVD Planet (www.dvdplanet.com)

Fantoma (www.fantoma.com)

First Run Features (www.firstrunfeatures.com)

Fox Home Entertainment (www.foxhome.com)

Image Entertainment (www.image-entertainment.com)

Iranian Movies (www.iranianmovies.com)

Kino Film on Video (www.kino.com)

Luminous Film and Video Wurks (www.lfvw.com)

MGM (www.mgm.com)

Milestone Films (www.milestonefilms.com)

New Yorker Films (www.newyorkerfilms.com)

1-World Festival of Foreign Films (www.1worldfilms.com)

Pimpadelic Wonderland (www.pimpadelicwonderland.com)

Something Weird (www.somethingweird.com)

Starz Home Entertainment (www.anchorbayentertainment.com)

Tai Seng Entertainment (www.taiseng.com)

The Twonky Video Collection (www.neetstuff.com)

Warner Home Video (www.warnervideo.com)

Yes Asia (www.yesasia.com)

Zeitgeist Films (www.zeitgeistfilms.com)

STORES

American Video Center, 14442 Union Ave., San Jose, CA 95124; 408-558-9545.

Amoeba Music, 2455 Telegraph Ave., Berkeley, CA 94704; 510-549-1125.

Evergreen Video, 37 Carmine St., New York, NY 10014; 212-691-7362.

I Luv Video, 4631 Airport Blvd., Austin, TX 78751; 512-450-1966.

Kensington Video, 4067 Adams Ave., San Diego, CA 92116; 619-584-7725.

Kim's Video, 6 St. Mark's Place, New York, NY 10013; 212-505-0311.

Lost Weekend Video, 1034 Valencia St., San Francisco, CA 94110; 415-643-3373.

Movie Time Video, 1118 S. Charles St., Baltimore, MD 21230; 410-528-8888.

112 Video World, 1761 Route 112, Medford, NY 11763; 631-758-9292.

Rain City Video, 464 N. 36th St., Seattle, WA 98103; 206-545-3539

Reel Video, 2655 Shattuck Ave., Berkeley, CA 94704; 510-548-1118.

Rocket Video, 726 N La Brea Ave., Los Angeles, CA 90036; 323-965-1100.

Scarecrow Video, 5030 Roosevelt Way NE, Seattle, WA 98105; 206-524-8554.

Le Video, 1231 9th Ave, San Francisco, CA 94122; 415-566-3606.

Video Americain, 400 W. Cold Spring Lane, Baltimore, MD 21210; 410-243-2231; five other stores in Maryland, D.C., and Delaware.

Video One, 1301 E. Colfax Ave., Denver, CO 80218; 303-832-4646.

Video Central, 1299 Bethel Rd., Columbus, OH 43220; 614-442-8273.

The Video Station, 1661 28th St., Boulder, CO 80301; 303-440-4448.

Videosmith, 275 Dartmouth St., Boston, MA 02116; 617-262-1144.

Vidiots, 302 Pico Blvd., Santa Monica, CA 90405; 310-392-8508.

Vulcan Video, 112 W. Elizabeth St., Austin, TX 78704; 512-326-2629; two other stores in Austin.

All Movie (www.allmovie.com)

Bright Lights Film Journal (www.brightlightsfilm.com)

Chicago Reader (www.chicagoreader.com)

Cinema Scope (www.cinema-scope.com)

Davekehr.com (www.davekehr.com)

DVD Beaver (www.dvdbeaver.com)

Facets Multimedia (www.facets.org)

Film Comment (www.filmlinc.com)

Kinoeye (www.kinoeye.org)

Masters of Cinema (www.mastersofcinema.org)

Movie Review Query Engine (www.mrqe.com)

Jim Emerson's Scanners (blogs.suntimes.com/scanners)

Senses of Cinema (www.sensesofcinema.com)

Sergio Leone and the Infield Fly Rule (sergioleoneifr.blogspot.com)

Sight & Sound (www.bfi.org.uk/sightandsound)

Strictly Film School (www.filmref.com)

Turner Classic Movies (www.tcm.com)

INDEX OF FILM TITLES

INDEX OF NAMES